HEROIC FORMS
Cervantes and the Literature of War

Before he was a writer, Miguel de Cervantes was a soldier. Enlisting in the Spanish infantry in 1570, he fought at the battle of Lepanto, was seized at sea and held captive by Algerian corsairs, and returned to Spain with a deep knowledge of military life. He understood the costs of heroism, the fragility of fame, and the power of the military culture of brotherhood.

In *Cervantes and the Literature of War*, Stephen Rupp connects Cervantes's complex and inventive approach to literary genre with his many representations of early modern warfare. Examining Cervantes's plays and poetry as well as his prose, Rupp demonstrates how Cervantes's works express his perceptions of military life and how Cervantes interpreted the experience of war through the genres of the era: epic, tragedy, pastoral, romance, and picaresque fiction.

(Toronto Iberic)

STEPHEN RUPP is an associate professor in the Department of Spanish and Portuguese at the University of Toronto.

Heroic Forms

Cervantes and the Literature of War

STEPHEN RUPP

UNIVERSITY OF TORONTO PRESS
Toronto   Buffalo   London

© University of Toronto Press 2014
Toronto Buffalo London
www.utppublishing.com

Reprinted in paperback 2017

ISBN 978-1-4426-4912-5 (cloth)   ISBN 978-1-4875-2254-4 (paper)

Library and Archives Canada Cataloguing in Publication

Rupp, Stephen James, author
Heroic forms : Cervantes and the literature of war / Stephen Rupp.

(Toronto Iberic ; 16)
Includes bibliographical references and index.
ISBN 978-1-4426-4912-5 (bound)   ISBN 978-1-4875-2254-4 (softcover)

1. Cervantes Saavedra, Miguel de, 1547–1616 – Criticism and interpretation.
2. War and literature – Spain – History – 16th century.   3. War in literature.
I. Title.   II. Series: Toronto Iberic ; 16.

PQ6348.A3R86 2014   863'.3   C2014-902566-1

University of Toronto Press acknowledges the financial assistance to its publishing program of the Canada Council for the Arts and the Ontario Arts Council, an agency of the Government of Ontario.

To the memory of

James Arthur McGeer (1892–1962)
Ada Mary McGeer Rupp (1915–99)

The Classics, it is the Classics! & not Goths nor Monks, that Desolate Europe with Wars.

William Blake, *On Homers Poetry* (ca 1822)

Contents

Acknowledgments xi

Note on Texts and Translations xv

Introduction   3

1 Warriors: Epic and Tragedy   31

2 Defenders: Pastoral and Satire   63

3 Captains and Saints: Lyric and Romance   100

4 Soldiers and Sinners: Picaresque   149

Conclusion   195

Notes   203

Works Cited   233

Index   245

Acknowledgments

This project began with an interest in Cervantes's writings on war and heroism in the context of the innovations in technology and tactics that shaped warfare in early modern Europe. I was initially concerned with war as an agent of historical change and with Cervantes's attitudes toward the old and the new in the culture of his time. Further research and teaching on Cervantes have led me to write this monograph on his presentation of warfare and soldiers' lives in a range of literary genres, both the canonical kinds explicated in Renaissance literary theory and such non-official forms as romance and picaresque fiction. This approach reflects my experience of teaching Cervantes in undergraduate classes and graduate seminars at the University of Toronto. Rewarding interactions with students have informed and enhanced my understanding of Cervantes and of the shaping and mediating force of imaginative literature in his works. Among my colleagues, Robert Davidson and Donna Orwin have shown a strong interest in this project and have encouraged me to complete it. I am grateful to Richard Ratzlaff at the University of Toronto Press for his assistance and encouragement, and to the anonymous readers who evaluated the manuscript for suggesting revisions that have improved the structure and development of my argument. My wife, Alison Keith, has read sections of the manuscript at many stages and has been unfailing in her support of my research and writing. Judith Schutz reviewed the manuscript for clarity and consistency and encouraged me to reword my argument on various points.

In 2007–8 Alison and I spent a productive year in North Carolina, where Alison held the Robert F. and Margaret S. Goheen Fellowship at the National Humanities Center. I am grateful to the Director, Geoffrey

Harpham, and the Deputy Director, Kent Mullikin, for providing me with a study for the year and to the fellows and staff of the Center for welcoming me to their community and for many helpful and engaging conversations. The participants in the Master Languages and Vernaculars Seminar – Catherine Chin, Mary Ellis Gibson, Alison Keith, Tim Kircher, Su Fang Ng, David Samuels, and Nigel Smith – read a preliminary version of chapter 4 and enhanced my understanding of languages and linguistic diversity in Cervantes.

I completed this book during a term as a Vice-Dean in the Faculty of Arts and Science. I am grateful to my Dean, Meric Gertler, and to my colleagues in the Dean's Office, Rob Baker, Anne-Marie Brousseau, Isaak Siboni, Suzanne Stevenson, and Sandy Welsh, for their confidence in my abilities and their support of every aspect of my administrative and scholarly work. It is a pleasure to work in an office so deeply committed to the open exchange of ideas and to the university's core purposes of teaching and research.

Sections of chapter 3 and chapter 4 have been published as articles: 'Remembering 1541: Crusade and Captivity in the Algiers Plays of Cervantes,' *Revista de Estudios Hispánicos* 32 (1998): 313–35; and 'Cervantes and the Soldier's Tale: Genre and Disorder in *El casamiento engañoso*,' *Modern Language Review* 96 (2001): 370–84. I thank the editors of these journals for permission to reprint this material in its present form.

In the course of my research I have read widely in the literature of war from the twentieth century. This material records the experience of war among modern soldiers and is the subject of illuminating works of contemporary criticism, such as Paul Fussell's *The Great War and Modern Memory* and Samuel Hynes's *The Soldier's Tale*. Hynes remarks that many books on modern war were written late in the lives of their authors, as a form of mature reflection on a young man's passage through military service. Alvin Kernan, one of my former teachers at Princeton University, is the author of *Crossing the Line*, a fine memoir of his naval service in the Pacific during the Second World War, and by reading his published work I have continued to learn from him.

I share with other scholars in the humanities an enduring debt to my many teachers. In this research I have maintained a long and rewarding dialogue with the Cervantes scholarship of Alban Forcione. As I prepared the manuscript for submission to the Press, I realized the extent to which I had returned to the work of the late Robert Fagles and to the questions about classical literature and its tradition that I had studied in his graduate seminars on epic and tragedy. I hope that I have been able to renew these questions and to make them my own, in a process that Professor Fagles would have recognized and understood. The choice of my epigraph from William Blake is an instance of open theft, from the Translator's Preface to Fagles's excellent version the *Iliad* – perhaps the sincerest form of scholarly tribute.

I have dedicated this book to the memory of my grandfather, who served in the Canadian Expeditionary Force in the First World War (Third Section, Fourth Divisional Ammunition Column, mobilized at Bouvigny Huts in June 1917), and of my mother, who loved him and kept his life story alive for my family.

Note on Texts and Translations

The texts of Cervantes's works that I have quoted appear in the list of works cited. I have cited two editions of *Don Quixote*: Murillo for the text and Astrana Marín for Diego Clemencín's extensive commentary. Translations are provided for all passages quoted in Spanish. I have used the Ormsby translation of *Don Quixote*, in the version revised by Joseph R. Jones and Kenneth Douglas for the Norton Critical Edition, and the translations of the *Novelas ejemplares* from the complete version prepared for Aris and Phillips under the general editorship of Barry W. Ife. All other translations from Spanish are my own. For primary sources in Latin, Greek, and Italian I cite published translations that appear in the list of works cited. Italian sources and Latin literary texts are cited in the original and in translation. Sources in Roman history are cited in translation, with reference to key terms and phrases in the original.

HEROIC FORMS

Introduction

Iridescence: shifting with colours as the observer moves – from the Latin for iris. Which is something you can't understand until you've seen the ruin of an eye, when it's out and split and the iris cut and wrong and shining by your boot. That's the trouble with education, it never stops. It is too much. Too much everything.

A.L. Kennedy, *Day* (2007)

A brief episode in the second part of *Don Quixote* (II. 24) describes an encounter with a young page who has abandoned the court for a life of service in the king's armies. Like a number of minor characters in Cervantes's novel, the page draws attention by presenting an unusual appearance and by speaking of his life in terms mediated by popular art.[1] He carries a sword across his shoulder with a bundle tied to its end. His attire is in the style of the court – a short velvet jacket, silk hose, and square-toed shoes – but his clothing is incomplete, since he is not wearing pantaloons to match his jacket. He lightens his journey by singing *seguidillas*, short poems in a popular style. When Don Quixote and his companions overtake the page, he is singing a lyric that speaks of his motives as he departs for Spain's wars:

> A la guerra me lleva
> mi necesidad;
> si tuviera dineros,
> no fuera, en verdad. (II. 24, 226)

4   Heroic Forms

> I'm off to the wars
> For want of pence,
> Oh, had I but money
> I'd show more sense.

This *seguidilla* suggests that poverty leads men to military service, and in conversation with Don Quixote the page expands on the economic disadvantages that he has endured. Although service to a member of the high aristocracy may promise material and social rewards, the page describes the masters whom he has known as negligent, more attentive to their own advancement than to the obligations of their rank. Life at court has left the page without means; the stipends that he has received have never been adequate, and he is carrying in his bundle the only pantaloons that he owns to spare them the wear and tear of the road. His intent is to enlist in the infantry and proceed with his company to the Mediterranean port of Cartagena, a standard point of embarkation for military service abroad. His expectation is that he will find superior masters and better conditions for advancement in the army: 'más quiero tener por amo y señor al rey, y servirle en la guerra, que no a un pelón en la corte' (I would rather have the king for a master and serve him in the wars, than serve some pauper at court) (II. 24, 227).

Don Quixote shows sympathy for the page, recognizing that he occupies a difficult position between a harsh past and an uncertain future (Fernández 109). He praises the page's decision to leave the court and offers counsel to support and comfort him in his chosen career, proposing that the life of arms extends to those who practise it the noble reward of honour. The nobility of arms and the limited material benefits of a military career are common topics in treatises on warfare from Cervantes's time (Serés 120), and Don Quixote concedes that the life of letters is more likely to provide wealth and property. He nonetheless claims that arms bear an intangible advantage over all other careers, and he advises the page to profit from the benefits of military service and to face its trials ('trabajos') without apprehension. The adversities of military life should not be feared, since the worst of these is death and warfare offers the prospect of dying well. On this point Don Quixote cites the authority of Suetonius's *Life of Caesar*: 'Pregutáronle a Julio César, aquel valeroso emperador romano, cuál era la mejor muerte; respondió que la impensada, la de repente y no prevista' (They asked Julius Caesar, the valiant Roman emperor, what was the best death. He answered, the unexpected death, which comes suddenly and unforeseen) (II. 24,

228).² He generalizes this statement by applying it to death inflicted by gunpowder weapons, under conditions of combat unknown to the Roman world: 'que puesto caso que os maten en la primera facción y refriega, o ya de un tiro de artillería, o volado de una mina, ¿qué importa?' (suppose you are killed in the first engagement or skirmish, whether by a cannon ball or blown up by a mine, what matter?) (II. 24, 228). Don Quixote recognizes both the dangers of modern warfare and its structures of authority and argues that observance of orders and of one's place in a chain of command will bring the traditional rewards of the soldier's life: 'tanto alcanza de fama el buen soldado cuanto tiene de obediencia a sus capitanes y a los que mandar le pueden' (the good soldier wins fame in proportion as he is obedient to his captains and those in command over him) (II. 24, 229). His intentions are to endorse the page's preference for the king's infantry over the court, assert the rewards and values associated with the life of arms, and send the page on his way with counsel and good will. Don Quixote perceives himself as inclined to the life of arms, and here he finds common cause with a youth who is bound for the wars.³

The narration of this encounter is typical of Cervantes in its engagement with several of the literary and rhetorical forms available to writers in early modern Spain. The page's decision to enlist under the king's standard can be linked to the two related literary forms of picaresque and satire. In his poverty and his chance appearance on the open road, the page is a picaresque figure, committed to making his own way in the world. Enlistment is a choice that he shares with the protagonists of late picaresque narratives, for whom Spain's armies offer the prospect of release from the restrictions and penury of civilian life. The road to Cartagena will take him on a well-established route that leads across the Mediterranean to the Spanish garrisons in Italy, and overland to active service in the Army of Flanders.⁴ The page departs from the social domain of the picaresque, however, in that he attributes his poverty not to the hardships of the lower tiers of society but to the self-interest and parsimony of the court. His choice of arms over a career at court places him within a strain of satire that finds in military service an ethical alternative to the venality of civil society. This strain recognizes the difficulties and dangers of the soldier's life, but attributes a positive value to its sharply defined ethos of male excellence and comradeship.⁵ In his condemnation of his noble masters and the illusory rewards of the career that he has abandoned, the page connects the praise of military life with a long tradition of anti-court satire.

When Don Quixote attempts to persuade the page that he has chosen well, he turns to rhetorical formulas and topics. He begins with a colloquial expression that endorses the page's complaint against his masters – 'Notable espilorchería' (What *spilorceria*!)[6] – and then shifts to a more formal linguistic register to offer assurance that his decision will lead to a favourable outcome: 'tenga a felice ventura el haber salido de la corte con tan buen intención como lleva' (consider yourself fortunate to have left the court with so worthy an aim) (II. 24, 228). To hold his auditor's attention and good will, Don Quixote addresses him in part through a series of commands that ask him to exercise his mental faculties – 'esto que ahora le quiero decir llévelo en la memoria' (bear in mind what I am about to say to you) ... 'advertir hijo' (remember, my son) – and he concludes with a traditional offer of hospitality to a stranger, inviting the page to ride with him to a nearby inn and share an evening meal (II. 24, 228–9). These gestures of common interest and benevolence frame a series of arguments, carefully stated in periodic sentences, on the traditional virtues and rewards of the soldier's life: honour, fortitude, fame. Don Quixote appeals to the authority of the classical past to support his views, citing Caesar's definition of a good death from Suetonius and a statement on the nobility of death in battle attributed here to the Roman playwright Terence: 'más bien parece el soldado muerto en la batalla que vivo y sano en la huida' (a soldier dead in battle cuts a better figure than when alive and safe in flight) (II. 24, 228–9).[7] This defence of the life of arms is notable in its application of classical precedents to the conditions of modern warfare. The weapons that Don Quixote mentions to the page – artillery and mines – are typical of wars of siege and attrition, and a substantial body of humanist moral and military thought regards such warfare as ethically suspect and non-heroic. In contrast to this line of moral critique, Don Quixote praises gunpowder as a sign of martial identity: 'al soldado mejor le está oler a pólvora que algalia' (it is better for the soldier to smell of gunpowder than of civet) (II. 24, 229). The purpose of Don Quixote's rhetorical address is to make a case for the nobility of the soldier's life, and his argument extends to the instruments and conditions of military service in Cervantes's time.

This dialogue between Don Quixote and the page invites reflection on the uses of genre. Their exchange centres on the motives and rewards of military service, and the statements of both interlocutors connect these subjects with a range of literary and rhetorical forms. The page's motives for enlistment can be related to picaresque fiction and satire, while Don Quixote's response draws on the conventions of classical rhetoric and the authority of classical texts. In this exchange established genres enable informed comment on the experience of war, including the attractions that draw men to military life and the kinds of counsel that will prepare them for the dangers of active service. Don Quixote forms a bond of common interest with the page and is able to draw on his extensive readings to offer him advice.[8] This confidence in the capacity of received forms to make sense of warfare presents a revealing contrast with narratives that centre on soldiers' lives in the large-scale wars of the twentieth century. The main character in A.L. Kennedy's *Day* – a tailgunner on a Lancaster bomber – finds his education inadequate to the violence and disorientation that he encounters on repeated missions over Duisburg and Hamburg. The knowledge that he has acquired cannot contain the destruction that he has witnessed but rather amplifies it, flooding his awareness with 'too much everything.' This disjunction between immediate experience and received culture is typical of modern war narratives. Modern soldiers approach military service on the basis of ideas and assumptions drawn from literary and popular sources: epic verse, Shakespearean drama, popular fiction, canonical lyric poetry.[9] Their experience of war reveals the inadequacy of these models, the stark contrast between war as young soldiers imagine it and the reality of combat (Hynes 29–30). In contrast, Cervantes finds in the literary and rhetorical culture of early modern Europe forms that can describe and give order to the experience of warfare.

The extensive body of literary texts and life writing on modern warfare can nonetheless illuminate some central concerns of Cervantes's writings on war in his time. Modern soldiers may experience unprecedented conditions of combat and new demands for determination and endurance, but they often share a sense of continuity with those who fought in the armies of earlier ages. This understanding of common commitments and interests can help us to grasp soldiers' views of the ethos and experience of warfare. In the epigraphs that introduce the chapters of this study, modern authors comment on aspects of war and military life that are also important for Cervantes: the unforgiving codes of conduct that soldiers share, the intrusion of martial violence into times and places of peace, the kinds of heroism that can be exercised under restrictive conditions, the sodality of common soldiers, and the persistence in memory of the costs and compensations of armed combat.

Over the course of his literary career Cervantes explores the ethos and representation of warfare through multiple genres, including forms that he inherits from the classical tradition and models that he adopts from the popular literature of early modern Spain. His early play *Tragedia de Numancia* combines the patterns of epic and tragedy to examine the challenges of heroic conduct in siege warfare and the instability of the rewards of fame and glory that classical epic offers to its exemplary warriors. Pastoral, a classical genre often placed in contrast to the high forms of epic and tragedy, creates a space that enables reflection on warfare and martial violence. A comic dialogue between Don Quixote and Sancho on the construction and commemoration of fame, and Don Quixote's encounters with two sheepflocks that he takes for armies and with the residents of a village who are in conflict with their neighbours, revisit the fragility of secular fame and examine the intrusion of epic violence into the green world of pastoral. Here the plain voice of pastoral offers satirical commentary on war and the nature of violence. In three texts that centre on Spain's conflict with the Ottomans in the Mediterranean and the experience of Spanish captives in Algiers – *El trato de Argel*, *Los baños de Argel*, and the captive's tale in *Don Quixote* – Cervantes uses the forms of romance and lyric to trace a transition from martial to spiritual heroism, asserting the value of an ethos of Christian constancy and endurance. Through a series of low mimetic characters – the returned soldier Vicente de la Rosa, the ensign Campuzano in the interlinked stories *El casamiento engañoso* and *El coloquio de los perros*, Ginés de Pasamonte in his roles as galley slave and puppeteer in *Don Quixote*, the false captives in *Los trabajos de Persiles y Sigismunda* – Cervantes engages the popular model of picaresque fiction to examine the culture of violence and solidarity among common soldiers. Canonical and non-canonical forms are used for different purposes. Classical kinds offer general reflection on warfare and the heroic ethos, while popular forms emphasize endurance and constancy and consider the military culture that unites soldiers in war and sets them apart from civil society. Scrutiny of heroism is a constant in Cervantes's works, with a particular focus on the kinds of heroism that could be practised under the limiting conditions of warfare and endemic imperial conflict in early modern Europe.

Hynes has characterized the soldier's tale as a retrospective account of 'the things men do in war and the things war does to them' (3).[10] One factor in Cervantes's literary engagement with warfare is his own experience of Spain's enduring conflict with the Ottoman Empire and with the corsairs of North Africa. We know of Cervantes's birth in Alcalá de Henares in 1547 and his death in Madrid on 22 April 1616, but reliable documentary evidence for most of his life is strikingly scarce.

We nonetheless have notarial documents, contemporary testimonies, and literary evidence for the period from 1570 to 1580, when Cervantes pursued a military career in the Mediterranean and spent five years as a captive in Algiers.[11] It is known that in 1569 Cervantes was living in Rome, at the court of Giulio Acquaviva. He enlisted in the infantry company of Diego de Urbina in the fall of 1570 and fought in Spain's engagements with Ottoman forces at Lepanto, Corfu, Tunis, and La Goleta. In 1575, during his return voyage to Spain, he was captured in an encounter with Turkish ships and taken to Algiers, where he spent five years as the captive of two renegades – first Dalí Mamí, then Hasan Pasha – Europeans who had converted to Islam and rose to prominence in the privateering economy of North Africa. In 1580 he was rescued through his family's payment of a ransom and the agency of the Trinitarian friars and returned to Spain. Testimony from Cervantes's fellow captives attests to his courage and constancy during this time and to his generosity and concern for others.[12] In his prologue to the *Novelas ejemplares* (1613) Cervantes reflects on his infantry service and his life as a captive, in a third-person description that might be placed beneath a portrait of himself:

> Fue soldado muchos años, y cinco y medio cautivo, donde aprendió a tener paciencia en las adversidades. Perdió en la batalla naval de Lepanto la mano izquierda de un arcabuzazo, herida que, aunque parece fea, él la tiene por hermosa, por haberla cobrado en la más memorable y alta ocasión que vieron los pasados siglos, ni esperan ver los venideros, militando debajo de las vencedoras banderas del hijo del rayo de la guerra, Carlo Quinto, de felice memoria. (51)

> He was many years a soldier, five and a half a prisoner, when he learned patience in adversity. He lost his left hand in the naval battle of Lepanto, from a blunderbuss wound, which, although it looks ugly, he considers beautiful, since he collected it in the greatest and most memorable event that past centuries have ever seen or those to come may hope to see, fighting beneath the victorious banners of the son of that glorious warrior, Charles V of happy memory.

Cervantes presents his record of service to the king in terms mediated through the literature of war. He follows a classical trope in describing the loss of his arm at Lepanto – an injury inflicted by a gunpowder weapon – as a wound that provides an external sign of his honourable participation in a historic battle.[13] The reference to the standards of Juan de Austria sets his dedication to arms in a tradition of martial excellence that extends back to the imperial armies of Charles V. He also recognizes the costs of war and the challenges that can delay homecoming, common themes in classical epic and tragedy. This passage speaks of what Cervantes has done in war and of what war has done to him, of the lessons of patience and endurance that he has drawn from the hardships of military service and captivity.

Cervantes responds with internal constancy to the uncertain conditions of military service in his time. Soldiers and strategists encountered instability and change in the wars of early modern Europe, and they reacted to innovations in the technologies, tactics, and structures of warfare that were embedded in and contributed to larger processes of social transformation. Some discussion of these military innovations and their broad impact will elucidate the historical context of Cervantes's work. Michael Roberts's influential account of warfare in the time of Maurice of Nassau in the Netherlands and Gustavus Adolphus of Sweden describes a revolution that began in theatres of war and extended to broad effects on the civilian population and the administration of society. Recent historians have criticized Roberts's approach for its lack of attention to continuities in technology and strategy, its selective treatment of the factors that contributed to social and military change, and its emphasis on the training and supply of large armies as determining factors in more general social processes. The work of Roberts and his critics nonetheless makes it clear that this was a period of alteration and adaptation in the conduct of wars and the experience of soldiers.

Gunpowder weapons changed the face of battle and shaped the experience of conflict and violence for common soldiers. Such innovations in weaponry are central to historical arguments for a military revolution. Roberts maintains that new 'weapons (technology)' required changes in 'doctrine and particular habits of war (technique)' (Black, *European Warfare* 32). He emphasizes the effectiveness of projectile weapons – the longbow and the musket – against lances and pikes, and the general superiority of massed infantry over the cavalry forces of medieval warfare. On the technical side, efficient use of small firearms depended on a disciplined order of fire, particularly the tactic of successive volleys that enabled parallel ranks of musketeers to fire, countermarch, load, and fire again as they advanced on the enemy. Developed by the Dutch in the 1590s, this technique required substantial numbers of active soldiers, trained through newly articulated drills and exercises. The complex strategies of infantry warfare demanded larger forces, and the rapid growth of European armies increased the costs of recruitment, maintenance, and management. To raise and administer their armies, European states established structures and procedures that advanced the consolidation of their centralizing powers, a developmental pattern that suggests a link between 'the modern art of war' and 'the creation of the modern state' (Black, *European Warfare* 33). For Roberts, the defining features of the military revolution are innovations in weapons and tactics, increased army size, new challenges in strategy and supply, and the broad social impacts of war and military organization (Parker, *Military Revolution* 2).

Geoffrey Parker's revision of Roberts's argument expands the temporal and geographical limits of the military revolution and locates its centre in Spain and in the European states with which the Hapsburg monarchy waged wars. Parker traces technological change to the development of mobile artillery in the fifteenth century and, more specifically, to the introduction of complex defence works for the purpose of protecting cities and fortresses against artillery sieges. First designed during Italy's wars against French invading armies in the early sixteenth century and commonly known as the *trace italienne*, this new system of defence combined low and wide enclosing walls with angled bastions and ravelins that extended outward to provide platforms for flanking fire. Later military architects elaborated on this design by adding supporting trenches and bastions outside the central core, but the elements of the system retained their basic functions: the broad and solid walls offered protection against cannon fire, while the bastions and other salient works enabled the defenders to fire on any enemy forces that attempted to assault or undermine their fortifications. Such defensive works were constructed on an extensive scale over the course of the sixteenth century, and they had a marked impact on the costs of war in terms of time and troops, since a campaign against a well-designed stronghold depended on tactics of encirclement and attrition: 'a chain of siegeworks had to be built and manned until either the defenders were starved out, or trenches were advanced near enough to the walls to permit close-range bombardment and an assault, or else tunnels were excavated under a bastion where gunpowder mines could be planted' (Parker, *Military Revolution* 13). The human and economic costs of war rose to an unprecedented degree, given that 'much of western Europe seemed locked into a military system in which defence and offence were almost exactly balanced' (14). These changes in fortification and siege tactics and the subsequent innovations in projectile weaponry altered the nature and scale of warfare, requiring new tactics, complex chains of command and supply, and large armies centred on infantry forces. For Parker, the core elements of the military revolution are fortification and siegecraft, firepower and infantry tactics, and a rapid increase in the size of armies. Parker also notes that 'all the evidence for radical military change' is concentrated in 'Spain, Italy, the Netherlands, and France' and that the lands held by the Hapsburgs and their neighbours can be described as 'the heartland of the military revolution' (24).

Common soldiers were subject to new forms of training and to the dangers of wounds from projectiles and war by attrition. The discipline of drill prepared men for new conditions of combat, in which the massed force of infantry and the strategic calculations of siege warfare often outweighed individual skill and distinction in the exercise of arms. These factors were significant in their scale and effect, but military historians have questioned the view that they represented a military revolution. In practice, new weapons and tactics were adopted in multiple stages, military affairs played a complex role in relation to the powers of the state, and military change took place within a complex cultural matrix.[14] In the development of technology and technique, the link was not linear. Tacticians learned to group musketeers in ranks in order to compensate for the limited accuracy and range of their weapons, and other instruments of siege and battle – cannons, pikes, polearms – had similar limitations and required parallel patterns of learning. Many of the technologies of early modern warfare had medieval antecedents, and changes took effect not in revolutionary events but through processes of adaptation to the features of particular weapons and the conditions of campaigns.

Such changes did not always work to the advantage of a centralizing state. The tradition of local levies of troops helped to sustain the authority of the landed nobility, and members of the aristocracy maintained their hold over their established tiers in the structure of large armies: the cavalry and the officer class. In addition, protracted campaigns generated demands for resources that could undermine political stability and control. In different contexts, military changes both advanced the powers of the state and preserved the interests of the nobility. Cultural factors consistently shaped the choices that led to the adoption of innovative weapons and tactics. The rediscovery of Roman military treatises such as Vegetius's *De re militari* encouraged reflection on questions of organization and strategy, and the printing press promoted the diffusion of new ideas in a format conducive to standardization and systematic approaches.[15] Printed manuals on the use of weapons and on tactical issues formed a common currency among European states. Military innovation involved complex processes of 'adoption, dissemination and adaptation,' in a culture that combined 'interests in new methods' with 'powerful elements of continuity' (Black, *European Warfare* 50, 53). In the case of Spain, innovations in weaponry, organizational changes, and matters of policy contributed to a long record of adaptation to the material and human conditions of waging war. To the tactical challenges of siege weapons and small arms and the demands of recruitment and supply, Spanish military leaders responded 'with a combination of professionalism and resilience' (Black, 'Military Revolutions' 29–30). Over successive campaigns Spain developed the capacity to conduct expeditionary wars and prevail in overseas conflicts. Its objectives were consistent with a political culture that equated security with territorial control and expansion and with traditional martial values of honour, glory, and the normative meaning of combat.

Writers and artists responded to the changes in weapons and strategy and in the ethos of war that soldiers knew as a matter of practice and experience. Treatises on the art of war review the uses of infantry and fortification and outline strategic methods and procedures for drill and training. While portraits of kings and generals gesture to a traditional iconography of equestrian excellence, drawings and engravings of armies and their baggage trains record the foot soldiers of early modern military campaigns and the camp followers who trailed in their wake.[16] In the case of imaginative literature, questions of war and its ethos present themselves in the first instance in genres traditionally associated with warriors and acts of arms. Michael Murrin has traced the literary response to the 'slow but complete revolution' in weapons and tactics through the shift in heroic poetry from chivalric romance to texts modelled on classical epic (8). This preference for epic in Renaissance poetics and in literary practice rests on the forms of warfare that it describes and on the questions about the use of force that it can entertain. The heroes of romance are mounted knights who practise the skills and tactics of combat by cavalry and project the ideals of an ascendant chivalric aristocracy; this genre celebrates a military system that was gradually displaced over the course of the sixteenth century.[17]

Classical epic, in contrast, presents hand-to-hand combat that parallels battles by infantry and lends itself to reflection on questions of military change: the challenges of new weapons and tactics, the shifting codes of heroic conduct, the limits of violence. In Murrin's view, the genre of epic responds to historical changes in the structure and values of war. Representation and scrutiny of warfare, however, are not limited to epic and chivalric romance. Renaissance lyric explores the internal conflict between the claims of service in arms and courtly devotion to the beloved. Pastoral retirement offers space for celebration of martial achievements and for reflection on the rewards of commitment to an active life. Picaresque narrative presents the lives of common soldiers in the lower ranks of Spain's armies and the lower tiers of the contemporary social order. Given the extension of war and its ethos across a broad range of genres, Cervantes's writings can be placed in the context of the concepts and practices that shape systems of genre and generic change.

At the core level of theory, literary forms can be traced to generic 'universals' or 'radicals,' based primarily on modes of presentation.[18] A traditional schema posits a threefold classification of epic, dramatic, and lyric modes; Northrop Frye's treatment of genre in the *Anatomy of Criticism* further divides the first of these into 'epos' and 'prose.' Creative practice, however, responds less to such universals than to the particular genres that can be developed within each mode, through differentiation in such features as scale, subject, setting, structure, and style.[19] In Claudio Guillén's formulation, genre offers 'an invitation to the matching (dynamically speaking) of matter and form' ('On the Uses' 111), a process that requires structural models of adequate distinctiveness and elaboration. The range of available models can be broad and diverse. The theoretically articulated poetics of a given period of literary history generally embraces and diffuses a particular set of genres. In practice, however, writers draw on a range of models that extend beyond the codified genres of their time, and this interplay between accepted norms and unwritten codes is central to the process of generic change. Genres develop over time in part through their shifting placement in relation to synchronic sets of accepted norms.

The literary culture of early modern Europe offers both a highly codified system of genres and multiple options for generic innovation. Neo-Aristotelian theory constructs a written poetics centred on the received genres that Alastair Fowler has classified as 'historical kinds.'[20] Although the list of kinds admits some variation, epic, tragedy, comedy, lyric, pastoral, and verse satire constitute a typical set. An awareness of tradition and precedent informs both theoretical reflection on these genres and practical engagement with them. They are generally identified by names drawn from classical texts and through reference to ancient origins and foundational authors. Each genre has a typical repertoire, defined in terms of formal features and characteristic themes or subjects. The various kinds reflect the core radicals of presentation – narrative, dramatic, and lyric – and they often depend on external and metrical structures. Contrasts in size and scale define them in relation to one another, and each kind employs a defined stylistic range. In addition, the kinds are associated with particular character types and thematic concerns, and they project sets of values deemed appropriate to their subject matter. In literary theory and creative practice, these defining features are interrelated. The concept of decorum links the three traditional registers of style – high, middle, and low – to the presentation of characters in accordance with the conventions of social class. The kinds themselves can be placed in a hierarchy, ranging from the low forms of pastoral and satire to the heroic genres of epic and tragedy. The progression of kinds can be defined as the stages in a literary career, corresponding to the skills that a writer develops as he moves through an ordered curriculum of genres.[21] These axioms attest to an articulated system of written poetics, based on classical authority and the imitation of traditional models.

The range of genres available to early modern authors nonetheless extends well beyond the historical kinds delineated in the written poetics of the time. The classical tradition also made available forms that were not recognized as canonical kinds, and the didactic tendency of humanist thought encouraged the imitation of ancient rhetorical structures: epistles, orations, discourses, dialogues (Colie 4). Classical texts also offered models for the composition of long and variegated narratives, particularly Greek romance and the intellectually cast, non-linear form known as Menippean satire.[22] Popular traditions traceable to the Middle Ages presented a wide range of non-standard forms: folktale, fable, morality play, ballad, fabliau. The exuberance and invention of early modern literature can be linked to this plenitude of available models and to the tension between canonical and non-official forms. Rosalie Colie has identified 'the imitation of formal models' as 'a factor for literary change and imaginative experiment,' arguing that 'there were many more kinds than were recognized in official literary philosophy' and that 'these competing notions of kind' informed 'the richness and variety of Renaissance letters' (8). As well, the boundary between one conception of kind and another was not fixed. As Guillén has observed, 'the process of generic description and classification is never quite closed,' and creative practice can play across the demarcations of official poetics and draw a non-canonical kind into the 'inner circle' of privileged forms ('On the Uses' 124–5). The simultaneous presence of Neo-Aristotelian poetics and a robust variety of popular kinds enabled such interchange. For Guillén, the 'theoretical restlessness' of sixteenth-century literary culture produced 'a moment of dynamic contact between traditional artistic principle and practical innovation' ('On the Uses' 109, 126).

Modern criticism of Cervantes has analysed in detail his engagement with Renaissance literary theory and his innovative use of canonical and popular forms. Such questions as the theoretical separation of poetry from history, the status of Ariosto's *Orlando furioso* as a modern epic, the structural challenges of episodic narrative, and the decorum of style and character shape his understanding of imaginative literature and the construction of his works.[23] Guillén offers illuminating commentary on Cervantes's integrative approach to matters of genre:

> We may assume that the pastoral novel still belonged to the circle of 'unwritten poetics' when Cervantes started *La Galatea*; that although the official class of the epic poem was available to every sixteenth-century poet, Cervantes chose not to compose an epic in *octavas reales* on the victory of Lepanto; that as far as the stage was concerned, he wavered between the accepted tragic structure and the developing popular forms; and that he confronted simultaneously the written and unwritten norms of the day – the whole expanding circle of contemporary poetics – when he wrote his most syncretic and original work, *Don Quixote*. ('On the Uses' 127)

Guillén stresses Cervantes's awareness of the entire range of genres available to him – whether codified in Renaissance poetics or disseminated through creative practice – and his interest in combining canonical kinds with non-official forms. Popular literature asserts its presence in Cervantine prose fiction in part through the interplay between two basic forms that modern critics have categorized as 'romance' and 'novel.' Cervantes writes with a keen understanding of the patterns and conventions of romance and of its capacity to adapt to and incorporate other forms; he draws on its imaginative freedom to explore the interaction between its paradigmatic plot of adventure and love, marked by repeated recognitions and reversals, and the nascent realism of narratives that follow the criterion of verisimilitude and the conventions of historical writing. The insistent presence of romance, in itself and in varying combinations with the novel, attests to Cervantes's interest in non-official forms.[24]

Cervantes's direct statements about genre and generic mixing nonetheless appeal to the historical kinds. In a frequently cited passage from his dialogue with the priest from Don Quixote's village (*DQ* I. 47–8), the canon of Toledo comments on the capacity of chivalry books to encompass other forms:

> la escritura desatada destos libros da lugar a que el autor pueda mostrarse épico, lírico, trágico, cómico, con todas aquellas partes que encierran en sí las dulcísimas y agradables ciencias de la poesía y la oratoria; que la épica también puede escrebirse en prosa como en verso. (I. 47, 567)

> the unrestricted range of these books enables the author to show his powers, epic, lyric, tragic, or comic, and all the moods the sweet and winning arts of poetry and oratory are capable of, for the epic may be written in prose just as well as verse.

The canon espouses a Neo-Aristotelian poetics of decorum and verisimilitude, and for the most part he is hostile to the inventive language and loosely articulated narrative structure of the romances of chivalry. Here, however, he concedes that the free composition of these books has a positive aspect, in that it allows for the display of authorial skill across a range of styles, high and low, in literary kinds and rhetorical registers. Epic is part of the traditional repertoire available to the writer of such an improved romance, and it provides a model for a work comprehensive in its handling of genres and well ordered in its narrative. The canon's aim is to compose a modern work in prose modelled on classical verse epic.

As an influential historical kind, epic is closely linked to the matter of war. Classical epic commemorates singular acts in open battle and the fame that rewards such accomplishments; the genre celebrates a sharply defined code of martial excellence and shapes a culture of reception based on male readers and the formation of male subjects.[25] In his treatment of epic, however, Cervantes often displaces its traditional material and ethos. As Michael Armstrong-Roche has shown, *Los trabajos de Persiles y Sigismunda* illustrates the complex interplay of epic, novel, and romance in Cervantes's writing, in the context of contemporary critical debates on the aesthetic and ethical failings of popular literature. Armstrong-Roche argues that Cervantes finds in the *Ethiopica* of Heliodorus an exemplary text that reconciles the adventures of Greek romance with the decorum and ethical intent that Neo-Aristotelian poetics associates with positive literary models. On the pattern of Heliodorus, the *Persiles* presents characters of high social status and engages serious themes from the epic tradition: arms and empire, religion, love. Its settings include a series of kingdoms – the Barbaric Isle, Policarpo's Isle, Thule – that announce a concern with epic matters of politics and the education of rulers. Each of these epic themes, however, is subject to interrogation and redefinition. The itinerary of Cervantes's protagonists from the northern Barbaric Isle to Rome reverses the traditional movement of imperial rule and ideology from Europe to its overseas possessions, and the survival in the Catholic South of archaic customs questions the civilizing ideal of an orderly government founded on the rule of law. The contrasting careers of Persiles and his elder brother Maximino revisit the proper objectives of the epic hero: Maximino represents traditional martial values of conquest and glory that Persiles must forgo if he is to consummate his love for Sigismunda in marriage and peaceful succession. The *Persiles* moves away from the patriarchal values of classical epic to celebrate the trials and rewards of domestic love and a politics grounded in Christian ethics. In the development of the text a revalorization of imaginative literature parallels this shift in values. A dream episode in Book II enables Persiles to discover his identity as a new kind of hero, and he enacts this role in part through his ability to understand and give voice to lyric verse. In its engagement with epic as an encyclopedic form, the *Persiles* explores a paradoxical reconciliation of the opposing values and ideals that shape the epic tradition.[26]

In the *Persiles* Cervantes responds to the extended tradition of epic as a historical kind. The practice of epic and the body of critical reflection on its characters and values link the composition of imaginative literature to matters of war and relate generic change to shifting perspectives on martial themes. Modern genre theory can elucidate the various processes of generic transformation that are present in Cervantes's works.[27] His variations on a single genre rest on such techniques as the introduction of new topics into an established generic repertoire, the aggregation of short works into a composite whole, and the counterstatement of a recognized form as an anti-genre. His experiments in multiple genres include the insertion of one form into another, the mixing of the structures and repertoires of distinct genres, and the use of hybrid forms that characterizes Renaissance drama. Cervantes's understanding of genre as a matter of poetic theory and creative practice consistently shapes his writing and his engagement with the literary culture of his time.

Canonical kinds and popular forms exert a marked influence on Cervantes when he writes about soldiers and warfare. He is drawn to the classical genres of epic and tragedy, but he also turns to such popular forms as romance and picaresque. The interaction of formal structures with issues of modern warfare can be examined in the first instance in the discourse on arms and letters that Don Quixote delivers to a select audience in one of the inns that brings him together with other characters who have experienced trials and adventures that parallel his own (I. 37–8). The topic of arms and letters is well established in the rhetorical tradition, and Don Quixote develops an argument in favour of arms within the structure of a classical oration and through rhetorical formulas and devices.[28] His discourse can be read as an exercise on a set theme, designed to present one side of a topical debate. His argument is nonetheless striking in its adaptation of traditional structures to the conditions of modern war. While praising the heroic ethos of the life of arms, Don Quixote recognizes the trials and accomplishments of those who fought in the Spanish armies of his own time. He presents a fusion of literary ideals and technical terms drawn from treatises on warfare (Castells 44).

Don Quixote articulates his comparison of arms and letters through four central concepts: the particular end or goal ('fin y paradero') to which each of these lives is directed, the trials ('trabajos') that each one imposes, the rewards ('premios') that each offers, and the costs ('aquello que más cuesta') that each exacts (I. 37, 465–6, 469). His discourse offers detailed comment on each of these ideas. The end of arms is peace – a proposition that seems curious to a modern reader, but one that enjoyed broad acceptance in Cervantes's time – while letters serve the cause of justice and good laws. Letters entail the trials of poverty and study; arms impose the sufferings of life on campaign and the risks of open battle. Letters promise the benefits of wealth and secular power; arms offer the uncertain rewards of delayed wages and seigneurial generosity. The cost of letters is minor suffering, in such forms as sleeplessness, light-headedness, and indigestion; service in arms may exact the cost of life itself. To reinforce these propositions Don Quixote uses a range of rhetorical topics and devices. He begins by appealing to his audience at the inn, promising that he will speak of 'grandes e inauditas cosas' (great and marvellous things) (I. 37, 465), and through repetitive phrasing he directs their attention as he moves from one concept to another: 'veamos ahora cuál de los dos espíritus, el del letrado o el del guerrero, trabaja más' (let us see now which of the two minds, that of the man of letters or that of the warrior, has the most to do) (I. 37, 466); 'veamos si es más rico el soldado' (let us see now if the soldier is richer) (I. 38, 468). He asserts three times that a greater measure of danger and expense confers a higher degree of value and honour, and in his conclusion he applies this formula to himself, proposing that he will achieve greater fame than the knights of the past because he has taken on greater perils. Don Quixote also appeals to the authority of received texts, most notably when he cites the New Testament to prove that peace is central to Christ's Gospel and represents the highest goal of earthly existence. These various arguments attempt to demonstrate the superiority of the life of arms to that of letters: the former is more noble in its ends, more changeable in its material rewards, and more demanding in its costs. This proposition has a traditional cast, yet it is developed in relation to the conditions and constraints of early modern society. This contrast is central to Cervantes's response to the mentality of this period. For J.A. Maravall, Don Quixote represents a strain of utopian thought that equates virtue with pre-eminence in arms and enshrines the conservative martial virtues of strength, valour, and loyalty. Through the archaic weapons that Don Quixote bears and the ideals of social and spiritual renewal that shape his speech and conduct, Cervantes critiques this aristocratic utopia of arms (116–19). The defence of the modern soldier's life in this discourse, however, strives to identify a core of heroic fortitude and endurance that can be maintained under the conditions of early modern warfare.

Don Quixote defines arms and letters in terms of two contrasting career paths: university study in Spain, and military service in the Mediterranean or Flanders. His discourse plays on the semantic range of the word 'letras.' Through the curriculum of letters the student acquires learning in the humanities ('letras humanas') and so becomes a 'letrado,' a term associated in early modern Spain with university graduates in law and, by association, with the lawyers who staffed the royal bureaucracy. Richard Kagan has shown that university students in Cervantes's time anticipated the rewards of bureaucratic employment and that influential Castilian universities traded in the coin of access to official circles, as in the motto of the University of Salamanca: 'Kings for Universities, Universities for Kings' (*Students* 212). 'Letras' in this specific sense can be compared to the 'armas' that modern soldiers bear in the king's name. On the basis of this semantic play, Don Quixote opposes the material comfort and worldly influence of the successful 'letrado' to the uncertain life of a soldier in Spain's imperial armies. He has transformed the traditional opposition of priestly studies and knightly arms into 'a more modern choice among thoroughly secular careers' (Quint, *Cervantes's Novel* 13).

The contrast between soldier and 'letrado' leads to ironic effects, often to the soldier's advantage. In comparing the two careers in terms of their particular trials, Don Quixote describes the privations of a military campaign:

> Y a veces suele ser su desnudez tanta, que un coleto acuchillado le sirve de gala y de camisa, y en la mitad del invierno se suele reparar de las inclemencias del cielo, estando en la campaña rasa, con sólo el aliento de su boca, que, como sale de lugar vacío, tengo por averiguado que debe de salir frío, contra toda naturaleza. Pues esperad que espere que llegue la noche para restaurarse de todas estas incomodidades en la cama que le aguarda, la cual, si no es por su culpa, jamás pecará de estrecha; que bien puede medir en la tierra los pies que quisiere, y revolverse en ella a su sabor, sin temor que se le encojan las sábanas. Lléguese, pues, a todo esto, el día y la hora de recebir el grado de su ejercicio: lléguese un día de batalla; que allí le pondrán la borla en la cabeza, hecha de hilas, para curarle algún balazo, que quizá le habrá pasado las sienes, o le dejará estropeado de brazo o pierna. (I. 38, 468)

> Sometimes his nakedness will be so great that a ragged leather jacket serves him for uniform and shirt, and in the depth of winter he has to defend himself against the inclemency of the weather in the open field with nothing better than the breath of his mouth, which I need not say, coming from an empty place, must come out cold, contrary to the laws of nature. To be sure, he looks forward to the approach of night to make up for all these discomforts on the bed that awaits him. This, unless by his own fault, never sins by being over-narrow, for he can measure out on the ground as many feet as he likes, and roll about to his heart's content without any fear of the sheets slipping off. Then suppose the day and hour have come for taking his degree in his calling. Suppose the day of battle has arrived, when they put on him a mortar board of bandages, to mend some bullet hole, perhaps, that has gone through his temples or left him with a crippled arm or leg.

Irony is in part a typical reaction of humanist observers to the conditions of early modern warfare. In his account of the siege of Metz in 1552, the court physician and surgical innovator Ambroise Paré remarks that the soldiers under his care fell victim to hunger, disease, and cold weather, even though they 'lodg'd at the signe of the Moone,' where 'each souldier had his field bed, and a covering strewed with glittering stares' (49).[29] Don Quixote argues that the trials of the soldier are the same in kind as those of the student – lack of clothing and other protection from the elements, hunger, broken sleep – but that they differ significantly in degree, since the soldier finds himself exposed to mortal danger. The ironic cast of the comparison is particularly pointed in the account of graduation day for the two professions. Where the 'letrado' collects in peace a degree obtained through book learning, the soldier acquires skills that must be demonstrated in practice and can only claim his diploma on the battlefield. The tattered bandage of the wounded recruit, substituting for the doctor's cap of the new graduate, confirms the greater trials and the superior status of the soldier's career.

It is interesting that the ironies here cut against the 'letrado,' and not against the general ethos of heroism. Although Don Quixote recognizes the harsh conditions of war in his time, he also places the conduct of common soldiers in a heroic light. In his section on the relative costs of the two careers, he offers two concise illustrations of heroic responses to the dangers of war:

> Y ¿qué temor de necesidad y pobreza puede llegar ni fatigar al estudiante, que llegue al que tiene un soldado, que, hallándose cercado en alguna fuerza, y estando de posta, o guarda en algún revellín o caballero, siente que los enemigos están minando hacia la parte donde él está, y no puede apartarse de allí por ningún caso, ni huir el peligro que de tan cerca le amenaza? Sólo lo que puede hacer es dar noticia a su capitán de lo que pasa, para que lo remedie con alguna contramina, y él estarse quedo, temiendo y esperando cuándo improvisamente ha de subir a las nubes sin alas, y bajar al profundo sin su voluntad. Y si éste le parece pequeño peligro, veamos si le iguala o hace ventajas el de embestirse dos galeras por las proas en mitad del mar espacioso, las cuales enclavijadas y trabadas, no le queda al soldado más espacio del que concede dos pies de tabla del espolón; y, con todo esto, viendo que tiene delante de sí tantos ministros de la muerte que le amenazan cuantos cañones de artillería se atestan de la parte contraria, que no distan de su cuerpo una lanza, y viendo que al primer descuido de los pies iría a visitar los profundos senos de Neptuno, y, con todo esto, con intrépido corazón, lllevado de la honra que le incita, se pone a ser blanco de tanta arcabucería, y procura pasar por tan estrecho paso al bajel contrario. (I. 38, 470)

What dread of want or poverty that can assail the student can compare with what the soldier feels when, beleaguered in some stronghold, mounting guard in some trench, or on the walls, he knows that the enemy is tunneling towards the post where he is stationed? He cannot under any circumstances retire or flee from the imminent danger that threatens him. All he can do is to inform his captain, who may try to remedy it by a countermine. Then the soldier stands his ground in fear and expectation of the moment when he will fly up to the clouds without wings and descend into the deep against his will. If this seems a trifling risk, let us see whether it is equaled or surpassed by the encounter of two galleys prow to prow, in the midst of the open sea, locked and entangled one with the other, when the soldier has no more standing room than two feet of plank on the ramming prow. He sees himself threatened by as many ministers of death as there are gunbarrels of the foe pointed at him, not a lance length from his body, and sees too that with the first heedless step he will go down to visit the profundities of Neptune's bosom. Still with dauntless heart, urged on by honor that nerves him he makes himself a target for all that musketry and struggles to cross that narrow path to the enemy's ship.

This text reflects on the conflictive role of martial ideals in early modern combat. The soldiers described here find themselves exposed to conditions typical of Spain's two main theatres of war in the sixteenth century: the siege of a walled city in the Low Countries and a battle of galleys at sea in the Mediterranean. Both cases involve weapons and strategies widely regarded as non-heroic in polemics of the time: the defensive and essentially static techniques of siege warfare and the gunpowder weapons held to be inimical to individual valour. Heroism nonetheless persists in these unpropitious conditions, although its expression may not satisfy the scale of epic: the sentry holds his post despite his fears that the enemy is mining the defensive wall beneath him, and the soldier on the galley, moved by courage and honour, attacks against the opposing fusillade. Here Don Quixote also revisits the heroic code of the romances of chivalry, with its emphasis on the deeds of the solitary knight-errant. On the salient ravelin or the galley's prow, the modern soldier experiences solitude, although he is surrounded by others and by the confusion of war. In the case of the galleys this experience repeats itself again and again, as one boarder falls after another: 'que apenas uno ha caído donde no se podrá levantar hasta la fin del mundo, cuando otro ocupa su mesmo lugar; y si éste también cae en el mar, que como a enemigo le aguarda, otro y otro le sucede, sin dar tiempo al tiempo de sus muertes' (no sooner has one gone down into the depths he will never rise from till the end of the world, than another takes his place. And if he too falls into the sea that waits for him like an enemy, another and another will succeed him without a moment's pause between their deaths) (I. 38, 470). This passage concedes that the privations of the common soldier grant limited opportunities for acts of heroism in the style of privileged literary texts, but it also suggests that under these conditions the heroic code must be redefined in terms of obedience and endurance. In modern warfare to remain at one's post or to stand against enemy fire is heroism enough, and the central martial virtue is 'fortaleza,' fortitude. Don Quixote describes the quality of the soldiers who charge one after another the weapons of the opposing galley as 'valentía y atrevimiento el mayor que se puede hallar en todos los trances de la guerra' (such courage and daring are the greatest that all the hazards of war can show) (I. 38, 470).

Although Don Quixote's oration takes as its primary objective the praise of arms, it also comments briefly on the positive attributes of letters. The traditional argument that letters conserve and transmit the fame that men achieve through feats of arms is generally present in the text of Cervantes's novel, particularly in the various passages in which Don Quixote expresses his desire to have his acts of chivalry recorded and memorialized in a book. Rather than reiterating this argument, however, the oration presents the case for the life of letters in terms consistent with the training and career of the 'letrado':

> dicen las letras que sin ellas no se podrían sustentar las armas, porque la guerra también tiene sus leyes y está sujeta a ellas, y que las leyes caen debajo de lo que son letras y letrados. A esto responden las armas que las leyes no se podrán sustentar sin ellas, porque con las armas se defienden las repúblicas, se conservan los reinos, se guardan las ciudades, se aseguran los caminos, se despejan los mares de corsarios, y, finalmente, si por ellas no fuese, las repúblicas, los reinos, las monarquías, las ciudades, los caminos de mar y tierra estarían sujetos al rigor y a la confusión que trae consigo la guerra el tiempo que dura y tiene licencia de usar de sus previlegios y de sus fuerzas. (I. 38, 469)

> letters say that without them, arms cannot maintain themselves, for war, too, has its laws and is governed by them, and laws belong to the domain of letters and men of letters. To this arms make the answer that without them, laws cannot be maintained, for by arms states are defended,

kingdoms preserved, cities protected, roads made safe, seas cleared of pirates. In short, if it were not for them, states, kingdoms, monarchies, cities, ways by sea and land would be exposed to the violence and confusions which war brings with it, so long as it lasts and is free to make use of its privileges and powers.

'Letras' are associated here with the professional expertise of the 'letrado.' Sixteenth-century Spanish jurists produced an influential body of writings on natural law and on the causes and limits of just war. Don Quixote alludes to this material when he states that war has its own laws and falls for this reason under the jurisdiction of 'letters and men of letters.' The response from the side of arms – that they alone can control violence and maintain the peace and order upon which good laws and civil society depend – concedes the importance of the rule of law for a wide range of human endeavours. This exchange of arguments points towards the reconciliation of arms and letters, in a gesture characteristic of the humanist tradition.[30] It is nonetheless striking that such reconciliation has less force than the many arguments that Don Quixote offers in favour of arms, and that it appears in the part of his oration classified in rhetorical theory as the *refutatio*, the section in which the orator presents and then refutes arguments opposed to his own. As Don Quixote states at the beginning of his discourse, his objective is to demonstrate the pre-eminence of arms.

The skills of a rhetorician include the ability to state and respond to countervailing arguments. Don Quixote's comment on the laws of war can be read in this light, as a demonstration of rhetorical completeness and the capacity to contain opposing propositions within a single discourse. The same interpretive principle applies to Don Quixote's brief invective against gunpowder weapons. The closing section of his oration condemns artillery as a 'diabolical invention' unknown to earlier, better-favoured ages, and deplores modern weapons that can enable a common infantryman to kill a noble knight through the distant and anonymous exercise of mechanized violence. Don Quixote applies these adverse circumstances to himself, lamenting his untimely effort to revive the lost skills and values of knight-errantry:

> considerando esto, estoy por decir que en el alma me pesa de haber tomado este ejercicio de caballero andante en edad tan detestable como es esta en que ahora vivimos; porque aunque a mí ningún peligro me pone miedo, todavía me pone recelo pensar si la pólvora y el estaño me han de

> quitar la ocasión de hacerme famoso y conocido por el valor de mi brazo y filos de mi espada, por todo lo descubierto de la tierra. (I. 38, 471)

> when I reflect on this, I am almost tempted to say that in my heart I repent of having adopted this profession of knight-errant in so detestable an age. For though no peril can make me fear, it distresses me to think that powder and lead may rob me of the opportunity of making myself famous and renowned throughout the known earth by the might of my arm and the edge of my sword.

The terms of this complaint reflect standard responses to the technological and tactical changes associated with the development and deployment of gunpowder weapons. Don Quixote criticizes both artillery and small firearms as inimical to a traditional martial ethos of honour and valour. It should be noted, however, that Don Quixote's anxiety here centres on his own desire to secure fame through valorous acts of arms, and that the general intent that informs his discourse is to assert the value of the life of arms in his time. Rather than condemning modern warfare as such, his argument defines modes of heroic conduct that can be reconciled with its specific demands and limitations. Samuel Hynes comments on how such heroism presents itself in Marc Bloch's memoir of his service as an infantry sergeant in 1915:

> The courageous act here is not some extreme individual gesture ..., but simply going back to the trenches and standing there, enduring the shells, the misery, and the privation, and *not trembling*. It is passive courage, a stoic endurance where there is nothing else to be done. Such courage doesn't win medals, but it is a fine and difficult virtue, as old soldiers know. (58)

Silent and patient in the face of the enemy's mines, the sentry who stands as one of Don Quixote's exemplary figures practises this difficult martial virtue.[31]

The discourse on arms and letters illustrates Cervantes's distinctive use of conventional forms. It presents a debate on a set theme in the structure of a formal oration, a model that humanist authors used to examine the various facets of rhetorical controversies and to compose both panegyrics and mock encomia.[32] Don Quixote's praise of arms admits some irony, given his absorption in the lettered world of books and readers and his lack of experience of warfare. Don Quixote nonetheless offers a forceful defence of the soldier's life that responds to the practical and ethical challenges of wars conducted with gunpowder weapons. The play of rhetorical structures and techniques allows Cervantes to construct a complex discourse that adapts a conventional theme to issues of the conduct and ethos of armed conflict in his own time. Similar kinds of play and invention inform the treatment of warfare and heroism across a broad range of canonical and popular genres in Cervantes's works.

The purpose of this study is to analyse the presentation of war and issues of heroism in Cervantes through the exploration and juxtaposition of multiple genres. Chapter 1 analyses the scrutiny of the classical ethos of heroism in the *Tragedia de Numancia*, through the interplay of epic and tragedy in its characters and dramatic action. Cervantes's historical subject is the resistance of the residents of Numantia to a long siege by Roman troops under the command of Scipio Aemilianus Africanus, an event that is accorded foundational significance for the Spanish nation in early modern historiography. In the terms that Tasso uses in his *Discorsi del poema eroico*, the Numantian characters display the elevated virtues of valour and magnanimity, while the Roman general Cipión is less secure in his possession of these virtues and subject to tragic error. The two sides share a commitment to an ethos of valour and martial fame that can be traced to sources in classical epic and Roman history, but they differ in their fidelity to the values of open war. The Numantians challenge their enemies to confrontation on the battlefield and respond to the restrictive conditions of the siege by turning their force and valour inward in an act of collective suicide. The Romans, in contrast, secure victory as a pragmatic end through tactics that depend on the avoidance of direct combat. The play's action ends in a double reversal, with the fall of Cipión and the rise of Numantia. Cipión's strategic approach responds to the constraints that he experiences as a military leader who must answer to the authority of the Roman Senate and limit the material and human costs of war. His role illustrates the limitations of the heroic ethos and the difficulties of sustaining traditional martial values under the conditions of centralized command and political rule.

Chapter 2 centres on the uses of pastoral in conjunction with other genres to interrogate the values that inform heroic literature and the exclusions that make the pastoral world pacific and orderly. A historical kind that occupies a low place in the Neo-Aristotelian hierarchy of genres, pastoral generally projects an idealized space of retirement, distant from the clash of arms and the ethos of war. From a perspective of detachment, pastoral speakers contemplate the demands and rewards of public life, sometimes commemorating achievements in the exercise of arms and letters and sometimes lamenting the disorder of the external world in a voice that assimilates itself to satire. By combining pastoral with other genres, Cervantes explores the instability of the values that pastoral celebrates and the implication of violence in its green world. In Don Quixote and Sancho's journey to El Toboso (*DQ* II. 8), the pastoral space of rural Spain provides a setting for a dialogue on the rewards of an active life that reveals the instability of the terms in which the fame of heroes is defined and recorded. In Don Quixote's assault on the sheepflocks (*DQ* I. 18) the literary conventions of epic and pastoral are juxtaposed with the concerns of practical pastoralists. Don Quixote persuades himself that he has found an opportunity to secure fame by displaying his valour in arms, but the shepherds defend their flocks through forms of violence alien to the literary conventions that have shaped his imagination. The adventure of the braying *regidores* (*DQ* II. 25–7) revisits questions of reputation and violence in rural life. Mockery leads to a conflict between two communities that is resolved only when Sancho offers himself as a scapegoat on which the offended villagers discharge their violence. In the style of Horatian satire, this episode considers the fragility of fame and the difficulties of containing violence once it has been released.

Chapter 3 discusses Greek romance, the saint's life, and lyric poetry as forms that Cervantes uses to represent and reflect on Spain's protracted conflict with the Ottoman Empire in the Mediterranean. Three interrelated texts that draw on Cervantes's direct experience as a soldier in the Spanish infantry and as a captive of the Algerian corsairs – *El trato de Argel*, *Los baños de Argel*, and the inset narrative of the Spanish captain Ruy Pérez de Viedma in *Don Quixote* (I. 49–51) – employ lyric verse for such purposes as lament, prayer, and heroic eulogy, and use the form of romance to explore heroic conduct in Spain's repeated military encounters with the Ottomans and in the restrictive conditions of captivity. These texts mark a shift from martial heroism to a spiritual endurance appropriate to romance. The captives in *El trato de Argel* request assistance from the Virgin through prayers and invest hope in the prospect of military relief by a new armada from Spain. In *Los baños de Argel* typological patterns associate the captives' experience with Old Testament exile and Christian martyrdom, and a romance narrative leads to flight from Algiers through the agency of an enigmatic Moorish woman. The tale of Ruy Pérez de Viedma combines an account of historical battles at Tunis and Lepanto with a narrative of captivity in Algiers and escape by sea to Spain. The first section praises the ideal of the aristocratic soldier-poet, an emblem in Renaissance literature of the union of arms and letters; the second centres on a female figure who devises the captives' release and is assimilated to the redemptive character of the Virgin. In each text the conventions of romance reinforce a heroism of Christian endurance and constancy and articulate the values of community and cooperation.

Chapter 4 turns to Cervantes's presentation of the ethos and conditions of service in the common ranks of Spain's imperial armies and the impact of returning soldiers on civil society. The Spanish state formed its armed forces by recruiting from the masses of labourers, peasants, vagabonds, and other occupants of the lower tiers of society and by conscripting slaves and convicted criminals into terms of forced military service. A culture of soldiers, based on a shared experience of violence and on freedom from the restrictive laws and customs of civilian life, attracted enlistment and created a distinct sodality among the lower ranks. This separation also generated social anxieties about the disorder that might be visited on civilians as returning soldiers asserted the liberties that they had acquired and boasted of the exploits that they had undertaken in the king's name. Among the popular genres of early modern Spain, picaresque fiction offers a model for writing about the classes that were subject to recruitment and conscription, the military culture in which they lived, and the anxieties that they provoked. To examine the lives of common soldiers, Cervantes turns to the picaresque, in combination with a number of related genres: pastoral, miracle narrative, autobiography, confessional writing, popular theatre. Vicente de la Rosa, a disruptive rival in the goatherd Eugenio's tale of his lost love for Leandra (*DQ* I. 51), has returned to his village from the wars and captivates his neighbours with his soldier's finery and his tales of great deeds in battle. Vicente's role revisits the proximity of warfare to the pastoral world, and his seduction of the innocent Leandra illustrates the attractions of soldiers' tales and their affinities to popular art. In *El casamiento engañoso* the ensign Campuzano uses the finery and bravado of a returned soldier as instruments of deception, to contract a marriage that promises to enrich him and improve his social position. The story that Campuzano tells about this stratagem incorporates multiple generic conventions into the frame of a picaresque narrative and stresses the distinctive culture of soldiers and their defiance of civilian norms. Such dislocation, however, is not the sole effect of the ensign's tale. In conjunction with the interlinking narrative of *El coloquio de los perros*, it attests to the pleasures of friendship and recreation. The convict and author Ginés de Pasamonte further illustrates the pragmatic uses of storytelling. His two appearances in *Don Quixote* (I. 22, II. 25–7) assert the value that he places on the narrative of his life that he has in progress – a picaresque text that relates truths rather than fictions – and on the skills that he exercises in his puppet theatre. Through his *Life* and his puppets, Ginés expects to realize material and practical gains, filling his purse and evading his term of service in the galleys. He represents the popular artist as trickster, reliant on his verbal wit and powers of invention. The two false captives in *Los trabajos de Persiles y Sigismunda* (III. 10) also intend to tell stories for pragmatic ends, but they lack the ingenuity and bravado of practised *pícaros*. They use external signs of the experience of captivity – a map of Algiers, chains, a whip – to solicit funds from a group of villagers, but when one of the local justices challenges them they are unable to sustain the fiction that they have returned to Spain after years of forced service among the Algerian corsairs. The justice is prepared to send them to the galleys, but they escape his wrath by revealing their true identity as students who have left Salamanca to pursue the life of arms in Italy and Flanders. Their intent to join the community of common soldiers puts aside the rigour of the law and invites compassion and the rites of hospitality.

1 Warriors: Epic and Tragedy

> He wondered how this had happened to him, how despite himself he had been imprisoned by this inflexible choice of winning or losing; for there seemed to be no compromise between the two in this barren place where there was a single definition of excellence.
>
> James Salter, The Hunters (1956)

An early modern author who chooses to reflect on the nature and rewards of a warrior's ethos will turn in the first instance to epic, a genre that offers canonical texts on martial themes and informs critical thought on central issues in Renaissance literary theory. Classical epic commemorates exemplary acts of arms and, in the case of Vergil and his Roman successors, explores the intersection between the ethos of heroic poetry and the public sphere of politics and history.[1] Renaissance poetics places epic at the highest position in its hierarchy of genres and often frames its commentary on such questions as decorum of style and character and the relationship between history and poetry in reference to canonical epic texts. The critical elevation of epic corresponds to its subject matter. Epic embodies an inflexible ethos that honours only the most excellent acts of martial violence and celebrates the fame that rewards those who accomplish such feats, inviting reflection on the narrow world of heroes and on the connections between martial ideals and the world view of empire. The singular hero can represent the totality of a people and their history. To define the best among warriors and to describe the foundation of systems of rule through heroic warfare are central concerns in the epic tradition.[2]

Epic is also closely aligned with tragedy, a second genre that is highly placed in Renaissance poetics.[3] Northrop Frye classifies epic as an 'encyclopaedic form' that explores the intersection of individual lives with the extended temporal rhythm that marks the existence of cities and empires. On this reading, tragedy selects from epic poetry the trajectory of an individual life, focusing on the hero's isolation and the narrowing of his freedom through the forces of fate and the law.[4] In Greek tragedy the forces that the hero encounters are often linked to his earlier acts of military excellence, so that tragedy exposes the costs that war exacts when the hero returns home. The uses of tragedy in epic are particularly clear in the *Aeneid*, a foundational work that engages symbolic and moral patterns from Aeschylus's *Oresteia*. In both Vergil and Aeschylus the underworld communicates with the sphere of human action and releases demonic energies that move men and women to anger and vengeance. Through the virtue of *pietas* Vergil's heroes have the potential to control the *furor* of demonic rage, but as in tragedy this moral opposition is not easily sustained: just anger declines into fury and fair retribution into vengeance. This moral uncertainty undermines the distinction between heroes and their antagonists and leads in both genres to a social and cultural crisis, in which violence escapes the sacrificial rites that contain it as part of an established order and extends itself through periodic and indiscriminate surges. The crisis of violence marks the killing of Turnus at the end of the *Aeneid* and is revisited in such later Latin epics as the *Bellum ciuile*, Lucan's epic of the disorder and brutality of Roman civil strife.[5]

Political issues and the moral challenges that they raise are prominent in epic poetry from early modern Spain. Armstrong-Roche places Cervantes's *Persiles* in creative opposition to a traditional martial ideology that subordinates love to war and projects myths of ancient foundations and providential forces 'in the service of empire' (66). In his last work Cervantes 'rewrites the script of empire' that links the Hapsburg monarchy to the translation across time of Rome's imperial practices and powers (Armstrong-Roche 73–4). Epic poems from this period speak to the intersection of heroic conventions and imperial ideas. Such works appeal to ideas of fame and glory drawn from Roman historiography and present an understanding of political community based on continuity with a past that is conceived in heroic terms (Lara Garrido 39–40). Spanish poets and theorists found in the dynastic concerns of Ariosto's *Orlando furioso* a means of reconciling the classical canon of epic and the precepts of Neo-Aristotelian poetics with the modern models of Italian Renaissance epic, and Spain's recent experience offered matters for genealogical and imperial praise: the victorious campaigns of

Charles V, the conquest of the New World, the containment of Islamic rebellion within Spain, and the conflict with the Ottoman Empire in the Mediterranean (Lara Garrido 70, 45–6).[6] Epic poetry contributed to a political program that sought to establish legitimacy for imperial rule, through its status as a canonical genre and its use 'as a vehicle for the construction of an imagined ethnic and political identity for Spain' (Davis 10). This project, however, led to tensions and contradictions of a tragic kind. Epic poetry constructed a single identity in opposition to the multiple others that Spain encountered in its campaigns of conquest and conversion. Since the 'ideological divisions' of this process could not be fully concealed, they undermined the discourse of unity and revealed 'the seams of the epic's dominant belief system' (Davis 12, 17). Alonso de Ercilla's *La Araucana* – an epic that exerted significant influence in its own time – illustrates the ideological uses and tensions of the form. Through prophecies of Spain's victories in France and the Mediterranean and an imagined map that celebrates its empire, Ercilla associates his subject of a minor war on the colonial periphery with the grand designs of empire (Nicolopulos 11–12). His acclaim for Spain's imperial program, however, is not unqualified, since his construction of the Spanish combatants and their Amerindian enemies engages three discourses – of service, virtue, and economic gain – that each admit internal contradictions and complicate the fundamental distinction between Spain and its others (Davis 60). High mimetic literature in Spain follows its classical predecessors in its concern with the ethical and cultural uncertainties of heroic action.

In his early play *La Numancia*, Cervantes dedicates his attention to a heroic theme from Iberian history: the fall of the Celtiberian city of Numantia in 133 BCE, following a protracted siege by Roman troops under the command of the Roman consul and general Scipio Aemilianus Africanus. A distinguished commander, Scipio could count Numantia among an impressive list of victories, including the storming and capture of Carthage at the end of the Third Punic War (149–146 BCE). The historiography of the siege emphasizes the striking heroism of the Numantian defenders, who offered sustained resistance to Rome and chose to destroy themselves rather than to surrender their persons and their wealth to Roman rule.[7] Histories and chronicles in early modern Spain often present the defence of Numantia as an exemplary case of courage and common purpose. In his continuation of Florian Ocampo's *Corónica general de España* – a history of Spain sanctioned by royal authority – Ambrosio Morales portrays the siege of Numantia as 'a founding moment in the history of his *patria*' (Schmidt, 'Development of *Hispanitas*' 32) and places the city's inhabitants among the first members of the political community that constitutes the Spanish nation and embodies such essential values as valour, strength, loyalty, resistance, and perseverance in the face of suffering (33, 35). This interpretation suggests that Numantia is a subject appropriate to epic. Like the fall of Troy in the *Aeneid*, the siege in *La Numancia* is an account of martial violence and destruction that leads to an imperial order, in a conjunction of martial themes and foundational narrative. Such recourse to specific historical events as a basis for paradigms of national identity is typical of learned epic in Spain (Lara Garrido 41–2). *La Numancia* takes the epic matter of war as its central subject and explores key issues related to the theory, causes, objectives, means, and ends of martial conflict (Endress). In its use of dramatic form, however, it presents affinities with other genres. The Romans and the Numantians endorse an epic ethos of martial excellence and fame, but Cipión's generalship aligns his character with tragic conventions, and this tragic aspect qualifies the play's celebration of the heroic ethos and prophetic claims of the epic tradition. Through the interaction of canonical genres, Cervantes explores the ethos of epic heroism and the conditions under which such heroism turns towards tragedy. As in other history plays from early modern Europe, tension between competing genres reveals the 'fault lines' of contemporary ideological constructs (Simerka 89–90).

La Numancia is central to the commitment to imaginative literature that marks Cervantes's life following his return from Algiers in 1580.[8] His interest in dramaturgy is directly related to the emergence at this time of Spain's first *corrales*, or public theatres. Sponsored by religious societies for charitable ends and occupied by companies of professional actors, these venues established Spanish theatre as a form of popular art and created the possibility that authors could earn an income by writing for the stage. The sale of a play transferred control of the text from the author to the director who had purchased it for his company, but usually offered better monetary returns than arrangements for printing a book, and Cervantes took advantage of this opportunity as he began to establish himself as a writer in Madrid. *La Numancia* and *El trato de Argel* are the two plays that remain extant from several that he wrote between 1580 and 1587.[9] As a dramatist Cervantes is sympathetic to the efforts of his contemporaries Juan de la Cueva and Cristóbal de Virués to produce high mimetic drama modelled on Senecan tragedy. In *La Numancia* Cervantes participates in this engagement with classical models and announces an interest in epic that will he will sustain over the course of his literary career.[10]

The play's action begins as Cipión takes command of the Roman army encamped outside Numantia's walls. Cipión recognizes the challenges of renewing an indecisive campaign that has lasted sixteen years, and he exhorts his troops to set aside the vices of an idle army and recover their Roman discipline and valour. Two Numantian ambassadors arrive to express their respect for Cipión and to propose a treaty between their city and Rome, but the Roman general rejects their offer of peace, asserting his commitment to open battle and his confidence that his army will prevail through force of arms. In a private conference with his brother and subordinate Quinto Fabio, however, Cipión reveals that he plans to encircle Numantia with a trench, in order to defeat its defenders through the prudent tactics of siege warfare. These opening scenes establish the pattern of the conflict between the two sides. Cipión, a general aware of his place in the Roman structure of command and his duties to the Senate, pursues a strategic victory that will limit losses among his troops. In contrast, the Numantians Teógenes and Corabino, leaders who respect the collective identity and will of the city's residents, remain faithful to an ethos of open force and valour. Corabino proposes two measures to break the siege: a single combat between champions chosen by the two sides and a concerted nocturnal assault on the Roman siegeworks. Although the men of Numantia support both measures, neither is put into practice, since Cipión rejects the unbridled violence of a single combat and the women of the city fear that they will be abandoned and enslaved if their men assault the enemy by night. In the face of the privations of the siege, the Numantians turn to acts of individual and collective heroism. The young Morandro crosses the trench with his friend Leoncio to find bread for his beloved Lira; Teógenes orders his people to burn their material goods and leads them in collective suicide to deprive the Romans of the substance of victory; Viriato, a child who has hidden during the suicide of his elders, resists Cipión's offer of Roman clemency and leaps to his death from a tower. As the dramatic action unfolds, supernatural agents reveal their foreknowledge of the end of the siege and its sequel in history. The personified figure of the river Duero delivers a prophecy of Spain's future triumph over Rome during the age of the Hapsburgs; a dead body, conjured to speak through the arts of necromancy, predicts that Numantia will turn its forces upon itself; the figures of War, Disease, and Hunger bear witness to the city's violent destruction and foresee both Cipión's immediate capture of the city and Spain's success over the long term as an imperial power. Viriato's death leads Cipión to recognize that the Numantians have denied his claim to military glory through their superior heroism. At the play's end, Fame appears to praise Numantia's force and valour as a fit subject for her song.

La Numancia addresses themes and conventions associated in Renaissance poetics with high mimetic genres. Elements of classical epic are present in its dramatic action: strategic consultations between Cipión and his subordinates; counsels of resistance within the city walls; embassies and parleys between the Roman general and the Numantian leaders; and prophecies of imperial rule and expansion. The Numantians' proposed recourses of single combat and nocturnal assault have clear precedents in the epic tradition and in Roman history.[11] At the level of style, the repetition of heroic epithets and the dominance of the hendecasyllabic line imitate the elevation of epic verse. Tragic conventions shape Cipión's character and conduct. To show concern for the aftermath of war; to anticipate war's effects on one's own reputation; to recognize the limitations of the tactics employed against the enemy; to accept that the moral outcome of an engagement favours the defeated: all these gestures are associated with tragedy. Analysis here of the play will begin with discussion of epic and tragedy in Neo-Aristotelian literary theory and proceed to consider three key aspects of the text: the heroic ethos of epic and the fidelity of the Romans and Numantians to this code; Cipión's tactics and his awareness of their limitations; and the shifting definitions of fame and glory as they apply to Numantia and to Rome and its general. The presentation of the conflict between the Numantians and their Roman besiegers examines the limits of martial violence and the fragility of the rewards extended to those who exercise it.

Torquato Tasso's *Discorsi del poema eroico* illustrate the principles that inform Cervantes's choice of the siege of Numantia as a subject appropriate to epic presentation.[12] Tasso's treatise confirms the eminence of epic in Renaissance poetics and carefully locates epic in relation to other canonical genres, particularly tragedy. Following the assumptions of Neo-Aristotelian theory, Tasso defines poetry as an imitation of human action. He distinguishes genres according to the kinds of actions that they imitate and the ends or effects that they produce for an audience. His definition of epic emphasizes the thematic and stylistic elevation of the form, as well as its association with the marvellous: 'Diremo dunque che 'l poema eroico sia imitazione d'azione illustre, grande e perfetta, fatta narrando con altissimo verso, affine di muovere gli animi con la maraviglia e di giovare in questa guisa' (We shall then say that the epic poem is an imitation of a noble action, great and perfect, narrated in the loftiest verse, with the purpose of moving the mind to wonder) (74). The *favola*, or plot of epic, has three essential components: reversal, or *peripeteia*, 'una mutazione dalla buona nella rea fortuna, o dalla rea nella buona' (a change from good to bad fortune or from bad to good); recognition, 'un passar dall'ignoranza alla notizia' (a passing from ignorance to knowledge); and pathos, 'la perturbazione dolorosa e piena d'affanni, come sono le morti e le ferrite e i lamenti e i ramarichi che possono muover a pietà' (a grievous perturbation full of anxieties, such as deaths and wounds and lamentations and complaints, which can move to pity) (74–5). This account of the epic fable reproduces the parts of the tragic plot as they are outlined in Aristotle's *Poetics*, and Tasso takes considerable care to distinguish epic from tragedy. Recognizing the high placement of these genres, he notes that they both present the actions of heroes, but he maintains that the actions imitated in epic are nonetheless more noble than those represented in tragedy. The pre-eminent form of epic requires the most elevated of subjects – that is, excellence at arms – and the most noble of human virtues: 'l'illustre dell'eroico è fondato sovra l'eccelsa virtù militare e sopra il magnanimo proponimento di morire, sovra la pietà, sovra la religione e sovra l'azioni nelle quali risplendono queste virtù' (epic illustriousness is based on lofty military valour and the magnanimous resolve to die, on piety, religion, and deeds alight with these virtues) (102). In contrast, the tragic plot depends on characters who are not so possessed of exemplary virtues and therefore subject to error: 'richiede la tragedia persone né buone né cattive, ma d'una condizione di mezzo' (tragedy demands persons neither good nor bad but in between) (102). The plots of epic and of tragedy both trace out patterns of reversal, but epic admits a more complex use of *peripeteia*. Reversal can involve change 'dalla prospera nell'avversa fortuna, o dall'avversa nella prospera' (from prosperous to adverse, or from adverse to prosperous fortune) (141). The first kind of reversal is appropriate to tragedy, while epic can present both kinds of reversal in a single work, 'altri passa da miseria in felicità, altri da felicità in miseria' (some people going from misery to happiness, others from happiness to misery) (142). For Tasso, one of the strengths of epic is its receptiveness to complex patterns of reversal: 'questa doppia mutazione conviene più all'epopeia ch'a gli altri poemi' (this double change of fortune is more suitable to epic than to other kinds of poem) (142). Epic also produces a specific response in the audience. While tragedy moves its audience 'co 'l terrore y con la compassione' (by terror and compassion), epic evokes a reaction of 'maraviglia' (wonder) at the narration of illustrious and marvellous events (72). The various distinctions that Tasso draws to separate epic from tragedy attribute more elevated subjects, more complex structures, and superior effects to the epic fable. His analysis appeals repeatedly to the related concepts of nobility and excellence.

In *La Numancia* Cervantes presents the siege of the Celtiberian city as an epic fable. The central concepts of excellence, nobility, and the marvellous inform the play's characters and dramatic action. The defence of the city is a noble action, in which the Numantians display military excellence and magnanimity. Their collective suicide at the end of the siege is both an act of self-sacrifice that confirms their extraordinary valour and a spectacle of martial violence that inspires wonder. While the Numantians display resolution and bravery, the Roman general is a middle character, subject to error in his strategic decision to reduce the city to Roman rule by siege. The dramatic action follows a pattern of double reversal, in that Cipión passes from a state of high and secure reputation to a condition of self-reproach at the prospect of returning to Rome, while the Numantians secure a moral victory over the Roman forces and so foreshadow the rise of Spain as an imperial power that will exceed Rome in its military force and geographical extension. A central irony is that the arrogance of investment in military victory leads to Cipión's tragic fall and to the Numantians' triumph in the voice of Fame (Martín 18–21). The unfolding of these reversals involves both recognition, in Cipión's realization that he has surrendered his glory to the opposing defenders, and pathos, in the lamentations of the Numantian women and the closing spectacle of the city's physical destruction. Incorporating the rise of Numantia's fame and the fall of Cipión, and drawing on diverse models from Latin epic and classical tragedy, the play presents an epic narrative in the form of high mimetic drama.[13]

Tasso also offers guidance on the selection and presentation of epic subjects. On Homeric precedent, he notes that the epic poet should take his subject from history (83); on the authority of Vergil, he asserts 'abbia ancora risguardo il poeta alla gloria della nazione, all'origine delle città e delle famiglie illustri, a' principi de' regni e degl'imperi' (the poet should also consider the glory of his country, the origin of cities and illustrious families, the beginnings of kingdoms and empires) (110). The use of historical distance as a means of balancing invention and verisimilitude is a central concern in the *Discorsi*. Tasso argues that subjects drawn from recent events limit the scope of invention, since the details of such events will be familiar to the poet's audience. In contrast, temporal distance confers freedom to complement and enrich the outline of a historical narrative with poetic invention. Such distant material nonetheless presents difficulties, since the poet's audience may find an account of remote customs tedious and unpleasant. Cervantes resolves the challenge of his historically distant subject by attributing similar customs and practices to the Romans and the Numantians, a technique that depends on poetic invention, particularly in the presentation of Numantia. In his play many of the inhabitants of Numantia have Latinate names. They invoke the Roman deities Jupiter and Pluto, and they attempt to foresee the outcome of their conflict with Rome through forms of augury well represented in Latin epic: appeals to divine knowledge, avian signs, dreams, necromancy.[14] On the lines of Tasso's counsel concerning the uses of invention in historical epic, Cervantes represents the remote social practices of Numantia by drawing on Roman customs widely known through the diffusion and translation of classical texts.

The ethos of open heroism is one of the classical ideals that Cervantes attributes to Rome and Numantia alike. Based on bravery displayed through direct force, and on military achievements exercised for the common good and rewarded through public praise and enduring fame, this ethos draws on ancient sources. The Roman soldiers and the defenders of Numantia favour open armed conflict and aspire to glory as the reward for illustrious acts of arms, but the two parties differ in their fidelity to the ethos of heroism. Over the course of the siege the Numantians are constant in their dedication to the demanding standards of open warfare, while the Romans turn to strategies that avoid open battle and so compromise their commitment to the heroic values that they espouse. This distinction aligns the Numantians with classical epic and Cipión with tragedy.

When Cipión assumes command of the Roman forces encamped outside Numantia, he affirms his commitment to the heroic values that sustain open warfare. The historical Scipio was well recognized for his skills in oratory and in war (Kahn 151). The harangue that Cervantes's character delivers to the troops follows a practice well established in Roman sources, and makes the case that decisive action will bring the protracted campaign against Numantia to a successful end.[15] As an experienced commander, Cipión proposes to reform his army by returning to a traditional code of self-denial and military discipline. Although the Romans should not be confident in their simple numerical superiority, the Numantians can be conquered through the concerted and prudent exercise of force ('el esfuerzo y cordura,' l. 101). These terms invoke the qualities linked to military leadership in medieval commentaries on the Homeric epics: valour *(fortitudo)* and wisdom *(sapientia)*.[16] The general stresses in his *peroratio* that each soldier has the capacity to shape his destiny on the battlefield:

> cada cual se fabrica su destino;
> no tiene allí fortuna alguna parte:
> La pereza fortuna baja cría;
> la diligencia, imperio y monarquía. (ll. 157–60)

> each one makes his destiny; fortune has no part in this: idleness produces humble fortune; perseverance, empire and dominion.

Cipión asserts that military force will bring rewards to the individual soldier and to the Roman Republic. In opposition to the fragile goods of fortune, he exhorts his troops to rely on the diligence and fortitude that inspire heroic conduct and guarantee political order and imperial rule. The insistence on these qualities suggests an intention to encounter the enemy with direct and open force. The general's appeal to the soldier's destiny is a call to arms. His subordinate Gayo Mario assures him that the troops have responded favourably to his words and are now prepared to sacrifice their lives in his service, moved by the 'brío' (spirit) of true Romans (ll. 195–6).

The Numantians share Cipión's stated commitment to martial excellence and open warfare. In internal councils of war and in parleys with the enemy, they express their intention to bring the conflict with Rome to a quick and decisive end. Confident in their own abilities as soldiers, they express their preference for acts over words (ll. 288–9) and their inclination to heroic acts: 'de guerras ama el numantino pecho' (the Numantian breast is enamoured of wars) (l. 304). This ethos is central to their identity as citizens and defenders of Numantia. It is common to their leaders Teógenes and Corabino, and to the unnamed warriors who speak in defence of the Numantian cause. Their statements and attitudes throughout the course of the conflict confirm their devotion to martial values and their readiness for open battle. Like the Romans, they pursue military advantages through moral reform, casting out vice from their city and offering a sacrifice to Pluto (ll. 633–40). This gesture is in part a ritual enacted to attract divine favour, and in part an augury performed to ascertain the future outcome of the war. When the results of the augury are not propitious for the Numantians, Leoncio counsels his companion Morandro against despair:

> Morandro, al que es buen soldado
> agüeros no le dan pena;
> que pone la suerte buena
> en el ánimo esforzado.
> Y esas vanas apariencias
> nunca le turban el tino:
> su brazo es su estrella o signo;
> su valor, sus influencias. (ll. 915–22)

> Morandro, the good soldier finds no grief in omens, since he relies on his valiant spirit for good luck. And these vain appearances never disturb his good sense: his arm is his star or sign; his valour, their influences.

The parallel with the Roman characters is clear. Like Cipión, Leoncio locates a warrior's fortune in the determination and force that he exercises in defence of his person and his cause. The 'star' that shapes a soldier's fate is the 'arm' with which he wields his weapons; its 'influences' depend on the valour that he shows in battle. Through these metaphors Leoncio opposes the idea that methods of augury can foresee the outcome of a military encounter. The true soldier claims his own destiny by force of arms.

Mutual dedication to the epic ethos informs verbal exchanges between the two sides. Cipión's assumption of command of the Roman troops leads to a parley in which the Numantian ambassadors present their case for a diplomatic peace. They salute Cipión as the strongest of Roman generals (l. 235), praise his 'virtue and valour' (l. 261), and announce their willingness to form a bond of allegiance with him as their 'lord and friend' (l. 264). In Cipión's recognized martial virtues and their own reputation for strength and valour, the Numantian ambassadors hope to find shared grounds for peace.[17] Cipión listens to their claims, but he rejects summarily their offer of concord and presses them to take up arms:

> Tarde de arrepentidos dais la muestra;
> poco vuestra amistad me satisface.
> De nuevo ejercitad la fuerte diestra,

> que quiero ver lo que la mía hace,
> ya que ha puesto en ella la ventura
> la gloria mía, y vuestra desventura.
> A desvergüenza de tan largos años
> es poca recompensa pedir paces:
> seguid la guerra, renovad los daños,
> salgan de nuevo las valientes haces. (ll. 267–76)

> You have delayed too long in showing your repentance; your friendship offers me scant redress. Once again exercise your strong right arm, for I want to see what my own can achieve, since fortune has placed in it my glory and your misfortune. For the shamelessness that you have shown over so many years, to sue for peace is little recompense: carry on the war, return to its harms, let the emblems of valour appear once more.

Cipión reaffirms his commitment to the use of open force, an instrument that will sustain his reputation and secure a Roman victory. He understands that the offer of friendship from Numantia is an attempt to establish a political alliance with the Republic, but he denies their proposal as a belated gesture that cannot redeem their long years of resistance to Roman authority.[18] The image of the right arm – a conventional metonym for the living body that the soldier delivers as an instrument of battle – incites the Numantians to renew their war with Rome. The general warns his enemies that he will lead his troops to victory in open battle, beneath the standards of Roman rule. In rejecting the diplomatic claims for peace, he reasserts the martial values of force and valour.

The ethos that the Romans and Numantians share can be traced to Latin epic. In Book XII of the *Aeneid*, an enemy archer strikes Aeneas and forces him to withdraw from battle. Aeneas chafes at the interruption in his assault on the enemy, and Venus intervenes to assist the Trojan healers in removing the arrowhead and restoring her son's wounded flesh, so that he can arm himself and pursue a decisive encounter with Turnus. In his impatience with his own wound and his eagerness to return to combat, Aeneas is an exemplary soldier and military leader. As he returns to the battlefield, he embraces his son Ascanius and offers him a lesson on the demands and benefits of the life of arms:

> disce, puer, uirtutem ex me uerumque laborem
> fortunam ex aliis. nunc te mea dextera bello
> defensum dabit et magna inter praemia ducet.

tu facito, mox cum matura adoleuerit aetas,
sis memor et te animo repetentem exempla tuorum
et pater Aeneas et auunculus excitet Hector. (XII. 435–40)

Learn fortitude and toil from me, my son,
Ache of true toil. Good fortune learn from others.
My sword arm now will be your shield in battle
And introduce you to the boons of war.
When, before long, you come to man's estate,
Be sure that you recall this. Harking back
For models in your family, let your father,
Aeneas, and uncle, Hector, stir your heart.

Aeneas praises the use of direct force against the enemy. Like Cipión, he opposes the fortitude and diligence of the true warrior to the trust that others place in fortune. Through the right arm that wields the sword – the 'diestra' that Cipión invites the Numantians to test against his army – Aeneas will protect his son and garner for family and state the rewards ('praemia') of successful military action. These include honour and public praise, forms of social capital obtained in war and subject to transmission through patrilineal succession. The proleptic exhortation that urges Ascanius, on reaching the age of maturity, to remember the exemplary conduct of his father and uncle emphasizes the passage of martial values and motives from one generation to the next. Public recognition secured through military success will form part of Ascanius's patrimony, and this symbolic inheritance will spur him to further accomplishments. Aeneas expounds here an ethos of male excellence bound to open warfare and sustained through the public honours of a militaristic society.

Historical sources also illustrate the influence of the Roman military ethos. In his *Pro lege manilia* – a speech in defence of the legislation that conferred supreme military command on Pompey in 66 BCE – Cicero appeals to Rome's tradition of military excellence: 'the glory of Rome ... has come down to you from your forefathers great in everything but greatest of all in war' (II. 6). Polybius stresses the Roman preference for decisive and determined military action: 'the Romans, to speak generally, rely on force in all their enterprises, and think it is incumbent to carry out their projects in spite of all, and that nothing is impossible once they have decided on it' (I. 37.7). Plutarch praises the martial values of the Republic and comments on the semantics of the Latin term 'virtus': 'in those days Rome held in the highest honour that phase of virtue which concerns itself with warlike and military achievements, and evidence of this may be found in the only Latin word for virtue, which signifies really *manly valour*; for they made valour, a specific form of virtue, stand for virtue in general' (*Life of Caius Marcius Coriolanus* I. 4). These sources attest to a code of military values that shaped the formation of Roman aristocrats, linking individual acts of war to the Roman patrimony.[19] The ethos that Cervantes attributes to both sides of the Numantian conflict involves this connection of political and personal attainments. Cipión pursues victory to augment his own reputation and to expand Rome's dominion in Iberia; he exhorts his men to fight with courage and determination as true Romans. The Numantians pursue liberty for their city, confident in their individual valour and their ability to secure victory through direct force.

As the Romans renew the conflict under Cipión's command, the Numantians reaffirm their commitment to the demands and rewards of martial heroism. They respond to the changing conditions of the war through collective decisions informed by their determination to maintain the integrity and reputation of the city and its citizen-soldiers. The progress of the siege causes them to redirect their force and valour. Enclosed by the Roman troops, they exercise their arms internally, destroying the wealth that they have collected within the walls of the city and inflicting death on the bodies that they have given over to war. These acts are intended to deny the Romans any reward for their victory, whether in the form of material spoils or of prisoners who can be brought in triumph to Rome. They are also feats of war inspired by a high standard of martial conduct. Through the destruction of their wealth, the nocturnal expedition of Morandro and Leoncio, and the mutual violence of their collective suicide, the Numantians remain faithful to a martial code that is essentially Roman in its definition and articulation.[20] Cervantes presents their resistance to the siege as a case study in the limits of epic heroism and the possibilities for heroic conduct under restrictive circumstances.

The Numantians make the definitive demonstration of their commitment to the code of martial excellence in their ritualized act of collective suicide. When they cannot break Cipión's siege, they turn their violence upon themselves, sacrificing the bodies that might be led in triumph through the streets of Rome. These acts demand courage and engage the forms of direct violence that the Romans have refused to employ. As the Numantians transform their city into a theatre of violence, Teógenes appears bearing a sword in each hand and commands his fellow citizens to release their fury on his body:

> ¡Valientes numantinos, haced cuenta
> que yo soy algún pérfido romano,
> y vengad en mi pecho vuestra afrenta,
> ensangrentando en él la espada y mano!
> Una de estas espadas os presenta
> mi airada furia y mi dolor insano;
> que muriendo en batalla no se siente
> tanto el rigor del último accidente. (ll. 2140–7)

> Valiant Numantians, imagine that I am some treacherous Roman, and avenge in my breast the outrage that you have suffered, staining your swords and hands with my blood! My wild fury and insane grief offer you one of these swords, since the final privation of life is less painful if one dies in battle.

Cervantes dramatizes the aggression of one Numantian against another as a form of surrogate combat. The direct combat that the Romans have avoided now releases itself in the streets and squares of the besieged city. Teógenes incites violence by posing as a 'treacherous Roman,' turning himself into a fit object for the rage of the city's defenders. The action here depends on a serious version of role playing, in which violent play releases the energies of Numantia's frustrated desire for vengeance on the Roman aggressors. Teógenes's willingness to die in ludic battle reflects a soldier's preference for sudden death by force of arms. Such a death also respects an ethos of force and unrestrained valour. For Teógenes, the forms of destruction that Numantia has unleashed are consistent with epic glory: 'ora me mate el hierro o el fuego me arda, / que gloria nuestra en cualquier muerte veo' (whether the blade slays me or fire consumes me, I see in any death our glory) (ll. 2174–5).

The Numantians remain faithful to the warrior's ethos of valour in open battle, but their collective suicide frustrates any adequate resolution of the disorder that warfare has brought to the city and its besiegers. Classical epic parallels tragedy in its representation of a cultural crisis that leads to endemic disorder and resolves itself through an act of violence that imitates rites of sacrifice. Since the warrior who dies by his own agency cannot be the sacrificial victim of others, the act of suicide denies the logic of sacrifice and its promise of stability. Like Cato's suicide in Lucan's *Bellum ciuile*, the death of the Numantians ends the immediate conflict without dissolving the risks of militarism.[21] The collective action that they undertake does not satisfy the conditions of ritual sacrifice and threatens a descent into a spiral of mimetic violence (Petro 768–9). In their fury and their insistence on vengeance, the Numantians exceed the bounds of just anger and augur future conflict for the Romans.

The contrasting fidelity of the warring parties to the heroic ethos prompts Cipión to consider the limits of his generalship during the conflict. His intention to reduce the city through tactical measures compromises his stated commitment to direct conflict and martial valour. The siege ends in Roman success, but on terms that mark Cipión as a tragic character. The unyielding heroism of the besieged leads to his recognition that he has secured victory by questionable means. Although Cipión explains his strategies in terms that engage the values of Vergilian epic, he realizes that his reduction of Numantia encumbers both Rome's moral authority and his personal claim to the rewards of fame and glory. As the siege comes to its planned conclusion Cipión experiences a 'moral fall' (Kahn 92–3), and this reversal reflects in turn on the central themes of empire, prophecy, and the nature of fame.

Cipión's understanding of his tactics can be traced through the play. In the face of Numantia's long-standing resistance to Roman aggression, Cipión is quick to modify his plans for engaging the city's defenders. In conference with Quinto Fabio he explains his intention to avoid open conflict and outlines the alternative strategy that he has devised:

> pienso de un hondo foso rodeallos,
> y por hambre insufrible he de acaballos.
> No quiero yo que sangre de romanos
> colore más el suelo de esta tierra;
> basta la que han vertido estos hipanos
> en tan larga, reñida y cruda guerra. (ll. 319–24)

> I intend to encircle them with a deep trench and to kill them with unbearable hunger. I have no wish that Roman blood shall further stain the soil of this land; let the blood suffice that these Spaniards have spilled in such a long, hard-fought, and merciless war.

Cipión appeals here to military pragmatism. The siege tactics that he proposes will work to his 'provecho' (profit, l. 316), in part by limiting further Roman losses in the long and harsh campaign against Numantia. In consideration of the blood that Roman soldiers have shed at the city's gates, Cipión will subject the Numantians to the slow and relentless methods of encirclement and starvation. He urges the troops to undertake the labour of constructing the siegeworks with determination and a sense of common purpose (ll. 325–36), a gesture that attempts to reconcile the strategy of the siege with the values that define martial excellence. The contrast between the defiant invitation to open war that Cipión delivers in his parley with the Numantian ambassadors and his pragmatic approach to encircling the city is nonetheless striking. Confronted with the proven risks of direct warfare against Numantia, Cipión is prepared to depart from the ethos of force and valour.

Critical responses to Cipión's strategic thinking reflect the ambiguities of his situation. His decision to spare the lives of Roman soldiers can be seen as an expression of a 'humanitarian' approach to war (Avalle-Arce, 'Poesía' 66) and of his obligations to the Roman Republic (de Armas, *Cervantes, Raphael* 106). This reading presents Cipión as an exemplar of prudence (*sapientia* or *cordura*), a virtue associated in the epic tradition with Odysseus, a hero of many wiles (de Armas 106). His pragmatism, however, invites a less positive view of his qualities as a soldier and commander. His explanation of his plans for the siege exposes a troubling 'discrepancy between his public bravado and his subsequently revealed intentions' and a willingness to mislead both the enemy and his own troops in pursuit of Rome's military objectives (Lewis-Smith 18–19). More generally, his logic depends on a calculus of means and ends that imparts to his conduct a Machiavellian cast (Avalle-Arce, 'Poesía' 66; Zimic 63). The conflict between strategic and ethical considerations is clear in these readings. Given this tension, Cipión's conduct can be discussed in relation to the well-recognized ethical challenges of siege warfare.

Cipión claims that his plan for reviving the Roman campaign involves new and unfamiliar tactics (ll. 347–8). His methods may be innovative in the context of the war with Numantia, but the siege was a standard instrument of ancient strategy in which the Roman army had long experience (Keegan 273). As Michael Walzer has noted, 'siege is the oldest form of total war' (160) and its tactics of encirclement and attrition are inevitably deployed in the face of widely recognized ethical challenges. A standing convention of war prohibits any direct attack on civilians. This convention concedes that military actions may endanger civilians who are in close proximity to them, but it states that such actions must be directed towards a legitimate military objective and that the risk to non-combatants must be incidental to this primary goal. Siege warfare is ethically suspect because its tactics make no distinction between soldiers and civilians, since the military objective of reducing a city is sought through harms inflicted on the civilian population. In Walzer's formulation, 'the goal is surrender; the means is not the defeat of the enemy army, but the fearful spectacle of the civilian dead' (161). Certain conditions can mitigate the ethical challenges of a siege, and some of these apply to Cipión's action against Numantia. The civilians inside the city are not subject to the will of a small corps of militant defenders, and they explicitly form common cause in resisting Rome's authority. It is also clear that the Numantians would not leave their city and place its defence in the hands of a soldier class, even if they were given the opportunity to escape the inhumane conditions of the siege.[22] Despite these qualifications, Cipión follows a strategic course that entails a clear ethical burden. He has chosen to act directly against the city as a whole, seeking to defeat its defenders through a mass spectacle of starvation and death.

Cipión knows that his strategic choices conflict with his stated commitment to the open use of armed force and that his measures expose his leadership to moral and military objections. The recourse to non-heroic tactics may compromise the general's authority and undermine the martial spirit of his troops. Cipión is also aware, however, that established forms of strategic thinking recognize the legitimacy of his position. As Walzer has noted, 'sitting and waiting is far less costly to the besieging army than attacking, and such calculations are permitted ... by the principle of military necessity' (162). Cipión appeals to the practical knowledge that he has acquired through years of waging war and argues that other experienced soldiers will approve of his tactics (ll. 1125–8).

Cipión also describes his motives in terms that reflect central values in Latin epic. He regards his enemies as a proud nation that he is subduing by force ('esta libre nación soberbia domo,' l. 1115); he compares them to wild beasts who must be caged and tamed ('habéis de ser domados,' l. 1191); he boasts of Rome's skill in overcoming such foes ('que de domar soberbios es maestra,' l. 1787). In his initial reaction to the collective suicide that marks the end of the siege, Cipión confirms his commitment to the values of Roman conquest and settlement. He laments that the Numantians despaired of the compassion that he was obliged to extend to them as an agent of Rome's authority:

> Mal, por cierto, tenían conocido
> el valor en Numancia de mi pecho,
> para vencer y perdonar nacido. (ll. 2303–5)

> Without doubt, they knew little in Numancia of the worthy spirit that lives in my breast, born to conquer and to pardon.

In a parallel gesture, he urges Viriato – the child who is the sole survivor of the city's mass suicide – to take the measure of his 'piedad' (clemency) (ll. 2330–2). These passages employ a lexicon derived from Latin epic: 'soberbia,' 'domar,' 'perdonar,' 'piedad.' Avalle-Arce has noted that Cipión's lament on Numantian pride alludes to a well-known line from the *Aeneid*: 'parcere subietcis et debellare superbos' ('Poesía' 69). This Latin text, however, exerts a force beyond local allusion, particularly if account is taken of its Vergilian context. In his long prophecy of the imperial lineage that the survivors of Troy will found on Roman soil, Anchises's spirit enumerates the generals and lawgivers who will extend its dominion across the known world. Near the end of his speech, Anchises directly instructs Aeneas in the arts of Roman rule:

> tu regere imperio populos, Romane, memento
> (hae tibi erunt artes), pacique imponere morem,
> parcere subiectis et debellare superbos. (*Aeneid* VI. 851–3)

> Roman, remember by your strength to rule
> Earth's peoples – for your arts are to be these:
> To pacify, to impose the rule of law,
> To spare the conquered, battle down the proud.

Anchises's counsel on the Roman arts of war and law anticipates Aeneas's words to Ascanius in *Aeneid* XII. In both cases, a father transmits a lesson in Roman dominion that the son is to recall in his progress through a life of military leadership and public service. The essential Roman task is to extend peace and law to other peoples, through measures that combine force and clemency. Cipión defines his conduct in these terms, assuming command of the army with the objective of subjecting the proud nation of Numantia to Roman rule. His successful siege turns the Numantians into a subjugated people, to whom he should extend Roman peace and clemency. Cipión regards his capacity for both conquest and clemency as a mark of his true valour and of his standing as a model Roman general.

For Cipión, the progress of the siege confirms his strategic judgment, since prudence alone offers sufficient means to tame the proud Numantians (ll. 1115–16). The concept of prudence is central to the play's lexicon of military leadership. The verbal network of this term and its correlates shows that the same action can be seen as exemplary of both prudence ('cordura') and guile ('maña'), and that actions undertaken in the name of discretion are subject to practical and ethical challenges. Romans and Numantians alike address Cipión as an 'illustrious' and 'prudent' general (ll. 170, 234, 1153), but they express opposing views on the significance of his actions. For Cipión and his subordinates, the tactics of the siege exemplify the 'cordura' that will enable Rome to win victory at an acceptable human cost; for the Numantian defenders, these strategies reveal a disposition to prevail through 'mañas,' a trait typical of Rome and embodied in the general that its Senate has dispatched against their city (ll. 1225–6). The differing views of the two sides suggest that the strategic advantages of prudence are not easily reconciled with a warrior's code of force and valour.

Readings that present Cipión as the tragic hero of *La Numancia* interpret his recourse to tactical calculation as a central error of judgment. This failing can be traced to an inappropriate confidence in the methods that he employs, or to an inaccurate perception of the strengths and values of the enemy. Cipión may place unwarranted trust in the military efficacy of prudence (de Armas, *Cervantes, Raphael* 112). His error may also lie in 'his unshakable assumption that the Numantians will surrender if imprisoned in their city and starved to the point of death,' a belief founded on his failure to grasp the valour and constancy of his opponents (Lewis-Smith 17). It is also clear that the general's experience produces the essential tragic patterns of recognition and reversal.

During the initial stages of the siege Cipión asserts that fortune favours his tactics and that his ability to subdue Numantia by prudence alone demonstrates the excellence of his generalship. The opportunity to encircle the city is a propitious occasion that he has been quick to seize (ll. 1117–20); his victory, gained at little cost to his troops, will bring satisfaction to Rome (ll. 1133–6). The Numantians' heroic and sustained resistance, however, gradually causes Cipión to recognize the limitations of his strategic measures. Confronted with the ruins of the city and with the Numantian bodies destroyed through collective suicide, he praises his opponents for their valour and skill in arms and admits that these superior martial qualities have forced him to conquer them through 'industria y maña' (invention and guile, ll. 2243–7). The general here adopts the lexicon of his adversaries, conceding that prudence has compromised the status of his victory and that the traditional code of heroic force favours the Numantians. He has come to realize the moral costs of military necessity.

Cipión's attempts to safeguard his reputation confirm his recognition of the Numantians' excellence in matters of arms and morale. The report that a single Numantian child has survived revives the general's hope of a ceremonial triumph in Rome. Cipión attempts to persuade the child to accompany him to Rome, promising him the freedom and wealth of life in the capital of the Republic, but he fails in his appeal. The child Viriato, declaring himself the last inheritor of Numantian valour, rejects the promised rewards and leaps to his death. This final mortal spectacle prompts Cipión to praise the exemplary valour embodied in the precocious child:

> ¡Oh nunca vista, memorable hazaña!
> ¡Niño de anciano y valeroso pecho,
> que no sólo a Numancia, mas a España
> has adquerido gloria en este hecho!
> ¡Con tu viva virtud y heroica, extraña,
> queda muerto y perdido mi derecho!
> ¡Tú con esta caída levantaste
> tu fama y mis victorias derribaste! (ll. 2392–9)

> Oh, unprecedented, memorable deed! Oh, child with an aged and valiant breast, with this feat you have won glory not only for Numancia but also for Spain! Due to your strong, heroic, singular virtue, my claim is quit and lost! With this fall you have raised up your fame and cast down my victories!

Cipión recognizes that Viriato, through his act of heroic virtue, has confirmed the superiority of Numantia's martial excellence over Rome's strategic calculus. He expresses his admiration through established rhetorical devices. Viriato is a *puer senex*, a child brave and mature beyond his years; in a variant of the topos of inexpressibility, his deed is said to surpass all others that the general has seen.[23] Cipión also articulates his praise of the child's achievement in the terms of the traditional heroic ethos that Rome shares with Numantia. Viriato's valorous act has its reward in 'glory' for his city and 'fame' for his person. Since one of the defining qualities of glory is its persistence in human memory, the impact of the child's heroism will extend from Numantia to Spain, the future nation that will inherit the city's tradition of valour and just force. For Cipión, the recognition of Numantia's glory marks a reversal. Through his bravery Viriato has undone Cipión's prospect of a triumph in Rome, casting down the reputation that the general has won through his long line of past victories. The pattern of simultaneous recognition and reversal portrays Cipión as a tragic hero. Since Viriato's fall also marks the rise of his city, the play's conclusion offers us a double reversal in which Cipión passes from prosperity to adversity and Numantia from adversity to prosperity. In his final words the general makes this doubling explicit, granting to Viriato the profit of victory and conceding that the child, in casting himself from the tower, has vanquished an adversary who aspired to the height of glory. In the fall of Cipión and the rise of Numantia, Cervantes's drama presents the pattern of double reversal that Tasso describes as uniquely suitable to epic poetry.

The fame that Cipión attributes to Viriato engages the epic themes of glory and political prophecy and subjects them to critical scrutiny. The child's heroic act anticipates the dominion and renown that Spain will acquire in the future, in part through the Italian wars of the early modern period. As they comment on the dramatic action, the play's personified figures deliver prophecies of Spain's destiny as an imperial power. This praise of the martial excellence of Spain and Numantia reinforces the reversal of Cipión's expectations of victory and of the honours that he will claim on his return to Rome. In winning fame for himself and glory for his nation, Viriato has denied the Roman general these rewards. The end of the siege and its relationship to prophecies of the Spanish Empire attest to the instability and uncertainty of fame.

The play's use of prophetic discourse is multiple and complex. As Emilie Bergmann has noted, its prophetic speeches 'do not participate in the action so much as reflect on time past, interpret time present, and envision the future' (87). This emphasis on abstraction and explication, rather than on the immediacy of the staged action, once again engages the conventions of epic poetry. Prophecy is well established in the epic tradition as a medium for 'dynastic encomium' and 'the construction of political and ideological legitimacy,' and writers of epic in early modern Spain apply this practice to acclaiming the imperial program of the Hapsburg monarchy (Nicolopulos 3–4). Through its prophecies of Philip II's victories in the battles of St Quentin and Lepanto, *La Araucana* evokes the scale of Spain's dominion across the Old and New Worlds and establishes a complex mode of imitation that draws eclectically on Roman and Hispanic models (Nicolopulos 83). In addition, political readings of Vergil's *Aeneid* and *Fourth Eclogue* reinforce the 'providential myths' of a universal rule of peace and harmony and the concept of the transfer of imperial authority from ancient Rome to Spain (Armstrong-Roche 66–8). Cervantes parallels Ercilla in his approach to epic imitation, and the prophecies in *La Numancia* vary in their effects according to the dramatic contexts in which they appear and the models that they invoke. The Numantians' necromancy, modelled on the dark prophecy extracted from the corpse of a dead soldier in Book VI of Lucan's *Bellum ciuile*, is ambiguous in its meaning and impact, predicting that neither side will conclude the siege with a clear victory (ll. 1073–80). A more positive strain of prophecy, however, informs the audience of the dominion and renown that Spain will attain in Numantia's name. Like the spirit of Anchises in *Aeneid* VI, the personification of the river Duero and the eschatological figure of War foresee a future of imperial rule under divinely sanctioned authority, inviting reflection on the past of the Roman Republic and the future of the Spanish Empire.[24]

The prospect of Spain's imperial regime confirms Numantia's glory and grants the city vindication in relation to Rome. These purposes are clear in the dialogue between the personified figures of España and the river Duero that closes the first act, an exchange motivated by the immediate threat of the siege. España praises the Numantians for their defence of Spanish liberty and asks the river to come to the city's aid. The Duero responds that Rome's victory in the siege is ordained in the stars and cannot be prevented, but that time will favour Numantia's descendants, granting them victory over the city of Rome in the long term. The river delivers a prophecy of the decline of Rome's ancient powers and the rise of Spain as a modern empire. In accordance with the conventions that inform the literary representation of prophetic discourse, the Duero's speech is elliptical in style and selective in its use of historical events. It passes from the Visigothic invasions of Iberia and Attila's assault on the Roman provinces to the sack of Rome by the troops of Charles V in 1527 and the Duke of Alba's treaty of reconciliation with Pope Paul IV in 1557.[25] This account emphasizes both Spain's military superiority to modern Rome and papal recognition of the religious mission of the Spanish monarchy. Its line of prophecy culminates in the Christian empire of the Hapsburgs. The civil afflictions that España identifies in the peoples of Iberia – discord, internal division, bondage to foreign powers – find their remedy in the reign of Philip II, who will impose union on the kingdoms of Spain and Portugal and raise the standard of imperial rule over a multitude of nations. The Duero's prophecy offers two distinct perspectives, contrasting the immediate defeat of Numantia's defenders with the dominion that Spain will acquire in a future distant from the events on stage. This interplay of times and places is central to the play's view of the transformations of imperial power.[26]

In the play's discourse of prophecy, Spain's dominion marks a return to the values associated with Latin epic and the early history of the Roman Republic. To unify the kingdoms of Iberia and expand their sovereignty over foreign nations, the Spanish monarchy will exercise military power, with due attention to the virtues and practices that attain victory in open warfare. The figure of War confirms that Spain's destiny is to prevail over Rome and asserts that the powers of the modern nation will be secured through the force of its armies:

> Que yo, que soy la poderosa Guerra,
> de tantas madres detestada en vano,
> aunque quien me maldice a veces yerra,
> pues no sabe el valor desta mi mano,
> sé bien que en todo el orbe de la tierra
> seré llevada del valor hispano,
> en la dulce sazón que estén reinando
> un Carlos, y un Filipo y un Fernando. (ll. 1984–91)

> I, powerful War, the vain object of many mothers' hatred – although to detest me is at times to err, without knowledge of my force and skill – well know that I will be transported by Spanish valour across the world, in the blessed time when a Charles, a Philip, and a Ferdinand will reign.

War appeals in her own defence to the calibre and scale of Spain's military endeavours, conducted under the aegis of Catholic monarchy. To reinforce the ideal of religious authority, the Hapsburg regimes of Charles V and Philip II are conflated with the earlier reign of the Catholic king Ferdinand V. War's prophecy reflects the ideological assumption that held Spain to be the bearer of Roman *pietas* and Rome's claim to universal empire.[27] At the same time, War claims that Spain's modern empire will sustain the military excellence displayed by Numantia's warriors. In defence of the ancient city and in the wars of imperial Spain, 'Hispanic valour' secures and justifies the use of military force. War finds in this constant and stable attribute a proof of her own value.

The prophecy of military power and expansion aligns *La Numancia* with a strain of imperialist discourse that celebrated the renewal of Roman dominion under the rule of the Hapsburg dynasty.[28] Cervantes nonetheless qualifies his endorsement of the privileged position that the Hapsburgs and their advisors claimed for themselves in the imperial tradition. Recent critics have argued that *La Numancia* articulates a 'counter-epic literary discourse' that responds to the 'competing visions of Spain's foreign policy' in Cervantes's time (Simerka 97–8) and that it presents a sharp critique of the 'tyrannical imperialism' of Philip II's government (Kahn 25–8). The play's focus, however, centres less on opposing the ethos of epic or the political designs of the Hapsburgs than on exploring the limits of traditional heroism under specific conditions of warfare, and the problem of fidelity to heroic values under changing social and historical circumstances. Cipión's strategic approach to the war with Numantia suggests that the values that define military excellence and sustain Spain's claims to imperial dominion are not immutable. The general's conduct reflects the ways in which he defines himself in relation to the responsibilities that the Senate has imposed on him and the rewards that it offers him. His departures from the martial ethos that Rome shares with Numantia can be linked to the demands of imperial command and to the established Roman system of offices and honours. The errors of his generalship are matters not only of his moral character but also of cultural practices and expectations, since they reflect 'his personal and inherited experience of human behaviour in war' (Lewis-Smith 16). In contrast to the Numantians, Cipión is a tragic figure, in part because he finds himself subject to the challenges of strategic calculation and to a structure of centralized command and recognition.

The tensions that subject the heroic ethos to change and compromise can be traced to the central idea of glory. Both Romans and Numantians act on the desire for glory, a motive that classical historians and poets identify as the basis of individual and collective merit. In the *Bellum Catilinae* Sallust attributes the strength and liberty of the early Republic to 'the thirst for glory that filled men's minds' (VII. 3). Leo Braudy has noted that in Roman society 'personal honor (*dignitas*) and national glory were linked' (56). In *La Numancia* Teógenes explains to his fellow defenders the economy that governs the exchange of glory between the opposing sides:

> Sólo se ha de mirar que el enemigo
> no alcance de nosotros triunfo o gloria:
> antes ha de servir él de testigo
> que apruebe y eternice nuestra historia;
> y si todos venís en lo que digo,
> mil siglos durará nuestra memoria:
> y es que no quede cosa aquí en Numancia
> de do el contrario pueda hacer ganancia. (ll. 1418–25)

> Our sole aim should be that our enemy obtains from us neither triumph or glory: instead our enemy should be a witness who endorses and renders eternal our history; and if all concur in what I say, our memory will endure for all time: and for this purpose nothing should remain in Numancia from which our enemy can take profit.

For Teógenes, glory depends on acts of bravery and the recognition of such acts by others. The destruction of the city's goods will have a dual effect on the Romans, denying them the rewards of victory and forcing them to bear witness to the physical and moral force of Numantia's resistance. Teógenes defines the glory that the Numantians will attain through their heroic defiance of Rome as the preservation of their deeds in historical memory. To prevail over a worthy enemy is to render one's history eternal and secure a place in timeless remembrance. The need for recognition implies a mechanism of exchange: as witnesses to Numantia's merits, the Romans will be constrained to admit their own loss of the rewards of victory. The concept of 'ganancia' (profit) reinforces this mechanism. By eliminating the material benefits that their city might yield to the Romans, the Numantians make their claim to the spiritual profit that follows from their valour and resolution.

The terms of Teógenes's exhortation are drawn from the lexicon of heroism that the Numantians share with the Romans. Cipión asserts that fortune will favour the force of Rome's army in open war, leading to glory ('la gloria mía,' l. 272); Quinto Fabio boasts that the time is now propitious for Rome, offering a secure prospect of glory for its soldiers and death for the Numantian defenders ('nuestra gloria y vuestra muerte,' l. 308). These statements share a confidence in the benefits of fortune and a commitment to the ethos of martial excellence. In their vaunts before the enemy, Cipión and his subordinates confirm their expectation that their soldiers will conquer fame through heroism in open battle.

As general and commander, Cipión might anticipate sharing in the glory that he projects for all the Romans who have fought against Numantia. His decision to besiege the enemy, however, causes him to reconsider the prize of victory and expect for himself a reward less clearly defined than the glory of an epic warrior. He is aware that his tactics may seem less than heroic, and he seeks recompense in the Roman system of public honours. He views the command of the campaign against Numantia as a duty with which the Roman Senate has charged him, and he looks back to Rome for due recognition of his leadership. When he reviews the progress of the siege with his subordinates Mario and Jugurta, he declares that his tactics are adequate to the challenges of the conflict with Numantia and consistent with a code of martial values:

> ¿Qué gloria puede haber más levantada
> en las cosas de guerra que aquí digo,
> que, sin quitar de su lugar la espada,
> vencer y sujetar al enemigo? (ll. 1129–32)

> What nobler glory can there be in the matters of war of which here I speak than to conquer and subdue the enemy without taking one's sword from its sheath?

Cipión attempts here to redefine the rewards of war in terms that acknowledge his position as a leader who acts under the authority of the Roman Republic.[29] For a general who must reduce the exposure of his troops and conserve the resources of the state, the highest glory lies in securing victory through a limited exercise of force rather than through a long and costly military campaign. This gesture demonstrates Cipión's respect for the traditional warrior's ethos and his intention to reconcile its values with the demands and duties of the Roman state. His claim that he can attain glory without engaging the enemy in open battle is nonetheless striking, given the established connection between glory and the expert use of direct force. Cipión aspires to win without significant risk to his troops a form of recognition that depends on the open exercise of violence. His tactics respond to the concerns of the Senate, but they demand a revision of the traditional rewards of victory.

The proposal to end the siege through a single combat prompts Cipión to reaffirm his trust in due recognition from the Roman state. The Numantians regard this contest as a means to end the war through controlled but heroic violence, and they tell the Roman general that he should readily agree to their terms, given his many declarations of trust in the strength and skill of his soldiers. Cipión nonetheless responds with a definite refusal, dismissing the proposal as risible and boasting of his ability to prevail by strategy alone. To the concern that these tactics may undermine his reputation for courage, he opposes the recognition that he will receive when the city surrenders. The 'vergüenza' (shame) of a campaign conducted through siegecraft is slight, particularly in relation to the 'Fama' (fame) of victory (ll. 1199–1200). Although the terms 'fama' and 'gloria' are semantically similar, Cipión's appeal to fame suggests a shift in the scale of his expectations. To seek glory is to demand recognition for acts that rival the epic feats of the past and attract the universal respect of other warriors; to seek fame is, in Cipión's case, to aspire to eminence within a graded system of public honours. For whatever cost the siege may exact from his valour, he will find recompense in the fame that his victory will grant him at Rome. As the Numantians intensify their resistance to the siege, Cipión turns his mind with increasing frequency to Roman honours. When he learns of the acts of self-destruction within the city, he insists that he will not be denied the formal rewards of victory. Although most of Numantia may be consumed by fire and the sword, the presence of a single survivor will guarantee the general his ceremonial triumph in Rome. The progress of the siege leads Cipión to focus his attention on maintaining his reputation as a general who receives orders and rewards from the Republic, in a shift from motives of 'patriotism' to those of 'personal advancement' (Kahn 162). Roman fame replaces the larger goal of universal glory.

This change is central to Cipión's role as a tragic character. Northrop Frye has observed that the tragic hero experiences 'the narrowing of a comparatively free life into the process of causation' in accordance with a calculus of ambition or retribution that he has chosen to accept (*Anatomy* 212). Cipión adopts the logic of military necessity and confronts the limitations that this principle imposes on his stature as a warrior. Over the course of the campaign against Numantia, his aspirations shift from epic glory to Roman fame, and the demands of the Roman system of honours centre his attention on the sole child who has survived as a physical token of his military success. This process of tragic

Warriors: Epic and Tragedy 59

narrowing ends in the reversal of Cipión's victory and in his recognition that Viriato's suicide has secured Numantia's glory.

Cervantes presents Cipión as an exemplary Roman general who responds to the will of the Senate and assumes command of the Numantian campaign with the intention of winning victory and glory. His objectives are consistent with Cicero's characterization of the Romans as 'seekers of glory (*gloria*) and greedy of renown (*laus*)' (*Pro lege manilia* III. 7). Cipión's experience, however, suggests that heroic forms of warfare are not easily reconciled with the command of an imperial army and that fame as a Roman honour may be a more limited reward than epic glory. Sources in Roman history attest to an awareness of the tension between heroic values and imperial authority. Cicero praises Manilius not only for his martial skills but also for his moderation in resisting the lure of Eastern luxury and riches. Manilius pursues the sanctioned Roman goals of victory and glory, while other leaders have sought causes of war as a pretext for indulging a 'lust for plunder' (*Pro lege manilia* XXII. 64–5). The singularity of Manilius's conduct shows that expansion into the rich lands of the East has compromised the traditional Roman virtues of force and self-control. This dislocation of values can be temporal as well as geographical. In the *Bellum Catilinae* Sallust contrasts the moral and military excellence of the past with the failings of his own time. He praises the early consuls for instructing young Romans in the skills and values of warfare:

> as soon as the young men could endure the hardships of war, they were taught a soldier's duties in camp under a vigorous discipline, and they took more pleasure in handsome arms and war horses than in harlots and revelry. To such men consequently no labour was unfamiliar, no region too rough or too steep, no armed foeman was terrible; valour was all in all. Nay, their hardest struggle for glory was with one another; each man strove to be first to strike down the foe, to scale a wall, to be seen of all while doing such a deed. This they considered riches, this fair fame and high nobility. It was praise they coveted, but they were lavish of money; their aim was unbounded renown, but only such riches as could be gained honourably. (VII. 4–6)

Rome owes its eminence to this ethos of valour and renown. The arts of war and of justice secured its internal integrity and its success in external wars. Male citizens embraced as their traditional goal the 'fair fame and high nobility' ('bonam fama magnamque nobilitatem') that could be won through feats of arms. Worldly dominion, however, exposed Rome to the vagaries of fortune and to moral confusion. In the face of these conditions, the thirst for glory ('cupido gloriae') has yielded to the lust for money and power ('pecuniae ... imperi cupido') (X. 3). The early Republic offers an example of heroic virtue that brings to light the licence and luxury of the present. In a parallel gesture, Plutarch in his *Life of Caius Marcius Coriolanus* stresses the valour and accomplishments of an earlier age ('in those days') (I. 4), suggesting by implication that present conduct is not equal to the heroic standard of the past. These accounts of the history of Roman values show a tendency to locate true glory in a distant past, removed from the challenges and enticements of imperial command and expansion.

The projection of an idealized past reflects tensions in the uses of fame and in the system of Roman honours.[30] The shifting and conflictive value of fame is a central concern in Latin epic and in the tradition that it inspires. The *Aeneid* distinguishes between the false fame of human rumour and gossip and the true fame that respects and enacts divine designs, and a critique of worldly fame can be traced in Stoic and medieval sources.[31] In its final scenes *La Numancia* is equally attentive to the mutability of fame. The disposition of the central characters reinforces the contrast between the public fame that Cipión hopes to claim from the Roman Senate and the warriors' glory that the Numantians have attained through heroic acts of resistance. Cipión recognizes that his trust in Roman honours has led to the moral reversal of his military victory; Teógenes embraces his death by fire, calling on 'clara Fama' (clear Fame) to preserve the memory of his last act of valour (ll. 2282–3). The lesser fame of the Roman general, dependent on Rome's authority, stands opposed to the greater, enduring fame of the city's defenders. In the play's final speech the personified figure of Fame celebrates and disseminates the heroic reputation of Numantia. Bearing a trumpet – a conventional object in the Renaissance iconography of fame – and speaking in her 'clara voz' (clear voice), Cervantes's figure incites in her auditors an admiration that will render eternal the memory of Numantia's achievement.[32] She commands the Romans to bear in honour the body of the child who has defied their imperial authority, and she declares her intention to spread the name and honour of Numantia to the corners of the known world.[33] Her statement makes explicit the qualities that have made Numantia worthy of her praise:

Hallo sola en Numancia todo cuanto
debe con justo título cantarse,

y lo que puede dar materia al canto,
para poder mil siglos ocuparse:
la fuerza no vencida, el valor tanto,
dino de en prosa y verso celebrarse. (ll. 2432–7)

I find in Numantia alone all that can be rightly sung, providing matter for my song that will engage its purposes forever: unvanquished force, unbounded valour, worthy of being praised in prose and verse.

Fame endorses the traditional ethos of heroism and offers the reward of enduring recognition. Through the sustained 'force' and indomitable 'valour' of its defenders, Numantia inspires celebration and remembrance. This martial achievement presents a theme that uniquely commands Fame's labour, persisting and renewing itself in the medium of eternal 'song.'[34] The terms of her commendation show that through their fidelity to the traditional ethos of war the Numantians have attained the honour of true warriors and that their deeds will survive in a long tradition of heroic literature. Fame's closing words reaffirm the play's engagement with classical forms and its aspiration to the ideals of Latin epic.

Through its characters and actions *La Numancia* engages the epic themes of excellence and nobility. The Numantians and the Romans ascribe to a common ethos that defines excellence in terms of the direct exercise of force against a worthy enemy. In the restrictive conditions of siege warfare the Numantian leaders remain faithful to this ethos and win fame for their city and for the nation that will rise from its ruins. Cipión, in contrast, is a less elevated figure who secures military goals through strategic means and equates glory with the public honours of the Roman state. In the terms that Tasso sets out in his *Discorsi del poema eroico*, the Numantians embody the exemplary virtues of epic, while Cipión is subject to compromise and to tragic error. Cipión's actions, however, reflect both his character and his position as a military commander who must shelter his human and material resources and answer to the Senate at Rome. Attentive to the structures of command that sustain and limit his authority, Cipión must consider both the tactical advantages and the practical costs of the use of direct force. Cervantes's play places the warrior's community of Numantia in confrontation with the organized military society of Rome and measures each against the heroic ethos of classical epic. The contrast between these two cultures presents the central issue that concerned theorists of empire in early modern Europe: 'the perennial question of how to sustain certain kinds of value over time' (Pagden 112). The Numantians and the Romans represent two distinct stages in the evolution of a martial social order, and the exigencies of Cipión's role illustrate the difficulties of sustaining an ethos of martial valour when responsibility for the conduct of warfare is extended through an articulated chain of command.[35] In contrast with the Numantians, Cipión's freedom to act on the values of martial excellence is constrained. The shifting nature of fame and the challenges of heroic conduct in limited circumstances are questions that Cervantes will revisit in his later works on war.

2 Defenders: Pastoral and Satire

The difficult passwords that the army was using at this time were a minor source of danger. They were those tiresome double passwords in which one word has to be answered by another. Usually they were of an elevating and revolutionary nature, such as *Cultura – progreso*, or *Seremos – invencibles*, and it was impossible to get illiterate sentries to remember these highfalutin' words. One night, I remember, the password was *Cataluña – eroica*, and a moonfaced peasant lad named Jaime Domenech approached me, greatly puzzled, and asked me to explain.

'*Eroica* – what does *eroica* mean?'

I told him that it meant the same as *valiente*. A little while later he was stumbling up the trench in the darkness, and the sentry challenged him:

'*Alto! Cataluña!*'

'*Valiente!*' yelled Jaime, certain that he was saying the right thing.

Bang!

However, the sentry missed him. In this war everyone always did miss everyone else, when it was humanly possible.
George Orwell, Homage to Catalonia (1938)

La Numancia is a study in high style. Imitating the rhetorical and poetic techniques of Latin heroic verse, it presents Roman characters of elevated social status and Numantian defenders who equal them in courage and nobility. Its dramatic action engages the patterns of epic and tragedy to examine the limits of the traditional heroic ethos and the mutability of the fame that classical sources offer as the reward for singular acts of valour. In its conception the play rests on the ideal of decorum: it entertains the serious themes of heroism and fame through the conventions of two classical genres that enjoy a privileged place in the Neo-Aristotelian hierarchy of literary forms. These interrelated themes, however, also appear in genres that are not traditionally ranked as high, and the treatment of serious themes through low forms allows writers to present the actions and ethos of warfare from other perspectives. This practice often involves play across the boundaries of canonical genres. In many cases low genres define themselves in opposition to the characters and concerns of such high forms as epic and tragedy. To introduce warriors and their values into low forms is to discover new means for representing the causes, acts, and rewards of war. A shift in genre can encourage scrutiny of martial conduct and of the ethos that sustains it.

Distance from the world of arms and warriors is a characteristic feature of pastoral, a genre that can be defined through style and through the habits and attitudes attributed to its characters.[1] The classical schema of the *genera dicendi* identifies pastoral as a genre in the low style, and Renaissance writers on poetics assign it a low position in the hierarchy of canonical genres.[2] Its origins lie in opposition to epic – in the *Idylls* Theocritus responds to Homeric verse from the cosmopolitan and cultured perspective of Alexandria – and its representative settings and characters are modest and non-heroic. Herdsmen stand at the centre of the pastoral landscape, a space in which the imagination seeks accommodation to the demands and concerns of life on the land. The two herdsmen of Vergil's first *Eclogue* are aware of the conditions of life in the aftermath of Rome's civil wars, but they regard its difficulties and constraints from a stance of detachment, one that recognizes their restricted control of the circumstances that have shaped their lives. The typical stance of the pastoral character is suspension, an attitude that suggests contemplation of conditions that the speaker can neither overcome nor resolve. In contrast with the force and independence of the hero in epic or tragedy, the herdsman has limited strength in relation to his circumstances and concerns himself with common dilemmas and sorrows, and he takes comfort in sharing these matters with his equals through colloquy and song. Pastoral literature brings its characters together through occasions for shared poetic expression.[3] A standard form of contact among herdsmen is the singing contest, in which two lyric speakers rival one another in developing a common theme. In their acceptance of limits and their celebration of shared experience, these core conventions also mark pastoral's preference for themes of peace and natural order. Pastoral speakers comment on the pleasures and worries of country life, including the typical cares that they experience through love. The herdsman's humility can also grant moral authority to his voice, assimilating certain variants of pastoral to the critical perspective of satire.[4]

Engagement with the themes and patterns of European pastoral is a central thread in Cervantes's works.[5] His interest in this historical kind stems in part from its potential to incorporate and scrutinize matters commonly associated with high mimetic genres, by having pastoral speakers comment on the concerns and affairs of external society from a detached perspective and by introducing heroic figures into the pastoral circle. Given its focus on song and poetic creation, pastoral can offer a space for reflection on singular acts in the outside world and on the capacity of poetry to commemorate such deeds. Calliope's song in Book VI of *La Galatea* centres in part on the soldier-poets who have united the arts of arms and letters in praise of Spain's martial attainments.[6] In combination with other genres, Cervantine pastoral can also offer a critical perspective on heroic values and the uses of violence. Pastoral episodes in *Don Quixote* explore competing variants of fame and the means through which they are created and transmitted, the entry of epic violence and its conventions into the pastoral world and the efforts of practical pastoralists to defend themselves and the animals in their care, and the sources and effects of violence among pastoral communities, including the propensity of violence to release its energies once they have been aroused. In these episodes pastoral enables both critical reflection on heroic themes and satirical comment on the causes and persistence of violence in human affairs.

Over the course of its long history pastoral literature projects varying versions of the interactions between the country and the culture of civic spaces and public duties that lies beyond its bounds. As Raymond Williams has noted in his perceptive analysis of the pastoral tradition in *The Country and the City*, these relations are part of a larger cultural history, 'not only of ideas and experiences, but of rent and interest, of situation and power' (7). In Williams's view the variants of pastoral differ in the degree to which they recognize specific conditions of landholding and rural labour. Vergil's *Eclogues* speak to tensions between 'the pleasures of rural settlement and the threat of loss and eviction,' acknowledging the pressures on land tenure in the time of Rome's civil wars and their aftermath (Williams 17). Renaissance pastoral, in contrast, often presents the countryside as an 'enamelled world' from which the 'living tensions' of labour and land use have been excised (18). The concept of a beneficent nature that supplies food and shelter without human agency depends on 'the simple extraction of the existence of labourers' (32). The idea of a moral order inherent in a rural landscape sets aside the processes through which land and its products are secured, held, and exchanged over time, attributing a fictive innocence to means of acquisition and use that have been elided or safely removed to a distant past (50). This idealization also sets apart the life of arms. In early modern Europe pastoral romance revisits the tensions of its Vergilian model,[7] in a pattern that opposes 'the peace of country life' to 'the disturbance of war and civil war' (17). Like the labour of those who tend the land, the harsh work of soldiers is often removed from the pastoral world.

In Renaissance literature pastoral nonetheless finds space for the concerns of the public sphere, revisiting the relationship between pastoral and the forms of epic and drama by introducing into its idealized rural landscape characters who know the heroic claims of justice and the exercise of power.[8] These figures bring with them the experiences and concerns of an active life, and they draw various benefits from their interactions with the herdsmen who properly live on the land. A knight or a courtier may find in the shepherd's life an alternative to the responsibilities and values that he has set aside by leaving his normal sphere of activity (Alpers 189). This change may mark the permanent adoption of another form of life or it may offer a temporary sojourn in a restorative place, effecting the moral transformation of a noble figure before he returns to a life of service to the court or a dynastic state. Renaissance epic presents both these patterns. In Tasso's *Gerusalemme liberata* Erminia enters the pastoral world in flight from an armed nocturnal expedition and withdraws voluntarily into the intimate and solitary life of a shepherdess. Here pastoral is a felicitous alternative to the desires and designs of princes and warriors. In Ariosto's *Orlando furioso* Ruggiero recovers from a shipwreck in a pastoral setting, under the tutelage of a hermit who prepares him to return to his duties in society, a formative process that 'leads to marriage, the achievement of a kingdom, and an entrance into the active life as warrior, husband and dynast' (Marinelli 68). Garcilaso de la Vega evokes this restorative model of pastoral retirement in the first of his *Églogas* when he invites Pedro de Toledo, his patron and Spain's viceroy in Naples, to take respite from the cares of the state and the work of war in the shepherd's songs that he presents in his text (*Obras completas* 264–302, ll. 7–42). In the case of permanent retirement to the country, an exile from public life can comment with the authority of direct experience on the failings of the sphere that he has left behind, strengthening the satiric potential of the pastoral voice. Such assimilation to satire discovers a defensive cast in pastoral literature. Pastoral characters defend the natural order that surrounds them by asserting its separation from external violence and by critiquing the moral and physical disruptions of external society. The need for this stance reveals one of the ironies of pastoral: as Marinelli notes in his discussion of the complex ways in which Renaissance pastoral places itself in relation to the labours and accomplishments of the active life, one of its features is 'the nearness of Sparta' (57).[9]

In *Some Versions of Pastoral* William Empson argues that over their long history pastoral conventions reflect the shifting cultural and economic relationships between persons of high and low social status.[10] George Orwell's account of his service in the Spanish Civil War with a Republican militia in the hills and trenches outside the Aragonese town of Huesca offers a modern version of an encounter between pastoral attitudes and the world of war. In the anecdote of the double password 'Cataluña – eroica,' the peasant Jaime Domenech cannot understand the sense of a word that lies outside his normal linguistic register. Orwell is able to supply the synonym 'valiente,' not because he has a fluent command of Spanish but because he is familiar with the literary and rhetorical traditions that have shaped the ideals of heroic combat and resistance. Since the exchange of passwords depends on the exact verbalization of specific terms rather than on an understanding of their meaning, the militia's sentry shoots at Domenech when he produces the synonym, but to everyone's good fortune the sentry misses. The peasant's humility and lack of education put him at risk, but this danger is mitigated by the general disorder of trench warfare, and Orwell is quick to draw out the ironies of this situation. The system of passwords endangers those whom it is intended to protect; Orwell's well-meaning explanation of its elevated rhetoric leads the sentry to fire on his fellow combatant; the shot misses because poor marksmanship is endemic to a conflict among fatigued and irregularly trained soldiers. Domenech's incomprehension of the word 'eroica' reveals the non-heroic cast of the war in which he and Orwell are engaged. The pastoral contrast of rural inexperience and the public culture that lies beyond it shapes this encounter, a satire of circumstance that expresses the confusions and missed communications of modern warfare.[11]

Three episodes in *Don Quixote* explore the uses of pastoral and bring its characters into contact with martial concerns that are traditionally placed beyond its bounds and associated with high genres. Pastoral offers a space for reflection on the rewards of heroic conduct during the account of the journey that Don Quixote and Sancho make to El Toboso (*DQ* II. 8). Don Quixote intends to visit Dulcinea in her residence, a dwelling that he imagines in terms of pastoral artifice, and on the road he finds leisure to debate with Sancho the nature and the benefits of fame. Knight and squire are concerned at first with their own reputations, but their conversation quickly turns to the conflict between the secular fame that Don Quixote locates in medieval and ancient exemplars and the heavenly glory that Sancho associates with Christian saints. Rhetorical play and linguistic confusion reveal the instability of the various terms through which the high matter of fame can be inscribed. Don Quixote's assault on the sheepflocks (*DQ* I. 18) is an encounter with the practicalities of the herdsman's life, as mediated through the bellicose conventions of epic and chivalric romance. The seasonal migration of sheep across Castile's central plateau was an important and habitual component of the rural economy of early modern Spain. Don Quixote, however, perceives the flocks as two armies closing for battle, describing the leaders and soldiers of both forces in a series of epic catalogues. Here the idealized images of epic and pastoral are juxtaposed with the daily labours of herdsmen, a contrast stressed when the episode ends in a form of violence entirely distinct from the one that Don Quixote has imagined. The potential for violence between rural communities presents itself in the tale of the braying *regidores* and its sequel (*DQ* II. 25–7).[12] The *regidores'* efforts to find a lost donkey draws their village into a conflict with a nearby town that threatens to lead to armed violence. Don Quixote takes his chance encounter with the villagers as an opportunity to employ his eloquence in the cause of peace, attempting to persuade them that they have no just cause for taking arms against their neighbours. The threat of violence is dispersed, however, only when Sancho offers himself as a scapegoat and the villagers turn their weapons on his body. This version of the pastoral world harbours violence and offers a satiric perspective on the dangers of reputation and the connections between warfare and fame. All of these episodes explore the effect of generic frames on the representation of violence. They also revisit some of the tensions that Renaissance pastoral sets aside. Cervantes recognizes that pastoral literature and chivalric romance project two complementary aspects of a single social ideal and that the image of a harmoniously ordered society of landholders and labourers had lost its practical force in his time. He offers a critique of the utopian world of pastoral, in parallel with his critique of the utopia of arms (Maravall 188–90). The combination of genres – pastoral, epic, chivalric romance, encomium, satire – invites scrutiny of the values that inform heroic literature and of the exclusions that render the pastoral world peaceful and beneficent.

The antecedents and transmission of fame are general themes in *Don Quixote*. From the moment when he first conceives of his adventures, Don Quixote intends to perform notable acts of an order that will secure and maintain a heroic reputation: 'poniéndose en ocasiones y peligros donde, acabándolos, cobrase eterno nombre y fama' (exposing himself to peril and danger from which he would emerge to reap eternal fame and glory) (I. 1, 75). His recurrent preoccupation with the record of his own deeds invites consideration of the theme of fame, particularly in Part II, where characters appear who have read the printed account of Don Quixote's adventures in Part I and know him by reputation. As Don Quixote learns about his book and meets its readers, he weighs the benefits and perils of fame and comments on the uncertain boundary between fame and vainglory. In addition, the pastoral world that he encounters in his travels provides him with an opportunity to reflect on the desire for fame that shapes many of the books he has read and motivates his own pursuit of adventures.

When knight and squire take to the road in Part II and Don Quixote announces his intention to visit Dulcinea in El Toboso, the desire for fame asserts itself. Don Quixote hopes to obtain from his beloved a blessing that will bring success to his adventures and, by extension, distinction to his name. Don Quixote shows his habitual awareness of the processes that secure fame, but Sancho provokes some confusion over Dulcinea's residence and occupations that causes him doubt. Elaborating on one of his own inventions from Part I – that he travelled to El Toboso and delivered to Dulcinea a letter describing Don Quixote's love-madness in the Sierra Morena (I. 30–1) – Sancho insists that he and his master will find Dulcinea winnowing wheat in a barnyard. Don Quixote protests that this place and task are inappropriate to his beloved's high status and proposes an alternate scene. Like the water nymphs in the third of Garcilaso's *Églogas*, Dulcinea must live in a crystalline dwelling and pass her days weaving tapestries of precious cloths and jewels. Don Quixote insists that Sancho has perceived Dulcinea falsely, misled by the transformations of evil enchanters. In the same vein, Don Quixote fears that the printed book that offers a record of his adventures may misrepresent his deeds, treating one event as interchangeable with another and mixing lies with the truth. Don Quixote transposes to his book the metamorphoses that he believes Dulcinea to have endured in life; he fears that both he and his beloved may suffer as a result of envy and falsehood.

The connection between reputation and the printed word informs Don Quixote's reflections on the dangers of envy and misrepresentation. From the beginning of his first sally Don Quixote has entertained the belief that a magus will compile a written record of his deeds, and early in Part II he learns from his mischievous neighbour Sansón Carrasco that a book of his adventures is in print and has attracted attention and comment from many readers. The knowledge that his book now exists prompts him to speculate that its author may be an evil enchanter rather than a benevolent magus and that his reputation as a knight may be at risk. To these concerns the pragmatic Sancho replies that he is content to be mentioned in print, regardless of what may have been written about him. This exchange leads to a dialogue between knight and squire on the subject of fame, developed through well-known arguments and examples.

Sancho understands that fame depends on the circulation of narratives and names, and Don Quixote is attentive to the forms of creation that sustain this process. Don Quixote begins with three anecdotes that illustrate the universal desire for fame. The first concerns a modern poet who, having written a harsh satire on the noblewomen of the court, incurred the reproach of a woman whom he had not included because of her questionable social status. The poet satisfied her complaint by extending his satire, incorporating her name among the infamous. The second is the ancient legend of Herostratus, who set fire to the temple of Diana in Ephesus so that he might place his name among those destined to endure through the ages. The third tells of a modern Roman nobleman who guided Charles V through the architectural wonders of the Pantheon and then confessed to having felt the temptation to seize the emperor and cast himself down from the height of its cupola, in order to make his name immortal in the world. Don Quixote caps these anecdotes by enumerating exemplary cases of bold acts committed to win fame: Horatius casting himself fully armed into the Tiber, Mutius thrusting his arm into the flames, Curtius leaping into the abyss, Caesar crossing the Rubicon, Cortés grounding his ships on the shores of Mexico.[13] Don Quixote argues that these various cases, ancient and modern, confirm the active force of fame as a motive in human affairs.

The rural road to El Toboso provides Don Quixote with a pastoral space in which he can consider the claims and rewards of public life. The turn to Roman models in this context is familiar in Cervantes. It is nonetheless striking that other Cervantine texts associate Roman culture with less noble ends. In the *Viaje del Parnaso* the personified figure of Vainglory traces her influence in the ruins of classical monuments – 'arcos, anfiteatros, templos, baños, / termas, pórticos, muros admirables' (arches, amphitheatres, temples, baths, / spas, porticos, venerable walls) (VI. 158–9) – and in the extreme acts of Mutius Scaevola and Marcus Curtius. The uncertain distinction between fame and vainglory leads Don Quixote to offer an eloquent defence of the honourable ends of knight-errantry. The deeds that he has enumerated are works of secular fame, but the true knight-errant pursues a higher goal:

Todas estas y otras grandes y diferentes hazañas son, fueron y serán obras de la fama, que los mortales desean como premios y parte de la inmortalidad que sus famosos hechos merecen, puesto que los cristianos, católicos y andantes caballeros más habemos de atender a la gloria de los siglos venideros, que es eterna en las regiones etéreas y celestes, que a la vanidad de la fama que en este presente y acabable siglo se alcanza; la cual fama, por mucho que dure, en fin se ha de acabar con el mesmo mundo, que tiene su fin señalado. (II. 8, 96)

All these and a variety of other great exploits are, were, and will be the work of fame that mortals desire as a reward and a portion of the immortality their famous deeds deserve. Nevertheless we Catholic Christians and knights-errant look more to that future everlasting glory in the ethereal regions of heaven than to the vanity of the fame acquired in this present transitory life. However long that fame may last, it must after all end with the world itself, which has its own appointed end.

According to Don Quixote, the knight-errant aspires to true Christian 'glory,' as opposed to the fame sought by the warriors of the classical past. Even as he praises the great deeds that he has enumerated as 'works of fame,' he concedes the limitations of any secular reward for singular achievement. Human agency seeks immortality through heroic acts, but the fame that can be won in this world is subject to the destined end of all earthly things. In *La Numancia* Cipión covets the contingent glory of public renown; in *Don Quixote* the knight-errant pursues the certain glory of the redeemed in heaven, a state that demands patience in this world but offers enduring rewards. Don Quixote's account of his

Christian and Catholic office modulates into allegory as he catalogues the mortal sins that the knight-errant must overcome through acts of martial and spiritual courage: the giants of pride, the storms of anger, and so on. This praise of knight-errantry attempts to substitute Christian glory for the secular values of reputation and public recognition.

Don Quixote's discourse implies an opposition between classical and Christian paths to fame, and Sancho is eager to question him on the relative advantages of these different itineraries. Sancho presses his master to state the disposition that death has brought to the heroes he has named and the character of the sepulchres in which they lie. In particular, Sancho asks if these structures are adorned with objects that traditionally signify religious vows and veneration: crutches, shrouds, locks of hair, waxen legs and eyes. While Don Quixote admits that the pagan heroes are in hell, he praises the scale and wonder of their monuments:

> Los sepulcros de los gentiles fueron por la mayor parte suntuosos templos: las cenizas del cuerpo de Julio César se puserion sobre una pirámide de piedra de desmesurada grandeza, a quien hoy llaman en Roma *la Aguja de San Pedro*; al emperador Adriano le sirvió de sepultura un castillo tan grande como una buena aldea, a quien llamaron *Moles Hadriani*, que agora es el castillo de Santángel en Roma; la reina Artemisa sepultó a su marido Mausoleo en un sepulcro que se tuvo por una de las siete maravillas del mundo; pero ninguna destas sepulturas ni otras muchas que tuvieron los gentiles se adornaron con mortajas ni con otras ofrendas y señales que mostrasen ser santos los que en ellas estaban sepultados. (II. 8, 97)

> The tombs of the heathens were generally sumptuous temples. The ashes of Julius Caesar's body were placed on the top of a stone obelisk of vast size, which they now call in Rome Saint Peter's needle. The emperor Hadrian had for a tomb a castle as large as a good-sized village, which they called the *Moles Adriani* and is now the castle of St. Angelo in Rome. Queen Artemisia buried her husband Mausolus in a tomb which was considered one of the seven wonders of the world. But none of these tombs, or any of the many others of the heathens, were ornamented with shrouds or any of those other offerings and tokens that show that they who are buried there are saints.

Don Quixote responds to Sancho in a single, carefully structured sentence. He mentions the monuments of three notable figures from the ancient world – Julius Caesar, Hadrian, Mausolus – in a well-defined sequence. Each monument has a distinct architectural form, and they are listed in order of increasing scale and splendour, from the 'vast size' of Caesar's pyramid and the castle in Rome that rivals a village to the eponymous mausoleum counted among the wonders of antiquity. Don Quixote reaffirms the paradigmatic place of the Greco-Roman past in establishing and transmitting exemplars of fame and glory. In their heroic actions and imposing monuments, the ancients illustrate the persistent human drive for fame. Don Quixote nonetheless concedes Sancho's central point: that none of the ancient monuments displays the external signs of the veneration of saints.

Sancho turns this admission to his advantage. The absence of devotional objects clearly signifies that neither pagan emperors nor knights-errant have produced miraculous events of the order that confer sainthood. True miracles have greater force than the feats at arms of secular heroes, and the acts and vessels of worship that adorn the tombs of the saints enhance the 'Christian fame' that they have won by raising the dead and granting sight to the blind (II. 8, 98). Sancho responds to Don Quixote's orderly account of pagan monuments with a variegated catalogue of objects that offer physical evidence of saintly intervention against human suffering: shrouds, crutches, icons, wigs, eyes, legs. When his master asks what lessons he should draw from this array of devotion, Sancho has a prompt reply: 'Quiero decir ... que nos demos a ser santos, y alcanzaremos más brevemente la buena fama que pretendemos' (My meaning is ... let us set out to become saints, and we'll get the fame we are striving after more quickly) (II. 8, 98). This statement recognizes that knight and squire may share a common desire for fame while proposing that a holy life offers the most secure path towards securing fame in its positive form. It is clear that Sancho has directed the conversation to favour his case for the saintly path to fame, and Don Quixote responds by defending his chosen profession in religious terms: 'religión es la caballería; caballeros santos hay en la gloria' (chivalry is a religion; there are sainted knights in glory) (II. 8, 98–9). It is indicative of Sancho's influence over the debate that Don Quixote now equates the Christian fame that the true knight should pursue with the immutable glory of the saints in heaven.

This episode is comic, and much of its effect follows from Sancho's role as an interlocutor who proves capable of shaping the dialogue despite his incomplete comprehension of its terms. Don Quixote supports his argument for the primary force of fame in human affairs through an extensive range of rhetorical topics – modern and historical anecdotes, classical exempla, allegorical images, chivalric ideals – and Sancho often finds himself at a loss that leads to comic confusion. His efforts to imitate his master's high rhetorical register reveal gaps and inconsistencies in his knowledge and in his use of language. Sancho conflates Roman generals and emperors with the heroes of medieval chivalry and pursues questions concerning ancient burial monuments that are framed in relation to Christian expectations. In his diction he resorts at times to the colloquial register that conventionally marks the speech of peasants in literary texts, as in his opposition of 'señorazos' (great lords) and 'frailecitos descalzos' (little barefoot friars) (II. 8, 97–8), and he strings together terms that he has had difficulty in understanding, as in his categorization of the better fame that he attributes to the saints as 'esta fama, estas gracias, estas prerrogativas, como llaman a esto' (this fame, these favours, these privileges, or whatever you call it) (II. 8, 98). Despite these confusions Sancho presses his master to admit the superiority of the peaceful and saintly path to glory over the violent road to secular honours, replacing a model of fame based on heroic literature and romances of chivalry with another based on the written and oral transmission of saints' lives.

Don Quixote's contributions to the dialogue introduce another form of comic confusion. His command of rhetoric is exemplary, but his logic displays inconsistencies and flawed connections. As Geoffrey Ribbans has shown through a detailed analysis of the structure of Don Quixote's argument, his historical and contemporary examples can be divided into three distinct groups. The first group illustrates 'fame at all costs, even notoriety'; the second offers memorable instances of heroic conduct, in which 'valor and the thirst for reputation are inextricably confused'; the third reconciles the pursuit of glory with Christian values, but 'without replacing worldly renown' (188). The lapidary phrase on chivalry and religion with which Don Quixote defends his chosen profession rests on two separate propositions: that knight-errantry is an alternate form of faith and that some knights-errant have won their way to heaven (189). For all its rhetorical and aesthetic force, Don Quixote's discourse does not respond well to analytical scrutiny; as Ribbans observes, 'the fallacies in this argument are evident' (188). On close reading, Don Quixote's discourse on fame presents the features of a mock encomium: the playful treatment of a standard rhetorical theme, the juxtaposition of linguistic registers, and the use of paradoxical language to expose the limitations and transience of received categories. The extended exchange with Sancho shows that fame has a broad range of meanings and can be perceived as leading to various ends. Over the course of the dialogue Don Quixote defines fame as distinction, reputation, public recognition, and notoriety, and he associates its ends with both the enduring renown that pagan heroes have won in this world and the glory of the Christian saints in heaven. As in *La Numancia* and the *Viaje del Parnaso*, fame is disclosed as an uncertain quality, challenging in its multiple meanings and difficult to distinguish from vainglory.

This dialogue on fame shares with *La Numancia* a preference for classical models, particularly those drawn from the history of Rome and from the legends and monuments of the surviving city. Don Quixote cites exemplary instances of Roman heroism to illustrate the force of the desire for fame in human affairs, and he finds this desire enshrined in three architectural structures: the Pantheon, the granite obelisk that long stood near the church of St Peter and was moved to the centre of the Piazza San Pietro in 1586, and the Castel Sant'Angelo. His account describes both the architectural features of these well-known monuments and the changes over time in their names and functions. The pattern set by the description of the Pantheon – 'en la antigüedad se llamó el templo de los dioses, y ahora, con mejor vocación, se llama de todos los santos' (called in ancient times the temple 'of all the gods,' but nowadays, by a better nomenclature, 'of all the saints') (II. 8, 95) – repeats itself in the case of the obelisk – 'a quien llaman en Roma *la Aguja de San Pedro*' (which they now call in Rome Saint Peter's needle) – and of the fortress – 'que agora es el Castillo de Santángel en Roma' (and is now the castle of St. Angelo in Rome). Don Quixote's view of Rome traces a process that Thomas Greene has identified as the humanist hermeneutic. In one of his Latin letters (*Familiares* 1.5) Petrarch recalls walking through the Rome of his time in the company of Giovanni Colonna de San Vito and describes the places that they visited, 'not as they appeared to the naked eye but as they prompted his historical imagination' (Greene 88). This perspective implies both a principle of historical distance and a desire to bridge this gap by pursuing a 'deeper historical reality' that lies beneath the 'modern appearances' of the city (88). For the purposes of such scrutiny, the disciplines of archaeology and philology provide parallel procedures, since the excavation of lost objects and structures corresponds to the recovery of ancient texts (92). Through discovery, translation, and imitation, humanist writers engaged the textual heritage of the classics, attempting to recognize and reanimate stylistic and moral attitudes that the passage of time had made alien. To recover lost voices and sensibilities is to enter into an 'intimate, delicate, and subtle conversation with the ancient past' (94). Cervantes alludes to this process when he has Don Quixote describe Roman monuments in terms of both their ancient consecration to pagan gods and rulers and the functions that they have assumed in the modern city. Don Quixote's mock encomium draws on a serious and attentive hermeneutics of historical recovery.

The transformation over time of Rome's monuments also complicates the distinction that Sancho tries to draw between the sepulchres of ancient heroes and emperors and the temples of the saints. A striking feature of urban culture in medieval Rome was the papacy's 'gradual appropriation of the power and authority previously wielded by the Roman emperors' (Osborne 95), a process achieved in part through the consecration of ancient sites for Christian purposes and the accretion of saintly myths and legends concerning such places. As Don Quixote shows in his attention to the contrast between past and present, the pagan monuments that he mentions have been turned to the celebration and defence of Christian faith. Each of the three structures presents a history of functional changes. The rededication of the Pantheon to the Virgin and the saints in 609 CE was an early instance of Christian appropriation of Rome's ancient patrimony. The obelisk, Egyptian in origin, had been transported during the imperial period to Alexandria and then to Rome. Medieval guidebooks identify this monument as a pyramid and record the popular legends that it commemorated Julius Caesar and housed his ashes in a bronze sphere at its peak. The medieval name of St Peter's Needle can be traced to the belief that Peter had been martyred near the site of the obelisk, as well as to a more general association between Caesar's foundational role in Roman imperial history and St Peter's parallel place in the origins of the papacy. Transferred to Rome from conquered territory in Egypt, the obelisk assumed in the Middle Ages a complex role in joint commemoration of ancient empire and Christian faith. The Castel Sant'Angelo presents a similar duality. Constructed on the orders of the emperor Hadrian (117–38 CE), this monument was designed as a sepulchre to honour Hadrian and his successors, in a structure that would rival the elegance and grandeur of the temple of all the gods in the Pantheon. Its location opposite central Rome on the Tiber, however, had obvious strategic importance, and by the late third century the Romans had started to fortify it for the protection of their city. In the middle of the sixth century the demands of war on the Ostrogoths transformed the imperial sepulchre into a fortress, and subsequent modifications enhanced its value for defence against invaders and for the protection of the popes. A series of significant papal renovations were completed during the early modern period, following developments in strategy and in military architecture. Nicolas V (1447–55) introduced fortifications for the use of gunpowder weapons and had an apartment built within the cylindrical body of the original sepulchre. Under Alexander VI (1492–1503) the four bastions of the surrounding walls were strengthened and the papal residence expanded. Under Pius IV (1560–5) the central sepulchre was enclosed within modern trace ramparts designed for siege defence. The historical image of the fortress associated it with the protection of the city in times of peril. Its popular name can be traced to a medieval legend that the Archangel Michael appeared on its ramparts during the papacy of Gregory the Great as a sign of deliverance from the plague, and Clement VII took refuge in its papal quarters during the sack of Rome in 1527.[14] In response to Sancho's query about the burial sites of illustrious pagans, Don Quixote traces an itinerary of Roman monuments that mark both the survival of the city's ancient patrimony and its transformation to Christian purposes. This argument assimilates Roman renown to Christian glory, blurring the distinction between these two ideals.

In Don Quixote's dialogue here with Sancho we find critical scrutiny of the terms that inform the ethos of classical epic and the historiography of ancient Rome and its empire: fame, renown, valour, glory. One of the techniques on which such scrutiny rests is the juxtaposition of genres, particularly the interpellation of the high matters of epic by low mimetic forms. The comic exchange between knight and squire on the pursuit of fame reveals the instability of the distinctions that attempt to separate good fame from bad or earthly renown from transcendent glory. A parallel juxtaposition of genres shapes Don Quixote's encounter with the sheepflocks. A typical scene from Castile's rural economy – the movement of sheep from winter to summer pasture, under the care of migrant labourers – is transformed through patterns drawn from chivalric romance and classical epic.[15] Here Don Quixote brings to the countryside the violence of his chosen literary models, but the pastoralists whom he engages are not the shepherd-poets of pastoral romance and they are prepared to take up simple arms in defence of their flocks. Don Quixote's intervention and the shepherds' response call into question the conventional opposition of pastoral peace and epic violence. This episode combines the genres of epic, chivalric romance, and pastoral to comic effect, and it also reveals the tensions inherent in Renaissance pastoral and the implication of pastoral in the literature of war.

The models of chivalric romance and pastoral shape many of the initial chapters of *Don Quixote*, in a pattern that reflects the relationship between Don Quixote's madness and his powers of perception. Through his addictive reading Don Quixote has filled his brain with images drawn from books, with the result that he can only recognize external objects in relation to literary models. The passages in the text that comment explicitly on this process refer to the romances of chivalry, but it is clear from the scrutiny of Don Quixote's library that he has read other kinds of books, and during the adventures in Part I he recognizes what he sees in terms of familiar generic models. In his mind windmills are giants and inns are castles, while an acorn engages the model of pastoral, prompting his discourse on the Golden Age (I. 11). In these cases the relationship between the external object and its corresponding literary image is straightforward, but the process leaves open the possibility that a given sequence of objects and events may evoke more than one model and that Don Quixote may conflate different conventions. The perceptions that Cervantes attributes to his central character reinforce his practice of generic mixing.

The encounter with the sheepflocks begins when Don Quixote sees a large cloud of dust rising in the distance from the road. Following his habitual practice in Part I,[16] he takes this visual stimulus as a spur to the high adventures that he has decided to pursue:

> Éste es el día, ¡oh Sancho!, en el cual se ha de ver el bien que me tiene guardado mi suerte; éste es el día, digo, en que se ha de mostrar, tanto como en otro alguno, el valor de mi brazo, y en el que tengo de hacer obras que queden escritas en el libro de la Fama por todos los venideros siglos. (I. 18, 218)

> This is the day, O Sancho, which will reveal the boon my fortune reserves for me. This, I say, is the day when as much as on any other shall be displayed the might of my arm and when I shall do deeds that will remain written in the book of fame for all ages to come.

This sentence reveals both the traditional goal that Don Quixote has set for himself and the high rhetorical register in which he expresses his intentions. Through the traditional image of the book of Fame, Don Quixote declares his desire to establish an enduring reputation by acts of arms. In a careful rhetorical structure he enumerates, in order of ascending importance, three factors that assure him of the particular promise of this encounter: his conviction that fate favours his ambitions, his faith in his own valour, and the prospect of fame. Don Quixote's noble purpose appeals to the traditional ethos of heroism that offers fame as the reward for martial accomplishments, while his rhetoric echoes the style of high mimetic literary genres.

Given his desire to show excellence in feats of arms, Don Quixote finds a martial source for the cloud of dust that he has seen, telling Sancho that a large and diverse army is approaching. The knight's convictions are confirmed when his squire explains that two armies must be meeting, since he can see another cloud in the opposite direction. Here the text describes the process that has led to Don Quixote's perception of two armies and then reveals the true causes of the clouds of dust:

> alegrándose sobre manera, pensó sin duda que eran dos ejércitos, que venían a embestirse y a encontrarse en mitad de aquella espaciosa llanura. Porque tenía a todas horas y momentos llena la fantasía de aquellas batallas, encantamentos, sucesos, desatinos, amores, desafíos, que en los libros de caballerías se cuentan, y todo cuanto hablaba, pensaba o hacía era encaminado a cosas semejantes. Y la polvareda que había visto la levantaban dos grandes manadas de ovejas y carneros que, por aquel mesmo camino, de dos diferentes partes venían, las cuales, con el polvo, no se echaron de ver hasta que llegaron cerca. (I. 18, 218)

> He rejoiced exceedingly, for he concluded that two armies were about to meet and clash in the midst of that broad plain. At all times and seasons his fancy was full of the battles, enchantments, adventures, reckless feats, loves, and challenges that are recorded in the books of chivalry, and everything he said, thought, or did had reference to such things. Now the cloud of dust he had seen was raised by two great flocks of sheep coming along the same road in opposite directions, which, because of the dust, did not become visible until they drew near.

This encounter involves an arbitrary choice between the patterns of chivalric romance and the conventions of pastoral. Given the strongly established associations between sheep and pastoral literature, it is reasonable to assume that sheepflocks, like acorns, would activate pastoral images in the protagonist's brain. Don Quixote, however, does not see the sheepflocks themselves but rather the clouds of dust that they have raised, and he interprets this visual impression in terms of armies and warfare. No amount of later evidence or argument from Sancho can shift this perception. Convinced that he sees two armies converging towards him, Don Quixote announces that he must intervene in the battle he sees unfolding and improvises a narrative to explain the conflict that has brought the warring parties to the battlefield.

His narrative begins with the patterns of chivalric romance. He identifies the leaders of the armies and describes the nature of their conflict. Alifanfarón, an Eastern lord and a 'fierce pagan,' has fallen in love with the Christian daughter of the African king Pentapolín. To protect his child, Pentapolín will not accept Alifanfarón unless he abandons the law of Mohammed and converts to Christianity. This account combines the conflict between the faiths of Islam and Christianity – a central thread in the captive's tale and in other Cervantine romance narratives set in the Mediterranean – with the traditional romance motif of the virgin imperilled by unwanted suitors.[17] It addresses a serious question in the laws of war – the *casus belli*, or occasion of conflict between the parties – while presenting well-known strategies of parody. Alifanfarón, the name assigned to the pagan enemy, combines 'Alí' with 'fanfarrón,' the term in Spanish that describes the attributes of the self-glorifying soldier, or *miles gloriosus*, a stock figure in classical comedy and in the Spanish *comedia*.[18] The setting given for the action – the remote island of Trapobana or Sri Lanka – is both exotic and comic in its effect. This passage is typical of Part I in its imaginative and parodic replication of romance conventions.

The generic pattern modulates when Don Quixote ascends a slight rise and describes to Sancho the two armies, 'viendo en su imaginación lo que no veía ni había' (seeing in his imagination what he did not see and what did not exist) (I. 18, 219). The survey of the armies as they close for battle introduces the epic device of the catalogue of warriors, a convention established in foundational texts by Homer (*Iliad* II. 494–877) and Vergil (*Aeneid* VII. 641–817). Drawing on images from books that have reshaped his cognitive abilities, Don Quixote generates two catalogues in an exuberant act of verbal improvisation: the first describes the leading warriors from each of the opposing sides; the second, the nations and ethnic groups that have contributed soldiers to the two armies. The parade of knights and giants that Don Quixote conjures forth recalls popular celebrations of the carnival season (Redondo 341–2). His catalogues can also be traced to multiple sources in classical and Renaissance literature, including Spanish versions of the *Iliad* and the *Aeneid,* Ariosto's *Orlando furioso*, Luis de Zapata's *Carlo famoso*, Lope de Vega's *Arcadia*, and the chivalric romances *El caballero del Febo* and *Palmerín de Ingalaterra* (McGaha, 'Intertextuality' 155, 157). Their methods of description suggest a particular debt to *Orlando furioso*, in which the siege of Paris provides the motive for two epic catalogues. In the first (X. 76–89) the paladin Ruggiero witnesses a parade of knights who have enlisted to come to Charlemagne's aid from the realms of northern Europe – England, Scotland, Ireland, Sweden, Norway, Iceland – as an unnamed guide identifies the warriors by describing the heraldic symbols on their ensigns and standards. In the second catalogue (XIV. 11–27) the battalions of the besieging Saracen army pass in review before their commanders Marsilio and Agramante, as the narrator enumerates the provinces and cities in Iberia and North Africa from which they have assembled. In his epic catalogues Cervantes emulates Ariosto's methods of heraldic and toponymic description; he also plays on the typical perspectives of epic and romance and introduces features from other genres to comic effect.

Don Quixote's first catalogue is a sustained passage of rhetorical description. He lists three champions from each army, improvising for each one a name and a cognomen, a unique code of arms, and a heraldic device. His invention depends on the related processes of 'pictorialization and visualization,' with an emphasis on colour and emblematic design that enhances the 'visual effect' of his spoken words (Selig, 'Battle' 106). Romance continues to assert its presence within the formal frame of the epic catalogue, since Don Quixote characterizes the warriors that he imagines with attributes modelled on the books of chivalry that he has read. The clear persistence of romance creates a revealing play of perspectives. Where epic poetry presents an objectified view of great heroes removed in status and time from its intended audience, Don Quixote's catalogue of knights presents the subjective perspective that Northrop Frye has identified as one of the typical features of romance.[19] Through his 'pictorially idiosyncratic notion of chivalry' Don Quixote grants to each warrior attributes that both individualize each figure and mirror his own situation as a novice in knight-errantry (Murillo, *Critical Introduction* 61).

Comparison with the catalogues in *Orlando furioso* shows the approach to epic conventions that Cervantes shares with Ariosto and illustrates his subjective recasting of traditional models. Ariosto is known for an inventive treatment of epic that disrupts its serious tone with descriptions and gestures that tend to irony and comedy. Like Don Quixote's catalogue of warriors, the account of the knights who have gathered in Charlemagne's aid provides an internal gloss, in which

Ruggiero's attention is directed to the ensigns that they bear and their significance. A characteristic stanza presents a series of English knights:

> Il conte d'Arindelia è quel c'ha messo
> in mar quella barchetta che s'affonda.
> Vedi il marchese di Barclei; e appresso
> di Marchia il conte e il conte di Ritmonda:
> il primo porta in bianco un monte fesso,
> l'altro la palma, il terzo un pin ne l'onda.
> Quel di Dorsezia è conte, e quel d'Antona,
> che l'uno ha il carro, e l'altro la corona. (X. 80)

> The one displaying a boat sinking at sea is the Earl of Arundel; there goes the Marquis of Berkeley, and next, the Earls of March and of Richmond: the first displays argent, a cleft mountain, the second, a palm, the third, a pine in the water. Over there is the Earl of Dorset, and there, the Earl of Hampton, the former with the chariot, the latter with the crown.

This description appeals to the impact of images and colours and to traditional signs of nobility. The devices assigned to the knights are concise visual emblems and evoke conventional associations of nobility and authority: the palm of the Earl of March, the chariot of Dorset, the crown of Hampton. Throughout this catalogue particular terms stress the patrician and martial qualities of the knights: the comely Zerbino, Prince of Scotland, is lauded for his prowess, grace, and strength ('virtù,' 'grazia,' 'possanza,' X. 84). Style and subject appear to be consistent with the principle of decorum. Yet the identification of each knight with a single emblem has a reductive effect. To strip a heroic description down to its minimal elements is a technique of parody, one that Ariosto uses here to qualify the epic tone of his catalogue.[20]

Don Quixote's description of the warriors marching into battle is also marked by parody, but it adopts the contrasting technique of amplification. With invention and energy, Don Quixote describes to Sancho the knights who have come to the aid of the imperilled Christian virgin:

> Pero vuelve los ojos a estotra parte, y verás delante y en la frente destotro ejército al siempre vencedor y jamás vencido Timonel de Carcajona, príncipe de la Nueva Vizcaya, que viene armado con las armas partidas a cuarteles, azules, verdes, blancas y amarillas, y trae en el escudo un gato de oro en campo leonado, con una letra que dice: *Miau*, que es el principio

del nombre de su dama, que, según se dice, es la sin par Miulina, hija del duque Alfeñiquén del Algarbe; el otro, que carga y oprime los lomos de aquella poderosa alfana, que trae las armas como nieve blancas y el escudo blanco y sin empresa alguna, es un caballero novel, de nación francés, llamado Pierres Papín, señor de las baronías de Utrique; el otro, que bate las ijadas con los herrados carcaños a aquella pintada y ligera cebra y trae las armas de los veros azules, es el poderoso duque de Nerbia, Espartafilardo del Bosque, que trae por empresa una esparraguera, con una letra en castellano que dice así: *Rastrea mi suerte*. (I. 18, 220)

But turn your eyes to the other side, and you shall see in front and in the van of this other army the ever victorious and never vanquished Timonel of Carcajona, prince of New Biscay, who comes in armor with arms quartered azure, green, white, and yellow, and bears on his shield a cat on a field tawny with a motto which says *Miau*, which is the beginning of the name of his lady, who according to report is the peerless Miaulina, daughter of the duke Alfeñiquén of the Algarve. The other, who weighs down and presses the loins of that powerful charger and bears arms white as snow and a shield blank and without any device, is a novice knight, a Frenchman by birth, Pierre Papin by name, lord of the baronies of Utrique. That other, who with iron-shod heels strikes the flanks of that nimble parti-colored zebra, and for arms bears azure vair, is the mighty duke of Nerbia, Espartafilardo of the Forest, who bears for device on his shield an asparagus plant with a motto in Castilian that says, *My fortune creeps*.

Favouring the conventions of chivalric romance over those of epic, Don Quixote casts his catalogue in a tone of unbridled hyperbole. In contrast with Ariosto's practice of assigning a single emblem to each knight, he supplies exuberant detail according to a set pattern that includes a coat of arms with its colours and a shield that displays a device with a motto. His heraldry resorts to an improvised code, in which cats and asparagus plants have displaced traditional symbols, and the names that he assigns to the knights are comic and undercut their characterization as heroic leaders.[21] The cat is also a carnivalesque creature, associated in popular festivals with seasonal licence and lust (Redondo 345). Beneath this hyperbolic surface lies a strain of self-identification that is typical of romance. Upon each of the heroes whom he describes here Don Quixote projects some aspect of his own condition. The first displays Don Quixote's devotion to a distant beloved; the second shares his status as a novice who bears his arms unadorned in anticipation of winning a heroic device; the third echoes his misfortunes in the ambiguous phrasing of the motto *Rastrea mi suerte*.[22] Comic in its exuberance and invention, Don Quixote's rhetoric inserts his own image into the epic catalogue of heroes.

Cervantes parallels Ariosto's second catalogue when he lists the groups that constitute the two opposing armies. Ariosto describes the mixed troops – first Iberian, then African – who have mustered to join the siege against Paris. Given the setting of *Orlando furioso* in a legendary medieval past, the Iberian troops are religious enemies of the city's Christian defenders. They parade before King Agramante, commander of the Saracen cause, to display their force in arms:

> Balugante del popul di Leone,
> Grandonio cura degli Algarbi piglia;
> il fratel di Marsilio, Falsirone,
> ha seco armata la minor Castiglia.
> Seguon di Madarasso il gonfalone
> quei che lasciato han Malaga e Siviglia,
> dal mar di Gade a Cordova feconda
> le verdi ripe ovunque il Beti inonda. (XIV. 12)

> Balugant was in charge of the troops from Leon, Grandonio commanded those from Algarve. Marsilius' brother, Falsiron, led the army of Old Castille. The men of Malaga and Seville, and those from the green valley of the Guadalquivir between the Bay of Cadiz and fertile Cordova followed the ensign of Madarasso.

Ariosto maintains the concision of his earlier catalogue. The troops, representative of the various regions of Spain, are identified by the most economical of means, through the names of their kingdoms and cities and through conventional attributes of physical geography ('Cordova feconda,' 'verdi ripe'). In this case Ariosto's techniques are faithful to canonical models. Classical epic makes use of traditional attributes and characterizes places by naming the rivers that water them, as in the catalogues of armies in Homer and Vergil. Here brevity is consistent with the style and matter of epic verse. As the review of the troops proceeds, however, the narrator recounts the reversals that have forced Agramante to reinforce and reorganize his forces, including the triumphs of the warrior-maiden Bradamante over the commanders from the Sudan and Tangiers. In this section the complications of romance intrude into the epic catalogue.

In Don Quixote's second catalogue (I. 18, 221–2) Cervantes maintains the exuberance and the subjective focus of his first, in part by following Ariosto's eclectic approach. Many of the groups in each of the two armies are identified by the rivers that water their lands, and this listing of rivers contrasts the multiple nations of the pagans – the Xanthus of Troy, the Thermodon of Cappadocia, the Pactolus of Lydia – with the common home of the Christian troops in Spain – the Tagus, the Guadalquivir (here identified as the Betis, as in Ariosto), the Guadiana. As David Quint has noted, the opposition of an ethnically diverse enemy to a unitary force of defenders is a rhetorical strategy characteristic of imperial epic.[23] Don Quixote also resorts to the epic technique of characterization through conventional attributes. Among the enemy troops the Persians are identified by the bows and arrows that represent their skill in archery; the Arabians by their movable houses. The narrator intervenes to call attention to the formulaic character of this catalogue and its debt to the protagonist's library: 'cuántas provincias dijo, cuántas naciones nombró, dándole a cada una, con maravillosa presteza, los atributos que le pertenecían, todo absorto y empapado en lo que había leído en sus libros mentirosos' (what a number of countries and nations he named! To each he gave its proper attributes with marvellous readiness, brimful and saturated with what he had read in his lying books!) (I. 18, 222). Here the protagonist draws not only on the conventions of his favourite romances but also on topographical and mythological knowledge of the kind made available in Renaissance miscellanies. Absorbed in the world that he knows from books, he surveys the defining features of places both distant and near, from the gold that lies buried in the deserts of Arabia to the golden sands of the Tagus and the hidden course of the Guadiana. By identifying the defenders of the imperilled princess as his compatriots, drawn from the provinces of Spain, Don Quixote maintains the patterns of self-identification and subjectivity that shape the perspective of romance. In this second instance Cervantes transforms the catalogue of armies into a generic farrago that presents a comic juxtaposition of epic, chivalric romance, and Renaissance topographical lore. His account of the heroes and their troops engages a striking range of conventional literary and rhetorical techniques: ekphrasis, enumeration, the epic catalogue, 'onomastic invention, word play and art-minded philology' (Selig, 'Battle' 107). These varied and multiple techniques interact with one another, creating 'a polychromatic tapestry of the mock-heroic, the heroic-comic, and the comic-heroic' (107).

Rich in visual impact and rhetorical invention, the two epic catalogues confirm the martial cast of the patterns that have filled Don Quixote's imagination. The rural plain appears not as a pastoral space but as a source of random stimuli that engage images and themes from his readings in heroic literature. The agency that Don Quixote attributes to the sheepflocks is wholly fictional, drawn from the typical romance plot of the imperilled princess. His vision also maintains the conventional perspective of pastoral literature, in that it allows no place for the labour of tending and driving the sheep. When Don Quixote takes direct action, however, his intervention leads to a reversal of this view. Faithful to his vow to defend the innocent, he charges on the flock that he perceives as the army under the command of the pagan aggressor: 'se entró por medio del escuadrón de las ovejas, y comenzó de alcanceallas con tanto coraje y denuedo, como si de veras alcanceara a sus mortales enemigos' (he dashed into the midst of the squadron of ewes and began spearing them with as much spirit and intrepidity as if he were transfixing mortal enemies in earnest) (I. 18, 223). The prospect of violence has been implicit in Don Quixote's vision from the beginning, and here his expectations of violence are fulfilled, although not in the heroic clash of arms that he has imagined. Alarmed at this unaccountable attack on the animals in their care, the shepherds and drovers turn on Don Quixote, first attempting to dissuade him with words and then deploying their slings as defensive arms. The stones that they cast are simple but effective weapons, and the clash between knight and shepherds ends in mutual damage. Don Quixote kills at least seven sheep, while the shepherds inflict a wound in his ribs and knock out several of his remaining teeth. This non-heroic encounter plays again on the framing of violence through literary genres. In response to the epic force that Don Quixote attempts to exercise, the characters who depend on the land and its animals for their economic existence recover the agency that the conventions of pastoral would deny them. The shepherds are practical pastoralists who know that they must defend their flocks, and they turn the weapons of the countryside on the knight who has suddenly brought epic violence into their midst.

The entry into Renaissance pastoral of characters who exercise the practical skills of husbandry and tillage disrupts the enamelled world of literary representation and questions the convention that links country life to peace and harmonious social relations. In the encounter with the sheepflocks Cervantes turns to such characters for the purposes of parody, juxtaposing the violence of slings and stones to the elevated forms of armed conflict that Don Quixote associates with classical epic and the romances of chivalry. In the episode of the braying *regidores* a group of villagers take up arms to counter the mockery of their neighbours. These rural characters depend on the land and on working animals for their living, and here the presence and actions of practical pastoralists construct a satirical view of the traditional ethos of heroism and fame. The mechanisms through which reputation is lost and gained are evident in the acts that offend the villagers and in the measures that they take to defend their community. As the story of the *regidores* spreads across the countryside, the villagers are quick to take offence, and they are equally quick to claim vindication when they turn the force of their vengeance on an innocent victim. Violence asserts its presence in the pastoral world, once again through means that depend on the interaction of pastoral with other genres. The armed recovery of the villagers' reputation revisits the antecedents and demands of fame, from the perspective of a satire on human folly and the general failings of moral conduct that beset human life.

Cervantes's presentation of the feuding villagers can be placed in the context of his general views on satire. The *Viaje del Parnaso* contains statements that suggest an ambivalent stance on his part towards a classical mode of satirical writing. Cervantes writes himself into this mock epic as the first-person narrator and as a soldier in the army that Apollo raises to defend the mount of Parnassus. At the beginning of Book IV, he recites to Apollo a summary of his career in letters, listing the works that mark his achievements and commenting on the principles that inform his poetics. Through a general opening statement – 'Suele la indignación componer versos' (Indignation's habit is to write verses) (IV. 1) – he concedes that emotion has moved him to defend himself and his works. This clear allusion to Juvenal I. 79 – 'si natura negat, facit indignatio versum' (though nature say me nay, indignation will prompt my verse) – appears to declare an affinity with the attitude of moral outrage that informs Juvenal's satirical voice. Cervantes's own voice nonetheless moderates into a frequently cited rejection of satire as a low and disreputable form:

> Nunca voló la pluma humilde mía
> por la región satírica, bajeza
> que a infames premios y desgracias guía. (IV. 34–6)

> My humble pen never flew through the zone of satire, a mean act that leads to odious rewards and misfortunes.

The *Viaje del Parnaso* qualifies this disavowal through its use of techniques associated with satire, including the narrator's appeal to his authority as a direct witness of the assault on Parnassus and of literary life among the Spanish writers who answer Apollo's call to arms, his claim to speak with humility and directness, and his inventive colloquial language.[24] The central focus of Cervantes's critique of satire rests on its typical purposes and targets. The satirical speaker asserts a moral intent that animates his work and justifies the extremes of his tone and diction. He may disclaim an innate disposition to anger, but he finds himself driven to bitter words by the moral or social corruption that he has chosen to attack (Lokos 61). For Cervantes this aggressive stance is one of the detrimental features of satire.

Cervantes also recognizes that the satirist's stance is not equally trenchant across all the variants of the form. In the discourse on the study of poetry that he delivers to Don Diego de Miranda (*DQ* II. 16), Don Quixote defends this art as a noble and virtuous form of knowledge. He nonetheless advises that the genre of satire is not always worthy of praise and imitation:

> Riña vuesa merced a su hijo si hiciere sátiras que perjudiquen las honras ajenas, y castíguele, y rómpaselas; pero si hiciere sermones al modo de Horacio, donde reprehenda los vicios en general, como tan elegantemente él lo hizo, alábele; porque lícito es al poeta escribir contra la invidia, y decir en sus versos mal de los invidiosos, y así de los otros vicios, con que no señale persona alguna. (II. 16, 156–7)

> If your son writes satires reflecting on the honor of others, chide and correct him, and tear them up. But if he composes discourses in which he rebukes vice in general, in the style of Horace, and with elegance like his, commend him. It is legitimate for a poet to write against envy and scourge the envious in his verse, and the other vices too, provided that he does not single out individuals.

Don Quixote appeals here to a well-established distinction between a variant of satire modelled on Juvenal that trades in harsh denunciation and invective and a Horatian variant that offers a general critique of moral or social failings. The two differ in focus and in stylistic register. Juvenal's variant directs a harsh and pointed rhetoric against individuals, while Horace's censures abstract vices in a style that respects the principle of decorum. Cervantes takes an interest in both of these variants, but adopts a particular approach to each one. In the *Viaje del Parnaso*, as in *El licenciado Vidriera* and *El coloquio de los perros*, Cervantes explores the limitations of Juvenal's kind of satire. In these works the satirical speaker employs the rhetoric of moral indignation while implicating himself in the system of rewards and values that he has chosen as the object of his critique.[25] Don Quixote's encounter with the *regidores* and their neighbours presents rural characters in the low style of pastoral and uses a rustic conflict to comment from a Horatian perspective on the failings that human communities show in their attachment to reputation and their propensity to violence.

The episode begins when Don Quixote, accompanied by Sancho and the humanist guide who escorted them to the cave of Montesinos, encounters a peasant leading a donkey laden with lances and spears. The peasant tells Don Quixote that the weapons are to be used the next day and announces that if they both spend the night at a nearby inn he will take the opportunity to recount 'maravillas' (wonderful things), a promise that appeals to Don Quixote's curiosity and his interest in matters of arms (II. 24, 225). The episode then unfolds in two parts. In the first the peasant tells a story from his village, indicating how it came to be identified with two *regidores* practised in the art of braying, what effect this reputation has had on the villagers, and why they now have need of arms to defend themselves against the mockery of their neighbours. This tale has the attraction of curious events and explains the introduction of weapons into the pastoral world. In the second part Don Quixote sees the villagers' zeal at first hand when he encounters a group of some two hundred men who have set out in a flourish of colours and military music to do battle with the residents of a neighbouring town. Don Quixote initially believes that he has come upon a regiment of soldiers on the march, but he quickly recognizes the diversely armed squadron as defenders of the *regidores*' village. Faced with this display of arms and of violent intent, Don Quixote and Sancho make separate attempts to persuade the villagers that they do not have a fair grievance against their neighbours. These verbal interventions lead the villagers not to lay down their arms but to redirect the use of them. Taken together, the two parts of this episode comment on the causes of conflict between groups, the difficulty of restraining the impulse to violence, and the tendency of armed force to seek an object on which it can be exercised.

The peasant's narrative begins with a *regidor* from his village who lost a donkey through a female servant's 'industria y engaño' (cleverness and roguery), both familiar qualities in folkloric tales about rural characters. Another *regidor* tells him that the donkey has been sighted in a nearby wood, and the two set out to look for the lost animal. Their search fails at first, and the *regidor* who believes that the donkey can be found in the wood announces that he is able to bray with remarkable skill and proposes that the two men walk separately braying at intervals, since this sound will draw the donkey forth from the most remote of hiding places. The first *regidor* praises the 'ingenio' (genius or wit) of this plan and agrees that they should intensify their efforts through braying. The renewed search, however, is no more effective in its outcome. The two *regidores* diligently trace a circuit around the wood and find one another, since each is drawn to the convincing call of the other. This pattern repeats itself until the searchers find the donkey's dead body in the heart of the wood, mauled by wolves and insensate to any call. Despite this disappointment, the *regidores* take pleasure in having discovered their shared talent in the art of braying and return contented to their village.

This inset narrative plays on standard comic techniques and conventions. Here the world of herdsmen offers a setting for a tale of peasant cleverness and ingenuity. The plan to locate the lost animal by imitating its natural call is humorous, and the implementation of this strategy produces a series of failed attempts in which the two searchers are bound to find each other. Each of the *regidores* describes the skills of the other in a rhetorical register of courtesy and mutual praise. The donkey's owner assures his fellow *regidor* 'de vos a un asno, compadre, no hay alguna diferencia, en cuanto toca al rebuznar' (between you and an ass there's no difference as far as braying goes) (II. 25, 231–2). The clever friend returns this praise, responding that the greater skill in braying lies with his companion and elaborating on the qualities that he has displayed in this unusual art:

> por el Dios que me crió que podéis dar dos rebuznos al mayor y más perito rebuznador del mundo; porque el sonido que tenéis es alto; lo sostentido de la voz, a su tiempo y compás; los dejos, muchos y apresurados, y, en resolución, yo me doy por vencido y os rindo la palma y doy la bandera desta rara habilidad. (II. 25, 232)

> by the God that made me, you could give a couple of brays by way of a handicap to the best and most accomplished brayer in the world. Your tone is deep, your voice is well sustained in both time and pitch, and your finishing notes come thick and fast. In fact, I consider myself beaten, and I yield the palm and banner to you in this rare accomplishment.

Renaissance literature presents pastoral characters who show a surprising command of courtly language and the forms of court etiquette. Convention may oppose court and country, but pastoral speakers are often able to express themselves in terms that reflect the ethos of courtiers. Cervantes's characterization of the *regidores* follows this pattern, and the humour of this passage rests on the application of courtly attitudes and values to the art of braying. The *regidores* display a courtier's grace and spontaneity in practising their skills and exemplary gallantry in deferring pride of place to one another.[26] The praise of the braying voice for its tone and measured timing echoes the emphasis on balance and proportion in the formal language of Neo-Aristotelian aesthetics. In the account of the *regidores*, braying is a rare art that rivals the attainments of life at court.

The peasant-narrator emphasizes both the satisfaction that the *regidores* take in their mastery of braying and the unintended consequences of their enthusiasm. The *regidores* are eager to boast of their skills, telling and retelling the story of their search in the woods. Over time, however, this reiteration leads others to identify them and their neighbours as residents of the town of brayers, a habit that leads to a sense of insult and grievance. When people from adjacent communities bray at them in mockery, the villagers turn to the threat of violence:

> ha llegado a tanto la desgracia desta burla, que muchas veces con mano armada y formado escuadrón han salido contra los burladores los burlados a darse la batalla, sin poderlo remediar rey ni roque, ni temor ni vergüenza. (II. 25, 233)
>
> so far has it gone with this miserable joke that several times the scoffed have come out armed and arrayed to do battle with the scoffers. Neither king nor rook, nor fear nor shame, can improve matters.

This account does not indicate the extent of the villagers' violence. They have armed themselves many times in the cause of reprisal, but it is unclear whether those who mock them have answered in kind.[27] That the peasant is transporting a large number of weapons to his neighbours nonetheless suggests some escalation in the conflict, and Cervantes's text revisits here the serious matter of the *casus belli*. The villagers define themselves as a separate and particular community; they perceive the mockery of others as an injury to the peace and integrity of their communal existence; they take up arms to defend themselves and admonish their enemies. The peasant's narrative explains the demand for his burden of arms and offers a justification for their use. The campaign against another village, planned to take place within a few days' time, is a fair defence of his community.

The cause of the villagers' recourse to arms is subjected to scrutiny in the second part of this adventure. Processes of perception and recognition again come into play when Don Quixote and Sancho encounter a group of men bearing arms on the road towards the Ebro. Don Quixote's initial impression that he has come upon a *tercio* of soldiers recalls the Spanish Crown's practice of transporting its armies for long distances across the countryside, at an economic and moral risk to the peasants who were obliged by law to billet the soldiers in their communities.[28] As in the episode of the sheepflocks, Don Quixote ascends a hill to survey the warriors that surround him. He sees the varied weapons that they are carrying, their colours and insignia, the banners of their cause – including one that shows a donkey with his tongue extended in a bray – and understands that he has not found an army in transit. Instead, Don Quixote and Sancho realize that the residents of the brayers' village have set out against their neighbours: 'conocieron y superion como el pueblo corrido salía a pelear con otro que le corría más de lo justo y de lo que se debía a la buena vecindad' (they perceived, in short, that the town which had been twitted had turned out to do battle with some other village that had jeered it more than was fair or neighbourly) (II. 27, 252). In contrast with the mental transformation of the sheepflocks into armies in Part I, Don Quixote has no need to improvise a system of heraldic identification (Selig, '*Don Quixote* II, XXIV–XXVIII' 137–8). He recognizes the villagers through their banners and grasps the issues of concord and conflict that have led them to take up arms. Given this focus on social relations, Don Quixote intervenes with words rather than arms.

Cervantes's knight acts here 'as an arbiter and instrument to restore order' (Selig, '*Don Quixote* II, XXIV–XXVIII' 139). He structures his speech as a formal oration, beginning with a formulaic appeal to the attention and good will of his audience: 'Buenos señores, cuan encarecidamente puedo, os suplico que no interrumpáis un razonamiento que quiero haceros' (Worthy sirs, I entreat you as earnestly as I can not to interrupt a speech which I wish to address to you) (II. 27, 252). He sets out a sequence of arguments to persuade the armed men that they have no fair grounds for the violence that they plan to exercise. He first turns to the principles that govern duels among private persons, stating that the villagers' circumstances neither demand nor justify vengeance, since no individual can affront an entire community. To supplement this point, he claims that the mild epithet that has attached itself to the villagers should give no offence, citing residents of other communities who have acquired similar epithets through parallel instances of peasant simplicity, such as the eggplant-eaters of Toledo, the whalers of Madrid, and the soapmakers of Yepes and Ocaña.[29] From this discussion of the particular causes of insult among individuals and local communities, he proceeds to a more general argument concerning the legitimate reasons that lead to strategic acts of violence:

> Los varones prudentes, las repúblicas bien concertadas, por cuatro cosas han de tomar las armas y desenvainar las espadas, y poner a riesgo sus personas, vidas y haciendas: la primera, por defender la fe católica; la segunda, por defender su vida, que es de ley natural y divina; la tercera, en defensa de su honra, de su familia y hacienda; la cuarta, en servicio de su rey, en la guerra justa; y si le quisiéremos añadir la quinta, que se puede contar por segunda, es en defensa de su patria. (II. 27, 254)

> There are four things for which sensible men and well-ordered States ought to take up arms, draw their swords, and risk their persons, lives, and properties. The first is to defend the Catholic faith; the second, to defend one's life, which is in accordance with natural and divine law; the third, in defense of one's honor, family, and property; the fourth, in the service of one's king in a just war; and if to these we choose to add a fifth (which may be included in the second), in defense of one's country.

Don Quixote expands here on the just causes of violence. He stresses that force is legitimate when its use is defensive, given the self-evident obligation of citizens to protect their faith, their lives, their patrimony, and their nations. He understands participation in a just war as service to one's monarch, in accordance with the general view in *Don Quixote* that the life of arms is an expression of loyalty to the royal house. Each of the causes that he enumerates posits the defence of a substantive entity, and this factor justifies the risk inherent in resorting to arms. His intention in outlining the general grounds for just conflict among citizens and nations is to convince the villagers that the terms of divine and positive law oblige them to abandon their common commitment to vengeance.

In citing just war theory to the irate villagers, Don Quixote applies a concept from the sphere of politics and diplomacy to a local conflict among pastoral characters. Such disjunction between rhetoric and circumstance is a typical source of comic effects in *Don Quixote*. Here Cervantes's comedy acquires the force of satire. The villager's initial account defines the dispute in terms that invite us to assess it by the principles that natural law theorists proposed to limit and govern conflict among states. This reading prompts us to reexamine the villagers' cause for arming themselves against their neighbours and to question the view that violence can be contained through discourse and rational argument.

The influential theologian and jurist Francisco de Vitoria outlines the core principles of just war theory in his treatise *On the Law of War* (1539), a text shaped by the philosophical and legal debate on Spain's claim to territorial possessions in the New World. Vitoria considers such questions as the right of Christians to wage war, the authority to declare and conduct war, the moral responsibility of individual citizens, and the measures that Christian nations may employ when waging war. Central to his discussion are the causes for which just wars may be fought and the moral duty that obliges princes to avoid conflicts that may arise from inappropriate or insufficient motives. For Vitoria, the law of war includes an obligation to deliberate and take due counsel.

Vitoria offers a particular formulation of the standard view among early modern jurists that war has peace as its end: 'the purpose of war is the peace and security of the commonwealth' (298). His statements concerning the just causes of war and the authority to declare and direct wars follow from the proposition that the commonwealth has a duty to protect public order and the safety of its members. For this purpose it can both defend itself and take retribution for injustices committed against its patrimony and its people. Defensive war is an extension of the individual's right to self-defence, but offensive war is a public prerogative and can only be waged to serve the common good: 'the commonwealth ... has the authority not only to defend itself, but also to avenge and punish injuries done to itself and its members' (300). The concept of injury is central to Vitoria's understanding of just war. Since external injuries can compromise the capacity to maintain order and safety, the commonwealth has the right and duty to sustain its authority: 'the commonwealth cannot sufficiently guard the public good and its own stability unless it is able to avenge injuries and teach its enemies a lesson, since wrongdoers become bolder and readier to attack when they can do so without fear of punishment' (300). The need to safeguard authority invests the right to declare war in the prince, who acts in all matters as 'the authorized representative of the commonwealth' (301).

Vitoria's argument assumes that just war is limited to conflict among substantive political entities. This point is clear in his definition of the commonwealth as a perfect community, 'one which is not part of another commonwealth, but has its own laws, its own independent policy, and its own magistrates' (301). This concept presents challenges, given the complex historical relationships between the traditional authority of the Iberian kingdoms and imperial command, and the role of custom in establishing and sustaining legal and political rights.[30] Vitoria's central axiom, however, is that a commonwealth must be 'complete in itself' in order to exercise the right to declare war (301). The causes of war must also be substantive, on the principle that an injury that leads to war must justify the inevitable harms of armed conflict: 'since all the effects of war are cruel and horrible – slaughter, fire, devastation – it is not lawful to persecute those responsible for trivial offences by waging war upon them' (304). To ensure that the principle of substantiveness is observed, potential causes must be assessed through fair and honest counsel by senior advisors who are morally bound to prevent inappropriate dangers and harms: 'if such men can by examining the causes of hostility with their advice and authority avert a war which is perhaps unjust, then they are obliged to do so' (308). The right to declare war on behalf of the commonwealth entails the responsibility to respect the limits of just cause: 'since princes have the authority to wage war, they should strive above all to avoid the provocations and causes of war' (326).

Cervantes's presentation of the conflict that centres on the village of the braying *regidores* recalls juridical principles concerning the causes and limits of just war. The villagers perceive the braying and name-calling of their neighbours as an injury that threatens the tranquility and order of their community, and they have armed themselves to exact retribution from their enemies. They believe that they are justified in taking action against the adjacent village that has been most active in mocking them, and they have set forth for battle under banners that declare their identity and purpose. The conviction of external damage to their public lives has united them in a common cause that speaks of their attachment to their local community. In a broader context, however, this conflict does not have sufficient substance to justify their recourse to arms. Their village is a small community that clearly can make no claim to its own laws and policies. The villagers are quick to take offence and passionate in their intent to admonish their neighbours, but their cause is a minor dispute that bears no proportion to the risks of armed violence. Although an encounter among pastoralists may not end in slaughter and devastation, the exercise of weapons brings an inevitable potential for serious harm. In his appeal for peace and order, Don Quixote argues that arms should not be taken up for insignificant motives:

> tomarlas por niñerías y por cosas que antes son de risa y pasatiempo que de afrenta, parece que quien las toma carece de todo razonable discurso; cuanto más que el tomar venganza injusta, que justa no puede haber alguna que lo sea, va derechamente contra la santa ley que profesamos, en la cual se nos manda que hagamos bien a nuestros enemigos y que amemos a los que nos aborrecen. (II. 27, 254)

> to take them up for trifles and things to laugh at and be amused by rather than offended, suggests that he who does so is completely lacking in common sense. Moreover, to take an unjust revenge (and there cannot be any just one) is directly opposed to the sacred law that we acknowledge, wherein we are commanded to do good to our enemies and to love them that hate us.

In his attempt to persuade the villagers to abandon the sally they have mounted against their neighbours, Don Quixote enlists the axiom that trivial injuries do not demand the remedy of violence. His arguments from reason and from Christian doctrine are consistent with Vitoria's views, as is his role as a counsellor who intervenes to avert an unjust conflict. Here Don Quixote applies his rhetorical skills to a practical end that reflects the confidence of humanist advisers and jurists in their capacity to limit and contain violence through rational argument.[31]

Sancho's efforts to support his master, however, suggest that the impulse to violence resists such containment. Sancho both endorses the rhetoric of just causes and undermines its impact. He praises Don Quixote as a prudent counsellor and soldier, versed in learning and experience of an order that should command the villagers' attention. His interest in his master's case is such that he cannot resist adding his own advice, asserting that the sound of braying should cause no offence and recalling the mastery of this practice that he commanded in his youth. He asks the villagers to observe that he has not lost his skill: 'que esta ciencia es como la del nadar: que una vez aprendida, nunca se olvida' (because this skill is like swimming: once you learn it, you never forget it) (II. 27, 255). When he begins to bray, the villagers take this gesture as renewed mockery and use their weapons to silence him.

Defenders: Pastoral and Satire 97

They fail to respond to Don Quixote's eloquent appeal to the principles of just war, and they are eager to exercise their arms when Sancho offers himself in place of the neighbours against whom they have taken offence. Sancho attempts to supplement his master's words by showing that braying is an innocent display of the practical skills that can be acquired in pastoral life, but the villagers misunderstand his intentions and attack him. The arms that they have collected and taken up urge them to commit violence, and Sancho unknowingly presents himself as its target. Don Quixote takes up his lance in Sancho's defence, but he flees in fear when the villagers launch a volley of rocks against him. Despite Don Quixote's confidence in the laws of war and in the eloquence through which he articulates them, violence is resolved here through a traditional pattern of scapegoating.[32]

Some standard sources of comedy in *Don Quixote* are present in this episode. Don Quixote's arguments from the tenets of just war theory are incongruous in this encounter with rural villagers, and his abandonment of Sancho demonstrates his tendency to retreat when low mimetic characters threaten him with direct violence, despite his commitment to heroic ideals and his quest for the fame that can be won through acts of war. The lack of correspondence between Don Quixote's intentions and the results that his words and acts produce in the fictional world around him is a common pattern in the text. The failure of the villagers to respond to the rational dismissal of their grievance against their neighbours reflects both the challenges that Don Quixote's elevated language presents to them and their immediate reaction to Sancho's ill-fated intervention. Cervantes's object here is not to parody the language of Vitoria and other theorists of just war, but to question the general proposition that violence among groups can be regulated and contained through an appeal to rational principles. The propensity to violence is presented as a general human weakness and an appropriate satirical object. Cervantes's approach reflects his conception of Horatian satire. The *regidores* are comic figures but they are not possessed of the venality and foolishness commonly attributed to village officials in the popular tradition, and the villagers as a group are not presented through mockery. The intrusion of arms into the pastoral world enables critical comment on the causes and development of violence and war.

The violence and the ambitions of the villagers also have their limits, even if they cannot be contained through language. The villagers are unfamiliar with the arms that they bear, and they are content to let Sancho retreat with Don Quixote. Cervantes suggests that these limits are in part a matter of context, and that in another time and place more might have been made of the rout of the unlikely knight and his garrulous squire. In a single, carefully constructed sentence, the text describes a day of quiet celebration:

> Los del escuadrón se estuvieron allí hasta la noche, y por no haber salido a la batalla sus contrarios, se volvieron a su pueblo, regocijados y alegres; y si ellos supieran la costumbre antigua de los griegos, levantaran en aquel lugar y sitio un trofeo. (II. 27, 256)

> The men of the troop stood their ground until night, and as the enemy did not come out to battle, they returned to their town triumphant and happy. Had they been aware of the ancient custom of the Greeks, they would have erected a monument on the spot.

The villagers persuade themselves to pursue no further action against their neighbours. The assault on the innocent squire has achieved what his master's words have failed to secure: the pacification of their desire for vengeance. When their opponents do not appear, they retire in satisfaction to their village. Rural life has not prepared them for violence on a large scale, and they accept their armed sally in defence of their reputation as a momentary interruption in the cycle of pastoral duties, taking modest pleasure in a victory that is largely self-declared. In the context of a traditional heroic ethos, however, the villagers might have insisted on committing their success to public memory, erecting a trophy that would enshrine the drive for renown that informs both classical epic and ancient history. The proposition that the villagers might honour this 'ancient custom' and that their assault on Sancho might give them grounds for raising such a monument questions once again the stability and the privileged status of the concept of fame.

In the texts discussed in this chapter, Cervantes turns to pastoral to place high and low forms in contact with one another and to explore the contrast between the artful idleness of shepherd-poets and the concerns of practical pastoralists. These practices allow him to scrutinize the ideals that inform high mimetic genres and examine the intrusion of violence into an imagined world of peace and poetic creation. Pastoral settings provide space for reflection on the rewards and demands of an active life. Don Quixote brings epic violence into the pastoral world. Characters who tend the land take up their arms to protect the animals in their care and defend the reputation of their villages. In the *Viaje del*

Parnaso and in *Don Quixote*, pastoral interacts with the conventions of other forms – epic musters and catalogues, epideictic rhetoric, chivalric emblems, topographical and ethnographical lore, the patterns of folkloric narrative – to explore the shifting character of fame, the motives of injury and scapegoating that can lead to conflict among communities, and the difficulties of containing violence once its stimuli have been engaged. In its assimilation to satire, pastoral questions both the fame that defines the ethos of heroic literature and the claim that violence can be contained through rational discourse and an appeal to theories of just war.

3 Captains and Saints: Lyric and Romance

> What effect this experience would have on our lives we could not imagine, but at least it was unlikely that we should survive without some sort of inner change. Towards this transformation of our personalities we now marched.
> Ernest Parker, *Into Battle 1914–1918* (1964)

Classical forms allow Cervantes to explore issues in infantry warfare and strategic command that were central to the wars that Spain waged to maintain its imperial patrimony in the Lowlands. Through the tragedy of the Roman general Cipión, *La Numancia* examines the limits imposed on epic heroism by the conditions of a campaign by siege and the constraints of military pragmatism. In combination with other historical kinds, Cervantine pastoral reveals the instability of the terms that define heroic values and the persistence of violence in settings conventionally associated with the lives of rural characters and peaceful retirement from a life of public engagement. In each case warfare is implicated in the canonical genres that early modern authors inherited from Greek and Latin literature. When Cervantes takes as his subject Spain's campaigns against Ottoman navies and fortresses in the Mediterranean and its southern littoral, he follows the practice of Garcilaso de la Vega and other court poets in accommodating epic themes to the forms of Renaissance lyric. He also turns to two other genres that enjoyed broad diffusion in early modern Spain: Greek romance and the saint's life. These forms have their origins in late antiquity and had become, in effect, popular genres in Cervantes's time, given their diffusion through print and popular theatre and their elaboration by authors.[1] They are also variants of romance, a form that lends itself to representing the changing conditions of conflict between Christians and Ottomans in the Mediterranean and to exploring the various forms of heroism and resistance appropriate to these circumstances. In its patterns of descent and recovery, romance can present alternatives to the martial heroism that honours the privileged models of classical epic and takes fame as its goal. Romance can also inform war narratives through its structure of three successive stages: a dangerous journey, a climactic struggle, and the transformation of the hero (Fussell 130). The movement of romance also creates a subjective focus on the reshaping of its central characters and the discovery of identity. In his memoir of service in the British infantry in the First World War, Ernest Parker remembers the anticipation of 'inner change' that he shared with his fellow soldiers as they approached the front.[2] In Cervantes, this transformation in times of war involves a commitment to a heroism based on endurance and spiritual constancy.

The uses of genre to explore conflict in the Mediterranean and forms of conduct under these conditions can be studied in relation to three Cervantine texts: *El trato de Argel*, an early play probably written shortly after Cervantes's return to Spain from Algiers in 1580, *Los baños de Argel*, a drama published in the *Ocho comedias y ocho entremeses* (1613),[3] and Ruy Pérez's account of his military service and captivity in *Don Quixote* (I. 39–41), a narrative commonly described as the captive's tale. These texts draw on Cervantes's own experience as a soldier and captive, and each one is notable for its accommodation of extensive historical detail to a framework defined by literary patterns and conventions. Starting with Jaime Oliver Asín's research linking Zoraida in the captive's tale to the daughter of the wealthy and influential Slavonic renegade Haji Murad, modern criticism has identified many of the characters in Cervantes's Algerian texts as historical figures, including the prominent corsair Aluj Ali and the Venetian renegade Hasan Pasha, king of Algiers and Cervantes's last master before his ransom from captivity.[4] A strong critical consensus assigns to these texts a common concern with the plight of Spanish captives in Algiers, articulated in terms of Cervantes's efforts as a survivor to resolve the trauma of his own captivity and, more generally, in relation to the dangers of torture and apostasy under Ottoman authority.[5] Cervantes combines the models of lyric poetry, the saint's life, and Greek romance in different patterns for this purpose. In *El trato de Argel* the captives use lyric forms to lament their imprisonment, express their hopes of rescue by an armada from Spain, and offer prayers to the Virgin. In *Los baños de Argel* the hagiographic model of child martyrdom is combined with a romance narrative of escape through guile and invention. In the extended tale of Cervantes's captive captain, the narrator evokes through lyric poetry the heroic figure of the soldier-poet, attributes to his beloved Zoraida saintly powers of relief and deliverance, and records his own escape from Algiers as an adventure marked by the motifs of Greek romance.[6] As Cervantes revisits and reworks his experience in Algiers, he turns increasingly to the structures and values of romance.

Cervantes's inclination to romance can be explained in relation to the form's generic features and its complex history. Northrop Frye has remarked that 'in Greek romance the characters are Levantine, the setting is the Mediterranean world, and the normal means of transportation is by shipwreck' (*Secular Scripture* 4). This pattern lends itself to creating texts populated by characters from the multi-ethnic society of Algiers, set in the cities and sea routes of the Mediterranean littoral, and dependent in their narrative movements on such elements as corsairs' raids, naval battles, capture at sea, separation of lovers and families, and shipwreck. As a city enriched by the profits of international privateering and a 'sophisticated urban conglomerate ... inhabited by a multiethnic lot constituted by Algerian Muslims, exiled Moriscos, Berbers, Turks, renegade Christians from every country in Europe, and Jews' (Garcés 32), early modern Algiers offered a rich setting for the fictional conventions of Greek romance. In its origins this genre has been linked to the complex cultures of late antiquity,[7] and it allows Cervantes to explore the conditions of hybridity and conflict among the Mediterranean cultures of his own time. The medieval genre of the saint's life attests to the shaping influence of ancient romance on Christian literature. Many romance patterns – the use of exotic settings, the counterposed movements of descent and ascent, the passage through trials and conflict to a transformative end – can be traced in hagiographic accounts of temptation, trials, and conversion. Saints' lives present 'adventure and high drama' and often stress the agency of female protagonists (Fuchs, *Romance* 59). Spiritual narratives and romance also share common rhetorical purposes, in that they 'stimulate an emotional investment in the story and an adherence to its values intensified by that emotional response' (Marshall 377). In Cervantes, this 'commerce of ethos and pathos' engages sympathy for the Christian captives and explores the values and modes of conduct available to them.[8]

In writing on questions of heroism and on the remedies for captivity in Algiers, Cervantes responds to historical changes in the conditions of engagement among the imperial powers of the Mediterranean. As Jean Canavaggio has argued, Cervantes's understanding of the history of his time reflects his awareness of Spain's gradual and progressive abandonment of its ambitious military program in this area, over the course of its repeated armed encounters with the Ottomans.[9] Cervantes articulates a response to this important historical shift through the balance between two types or modes of heroism. The first is armed aggression against an appropriate enemy; the second, Christian fortitude and resistance in the face of suffering. A traditional ideological gesture combines these two modes in the ideal of crusade, urging upon Christian princes and soldiers an ethos of martial valour and religious values that will lead to triumph over the infidel. In *On the War against the Turks* Erasmus sets outs the conditions of a spiritual reform intended to secure both justice and victory for the Christian side: 'that, first of all, God's anger be appeased, that our intentions be pure and honourable, and all our trust placed in Christ; that we fight beneath his standard, that he triumph in us, and that we obey the commandments of our God and attack the enemy as if he were watching over our every movement' (327). Despite his program for peace among the Christian princes of Europe, Erasmus endorses the crusading ethos of war on the infidel.

In his works on Algiers Cervantes questions the synthesis that underlies this ethos by shifting his focus from martial to spiritual heroism. In *El trato de Argel* the prospect of a new armada from Spain offers the captives hope of general deliverance, while spiritual constancy sustains them in the daily trials of captivity. *Los baños de Argel* diminishes the appeal of martial valour and intensifies the pattern of Christian suffering and endurance. The captive's tale celebrates Spanish bravery at Lepanto and offers poems in praise of the heroic defenders of Tunis, but stresses in the last analysis the spiritual practices that sustain Ruy Pérez and Zoraida and secure their deliverance from Algiers. This shift from valour at arms to spiritual fortitude suggests a complex engagement with the conditions and ideologies of Spain's endemic conflict with the Ottomans. By examining the modes of heroism evoked in this conflict, Cervantes puts asunder the two sets of values – martial and spiritual – that are joined together in the traditional crusading ethos.

Aurelio's discourse on the Golden Age in Act II of *El trato de Argel* (ll. 1313–72) illustrates the conditions that underlie Cervantes's scrutiny of heroism in the context of conflict in the Mediterranean. As Zimic has argued, the significance of this discourse rests not so much in its parallels to Don Quixote's set address on the same topic (*DQ* I. 11) as in its protest against war. Zimic notes echoes here of Erasmian pacifism.[10] Aurelio nonetheless directs the force of his argument not against warfare in all its forms but rather against wars waged in pursuit of material gain, taking as his point of departure the contrast between the 'sweet liberty' of a remote Golden Age and the painful servitude of his own time. His account attributes this decline to blind avarice, the discovery of gold, and conflict over the acquisition of wealth. Such conflict takes its most destructive form in war, and Aurelio accuses war's followers of caring only for material profit:

> y sus fieros ministros, codiciosos
> más del rubio metal que de otra cosa,
> turban nuestros contentos y reposos,
> y, en la sangrienta guerra peligrosa,
> pudiendo con el filo de la espada
> acabar nuestra vida temerosa,
> la guardan de prisiones rodeada,
> por ver si prometemos por libralla
> nuestra pobre riqueza mal lograda. (ll. 1343–51)

> and her harsh ministers, more covetous of fair-coloured metal than of anything else, disturb our contentment and rest, and, although they can end our fearful lives with the edge of the sword in bloody and perilous war, they keep it bound in shackles, to see if we will pledge for liberty our paltry and ill-won wealth.

Aurelio reflects on the constraints that war in his time has placed on the traditional ethos of martial heroism. The logic of this passage appeals to an ancient convention of war that allows the victor to claim ransom in legitimate exchange for sparing the life of a captured enemy combatant. The substance of Aurelio's complaint is that this convention now so dominates armed conflict that war is waged for ransom alone. Under such conditions the glory of death by the sword's edge has given place to the indignity of being held in pawn for gold. Aurelio is lamenting his own situation as a captive whose poverty prevents him from purchasing his freedom; he is also speaking against an age that has rendered war non-heroic by sacrificing honour and heroism for financial interest.

In bemoaning war's decline into mercantile exchange, Aurelio looks back to a remote Golden Age and also to a more recent period of heroic warfare, large in its scale and honourable in its aims. The decline of heroism is a common theme in Renaissance treatises on war, but the contemporary pattern of Mediterranean conflict has a specific bearing on Aurelio's complaint. When imperial conflict along the Ibero-African frontier began in the 1530s, the Hapsburgs and the Ottomans confronted each other as parallel powers, moved by expansionist objectives and possessed of similar resources for waging war in the Mediterranean and along its coasts. As Andrew Hess has demonstrated, over the next fifty years both empires gradually abandoned their grand military designs in this area, in response to changes in the economic and political conditions required for sustaining effective warfare. New fortifications against sieges, improvements in naval artillery, land and sea forces of increasing size, and general economic inflation produced sharp rises in the cost of large-scale military campaigns. On the political front, both empires faced internal division – in such events as the Second Rebellion of the Alpujarras (1568–70) and the janissaries' revolt in Algiers (1557) – as well as military and economic demands from other regions of imperial rule. These factors led over time to mutual disengagement. By the 1560s Spain had begun to direct its military policy towards its Atlantic fleets and its war for the Hapsburg patrimony in the Netherlands; in 1577–8 the Ottomans turned to an eastern campaign against Persia. Hess has described the prominent naval engagements of the late sixteenth century – the victory of the Holy League at Lepanto (1571) and the Ottoman conquest of Tunis (1574) – as 'the proper ceremonial exits for empires that wished to confirm an early modern line of division between two civilizations' (71).[11]

The shift away from large-scale warfare brought in its train a change central to the context of Aurelio's complaint. As the major powers abandoned grand naval expeditions, conflict turned to secondary forms of war: brigandage, piracy, privateering (Braudel 865). Such irregular warfare was practised in the Mediterranean throughout the early modern period, but reached a heyday of activity between 1570 and 1620 (Lynch 1:220). Braudel tells us that privateering had its own geographical centres – Algiers, Malta, Livorno, Pisa – and its own long-standing customs and conventions (865, 867). The market in captives depended on habitual exchange between Europe and North Africa. In the case of Spanish captives, the orders of redemptionist friars raised funds in Spain for paying ransoms, through the charity of individuals and grants from councils of state; they supplemented this income by conveying trade goods to North Africa and selling them at a profit; under regulation from the Council of Castile they maintained detailed records of their transactions with the captors.[12] In these circumstances the trade in captives established itself as part of the maritime economy. Privateering became 'a means of forcible exchange throughout the Mediterranean,' and as such it prospered in parallel with other forms of trade (Braudel 883–4). Aurelio's claim that gold is now the sole object of war reflects this shift to a commercial circuit based on the exchange of funds and goods for captives. Although its motives should not be reduced to simple greed, secondary warfare demanded accommodations ill suited to the military ideals of crusade against the infidel. As Braudel has observed, 'privateering often had little to do with either country or faith, but was merely a means of making a living' (867). *El trato de Argel* displays the financial realities that bear on the lives of the Spanish captives. Garcés has noted that the term 'trato' in its title refers both to the captives' way of life in Algiers and to the process of commercial negotiation to which they are subjected (135–6). The armed conflict between Spain and the Ottomans lies in the background of the captives' experience, but their deliverance generally depends on a mercantile calculus of profit and loss. The presentation of this dynamic reflects a general concern in Spanish discourses on privateering and captivity with 'the nation's providential mission and the challenges to it from compromised religious identities and unheroic commercial transactions' (Fuchs, *Mimesis* 140).

The material conditions of warfare and captivity motivate the shift from martial to spiritual heroism in Cervantes's texts on Algiers. They also influence the representation of violence and its costs in human suffering. As Elaine Scarry has noted, the very limited capacity of the standard lexicon to express the experience of pain leads to a 'language of agency' in which pain is displaced onto the 'external agent' that has produced it or the 'bodily damage' that accompanies it (15). Such displacement is a core feature of writings on warfare. War produces and depends on injury to human bodies, but it is described in language that makes this injuring disappear, through such rhetorical techniques as omission, transference of human action to inanimate instruments, and marginalization by means of a range of conventional metaphors (injury as a by-product, as an intermediate step towards a final goal, as something that turns in on itself, and as a 'prolongation' of another phenomenon) (80–1). In the sections of his Algiers texts that evoke feats of arms and a traditional ethos of heroism, Cervantes describes acts of violence through techniques that mask the centrality in war of human injury, including metaphors that equate wounding with inanimate weapons and displace injury to material objects or to corporate bodies. In the sections that describe the conditions of the captives in Algiers, however, Cervantes provides a more direct and immediate account of pain and injury. In this context spiritual heroism involves a marked awareness of human suffering and a compassionate intention to alleviate the pain of others. These practices are closely related to the forms of conduct that romance endorses and to its characteristic gestures of participation and inclusion.

Through its complaint against non-heroic forms of warfare and its tableau of suffering in Algiers, *El trato de Argel* offers a point of departure for an analysis of captivity and its remedies in Cervantes. In this play spiritual constancy offers the most secure form of resistance and deliverance. Edward Friedman has isolated the principle that informs the captives' conduct: 'Slavery tests spiritual devotion; the enemy may inflict physical torture, but the soul of the resolute Christian remains unscathed' (26). Aurelio articulates this ethos, invoking it for his own consolation and in the counsel that he offers to others, in a language that often draws on conventional images of Stoic fortitude. He describes captivity as a 'touchstone' that reveals the temper of true Christian 'patience' (ll. 17–18), and he resolves to stand as firmly in his faith as a rock battered by tempestuous seas (ll. 327–8). Aurelio also takes comfort in prayer and praises the practice of giving alms, a 'holy work' that has the power to release the captives from temptation and physical suffering (ll. 1874–85). The most compelling example of Aurelios's constancy is his rejection of the easy deliverance set before him by Occasion and Necessity. When he dismisses the goods that these personified characters offer him as false, Aurelio takes possession of his soul and asserts his commitment to a firm and public faith: 'Cristiano soy, y he de vivir cristiano' (I am a Christian, and I must live a Christian life) (l. 1795), a declaration that 'underlines the victory of Christian fortitude in this drama' (Garcés 170). Here, as throughout the play, Aurelio bears witness to a heroism of spiritual resistance and a Christian life.

The other Christian characters act on the principle of resistance through faith. The community of Christians has been identified as the play's collective protagonist (Meregalli 403–4; Zimic 37–8; Garcés 170), and the captives are united in their active devotion. Individual speakers emphasize the power of belief and spiritual practice, and their general recourse to prayers of deliverance confirms the centrality of faith. In Act II a Christian family is divided through an auction of captives.

The mother asks her son to seek freedom through devotion to the Virgin: 'que esta Reina de bondad, / de virtud y gracia llena, / ha de limar tu cadena / y volver tu libertad' (for this Queen of goodness, full of virtue and grace, will surely file away your chain and make your liberty return) (ll. 959–62). The conceit of the file and chain – typical of Spanish devotional poetry – applies the powers of intercession to the immediate conditions of captivity. Such confidence in the Virgin as an agent of redemption in this world is common among the captives. Aurelio prays for the Virgin's 'light' to lead him from the 'deep valley' of servitude to the 'summit' of freedom (ll. 293–300); a Christian fugitive seeks the guidance of her 'star' in his journey from Algiers to the Spanish presidio in Oran and attributes the miraculous appearance of a companionable lion to her intervention (ll. 1974–9, 2052–6); three unnamed captives join Aurelio in concluding the play with a chorus in praise of her mercies, as the ships of the ransoming friars approach from Spain (ll. 2498–529). The captives' devotion to the Virgin and their assurance of her special concern for their plight confirm the importance of spiritual constancy as a remedy for the afflictions of Algiers. As Fothergill-Payne has observed, the play demonstrates repeatedly that 'sólo la Fe conducirá a la libertad' (only Faith will lead to liberty) (178).

The captives' hope of liberation through an armed assault on Algiers nonetheless presents itself in parallel with their recourse to spiritual remedies, appealing to the ideal of martial heroism. The prospect of such intervention appears when a group of captives discusses military preparations in Spain. Leonardo reports that a newly captured soldier has brought news of a muster of troops under Philip II's command in Badajoz (ll. 369–92). Although the captives know nothing of the king's intentions, they take heart in this show of military strength and assume that the troops may have an assault on Algiers as their objective. Leonardo announces that the soldier's reports have given life to his 'dead hope' of freedom (l. 374); his companion Saavedra speaks at length of the general longing for deliverance by force of arms (ll. 393–462).

Saavedra makes his plea for military action through a rhetoric of remembrance and exhortation. His appeal to memory is grounded in a specific historical incident: the failure in 1541 of a large naval expedition against Algiers under the generalship of Charles V. Since Saavedra's discourse recalls significant details of this occasion, its literal meaning can be elucidated through comparison to an immediate account of the expedition. For this purpose I have consulted the emperor's own version of events, in a letter to his ambassador in Venice, Diego Hurtado de Mendoza (2 November 1541).[13] The emperor reports the movements of ships and of men. The ships of the armada set sail from Spain and the Balearic islands and gather off the Barbary coast; they proceed against contrary winds to the outskirts of Algiers and disembark the infantry, although rising seas prevent them from landing sufficient food and horses to support the troops. The Spanish forces take a hill and a section of the shoreline close to the city; Algerian defenders reclaim the hill, but the invaders maintain their position on shore. Storm conditions at sea drive some of the galleys aground and force other vessels to lighten ship by casting weapons and tackle overboard. The ships and the landed infantry withdraw together to a sheltered cape, where the soldiers at last receive food and reckon their casualties. Faced with further losses of men and supplies, unremitting storms, and potential unrest in other parts of his realms, the emperor decides to order a general retreat, 'dexando por agora la empresa para otro tiempo que ... se podrá más conuenientemente hazer' (leaving the venture for now, until another time ... when it can be undertaken more profitably) (Fernández Alvarez 2:74).

Saavedra opens his discourse on invasion with a dual act of remembrance, framing the history of the failed armada within his personal recollections of his arrival in Algiers as a captive (ll. 396–410). He describes the features of the city and its surroundings that brought to his mind the lost heroism of the 1541 expedition. In its use of physical space as an incitement to memory, this passage parallels the Renaissance tradition of poetry on classical ruins and, as in such verse, the past is invoked for its exemplary value. Saavedra's act of recollection attests to the armada's persistence in Spanish memory and its force in renewing the call to arms. His verses also illustrate the tendency of discourses on war to deny human agency and the irreducible fact of human injury. In recollecting the armada of 1541, Saavedra uses techniques of metonymy and displacement:

Ofrecióse a mis ojos la ribera
y el monte donde el grande Carlos tuvo
levantada en el aire su bandera,
y el mar que tanto esfuerzo no sostuvo,
pues, movido de envidia de su gloria,
airado entonces más que nunca estuvo. (ll. 402–7)

There appeared before my eyes the shore, and the mountain where the great Charles held his standard raised in the air, and the seas that could not bear so much force, since, envious of such glory, they turned more violent than ever.

In his memory Saavedra sees the battle standard that represents by convention the empire's authority and its valour. He attributes human affect and agency to the sea, stating that it destroyed Charles V's armada through envy of Spanish force and grandeur. The claim that the sea showed unprecedented fury is a variant of the standard rhetorical undertaking to speak of things not heard before. This heroic rhetoric contrasts with the direct descriptions elsewhere in Cervantes's play of the privations and wounds inflicted on the bodies of the Christian captives.

The rest of Saavedra's speech reinforces the idea of the failed expedition as an incitement to renewed military action. Imagining a future in which he will return to Spain and secure an audience at the royal court, Saavedra delivers to his companions the speech that he would direct in such circumstances to Philip II. In this projected scene he casts himself as a modest and truthful counsellor, speaking in accordance with standard rhetorical conventions. Composed in an elevated style appropriate to its theme and intended recipient, Saavedra's discourse presents a structure of three formal sections. The opening *exordium* appeals to the king's attention and benevolence, praising his power to command obedience and tribute from the peoples of the New World. The *narratio* describes the inferior state of readiness among the Turks and their fear of another Spanish invasion, and refers to the 'harsh and bitter prison' of the *baños*. The conditions recounted here lead to the concluding *petitio*, in which Saavedra speaks for all the captives in exhorting the king to mount a new armada:

> y pues te deja agora la discordia,
> que tanto te ha oprimido y fatigado,
> y amor en darte sigue la concordia,
> haz, ¡o buen rey!, que sea por ti acabado
> lo que con tanta audacia y valor tanto
> fue por tu amado padre comenzado.
> El sólo ver que vas pondrá un espanto
> en la bárbara gente, que adivino
> ya desde aquí su pérdida y quebranto. (ll. 444–52)

> and since you are now free of the discord that has so oppressed and wearied you, and love continues to grant you peace, may you finish, o good king! what was begun with such audacity and valour by your beloved father. Simply to see that you are setting forth will terrify the barbarous people, whose ruinous and severe loss I foretell here and now.

Through this appeal the heroic past completes its claim on future designs. The earlier expedition against Algiers has left the painful memory of an incomplete conquest; the ruling monarch can close the circle of remembrance by attacking the city once again. In encouraging Philip II to temper his prudence with his father's 'audacity and valour,' Saavedra promotes the case for a Christian assault on Algiers and expresses the hope that the captives have invested in such military action.

The force of Saavedra's appeal depends in part on its connections with other Cervantine texts and its relationship to the Renaissance lyric tradition in Spain. Cervantes assigns the name Saavedra to two other characters: the protagonist of *El gallardo español*, and a captive Spanish soldier praised by Ruy Pérez in his narrative in *Don Quixote*. During the mid-1580s Cervantes himself began to use this name as a second surname, that is, to sign official documents as Miguel de Cervantes Saavedra. Garcés has discussed the significance of this name in relation to the broad range of naming practices in early modern Spain and the potential motives for Cervantes's choice. She identifies the surname Saavedra with a noble family that acquired fame in late medieval Spain for feats of arms on the border with the kingdom of Granada, a reputation reflected in the ballad tradition by the legendary figure of Juan de Saavedra (189–90). She argues that by adopting this name Cervantes associated himself with the warriors who fought on Spain's medieval frontiers and with their heroic resistance to 'the threats and temptations of Islam' (200). For Garcés, the name Saavedra is a 'cry of war' that records Cervantes's service in the Spanish infantry and registers his 'catastrophic experience' of captivity (200). Saavedra's call for deliverance by force of arms in *El trato de Argel* evokes this heroic ethos. It recalls the militant stance of Spanish imperialism during the reign of Charles V and engages the Renaissance ideal of the soldier-poet. In Spain this figure finds its most influential representative in Garcilaso de la Vega, a poet quickly embraced as canonical and repeatedly made present through citation and allusion in Cervantes's works. In its language and poetic form, Saavedra's appeal uses the court style cultivated by Garcilaso and his successors. It has long been recognized that Saavedra's words reproduce the final section of the 'Epístola a Mateo Vázquez,' a verse letter on military service, capture at sea, and captivity in Algiers addressed to Philip II's secretary of state and attributed to Cervantes.[14] The verse epistle is a classical form that enjoyed currency among Spain's soldier-poets. Garcilaso wrote an epistle to his fellow poet Juan Boscán from North Africa, and Francisco de Aldana composed extensively in this form. In the context of *El trato de Argel*, epistolary rhetoric is used to present a petition for military action.

Although *El trato de Argel* extends the prospect of invasion from abroad, it does not offer an unequivocal endorsement of martial heroism. The historical and dramatic context of Saavedra's discourse qualifies his enthusiasm for military endeavours. His argument echoes Charles V's intention to return to Algiers on a more propitious occasion and assumes that Philip II may be persuaded to execute this project, yet at the time of the play's composition the Spanish monarchy was unlikely to redeem hopes of the kind that Saavedra expresses. The military preparations that the captives discuss in *El trato* have a definite historical referent in a large muster of Philip II's troops in Extremadura (Stagg, 'Date and Form' 185), an army that was raised not for imperial adventures in North Africa but for the forced annexation of Portugal in 1580. On the Mediterranean and its littoral Philip II's policy of 'prudence and calculation' had reduced Spain's objectives to maintaining the system of armed presidios (Braudel 855). As Canavaggio has observed, Saavedra's enthusiasm cannot mask the transience of the grand endeavour that he projects, since the conquest of Algiers had lost any genuine strategic value for the Spanish crown (*Cervantès dramaturge* 386). Military designs have a diminished presence in *El trato*, and the Christian characters place most of their confidence in the spiritual remedies for captivity. This preference for spiritual heroism suggests an early awareness on Cervantes's part of Spain's gradual abandonment of the ideals and objectives of crusade in North Africa.

The separation of martial and spiritual heroism is more pronounced in *Los baños de Argel*. Both modes appear in this play, and they are presented through a complex set of literary conventions and through dramatic techniques modelled on the *comedia nueva*.[15] In contrast with *El trato*, each mode has an independent sphere of action, marked in part through generic conventions. Military excellence of the order celebrated in classical epic is evident in the text, but it is represented exclusively through the actions of the Algerian corsairs. Spiritual constancy is the sole remedy for the Spanish characters in captivity, who practise Christian devotion with a marked intensity. In *El trato* the captives resort to contemplation and prayer; in *Los baños* the central Christian characters model their actions on Scriptural precedent, reproducing typological patterns of imprisonment (Israel's exile in Egypt) and sacrifice (Christ's Passion). The captives take support and guidance from the example of their martyred companions and from the liberating agency of Zara, a clandestine Christian who intervenes on their behalf. The heightened representation of heroism in its martial and spiritual forms enhances the play's dramatic effectiveness; the division of these modes between corsairs and Christians indicates a more decided scepticism about the marriage of the two in the traditional crusading ethos. This contrast also stresses the shift from epic force to the forms of heroism associated with romance and its popular Spanish variant, the *comedia de santos*.

Los baños de Argel opens with an armed assault. Under the guidance of a Morisco scout, Algerian corsairs attack a coastal village in Spain by night, set its houses on fire, and load their ships with plunder and captives seized from its population (ll. 1–226). The text emphasizes the martial skills of the corsairs, the inadequacy of the Spanish defences, and the innocence of the villagers. The corsairs follow a set order of attack, exploiting the advantages of darkness and silence, and they evade the guards who survey the sea from watchtowers and the soldiers charged with defending the coast. At the moment of attack the villagers react with confusion and dismay. An old man, half-naked, appears on the walls to sound a belated alarm; later, as he attempts to lead his two small sons to safety, he follows a path that entraps the family in the corsairs' hands. The other villagers are equally defenceless before their enemies. Taken as a whole, the initial scenes depict a vulnerable rural population subject to the directed and disciplined force of the corsairs. As the scout Hazén assures his marauding companions concerning the local coast, 'sé bien sus entradas y salidas / y la parte mejor de hacerle guerra' (I know well its ways of access and of flight and the best place to make war on it) (ll. 11–12).

This initial sequence clearly reflects the conditions of making war on Spain's Mediterranean frontier during the sixteenth century. Historical evidence confirms the threat of African piracy for civilian populations and the dangers and difficulties of coastal defence. The enforced flight of the Morisco minority from Spain to North Africa benefited the corsairs, since exiled Moriscos could serve as spies or guides in raids on their native regions. The significant fraction of Spanish captives taken from coastal villages attests to the frequency and success of the corsair expeditions, as does the reiterated concern in Spain with successful defence along the Mediterranean coastline. Measures of improvement in this area were both various – programs for the construction of watchtowers and new fortifications, the raising of local militias – and of limited effectiveness. Local guards were exposed to violence and seizure during sudden raids, followed occasionally by periods of captivity in North Africa.[16]

Los baños de Argel dramatizes these historical elements through stagecraft and literary allusion. Cervantes's staging draws on techniques commonly employed in Renaissance drama to create the illusion of rapid action on a large scale: brief exchanges of dialogue, successive entrances and exits that indicate minor changes of scene, sudden effects that depend on sound and movement. The nocturnal raid on the peaceful village offers another instance of a pastoral world compromised through the intrusion of epic violence. The assault on a walled urban space and the villagers' flight from the fires of war clearly evoke the model of classical epic. Zimic notes the parallels between the destruction of the village and the legendary sack of Troy, and argues for the 'Homeric inspiration' of the sequence's action and elevated poetic style (149–51). A more immediate model can be found in Vergil's reworking of this Trojan material in Book II of the *Aeneid*. The Vergilian pattern is refracted through various characters. The old father compares himself to 'a Christian Aeneas,' hoping to bear his sons to safety (ll. 31–4). The distraught Don Fernando surveys the ruined village from its walls and looks for traces of his lost Costanza:

> Puntas de cristal claro y no de almenas,
> murallas de bruñido oro y rico argento,
> que guardaste[i]s un tiempo mi esperanza,
> ¿dónde hallaré, decidme, a mi Costanza?
> Techos que vomitáis llamas teosas,
> calles de sangre y lágrimas cubiertas,
> ¿adónde de mis glorias ya dudosas
> está la causa, y de mis penas ciertas? (ll. 147–54)

> Crests of clear crystal and not of battlements, walls of burnished gold and rich silver, which sheltered at one time my hope, tell me, where will I find my Costanza? Roofs that spew forth resinous flames, streets covered with blood and tears, where is the cause of my now uncertain bliss and of my certain pain?

The panorama that Fernando evokes of houses in flames and bloody streets and the anguish that he expresses at his separation from his betrothed recall Aeneas's flight through the burning ruins of Troy and his loss of Creusa.[17] In its style and descriptive details this lament marks the high point of the epic program that informs the play's opening sequence.

Don Fernando's description is typical of heroic rhetoric in its denial of injury and suffering. Damage and agency are displaced from human subjects to inanimate objects. The houses of the village 'spew' flames from their rooftops and its streets are marked with 'blood and tears.' In both cases the damage inflicted by the corsairs' violence is associated with the village as a constructed space rather than with its suffering residents. Fernando sustains this perspective when he turns to watch the Algerian ship on which Costanza has been taken captive:

Ya a descubrir se empieza
la máquina terrible
que con ligero vuelo
la carga de mi cielo
lleva en su vientre tragador y horrible;
ya las alas extiende,
ya le ayudan los pies, ya al curso atiende. (ll. 181–7)

Now the terrible machine makes itself visible, that in its swift flight carries my adored cargo in its devouring, horrible belly; now it stretches its wings, now its feet aid its progress, now it turns on its course.

The attribution here of animate actions to an inanimate object conveys Fernando's alarm and confusion at the loss of his home and his beloved; it also transfers agency for these acts from the human beings who have assaulted the village to the material instruments of their violence. In its displacement of injury to physical objects and weapons, Fernando's language participates in a rhetoric of denial.

The text of *Los baños* consistently associates martial excellence – the defining attribute of epic heroes – with the corsairs. In the Algerian society that it portrays, skill at arms is the main antecedent of public reputation. The corsair captain Cauralí is praised for his courage, strength, and cunning (ll. 630–3); the Morisco scout Yzuf is described as 'a good Moor and a good soldier' (l. 636). It is striking that the values and conventions of classical epic are invested principally in the corsairs (the agents of secondary warfare) rather than in the janissaries (the dominant warrior class of Algiers).[18] A captive villager refers to the social prestige of the janissaries (ll. 1197–206), but the only armed action attributed to them in the play is a cruel and needless attack on the *baños*. The evocation of Vergilian models in the staging of the corsairs' raid and the contrast between corsairs and janissaries displace the martial ethos of classical epic onto the actions and agents of non-heroic warfare.

In *Los baños* the Christian characters show no confidence in martial heroism. No spokesman holds up the prospect of a new armada from Spain, nor is there any general hope of a large-scale rescue by force of arms. As in *El trato*, the play dramatizes the bodily condition of captivity, presenting the physical cruelty of the Algerian masters and the sufferings of the captives. Violence asserts its presence through visual and verbal means. A captive who has taken ill is beaten for his incapacity to work. A victim of mutilation appears on stage, his head bound with a bloody bandage. The renegade Hazén turns against the Algerian authorities and is executed by impalement. The janissaries, seized by fear at the false sighting of an armada, indulge in a fury of injury and death. In contrast to the rhetoric of displacement through which Don Fernando describes the corsairs' raid, the presentation of violence when the scene shifts to Algiers is open and direct, and conveys its multiple effects on the captives' physical and mental lives. Faced with these circumstances the captives invest their energies in spiritual remedies, and Christian constancy assumes a more active aspect than in *El trato de Argel*. Prayer consoles and strengthens the captives and also offers them models of conduct that they repeatedly enact in resisting their Algerian captors. The text shows a corresponding shift in literary technique, in a systematic use of correspondences drawn from biblical typology to describe the conditions and remedies of the captive state.

Ossorio, one of the Christian captives, describes the city of Algiers as a type of Noah's ark:

> Argel es, según barrunto
> arca de Noé abreviada:
> aquí están de todas suertes
> oficios y hablidades,
> disfrazadas calidades. (ll. 2064–8)

> Algiers, as I suppose, is an abbreviated version of Noah's ark: here is every kind of trade and skill and hidden rank.

In the first instance Algiers evokes the biblical image because of the human diversity of its population. In addition, the reference to the ark suggests the captives' hope of deliverance and anticipates their flight from captivity. Many of the Christian characters articulate their aspiration to escape through another common typological pattern, comparing their situation to Israel's exile in Egypt and Spain to the spiritual home of Zion. Hazén, a Spanish renegade, hopes to reclaim his faith and his homeland: 'quizá hallaré ocasión / para quedarme en la tierra, / para mí, de promisión' (perhaps I will find an opportunity to stay in the land that I see as promised) (ll. 397–9). Longing for Spain also informs the ballad sung by a group of captives in Haji Murad's garden in Act II (ll. 1395–1420), a lyrical composition that casts reminiscences of Psalm 137 (Psalm 136 in the Vulgate) in the mould of Spanish popular verse.[19] The captives sing their lament by the Mediterranean ('A las orillas del mar' [by the shores of the sea]), as the Israelites mourn by the rivers of Babylonian captivity ('By the waters of Babylon, there we sat down and wept'); their yearning for the homeland ('¡Cuán cara eres de haber, oh dulce España!' [How dear you are to possess, o sweet Spain!]) recalls the Psalmist's solemn remembrance of Zion; their curse on tyrants ('tanto Datán y Virón' [so many of the kind of Dathan and Abiram])[20] echoes Israel's cry for revenge on their captors. Through the identification with Israel in exile, the captives express the depth of their suffering and their trust in spiritual remedies.

Zara's intervention in the fate of the captives conforms to romance conventions and revisits the typology of Exodus. The daughter of a rich renegade, Zara has been raised as a secret Christian in her father's house. She identifies the Spanish captive Don Lope as an agent who will take her to a country where she can openly practise her devotion to the Virgin Mary (whom she knows as Lela Marién) and as her chosen husband. From the seclusion of her father's house she communicates silently with Don Lope, passing him messages and bundles of coins with a length of cane. Through this assistance Don Lope ransoms himself and arranges for Zara and a group of his fellow captives to escape by sea. Zara's actions are those of a typical romance heroine, as Frye describes this role in *The Secular Scripture*. She is an isolated virgin who nonetheless chooses freely from her real and potential suitors, and she manages to arrange her marriage and her flight to Christian lands from the seclusion of her father's house. She pursues her goals through indirection and guile, the characteristic strategies of the imperilled and virginal heroine.[21] Don Lope and his companions follow another common romance pattern in interpreting Zara's agency in leading them to freedom as a miraculous and providential intervention, in terms that appeal to the typology of deliverance.[22] Don Lope describes the first coins that he receives from Zara's hand as 'maná del cielo' (manna from heaven) (l. 343), and her designs are consistently seen as an expression of God's 'gracia' (grace) and 'maravillas' (marvels) (ll. 470–6, 575–6,

1515–21). As the fortunate captives make their final preparations for flight, Vibanco reviews the meaning of their experience:

> Que habemos bien negociado,
> pues siendo una caña vara,
> y otro nuevo Moisén Zara
> de este Egipto disoluto,
> pasamos el mar enjuto
> a gozar la patria cara. (ll. 2609–14)

> For our business has gone well, since with a cane for a rod, and Zara for a new Moses, we have crossed a dry sea from this dissolute Egypt to possess our precious homeland.

The multiple parallels drawn in this passage – cane : rod; Zara : Moses; Algiers : Egypt; the Red Sea : the Mediterranean – reinforce the pattern of slavery and Exodus in the captives' efforts to return to the promised land of Spain.

The pattern of the Passion is more prominent in the play and asserts itself through two characters who cast themselves as martyrs: the renegade Hazén and the child Francisco. Critical scrutiny has stressed the thematic correlation of these two, noting that both demonstrate a 'vocation for martyrdom' (Casalduero 93) and a 'distinctly Christian courage' (Edward Friedman 27). Within the text's dramatic structure their actions establish a pattern of internal figural repetition, in that Hazén's public sacrifice finds its mirror and fulfilment in the subsequent death of Francisco. In each case a martyr's death recalls the order of the Passion, and each character also associates his sacrifice with previous forms and motives of martyrdom. Taken together, their exemplary deaths reinforce the figural representation of Christian heroism in *Los baños*.

Faith and patriotism are of equal importance in Hazén's conversion. He dies following a violent confrontation with his counterpart Yzuf – the Morisco who has led the corsairs in raiding the Spanish coast – in which he reproaches Yzuf for his treachery and puts him to death in an open act of Christian militancy. When the Cadí demands immediate public retribution for the killing of Yzuf, Hazén embraces the death sentence as an opportunity to bear final witness to his restored faith:

> Dame, enemigo, esa cama,
> que es la que el alma más ama,

> puesto que al cuerpo sea dura;
> dámela, que a gran ventura
> por ella el Cielo me llama.
> No le mudes la intención,
> buen Jesús; confirma en él
> su intento y mi petición,
> que en ser el cadí cruel
> consiste mi salvación. (ll. 847–56)

> Give me, my enemy, that bed, the one that the soul loves most, although it is hard for the body; give it to me, since Heaven summons me by means of its harshness to great happiness. Dear Jesus, do not change his intentions; confirm his purpose and my plea, since the Cadí's cruelty is my salvation.

In a sequence of four commands – two addressed to his worldly 'enemy' and two to his spiritual Saviour – Hazén dwells on the sacramental aspect of his own death. The stake to which he has been condemned is a place of rest for the soul, from which it will rise in redemption. Hazén asks that divine agency reinforce the Cadí's will because the cruelty of his enemy advances the end of his salvation. By modulating into a voice of Christian prayer and tracing a trajectory of persecution and deliverance in his own experience, Hazén assimilates his death at the infidel's hand to the Passion.

The scenes that lead to Hazén's death indicate complementary sources for his motives of self-sacrifice. In his confrontation with Yzuf, Hazén presents himself as committing an act of Christian patriotism and an open affirmation of faith. Against the apostasy of his youth, he offers in recompense this defiance of the religion and power of the Ottomans:

> ¡Buen Dios, perdona el exceso
> de haber faltado en la fe,
> pues, al cerrar del proceso,
> si en público te negué,
> en público te confieso! (ll. 832–6)

> Dear God, pardon my excess in having defaulted on my faith, since, at my trial's end, if I denied you in public, in public I confess my faith in you!

New scriptural resonances are present in these lines. The emphasis on public denial and public confession recalls the distinction in the

Gospels between those who acknowledge Christ before other men and those who deny him (Matthew 10:32–3, Luke 12:8–9). Hazén's conversion also retraces the spiritual course of St Peter in its movement from denial to repentance. As Casalduero has noted, Peter supplies the 'paradigm' and 'example' that Hazén follows in his spiritual transformation (82), and his encounter with Yzuf may be read figurally in relation to the conflict between the faithful apostle Peter and the traitor Judas (83). In turning to Peter and Christ so that he may imitate the pattern of their sacrifices, Hazén offers a model of heroic conduct grounded in scriptural precedent.

This model asserts itself more intensively in the death of the child martyr. Abducted from Spain in the corsair raid, Francisco becomes central to the dynamics of resistance to Islam. Early in the play his father expresses concern for the spiritual integrity of his two sons (ll. 1167–72, 1207–16), comparing their situation to that of seven brothers in the Old Testament who endured torture and death for their fidelity to the law of Moses (2 Maccabees 7:1–42).[23] Unlike his conterpart Juan in *El trato de Argel*, Francisco remains steadfast in his faith, showing a determination that incites the vengeful wrath of the Cadí. In the play's last act a Christian messenger arrives to relate the torments visited on the child for defying the 'ingenuity' and 'authority' of his captors:

> Atado está a una coluna,
> hecho retrato de Cristo,
> de la cabeza a los pies
> en su misma sangre tinto:
> témome que habrá expirado,
> porque tan cruel martirio
> mayores años y fuerzas
> no le hubieran resistido. (ll. 2373–80)

> He is bound to a column, turned into a portrait of Christ, stained in his own blood from head to foot: I fear that he has died, since someone more mature in years and of greater strength would not have withstood such cruel torture.

Casalduero has commented on the iconography and the dramatic placement of this scene. The messenger's account evokes the visual image of Christ's body on the cross, and his arrival brings to a tragic end the inset *comedia* that the captives have been performing for the Easter festival (96). Imagery and setting combine to reproduce the pattern of the Passion; as a 'portrait' of the Saviour, Francisco re-enacts Christ's torment at the command of imperial authority and his final sacrifice. The captive father, determined to witness his son's death directly, calls our attention to the figural roles of Cadí and child: 'veré en su ser a Pilatos / y en figura veré a Cristo' (I will see the essence of Pilate and I will see Christ in a figure) (ll. 2387–8). In a later scene the child's body appears in a theatrical discovery reminiscent of a *comedia de santos*, and the father instructs his son in the necessary significance of his suffering: 'de aquesa manera / más a Cristo has de imitar' (in that way you must imitate Christ more) (ll. 2258–9). In its explicit figural language and its visual spectacle of sacrifice, Francisco's martyrdom offers the play's definitive instance of saintly heroism in imitation of Christ.

In the case of Francisco's resistance to Islam, the text continues to invoke other figures of martyrdom and complementary antecedents of heroic conduct through prayer. The father indicates a figural correspondence to the Old Testament when he refers to the seven brothers in Maccabees, and Francisco compares himself and his brother to the early child martyrs Justo and Pastor (ll. 882–4, 1997–2001). In rejecting the temptations of their master, the captive children draw strength from Catholic devotional practices. At the end of Act II the two brothers appear; both are in Moorish dress, and Francisco is playing with a top. Although he has accepted the Cadí's gifts, Francisco asserts that he remains a 'Spanish Christian' (ll. 1867–70) and that 'divine force' will enable him to resist the 'human tyrannies' of his captors (ll. 1874–6). Together the brothers review the four prayers that they learned in their homeland: the Ave Maria, the Paternoster, the Credo, and the Salve Regina. This rehearsal prepares Francisco for interrogation by the Cadí at the end of the scene. To his captor's questions and challenges, the child replies by citing appropriate lines from each of these prayers. The dramatic recitation of prayer – a technique characteristic of the *comedia de santos* and the *auto sacramental* – sustains Francisco in his defiance:

Para vuestras confusiones,
todas las cuatro oraciones
sé, y sé bien que son escudos
a tus alfanjes agudos
y a tus torpes invenciones. (ll. 1977–81)

To confound you I know all four prayers, and I know that they are shields to protect me from your sharp blades and your dishonest inventions.

The child's verbal challenge affirms once again the idea of a militant faith. Francisco will use the 'four prayers' as spiritual 'shields' to deflect the Cadí's sword and to confound his 'dishonest inventions.' By internalizing the essential practices of Christian devotion, Francisco prepares himself for his heroic imitation of Christ and the early child martyrs.

Neither Hazén nor Francisco survives to escape from Algiers. It is nonetheless clear that their example guides and inspires the other captives in the exodus that they all desire. This point is explicitly made in the case of the child. The grieving father twice describes his lost son as a saint who presides over the fate of his compatriots: once when he asks Francisco's soul to intercede with Christ so that the captives may be sustained in their faith (ll. 2575–9), and again when he bears the child's remains as 'holy relics' to the point of embarkation for Spain (ll. 3013–15). Other characters who contribute to the final deliverance of Don Lope and his companions share in this spirit of devotion and self-sacrifice. Zara has learned the four Christian prayers that sustained Francisco (ll. 576ff), and her role unites the pattern of providential intervention with the romance motif of escape from paternal authority through marriage to a freely chosen partner. *Los baños* is striking in its programmatic exposition of spiritual heroism and in its separation of such heroism from acts of arms.

The captives in the Algiers plays practise the heroism of the saints. Aurelio and his companions in *El trato de Argel* are constant in their devotion to the Virgin and their hope of deliverance, and the typological language in *Los baños de Argel* presents Hazén and Francisco as martyrs who sacrifice themselves for the redemption of others. In each of these plays the dramatic action traces the trajectory of a hagiographic narrative, with its romance patterns of descent to a realm of suffering and persecution, a passage through trials and temptations, and a final transformation. The captive's tale in *Don Quixote* offers us a similar narrative, with a focus on the devotion and agency of the enigmatic Zoraida. Here the redemptive heroine is presented as a type of the Virgin, and the unfolding of a complex narrative enables the captives to return to Spain and to reclaim their Christian liberty and identity.

Many of the themes and concerns of the Algiers plays are present in the captive's tale. As a former galley slave and captive who has returned to Spain, Ruy Pérez bears witness to the suffering of the Christians in Algiers. He speaks of the violence inflicted on his companions and the remedies they pursue against the trials and temptations of life in the *baños*. His own liberation depends on Zoraida's intervention. In her role as a clandestine Christian and in her determination to flee with her chosen partner to Christian lands, Zoraida is a counterpart of Zara in *Los baños de Argel*. The extended prose narrative in *Don Quixote*, however, allows for more detailed development of her character and for fuller elaboration of romance form. Zoraida is described in detail as a romance heroine, and her agency is assimilated to Marian intervention. Her plan of escape entails the perils of storms and shipwreck and engages the typical movement of romance towards heightened participation. The captive's tale also parallels the Algiers plays in its treatment of heroism. The trajectory of Ruy Pérez's experience demonstrates the limits of martial heroism and the efficacy of faith and constancy as spiritual remedies and as means of deliverance.[24]

The captive's tale offers a detailed realization of romance form, both in the presentation of its characters and in its narrative structure. In *The Secular Scripture* Frye argues that the form of romance is based on conventional and formulaic units and that such structures are always close to its narrative surface (36–7). He also notes the affinity of romance in all its variants to folktales and popular legends (7). Insistent patterns and folkloric elements are clearly present from the opening of the captive's tale (Murillo, 'Cervantes' Tale' 231). Ruy Pérez begins his story at the point when he and his two brothers have reached the age to choose a path in life. Their father divides his wealth among the three siblings and cites a popular saying that dispatches them from their native village in pursuit of three distinct careers. Each career has its own end and each implies a particular point of departure; as a result, the three brothers set out for different places in Spain: Salamanca for study and letters, Seville for the life of trade, Alicante for arms and military service. The division of the patrimony is a familiar motif from folktales. The separation of family members is a common motif in romance and suggests that the family will be reunited through an act of recognition at the tale's end (Frye, *Secular Scripture* 111). Ruy Pérez and his family in León stand at one axis of his narrative; the other axis is Zoraida, the Moorish woman raised in Algiers as a secret Christian by a slave in her father's house. The figure of Zoraida also has folkloric roots, in the traditional the tale of the devil's daughter (Chevalier) and in medieval legends concerning a Jewish or Moorish woman favoured by the Virgin Mary (Márquez Villanueva 102–6). Ruy's flight from captivity through her agency can be traced to 'the universal folk motif of "miraculous release and escape of a prisoner" and "escape with the enemy's daughter who falls in love with a prisoner"' (Murillo, 'Cervantes' Tale' 232–3), and her segment of the tale is marked by the patterns and formulas of romance narrative. Her first contact with Ruy Pérez and the other captives is a ritualized test in which each of the male characters approaches the narrow window of her father's house so that she can choose among them by gesturing with a cane. Zoraida resorts again to the cane to transfer to Ruy Pérez the incrementally segmented sums of money required for their plan of escape. The captives' flight begins with two visits to her father's garden outside the city, and in each case Zoraida appears in a splendid display of beauty and wealth. The path of escape leads the captives and Zoraida to liberty and familial restoration in Spain, after a long passage of what Frye would call transport by shipwreck. In each of these features Ruy Pérez's tale shows its affinities with folktales and legends and its reliance on repeated formulaic units.

Frye's analysis of romance confirms its appropriateness to a tale centred on captivity and deliverance. Frye argues that all romance narratives share a common trajectory, one that traces a descent to a lower world of confusion and immobility followed by an ascent to a higher world of clarity and freedom. Clearly delineated at the level of formal structure, this trajectory is related to questions of identity and ideology. Frye offers a concise summary of the core structure of ascent and descent:

> Romance, the kernel of fable, begins an upward journey toward man's recovery of what he projects as sacred myth. At the bottom of the mythological universe is a death and rebirth process which cares nothing for the individual; at the top is the individual's regained identity. At the bottom is a memory which can only be returned to, a closed circle of recurrence: at the top is the recreation of memory. In romance violence and sexuality are used as rocket propulsions, so to speak, in an ascending movement. Violence becomes melodrama, the separating of heroes from villains, angels of light from giants of dark. Sexuality becomes a driving force with a great deal of sublimation in it. In the traditional romance, where the heroine is so often a virgin reaching her first sexual contact on the last page, the erotic feeling is sublimated for the action of the story. (*Secular Scripture* 183)

The captive's tale presents a complete version of this structure. Ruy Pérez descends into the suffering of captivity and ascends to freedom and reunion with his community in Spain. The lowest point of his experience is Algiers, the place of his imprisonment in Hasan Pasha's *baño* and of Zoraida's seclusion in her father's house. His love for Zoraida provides both the motive and the means of his escape. His return journey is marked by the melodramatic violence of the French pirates who attack and sink his ship off the Spanish coast, while the surprised horsemen who come upon the shipwrecked sailors on a road in Andalusia are his welcoming angels. His desire for his beloved is always present and consistently sublimated. His descriptions of Zoraida stress her extraordinary beauty and her miraculous agency in releasing him and his companions from captivity, while the promised marriage at the tale's end anticipates the surrender of the virginity that she has protected throughout her life in Algiers and her perilous flight to Christian lands. Ruy Pérez's narrative traces the vertical movement of romance, concluding in return and recognition.

Frye's opposition between 'a closed cycle of recurrence' at the bottom of this trajectory and 'the recreation of memory' at the top indicates the affinity of romance to the psychology of trauma and recovery. Garcés's psychoanalytical reading has traced in the captive's tale patterns of recollection and working-through that can be assimilated to the structure of descent and ascent in romance. For Garcés, Cervantes's literary treatment of captivity demonstrates both 'the repeated return of the traumatic event' in his life experience and his commitment to 'the therapeutic process set in motion by the reconstruction of the narrative' (9). In the captive's tale the trajectory of romance offers a model for the recovery and transformation of trauma through literary creation.

It should be noted, however, that in *The Secular Scripture* Frye assigns specific meanings to the terms 'identity,' 'recreation,' and 'recovery of myth.'[25] These terms are relevant to the captive's tale, given its detailed realization of romance form. Frye classifies myths as stories that have stuck together and acquired acceptance 'as structures of belief or social concern' (12). A society expresses and propagates its values and beliefs through such stories, and membership in a community implies subscription to a particular body of myths, whether they are sacred myths that describe a relationship with the gods or national myths that are assigned a privileged place in history (8). In both cases, myths are distinguished from folktales, legends, and other kinds of stories by the social authority invested in them. The concept of identity is central to the relationship between the heroes and heroines of romance and the myths of their society. Frye notes that 'identity means a good many things, but all its meanings in romance have some connection with a state of existence in which there is nothing to write about' (54). The pattern of descent in romance marks a loss of identity and an entrance into a night world of dangers and adventures; the opposing pattern of ascent is a movement towards a settled and stable existence, generally presented as lying just beyond the temporal frame of the narrative. Identity in this sense implies individual fulfilment and freedom, since as Frye astutely remarks, 'the individual alone can experience freedom' (172). One aspect of the freedom inherent in the identity that romance confers on its protagonists is the transcendence of social mythology, a process achieved in part through moving beyond conventional social prejudices and unexamined values, and in part through incorporating at an individual level the serious beliefs of the community, transforming them 'from accepted social values into the axioms of one's own activity' (170). In romance the individual claims his or her identity through the internal recreation of belief in a context beyond established authorities and hierarchies. The ascent to liberty involves the personal recovery of what has been projected as a body of social myths.

The recovery of myth can be traced in the experiences of Ruy Pérez and Zoraida, and in the last analysis it informs the version of heroism that each one of them practises. It is important to note that Zoraida stands at the centre of the captive's tale. Her initial appearance at Juan Palomeque's inn prompts Dorotea to raise a troubling question – '¿esta señora es cristiana o mora? (is this lady a Christian or a Moor?) (I. 37, 462) – and the narrative is set out to resolve the issue of her identity. In her private faith Zoraida has been a Christian from early childhood; she acts on this faith when she chooses Ruy Pérez from among the captives in Hasan Pasha's *baño* and helps to engineer their joint escape to Spain. Like her counterpart Zara, Zoraida conforms to the romance pattern of the imperilled virgin who insists on marrying the man whom she has chosen from her real or potential suitors. She directs a good deal of the action in Algiers from the hidden interior space of her father's house, using her cane to communicate with Ruy Pérez and to give him the funds to secure their escape. In her seclusion and her perilous voyage across the Mediterranean, Zoraida sustains herself through the three qualities that define heroism in the world of romance: suffering, persistence, and patience (Frye, *Secular Scripture* 88). In her case, these are assimilated to Christian faith and, more specifically, to devotion to the Virgin Mary, whose name Zoraida assumes on her arrival in Spain.

Ruy Pérez brings Zoraida to the inn mounted on a donkey, in a scene that recalls the figures of Joseph and Mary, and in his tale she assumes a redemptive role analogous to Marian intercession.[26] She appears to

Ruy Pérez in her father's garden as 'una deidad cielo, venida a la tierra para mi gusto y para mi remedio' (some heavenly being come to earth to bring me relief and happiness) (I. 41, 497). When the captives unite in the same setting on the night of their escape, they greet her as the agent of their deliverance (I. 41, 502). During the return voyage to Spain, a Spanish renegade tells Zoraida's father that she has been 'la lima de nuestras cadenas y la libertad de nuestro cautiverio' (the file for our chains and our deliverer from captivity) (I. 41, 505). In his extended discussion of the heroines of romance, Frye relates the figure of the redemptive virgin to such classical antecedents as Persephone and Euripides's Alcestis, and ultimately to 'the ancient ritual which in Greek religion is called the anabasis of Kore, the rising of a maiden ... from a lower to a higher world' (*Secular Scripture* 86–8, 163). In mythological terms, Zoraida's role can also be related to 'the marvelous initiator and the guide who ... has the keys that literally lead to another world – to freedom' (Garcés 217). On the model of the saints' lives, this pattern is adapted in the captive's tale to a Christian context. By transforming the beliefs that she has learned from her Christian nurse into personal agency, Zoraida discovers in herself a spiritual heroism that delivers her and the captives to safety in Spain. As in *Los baños de Argel*, a figural association with a scriptural exemplar links Zoraida's role to the unfolding in current history of Christian revelation (Gerli 46).

Ruy Pérez comes to practise the same kind of heroism, but his recovery of the myths that surround him follows a longer and less direct path, a difference that reflects his choice of a career or estate at the time of the division of his father's wealth. The saying that dispatches the three brothers into the world does not explicitly indicate the three paths that they are to follow. Their father makes his traditional saying relevant to the social conditions of early modern Spain by adding a commentary:

> Hay un refrán en nuestra España, a mi parecer muy verdadero, como todos lo son, por ser sentencias breves sacadas de la luenga y discreta experiencia; y el que yo digo dice: Iglesia, o mar, o casa real, como si más claramente dijera: 'Quien quisiere valer y ser rico, siga, o la Iglesia, o navegue, ejercitando el arte de la mercancía, o entre a servir a los reyes en sus casas'; porque dicen: 'Más vale migaja de rey que merced de señor.' Digo esto porque querría, y es mi voluntad, que uno de vosotros siguiese las letras, el otro la mercancía, y el otro sirviese al rey en la guerra, pues es dificultoso entrar a servirle en su casa; que ya que la guerra no dé muchas riquezas, suele dar mucho valor y mucha fama. (I. 39, 474)

In this Spain of ours there is a proverb, to my mind very true – as they all are, being short aphorisms drawn from long practical experience – and the one I refer to says, 'The church, or the sea, or the king's house.' As much as to say, in plainer language, whoever wants to flourish and become rich, let him enter the church or go to sea, adopting commerce as his calling, or go into the king's service in his household, for they say, 'Better a king's crumb than a lord's favor.' I say so because it is my will and pleasure that one of you should become a scholar, another a merchant, and the third serve the king in the wars, for it is a difficult matter to gain admission to his service in his household, and if war does not bring much wealth, it confers great distinction and fame.

This gloss expands on the saying's three terms, linking each one to an early modern career that promises both a position in the social order and material well-being. 'Iglesia' points to the religious life and the preparation it requires through university study in sacred and humane letters. 'Mar' indicates not simply navigation, but also trade and the material rewards of the merchant's life. 'Casa real' is interpreted as the life of arms, that is, as service in the king's armies rather than in the royal household. The father's warning here against service to the aristocracy echoes conventional complaints in Renaissance satire on the privations of life at court that shape Don Quixote's encounter with the page who has set out for the wars (*DQ* II. 24), while his description of warfare as a school of honour and fame recalls the positive value that can be assigned to the soldier's life in satirical writing. The father's direct experience also informs his advice. A veteran himself, he has chosen to divide his patrimony as a remedy for the profligacy that he acquired in the company of other soldiers.

Of the three careers outlined in his father's commentary, Ruy Pérez chooses the life of arms. His narrative begins with an account of his experiences of military life, first as an infantry officer in Flanders and the Mediterranean and then as a slave in the Ottoman galleys. He witnesses events central to the imperial conflicts of the Hapsburg monarchy: the execution of the rebels Horn and Egmont in the Lowlands (1568), the battle of Lepanto (1571), and the destruction of the Spanish troops that occupied Tunis and La Goleta (1574). His narrative describes acts of courage and presents figures who embody the ethos of epic heroism. In Flanders he serves under 'a famous captain of Guadalajara, Diego de Urbina by name' (I. 39, 476); among the defenders of Tunis he praises Juan Zanoguera, 'a Valencian gentleman and a famous soldier,' and

Gabrio Cervellón, 'a Milanese gentleman, a great engineer and a very brave soldier' (I. 39, 481).[27] Through their values and feats of arms these characters exemplify the traditional ethos of martial heroism. As he recounts his career, divided between military service in Spain's imperial armies and captivity in Algiers, Ruy Pérez praises the ethos of his fellow soldiers and then turns to a heroism of constancy and spiritual practice. In the course of his experience one mode of heroism supersedes the other.

This transition from martial to spiritual heroism can be related to the forms of violence that Ruy Pérez experiences during his career. At Lepanto he leads an infantry assault against an enemy galley and suffers multiple wounds from the Ottoman soldiers who take him prisoner. At Tunis and La Goleta he observes the siege tactics of the Ottomans and the heroic resistance of the Spanish defenders, who exact heavy losses from an enemy force far superior in numbers. In the Ottoman galleys and the prisons of Algiers he sees the violence of masters against captives, an instrument of terror and control that sustains the economy of human exchange through capture and ransom. His itinerary through the Mediterranean makes Ruy Pérez a witness to warfare and torture. As Scarry has shown, these two forms of controlled violence share a common structure based on the simultaneous infliction and denial of bodily injury and pain.[28] In his narrative Ruy Pérez uses different discursive strategies to represent these two forms of violence. His celebration of Spanish valour at Lepanto and Tunis demands a traditional rhetoric of heroism that displaces the reality of injury, but his experience in Algiers leads him to recognize and describe the bodily suffering of his fellow captives. This movement from one mode of heroism to another is based in part on his increasing awareness of the pain of others. In Scarry's analysis, such recognition of the reality of pain is one form of resistance to the structures that sustain the use of violence: 'An act of human contact and concern, whether occurring here or in private contexts of sympathy, provides the hurt person with worldly self-extension ... By holding that world in place, or by giving the pain a place in the world, sympathy lessens the power of sickness and pain, counteracts the force with which a person in great pain or sickness can be swallowed alive by the body' (50).

When Ruy Pérez describes military engagements in the Mediterranean theatre, he consistently praises the conduct of Spanish soldiers. He presents Lepanto as a victory of Christian valour over Ottoman arrogance and pride,[29] and he stresses the fortitude and courage of the

Spanish troops at Tunis, who attempted to defend the city's fortresses against the vast invasionary force of the Ottomans. As in Saavedra's call for an assault on Algiers in *El trato de Argel*, the heroic ethos is invoked most forcefully when it is linked to lyric forms and to the Renaissance figure of the soldier-poet. Ruy Pérez praises the accomplishments of Don Pedro de Aguilar, a Spanish ensign captured at Tunis whom fate brought to the bench of the Turkish galley where our captive rowed as a slave. As a 'soldado de mucha cuenta y de raro entendimiento' (soldier of great repute and rare intelligence) (I. 39, 482), Don Pedro has won fame through his martial career while showing complementary intellectual gifts. Like Don Quixote's discourse on arms and letters, the characterization of Don Pedro confirms that the life of arms demands not only physical force but also mental acuity and fortitude. In addition, Don Pedro's gifts have distinguished him in the republic of letters. In the words of the captive, his companion 'tenía particular gracia en lo que llaman poesía' (had in particular a special gift for what they call poetry) (I. 39, 482). Through his skills in the sphere of warfare and letters, Don Pedro has survived the loss of Tunis and celebrated in verse his fallen comrades.

Ruy Pérez states that when Don Pedro was serving at his side in an Algerian galley he wrote two commemorative sonnets on the fall of Tunis. The text of *Don Quixote* offers us these poems, through the intervention of Don Fernando, a character who has come to Juan Palomeque's inn through the trials and turnings of another romance plot and who identifies himself as Don Pedro's brother. After reporting that Don Pedro escaped from captivity and has established a settled existence with a wife and children in Andalusia, Don Fernando recites the two sonnets from memory. The first, on the defenders of La Goleta, is typical of both poems in its heroic themes and martial rhetoric:

> Almas dichosas que del mortal velo
> libres y esentas, por el bien que obrastes,
> desde la baja tierra os levantastes,
> a lo más alto y lo mejor del cielo,
>   y, ardiendo en ira y en honroso celo,
> de los cuerpos la fuerza ejercitastes,
> que en propia y sangre ajena colorastes
> el mar vecino y arenoso suelo;
>   primero que el valor faltó la vida
> en los cansados brazos, que, muriendo,

con ser vencidos, llevan la vitoria.
   Y esta vuestra mortal, triste caída
entre el muro y el hierro, os va adquiriendo
fama que el mundo os da, y el cielo gloria. (I. 40, 483)

   Blest souls, that, from this mortal husk set free,
In guerdon of brave deeds beatified,
Above this lowly orb of ours abide
Made heirs of heaven and immortality,
   With noble rage and ardor glowing ye
Your strength, while strength was yours, in battle plied,
And with your own blood and the foeman's dyed
The sandy soil and the encircling sea.
   It was the ebbing lifeblood first that failed
The weary arms; the stout hearts never quailed.
Though vanquished, yet ye earned the victor's crown:
   Though mourned, yet still triumphant, was your fall;
For there ye won, between the sword and the wall,
   In Heaven glory and on earth renown.

As in classical epic, the central theme here is military excellence, a demanding code of achievement that offers significant rewards and exacts high costs. Addressing the Spanish defenders as 'blest souls,' the speaker laments the loss of their lives while stressing the 'noble ardor' that they have shown in a just conflict and the positive value of their resistance to the Ottoman assault. This perspective on their deaths depends on rhetorical techniques of displacement and metonymy. Although the speaker recognizes that the defenders have exercised bodily force, he describes their efforts by treating the body as an abstracted entity and by referring to the material instruments of conflict. The images of Spanish and Ottoman 'blood' and of 'weary arms' displace the reality of injury from individual soldiers to the two warring armies, projected here as corporate bodies. The terms 'wall' and 'sword' (in Spanish 'hierro,' iron) describe by metonymy the circumstances of the assault, standing respectively for the defensive works of the fort at La Goleta and the weapons of the Ottoman invaders. These lines evoke the difficult situation of soldiers trapped between their own fortifications and the enemy's weapons, but they achieve this effect through a technique of displacement, attributing violence to instruments of assault and defence rather than to human agency. In its praise of epic heroism, the sonnet denies war's central dependency on bodily injury and pain.

Displacement of the body is also central to the sonnet's rhetoric of transcendence and paradox. A vertical axis in the text marks the ascent of the fallen defenders from the 'lowly orb' of the earth to the height of the redeemed. In this context, death becomes the soul's liberation from the body's 'mortal husk.' As in *La Numancia*, the strategic loss of a stronghold is simultaneously a moral victory for its defenders. The text shifts in its closing tercet from recalling heroic deeds in the past to registering in the continuous present the dual rewards of this paradoxical defeat. The loss of La Goleta now confers on the fallen soldiers secular 'renown' (in Spanish 'fama,' fame) and eternal 'glory.' The sonnet compresses the central thematics of martial epic into lyric form and brings together the highest of classical and Christian values in praise of Spanish heroism.

Pedro de Aguilar embodies the Renaissance model of joint achievement in the spheres of arms and letters. The sonnets assigned to his hand can be compared to similar texts by the soldier-poets of Cervantes's time. When such poets combine epic and lyric, they write principally in the lyric mode, stressing such features as the subjective perspective of the speaker and the examination of inner thoughts and emotional states. Garcilaso's sonnet XVI is a commemorative poem, written on the death of his younger brother Hernando de Guzmán during the siege of Naples in 1528:

> No las francesas armas odïosas,
> en contra puestas del ayrado pecho,
> ni en los guardados muros con pertrecho
> los tiros y saetas ponçoñosas;
> no las escaramuças peligrosas,
> ni aquel fiero rüydo contrahecho
> d'aquel que para Júppiter fue hecho
> por manos de Vulcano artificiosas,
> pudieron, aunque más yo me ofrecía
> a los peligros de la dura guerra,
> quitar una ora sola de mi hado;
> mas infición de ayre en solo un día
> me quitó al mundo y m'ha en ti sepultado,
> Parthénope, tan lexos de mi tierra. (*Obras completas* 110–11)

> Not the hateful arms of France
> Directed at this spirited breast,
> Nor on the well-armoured walls
> The assault of guns and poisoned arrows;
> Not the skirmishes of perilous war,
> Nor the frightful sound that counterfeits
> The thunder made for Jupiter
> By Vulcan's artful hands,
> Were able, for all that I cast myself
> Into the dangers of harsh war,
> To take a single hour from my fate;
> But fever of the air in a single day
> Took me from the world and has buried me in your tomb
> Parthenope, so far from my native land.

This poem takes the traditional form of a lapidary inscription, in which the soul of the commemorated individual speaks from the grave.[30] The text is inventive and rhetorically accomplished, but playful in its tone and effects. Epitaphs of this kind are usually directed to the reader, imagined by convention as a surviving family member or as a passer-by who has come upon the gravestone. Here the speaker addresses the city of Naples, personified as the siren Parthenope, in a variation on the traditional pattern that is particularly effective because the relationship between the lyric speaker and the addressee is not revealed until the sonnet's last line. The poem's central argument plays on a circumstantial irony. Although the speaker lived as a soldier and met his death in a besieged city, he has died not by force of arms but of the plague. The anaphora of 'no' and 'ni' in the two quatrains stresses that instruments of war have had no place in his sudden death. The treatment of epic heroism is also oblique. The speaker evokes the conditions of modern warfare – including sieges, skirmishes, and the artificial thunder of gunpowder – but in describing his conduct he stresses only his willingness to be exposed to the dangers of combat. Any comment on his own valour is indirect. Although the lyric speaker, like Garcilaso himself, has fought in Spain's imperial wars, he understates heroic themes and situations. This text prefers lyric irony and indirection to the elevated style of classical epic.

Lyric is also the dominant mode of Garcilaso's sonnet XXXIII. Addressed to his friend and literary collaborator Juan Boscán, this poem evokes Garcilaso's own service under Charles V in the assault on Tunis in 1535, a successful military action that placed the city under Spain's authority:

> Boscán, las armas y el furor de Marte,
> que con su propria fuerça el africano
> suelo regando, hazen que el romano
> imperio reverdezca en esta parte,
>   han reduzido a la memoria el arte
> y el antiguo valor italïano,
> por cuya fuerça y valerosa mano
> África se aterró de parte a parte.
>   Aquí donde el romano encendimiento,
> dond' el fuego y la llama licenciosa
> solo el nombre dexaron a Cartago,
>   buelve y rebuelve amor mi pensamiento,
> hiere y enciend' el alma temerosa,
> y en llanto y en ceniza me deshago. (*Obras completas* 152–3)

>   Boscán, the arms and rage of Mars,
> Which, watering the African soil
> With their own force, make Rome's
> Empire green again in this land,
>   Have recalled to memory the art
> And venerable valour of Italy,
> By whose force and courageous hand
> Africa shook from end to end.
>   Here where Rome's incendiary force
> With fire and licentious flames
> Left nothing of Carthage but the name,
>   Love disrupts and disturbs my thoughts;
> It wounds and inflames my fearful soul
> And I dissolve in tears and ashes.

Generic markers are aligned here with the sonnet form. As Richard Helgerson has shown in his monograph on this sonnet, the adverb 'aquí' (here) marks a turn from the epic matter of warfare and valour to a lyric preoccupation with the emotional state of the speaker, the central subject of Renaissance love poetry in the Petrarchan tradition (48–9). The articulation of these themes follows Roman historical and literary models as they are transmitted through classical epic and vernacular texts in Italian. Through his strategic assault on Tunis, Charles V has revived the force and valour that Rome exercised in Africa during the Punic wars, making green again the example of imperial rule. In Carthage, the city that 'stands for all that empire destroys and leaves behind,' the speaker finds himself undone through the passions of love, in an act of identification with the victims of epic violence (40, 52). Garcilaso follows Vergil in his description of war and his account of the effects of passion. His reference to 'the arms and rage of Mars' echoes the opening half-line of the *Aeneid*, modified through a distinctive emphasis on the 'large, impersonal forces' of war (22). In Carthage love 'wounds and inflames' the speaker, recalling the wound and fire that announce Dido's enamourment at the beginning of *Aeneid* IV (49). In a parallel reading of this sonnet, José María Rodríguez García has noted the speaker's identification with Dido as a victim of imperial force, in the context of the compression of 'historical epic into introverted lyric' (164). In its complex historical and generic engagements, Garcilaso's text admits various interpretations. The 'Italian art' that it celebrates is both an art of war and an art of poetry, and the first can be seen as 'deeply at odds' with the second, in witness to Garcilaso's divided loyalties to arms and letters and the larger tension in early modern culture between imperial designs and sensual desires (Helgerson 37–9, 14). At the same time, however, the speaker's presentation of himself as a poet-lover, subject in the midst of war to love's pain and confusion, can be read as a gesture of courtly detachment from the practical labours of war and public life.

A parallel sonnet by Gutierre de Cetina (ca 1510–ca 1554), a contemporary of Garcilaso who saw active military service in Italy, northern Europe, and New Spain, also favours lyric themes over epic heroism:

 Entre armas, guerra, fuego, ira y furores,
que al soberbio francés tienen opreso,
cuando el aire es más turbio y más espeso,
allí me aprieta el fiero ardor de amores.
 Miro el cielo, los árboles, las flores,
y en ellos hallo mi dolor expreso,
que en el tiempo más frío y más avieso
nacen y reverdecen mis temores.
 Digo llorando: ¡Oh dulce primavera,
cuándo será que a mi esperanza vea

ver de prestar al alma algún sosiego!
   Mas temo que mi fin mi suerte fiera
tan lejos de mi bien quiere que sea,
entre guerra y furor, ira, armas, fuego. (*Sonetos y madrigales* 104)

   Amid arms, war, fire, rage, and frenzy,
Which hold the proud French in check,
When the air is heaviest with smoke and mist,
Then am I afflicted with love's cruel ardour.
   I look at the sky, the trees, the flowers,
And in them I find my sorrow expressed,
For in the coldest and cruelest time
My fears are born and thrive again.
   I say as I weep: Oh sweet spring
When will I see that hope
May grant my soul some measure of peace!
   But I fear that my harsh fate
Wishes my end to come so far from my beloved
Amid war and frenzy, rage, arms, fire.

The speaker is a poet-lover who finds himself in the conditions of a winter campaign. Surrounded by the 'arms' and 'fire' of war, by air thick with the smoke of battle, and by a bare and inclement nature, he burns with love and trembles with fear. The placement of first-person forms in the second quatrain and in the two tercets ('Miro,' 'Digo,' 'Mas temo') stresses this shift to an inward perspective, a movement reinforced by an inner address to the personified season of spring. With the characteristic subjectivity of the Petrarchan voice, external conditions reflect by parallel or contrast the speaker's inner state. The barrenness of nature offers a visual analogue for the pain of absent love; the depth of winter marks a paradoxical rebirth of the speaker's fears; the 'sweet spring' that he invokes with longing holds the fleeting promise of new hope and of emotional peace. In the pattern of the Petrarchan tradition, the poet-lover's preoccupations are his absence from his beloved and his fear of never returning to her. The sonnet's last line reiterates the five terms set out in its initial line, yet the speaker's unfolding account of his emotional state changes the significance that these terms convey to the reader. The theme of martial force exercised against the enemy gives way to a lover's fear of separation and loss, and the matter of contemporary warfare is transformed through the sonnet form and its conventional lexicon into 'something quite different, namely, the enabling pretext for a lament about amorous longing' (Middlebrook 110). The poem subsumes epic elements to the subjective model of the Petrarchan love lyric.

These parallel texts by Garcilaso and Gutierre de Cetina offer a revealing contrast to the sonnets attributed to Don Pedro de Aguilar. The two historical soldier-poets subordinate epic material to lyric forms and conventions, but Cervantes's fictional counterpart of this type adapts the lyric form of the sonnet to the objective perspective, elevated style, and heroic themes of epic poetry. Don Pedro is of noble status, but he does not embrace an aristocratic conception of poetry. The sonnets of Garcilaso and Cetina are informed by a courtly understanding of poetic craft.[31] In the refined version of the arms and letters debate in Castiglione's *Libro del cortegiano*, Count Ludovico proposes that the perfect courtier should be 'versato nei poeti e non meno negli oratori ed istorici ed ancor esercitato nel scriver versi e prosa' (very well acquainted with the poets, and no less with the orators and historians, and also skilled at writing both verse and prose) (I. 44, 87), but that he should treat these skills with diffidence and modesty, as an 'ornamento' (adornment) to the professions of arms (I. 44, 88). Garcilaso and Cetina demonstrate these qualities through detachment and understatement. To mark the irony of a soldier's sudden death from the plague or to insist that the prospect of lost love has greater force than the arms of the enemy is to cultivate the *sprezzatura* that Castiglione defines as the essential quality of the courtier. Don Pedro, in contrast, does not share this courtly view of poetry. The attitude that informs his sonnets is not aristocratic detachment, but rather a commitment to the values of military excellence.

These sonnets also demonstrate Cervantes's awareness of the changing conventions of the Renaissance lyric tradition in Spain. The compression into lyric forms of the high style and imperial themes of Vergilian epic is a notable feature of late sixteenth-century verse written under the aegis of humanist poetics. Fernando de Herrera (ca 1534–97), a critic and poet who writes in the humanist tradition of imitation informed by classical learning, offers several examples of this tendency. Pedro de Aguilar's poems on the loss of Tunis can be compared to Herrera's sonnet on the defeat of combined Portuguese and Spanish forces at the battle of Alcazar-el-Kebir in Morocco (1578):

> Con triste voz, ô triste Musa, suena
> d'estos ecelsos Éroes la memoria;
> de quien recela el Hado la vitoria,
> i las mustias esequias mustia ordena.

> Por que pueda cantar (si en tanta pena
> da lugar el dolor) la ingrata istoria;
> esparze'n tanto en onra suya i gloria
>   el Iacinto, Amaranto i Açucena.
> Vos, no rendidas almas generosas,
> con desigual assedio i dura suerte,
> en la ribera Libia; qu'el mar baña,
>   Al cielo id veneradas, id dichosas;
> que n'osarà negar soberbia Muerte;
> que sois eternal luz i prez de España. (*Obra poética* 101–2)

> With a sad voice, o sad Muse, sound
> The memory of these sublime Heroes,
> The victory of those who trust not in Fate,
> And sombrely dispose the sombre exequies.
>   So that I may sing (if sorrow grants leave
> Amid so much pain) their doleful history,
> Scatter in their honour and glory while I sing
>   The Hyacinth, Amaranth, and Lily.
> You, magnanimous souls unconquered
> In uneven battle and by cruel fortune
> On the sea-bathed Libyan shore,
>   Rise to heaven in veneration, rise in bliss;
> For proud Death will not dare deny
> That you are Spain's eternal light and glory.

A devastating defeat in the face of superior Moorish forces, the battle of Alcazar-el-Kebir marked the end of Iberian territorial ambitions in North Africa.[32] As in Don Pedro's sonnets on Tunis, the poet's task here is to transform a military defeat into a moral and spiritual victory. To this end Herrera juxtaposes the conventions of classical heroic verse with a Christian ethos of redemption and devotion. The speaker invokes in the quatrains the aid of the Muse, asking her to sound a lament for the fallen heroes and recount the sad chronicle of their loss. The argument here rests on the values of classical epic, both in the rewards extended to the fallen and in the heroic stance attributed to them. The Muse will conserve the public 'memory' or fame of the dead, who have won a moral victory through a Stoic mistrust of fortune. The request that the Muse scatter flowers in their honour recalls the famous lament for Marcellus at the end of Anchises's imperial prophecy in *Aeneid* VI:

'manibus date lilia plenis / purpureos spargam flores animamque nepotis / his saltem accumulem donis, et fungar inani / munere' (Let me scatter lilies, / All I can hold, and scarlet flowers as well, / To heap these for my grandson's shade at least, / Frail gifts and ritual of no avail) (ll. 883–6). The speaker's sad obligation to commemorate the dead of Alzacar-el-Kebir parallels the debt that Anchises acknowledges to Marcellus; the naming of three flowers associated with immortality varies the privileged Vergilian model. The direct address in the tercets to the soldier's 'unconquered souls' marks a shift from classical fame to Christian immortality. The repeated imperative 'id' announces their ascent from the site of earthly defeat to a state of veneration and bliss, a transformation that anticipates the sanctification of the fallen as martyrs of a just war. This sonnet illustrates Herrera's command of the humanist poetics of imitation and amplification, as well as his ability to employ his learning for ideological ends. The soldiers' triumph over death confirms the glory and honour of Spain's imperial destiny.

Herrera's poem demonstrates various parallels to the sonnet on La Goleta that Cervantes attributes to Pedro de Aguilar. Both address the souls of fallen soldiers, praising the qualities of valour and fortitude that have led them to spiritual victory. Both displace war's violence onto the instruments and sites of conflict: the fortified 'wall' of La Goleta and the 'iron' of the enemy's weapons, or North Africa's fatal 'shore' and 'sea.' Both present a shift in verbal tense in the closing tercet, in order to stress the enduring nature of the fame and honour that the fallen have won. In its preference for the epic mode and its adaptation of a classical heroic ethos to Christian ends, Don Pedro's commemorative poetry is closer to Herrera's humanist verse than to the courtly sonnets of Garcilaso and Gutierre de Cetina.

This affinity with Herrera speaks to Cervantes's awareness of the ideological tensions that beset the idealized figure of the soldier-poet in the later sixteenth century. As Ignacio Navarrete has shown, Herrera's extensive *Anotaciones* challenge the pre-eminent status of Garcilaso's poetry in the Spanish literary canon, in part by questioning his well-attested reputation as the first writer in Spain to practise with equal dexterity the skills of warfare and poetry. Herrera cites multiple sources from classical and Renaissance authors for the themes and rhetorical figures of Garcilaso's poetry, and he proposes that an erudite poetics is crucial to Spain's interest in claiming fair recognition for its martial accomplishments. Navarrete agues that in linking the subject of his commentary to a strikingly broad range of poetic predecessors, 'Herrera would have us see Garcilaso's poems not as acts of *sprezzatura*, but instead as the results of much labor and scholarship' (142). He also reviews Herrera's argument that Spain's military accomplishments now demand commemoration in learned verse: 'What Spain needs are men dedicated entirely to letters; the scholar-poet is not inferior to the man of arms, but instead his fitting successor, the only one capable of completing the ascendancy of Spain' (149). This commitment to celebrating Spain's military eminence informs Herrera's own poetic production, in such texts as his sonnet on Alcazar-el-Kebir and his long heroic ode on the Christian victory at Lepanto.[33] Ruy Pérez presents Pedro de Aguilar as an exemplary soldier-poet, but the sonnets attributed to him follow the pattern of humanist poetry written in the service of empire. The heroic ethos that Don Pedro espouses responds to the demands of imperial ideology rather than to the circumstances of the soldiers who fight in Spain's wars.

Cervantes's captive captain does not express a positive view of Spain's imperial ambitions in the Mediterranean. Despite his admiration for the fortitude and courage of the defenders of Tunis, he does not hesitate to criticize the emptiness of the strategic objective for which they have surrendered their lives:

> Pero a muchos les pareció, y así me pareció a mí, que fue particular gracia y merced que el cielo hizo a España en permitir que se asolase aquella oficina y capa de maldades, y aquella gomia o esponja y polilla de la infinidad de dineros que allí sin provecho se gastaban, sin servir de otra cosa que de conservar la memoria de haberla ganado la felicísima del invictísimo Carlos Quinto, como si fuera menester para hacerla eterna, como lo es y será, que aquellas piedras la sustentaran. (I. 39, 480–1)

> But many thought, and I thought so too, that it was special favor and mercy which Heaven showed to Spain in permitting the destruction of that source and hiding place of mischief, that devourer, sponge, and moth of countless money, uselessly wasted there to no other purpose except preserving the memory of its capture by the invincible Charles V. As if to make that eternal, as it is and will be, those stones were needed to support it.

Ruy Pérez claims that his judgment enjoys general currency, and his rhetoric here recalls widely diffused arguments against warfare. His critique of the presidio at Tunis as a school of sinfulness and waste draws on the negative image of military life in Renaissance satire. His view that an act of divine mercy has taken from Spain this outpost of wickedness is a variation on the argument – often stated in Renaissance treatises on war and its causes – that the violence of the infidels is an instrument through which God has castigated Europe's Christian princes for their sins and presumption.[34] Like the captive Saavedra in *El trato de Argel*, Ruy Pérez appeals to the heroic memory of Charles V. The purpose for which he invokes this memory, however, differs radically from Saavedra's plea that Philip II mount a new armada against North Africa. Where Saavedra presents recollection of the 1541 armada as an incitement to further military action, Ruy Pérez argues that the memory of the emperor's victory over Tunis in 1535 is now eternal and does not require the material testimony of the stones that have been defended through an unacceptable expenditure of funds and human lives. This disillusion with Spain's wars in North Africa marks a separation from the imperial age of Charles V and its ethos of martial heroism.

The ethos celebrated in the sonnets of Pedro de Aguilar also presents a marked contrast to the heroism that Ruy Pérez practises after his capture at Lepanto. As a slave in the enemy's galleys and a prisoner in Algiers, Cervantes's captain witnesses the violence of the Ottoman masters and the suffering of his fellow captives. He responds to these difficult conditions by reasserting his hope of liberty. His intentions affect others who share his state of captivity, since Zoraida's intervention leads to a plan of flight that involves many beyond her intended husband: the other captives from the courtyard of Hasan Pasha's *baño*, the renegade from Murcia who acts as their interpreter, and the twelve Spanish captives whom Ruy Pérez recruits as oarsmen for the voyage across the Mediterranean. After the conventional perils of piracy and shipwreck, the sea voyage ends in an affirmation of liberty and a festive return to the communities of faith and family. Spiritual heroism here initiates the ascending movement of romance and engages its celebratory conventions.

Although Ruy Pérez praises the military skills and humane qualities of some of the Algerian leaders, he also stresses the cruelty of others, noting their propensity to violence and their use of torture to control their slaves and improve the prospects of a high ransom. In his account of a naval encounter at Navarino, he describes the death of one of the sons of Barbarroja at the hands of his own crew. In the confusion of battle the galley slaves abandon their oars and turn their bodies against their master's: 'pasándole de banco en banco, de popa a proa, le dieron bocados, que a poco más que pasó del árbol ya había pasado su ánima al infierno: tal era, como he dicho, la crueldad con que los trataba y el odio que ellos le tenían' (they passed him on from bench to bench, from the poop to the prow, biting him, so that before he had got much past the mast, his soul had already gone to hell. So great, as I said, was the cruelty with which he treated them and the hatred with which they hated him) (I. 39, 479). This statement is striking in its rhetorical force and its evocation of conditions in the galleys. Chained to their rowing benches and exposed to storms and plagues at sea and to injury and death in battle, galley slaves served under terms of forced labour and were often not free to defend themselves even during active engagements. This servitude was particularly marked on Ottoman ships, where all on board – the oarsmen and seamen, the armed janissaries, and the naval commander – were subject to the direct authority of the sultan (Hanson 249). The galley slaves pass the body of Barbarroja's son from bench to bench because they are shackled in their places; they assault him with their hands and teeth because they can secure no other weapons. Ruy Pérez describes this extreme act as an exchange of one form of violence for another, in which the Christian slaves repay their master's cruelty by putting him to death. The assault of their many bodies on the hated body of their master insists on the primacy of injury in warfare and on the central role of the human body in acts of war and torture.

Bodily harm remains present for Ruy Pérez throughout his imprisonment in Hasan Pasha's *baño*. Although he is treated with some favour as a captive likely to bring a high ransom, he and his companions are well aware that other Christians are subject to extraordinary cruelty:

> aunque la hambre y desnudez pudiera fatigarnos a veces, y aun casi siempre, ninguna cosa nos fatigaba tanto como oír y ver a cada paso las jamás vistas ni oídas crueldades que mi amo usaba con los cristianos. Cada día ahorcaba el suyo, empalaba a éste, desorejaba aquél; y esto, por tan poca ocasión, y tan sin ella, que los turcos conocían que lo hacía no más de por hacerlo, y por ser natural condición suya ser homicida de todo el género humano. (I. 40, 486)

> Though at times, or rather almost always, we suffered from hunger and scanty clothing, nothing distressed us so much as hearing and seeing at every turn the unexampled and unheard-of cruelties my master inflicted upon the Christians. Every day he hanged a man, impaled one, cut off the ears of another, and all with so little provocation, or so entirely without any, that the Turks acknowledged he did it for its own sake and because he was by nature murderously disposed toward the whole human race.

Here Cervantes makes striking use of a standard rhetorical topos. The conventional claim to tell of things not seen or heard before is evoked to stress the frequency ('at every turn') and brutality of the cruelties that Ruy Pérez has witnessed in Algiers. His language stresses bodily suffering, both the endemic hunger and exposure of the captives in the courtyard and the wounds inflicted on others. By naming bodily injuries – hanging, impaling, mutilation – Cervantes's captive expresses his awareness of the pain of others and of the connection between such suffering and the arbitrary authority of a master who resorts to torture without cause.

Ruy Pérez responds to the violence and privations of captivity by maintaining his hope of escape, a desire heightened by the proximity of Algiers to his home in Spain:

> pensaba en Argel buscar otros medios de alcanzar lo que tanto deseaba, porque jamás me desamparó la esperanza de tener libertad; y cuando en lo que fabricaba, pensaba y ponía por obra no correspondía el suceso a la intención, luego, sin abandonarme, fingía y buscaba otra esperanza que me sustentase, aunque fuese débil y flaca. (I. 40, 485)

> In Algiers I resolved to seek other means of effecting the purpose I cherished so dearly, for the hope of obtaining liberty never deserted me. When in my plots and schemes and attempts the result did not answer my expectations, without giving way to despair I immediately began to look out for or to think up some new hope to support me, however faint or feeble it might be.

For Cervantes's captive the practice of hope is a form of heroism. In the extreme conditions of Algiers, hope leads to action. It is asserted repeatedly, as plans that have failed to realize the intention of successful flight are replaced with new designs. Ruy Pérez insists that he has found constant support in his intentions to regain his freedom and that in his experience even faint hope has value. In this practice he parallels the constant Zoraida, who hopes to escape from the restrictions of paternal and religious authority. Just as Zoraida holds firm to her faith that the Virgin will deliver her to Christian lands, Ruy Pérez maintains his hope of liberty and homecoming. Both characters embody a heroism of spiritual practice and endurance.

The hope of liberty, although centred on Ruy Pérez and Zoraida, clearly extends to other characters. The term 'libertad' appears repeatedly in the captive's narrative of Algiers, often in contexts that stress its importance as a common purpose and motive. As Ruy Pérez executes the plan of escape that Zoraida has made possible, he enlists assistance and support from other characters, including his companions in the courtyard and others who possess skills essential to the plan's success. This process is particularly delicate in the case of the Spanish renegade who translates Zoraida's letters into Spanish and prepares responses to them in Arabic. Don Lope and Zara have no need of such assistance in *Los baños de Argel*, and the renegade in the captive's narrative introduces a new role and an original character type (Márquez Villanueva 95–6). The captives depend on the renegade for his local knowledge and his linguistic skills, but they are mistrustful of him because he has acquired these capacities by abandoning his original faith and assuming a place in Algerian society. Renegades are liminal types who live at the intersection of cultures and languages and can act as translators or agents between groups (Garcés 97, 190–1). As 'figures of change and mimetization,' they threaten a concept of Spanish identity based on a firm and unchanging confessional union (Fuchs, *Mimesis* 140). In the case of Cervantes's renegade, the prospect of freedom elicits a public declaration of interior faith. Ruy Pérez and his companions show him Zoraida's first letter under a pretext, saying that they have found the papers by chance. When the contents of the letter suggest that this explanation is improbable, the renegade asks the Christians to confide in him and to reveal the circumstances surrounding this astonishing document: 'y así, nos rogó que si era verdad lo que sospechaba, que nos fiásemos dél y se lo dijésemos, que él aventuraría su vida por nuestra libertad' (he begged us, if what he suspected were the truth, to trust him and tell him all, for he would risk his life for our freedom) (I. 40, 490). He produces a crucifix and swears by it that he will be loyal to the captives and reveal nothing of what they disclose to him. Through this confession the renegade risks reprisal from his masters and declares common cause with the captives who have sought his aid. Zoraida's letter, with its promise of flight, is the motive for his actions: 'porque le parecía, y casi adevinaba, que por medio de aquella que aquel papel había escrito había él y todos nosotros de tener libertad' (for he thought and almost foresaw that, by means of her who had written that paper, he and all of us would obtain our liberty) (I. 40, 490). The renegade recognizes Zoraida's agency and hopes to benefit from it. He first promises to place himself in danger for the freedom of others and then includes himself among those who will escape to Spain.

Captains and Saints: Lyric and Romance   145

The meeting of the captives on the evening of their embarkation shows us once again the formation of common cause among them. To protect himself and his companions, Ruy Pérez has recruited singly the oarsmen who will man the ship on its voyage of escape. On his instructions they are brought together for the first time in Haji Murad's garden, outside the walls of Algiers and in sight of the sea:

> Todos estaban suspensos y alborozados aguardándome, deseosos ya de embestir con el bajel que a los ojos tenían; porque ellos no sabían el concierto del renegado, sino que pensaban que a fuerza de brazos habían de haber y ganar la libertad, quitando la vida a los moros que dentro de la barca estaban. Sucedió, pues, que así como yo me mostré y mis compañeros, todos los demás escondidos que nos vieron se vinieron llegando a nosotros. Esto era ya a tiempo que la ciudad estaba ya cerrada, y por toda aquella campaña ninguna persona parecía. (I. 41, 500–1)

> They were waiting for me, anxious and elated, and eager to attack the vessel they had before their eyes, for they did not know the renegade's plan but expected to gain their liberty by force of arms and by killing the Moors on board. As soon, then, as I and my comrades made our appearance, all those in hiding came out and joined us. It was now the time when the city gates are shut, and no one was to be seen anywhere outside.

This passage records the anxiety that the recruits experience while they wait as individuals and the unifying gesture that gathers them together as a group. The appearance of Ruy Pérez and the captives from the *baño* draws the oarsmen from their hiding places. His narration, through its use of the continuous past ('se vinieron llegando a nosotros'), evokes a visual image of motion towards a single point of recognition and reunion. The closed gates of Algiers and the emptiness of the countryside around the garden emphasize the separation of the Christians as a group from the alien city in which they have been held in a state of suffering and immobility. The meeting in the garden initiates a common voyage towards liberty.

Northrop Frye remarks that such 'increased participation' is typical of the ascending movement that brings the structure of romance to closure (*Secular Scripture* 183). As Ruy Pérez and his companions approach the end of their long return voyage, they celebrate their reclaimed liberty, express gratitude for the divine agency that has granted them deliverance, and prepare to return to their homes and families. Through these actions they seek reconciliation with the communities of faith and of human society, in a general mood of pleasure and festivity. The captives rejoice at their first sight from the sea of the Spanish coast, a prospect that redeems their many trials and privations, 'tanto es el gusto de alcanzar la libertad perdida' (such is the delight of recovering lost liberty) (I. 41, 509). At their point of landing they make a joint affirmation of Christian faith and of gratitude for their freedom, a human and spiritual good of incomparable value. A propitious coincidence hastens their reconciliation with family members. When a troop of fifty horsemen meets them on the road, one of the captives recognizes his uncle among the riders and realizes that he is close to his home in Vélez Málaga. In a scene of mutual recognition, the rider greets his nephew, giving thanks that the members of the family have survived to witness his return from Algiers and recognizing the extraordinary nature of his redemption: 'por las señales y muestras de tus vestidos, y la de todos los desta compañía, comprehendo que habéis tenido milagrosa libertad' (to judge by your garments and those of everyone here, I conclude that you have had a miraculous restoration to liberty) (I. 41, 512). The people of Vélez Málaga welcome kin and strangers alike with equal generosity, offering them refuge until each is prepared to seek out the settled existence that lies beyond the end of romance. In the village community the returned captives find the gifts that faith can confer, 'the Christian blessings of peace, harmony, and love' (Gerli 47). The narrative ends in a celebration of faith and fraternity, and of the miraculous freedom that Zoraida and Ruy Pérez have secured through Christian endurance and devotion.

The Algiers plays and the captive's tale share with *Don Quixote's* discourse on arms and letters an attempt to define forms of heroism that can be practised under the conditions of endemic conflict in the Mediterranean world. Cervantes's soldiers and captives respect a traditional martial ethos and invest hope in deliverance by force of arms, but spiritual heroism offers the most effective remedy for their suffering and the best prospect of their return to Christian lands. In the galleys of the Spanish and Ottoman navies and the *baños* of Algiers, these characters turn to fortitude and Christian devotion, practices that enable them to resist the forms of violence that they encounter: naval battles by grappling and boarding, corsairs' raids, arbitrary torture at the command of their masters, piracy and capture at sea. In the case of *Don Quixote*, the narrative frame connects the captive's tale with the discourse on arms and letters through an encounter that revisits the relative rewards of these two paths in life. In the chapter that follows the end of Ruy Pérez's narrative, a judge named Juan Pérez de Viedma arrives at Juan Palomeque's inn. The coincidence of surnames is striking, and the judge proves to be the brother who has followed the path of letters, not to ecclesiastical office but to a career as a lawyer, or *letrado*. The judge offers an account of his rise in the *letrado* hierarchy, in part through his own efforts and in part through assistance from the third brother, who has become a rich merchant in Peru. Enriched in material terms and social status, Juan Pérez is on his way to assume a high position in the courts of New Spain. The parallel lives of Cervantes's captive captain and his brothers confirm the material advantages of the life of letters. Ruy Pérez nonetheless obtains a less tangible but more admirable reward. Through his acts of hope and endurance he has secured for himself and others a miraculous liberty, a benefit that his narrative places among the highest of spiritual and secular goods.

Cervantes links the spiritual heroism of his Christian characters in Algiers to two variants of romance that circulated widely in his time: saints' lives and Greek romance. The road to freedom follows the trajectory of trials and wanderings defined by romance conventions. This pattern of descent and ascent and the parallel processes of the reclaiming of identity and the recovery of myth are particularly clear in the captive's tale. By transforming Christian principles into axioms of personal conduct, Ruy Pérez and Zoraida resist the conditions of captivity in Algiers and claim freedom for themselves and others. Cervantes's ultimate insistence on the shared goals of liberty and community, rather than on individual fame, asserts the value of romance in relation to canonical literary genres that celebrate the values and rewards of warfare. Where classical epic embraces an unforgiving code of distinction and singularity, romance celebrates an ethos of human unity and common cause. In Frye's words, 'romance's last vision seems to be that of fraternity, Kant's kingdom of ends where, as in fairy tales, we are all kings and princesses' (*Secular Scripture* 173). The captive's tale begins as a folkloric narrative and ends with the captives' welcome to the fraternity of village and church in southern Spain. The two Algiers plays also conclude with the prospect of Christian community, as the captives embark for their voyages of return. Through the recovery of myth romance also displaces the conventional literary hierarchies that privilege the genres of epic and tragedy. For Frye, the place granted in the works of Homer and Shakespeare to 'the wandering tribes of folktale and anecdote, of popular story and ballad and nursery rhyme' speaks for the wholeness of the mythological universe, a construction of human fears and desires that is 'not an ordered hierarchy but an interpenetrating world' (187). Cervantes also celebrates the completeness of this universe, through the interplay of canonical genres and popular forms. In his works romance interpenetrates with epic and with humanist lyric, challenging the hierarchies that find the noblest material in feats of arms and an ethos of martial excellence.

4 Soldiers and Sinners: Picaresque

> The gods of war love nothing more than irony, and to be so blind to where and what we were was downright dangerous.
>
> Alvin Kernan, *Crossing the Line* (1994)

The captive's tale is faithful to the conventional preference in romance for characters of high social standing. Ruy Pérez reports on his experience as a soldier and captive by recording the military commanders and important masters under whom he has served, and his beloved Zoraida is the daughter of a wealthy renegade who holds a prominent place in the society of Algiers. In the course of his military career he rises to the rank of captain in the infantry, and during his service in the Mediterranean he maintains contact with other officers who belong to the aristocracy. Don Pedro de Aguilar, the soldier-poet who rows beside him in the Ottoman galleys, proves to be the brother of Don Fernando, a highly placed member of the Andalusian nobility. The captive's narrative is in part a story of social ascent. Although Ruy Pérez does not enrich himself with spoils of war, and the wealth in jewels and coins that Zoraida takes from her father's house is lost during the voyage to Spain, he has acquainted himself with a social circle that extends well beyond his birthplace in the provinces. He does not enjoy the material rewards that his brothers have achieved through lives in trade and the law, but he has improved his standing in the stratified society to which he has returned. His experience confirms the wisdom of the proverb that his father glossed when he sent his three sons into the world: 'Iglesia, o mar, o casa real' (The church, or the sea, or the king's house). Like the study of letters at Salamanca and the practice of commerce through the trading houses of Seville, service in the king's armies can improve an individual's position in the social order and enhance his social worth.

The promise of ascent in society is consistent with the narrative trajectory of romance, but in practical terms the rewards of military service in early modern Spain lay principally in escape from the economic and social restrictions of civilian existence and in the sodality of soldiers. When Cervantes writes about common soldiers who fight in the lower ranks of the Army of Flanders and the naval forces of the Mediterranean, he is attentive to the motives that draw men to military service and to the disruptive presence of soldiers and veterans in civil society. Here he recognizes what his best-known character often denies: the rough conditions of service in early modern armies and the impact of a culture of violence on the men who served and on the communities from which they were recruited. In exploring the ways in which soldiers tell their tales, Cervantes examines the strategies and intentions that inform such stories and the effects that they have on both narrators and audiences. The pastoral episode narrated by the goatherd Eugenio in *Don Quixote* (I. 51) shows the disruptive influence of a returned soldier on an idealized rural community devoted to the pursuits of husbandry and courtship. The ensign Campuzano in *El casamiento engañoso* relates an intricate tale of deception and reversal that again illustrates the disorder that soldiers and their hangers-on visit upon civil society, a theme revisited in the interlinked narrative of *El coloquio de los perros*. The two principal appearances of Ginés de Pasamonte in *Don Quixote* (I. 22, II. 25–7) present a criminal condemned to the galleys who is recording his life in a book and who uses strategies of narration and diversion to postpone his sentence of military service. The episode of the false captives in *Los trabajos de Persiles y Sigismunda* (III. 10) examines the purposes of storytelling and the benefits that stories can yield. Here the recitation of an invented narrative about captivity and forced service in the galleys leads through its aesthetic qualities to a scene of reconciliation and forgiveness. These texts share an interest in the nature of soldiers' tales and in the uses of narrative art. Cervantes recognizes that soldiers' lives are conducive to disorder and deception, but he insists on the pleasures of appreciation and human community that their stories can confer. He also explores the genres that lend themselves to representing the storytelling of common soldiers, including confession, autobiography, and picaresque fiction.

Cervantes's fiction responds to the social practices and class divisions that shaped the structure of armies and recruitment in his time. In early modern Europe the continuing influence of the medieval theory of estates sustained the expectation that members of the nobility would defend the realm in wars (Hale, *War and Society* 75), and the command structure of Spain's armies depended in large measure on the landed aristocracy. Members of the high nobility and professional soldiers formed the high command, while the officers' corps came principally from the lower nobility. Although recruiters for the Army of Flanders were encouraged to enlist a number of gentlemen or *particulares* as common soldiers, the majority of soldiers were drawn from the lower tiers of society. Methods of filling the lower ranks depended on a complex network of central and local jurisdictions. Commoners were recruited into the king's armies, and the Crown granted commissions that gave captains authority to enlist men beneath the colours of their regiments, under a royal patent that would indicate specific municipalities as sites of recruitment. Local officials were expected to assist captains in executing these commissions, and they could also receive direct royal orders to supply men for periodic military levies, both through voluntary recruitment and through lotteries that selected among residents eligible for service. This reliance on localized methods involved the Crown in extended negotiations with municipal officials, in the context of laws and political practices that generated 'simultaneity of authority' as an operating principle (MacKay 14). Spain was governed by multiple jurisdictions and tribunals and by laws that occasionally conflicted with one another, including regional codes and special privileges that the Crown had granted to specific communities. Contemporary political theory sustained the rights of subjects to question unjust orders by informing the king and postponing compliance pending resolution of the objections that they had raised. This combination of law and practice provided institutional means to limit royal authority in raising armies. Recruitment imposed moral and financial burdens on local officials, and they could respond by invoking jurisdictional arguments or local rights and privileges, in order to negotiate deferrals in executing royal orders or reductions in the number of men that they were expected to supply. Since legal rights were understood to extend to individual subjects, residents selected by lottery could also petition for exemption from military service, appealing to administrative abuses or to personal circumstances, and they could expect that their claims would receive

152 Heroic Forms

official responses. The system of recruitment generated challenges of accommodation and negotiation:

> From all the quarreling, the miscarriage of justice, the complaints, and the subterfuge, there emerges a vision of a complex society which at every level used the tools and arguments of jurisdiction, privilege, and office to define and redefine the limits and nature of royal authority. Using an idiom of justice, arguing that the king's duty to protect was equal to the vassal's duty to obey, individuals and corporations fought for what they understood to be their rights. (MacKay 135)

As the Spanish monarchy resorted to frequent levies to support its military campaigns, it encountered legal disputes and procedural delays both from municipalities and from individual subjects.[1]

In spite of the recourses available to unconsenting or reluctant recruits, many men enlisted willingly to serve in the king's armies. Some destinations of service were more likely to attract recruits. The Spanish garrisons in Italy were popular among common soldiers and provided a training ground for troops who could be sent on campaign to France and the Lowlands. The Army of Flanders could be maintained with volunteers, at least until the 1590s, when disease and the depopulation of the countryside substantially reduced the pool of available men.[2] In these cases captains of infantry could draw men to the colours and wages of their regiments, but service in the galleys of the Mediterranean was clearly less attractive. Here the Crown could not bear the expense of free oarsmen and turned to forced labour. By the end of the sixteenth century, the crews of the galleys consisted of slaves under the Crown's authority (*esclavos del rey*) and convicts sentenced to penal servitude (*forzados*). Drifters not drawn into infantry service by recruitment or municipal lotteries could be convicted of vagabondage and sent to the galleys, and sentences of galley service were imposed on a broad range of criminals, including bigamists, gamblers, perjurers, and male procurers.[3]

The promise of soldier's pay was a strong motive among those who volunteered for the infantry. Despite the notorious irregularities in the army's arrangements for remuneration, the basic wage rate, combined with bonuses for enlistment and for long service, offered sufficient incentive for men subject to economic privation in towns and villages compromised by depopulation and uncertain harvests. Siege warfare in Flanders also extended the prospect of quick enrichment through plunder or the taking of rich prisoners.[4] The accounts that Spanish soldiers have left of their lives confirm the economic motives for enlistment and also point to less material factors, including restlessness in the face of limited opportunities and a propensity to violence. Jerónimo de Pasamonte is orphaned at the age of ten. After living with two guardians and with an uncle in Soria, he moves to be with one of his brothers in Zaragoza, where he decides to travel to Rome to study in preparation for an ecclesiastical career. In Barcelona, however, he realizes that he has no income from lands to support him during the studies that he has planned and chooses instead to serve the king, enlisting in the company of Enrique Centellas (*Vida y trabajos* 7). Miguel de Castro is born in a village near Plasencia and passes a peripatetic childhood with his parents and his uncles in Orense, Lugo, Salamanca, Ampudia, and Valladolid. He encounters by chance an infantry captain, Alonso Caro, but shows little interest in military life at this time. He seeks assistance from an uncle in Segovia but receives a cold reception, and on his return journey to Valladolid he enlists in the company of Antonio de la Aya and proceeds to Cartagena to begin his career as a soldier (*Vida* 487–8). The *Discurso de mi vida* of Alonso de Contreras connects early experience with an inclination to military service. Contreras's childhood in Madrid is marked by violence when he kills a classmate with a penknife and is banished for five years to Ávila. He returns to Madrid to confront the straitened circumstances of his family. Apprenticed to a silversmith, he shows no interest in this trade, fights with his master, and leaves Madrid in the retinue of the Cardinal Prince. He follows this group on its journey through Barcelona and Genoa to the road for Flanders, enlisting in a company of infantry under Captain Mejía. In advance of their arrival in Flanders, he is drawn away from Mejía's troops by a corporal with little interest in seeing combat, and he travels south to Naples and Sicily, where he enlists for a second time in another infantry company in Messina, an act that initiates his military career in the Mediterranean (Contreras 18–26). Economic hardship, a life of movement and displacement, and a disposition to arms and violence influence the choice of these Spanish subjects to enlist in the king's armies.

Military service also offered release from the restrictions of life in civil society and involved practices that set men apart from their civilian peers. Enlistment under a captain's colours invited recruits to identify with the regiments in which they served, and some of the Spanish *tercios* in the Lowlands acquired nicknames that expressed martial solidarity. Informal fellowships among groups of five or six – a captain and his men, or a group of common soldiers – encouraged the sharing of war's misfortunes and its profits. Given the difficulties of maintaining regular wages and the potential for sudden windfalls at the end of a successful battle or siege, soldiers were exposed to extremes of poverty and riches, and in times of wealth they enjoyed unusual opportunities to make use of their earnings. Exemption from the sumptuary laws that bound civilians and the army's virtual monopoly on gambling encouraged men to exploit and display the winnings of war. The flamboyant soldier, dressed in bright colours and decked in gold chains, is a standard figure in Renaissance comedy and visual art.[5]

Interactions between soldiers and civilians were varied. Spanish troops were less effective in their homeland than on campaign elsewhere, and Spanish commanders complained of the temptations of desertion in local actions. Military demands and customs nonetheless disturbed civilian life, and common soldiers stood apart as a distinct and defiant social group. Municipal officials resented the disruptive presence of recruiters and lotteries, and the practice of billeting troops in transport in local households was widely regarded as 'a traditional scourge in Castile' (MacKay 152–3). Both soldiers on billet and returned veterans could bring disorder to settled communities. Men accustomed to violence, bravado, and a life of quick gains and even quicker losses came into conflict with the traditional values and customs of the communities that they had left behind when they enlisted to serve the king.[6]

This pattern confirms John Keegan's observation that warfare both reflects the culture that surrounds it and creates a martial culture of its own (11–12). The culture of violence among common soldiers is a standard concern for critics of war and its human costs. In *War is sweet to those who have not tried it* (1515) Erasmus laments the transformation of Christian subjects into ruthless warriors:

> Those are called soldiers, who rush of their own accord to the fight in the hope of a small profit, and fight on either side, like gladiators, though they may be brothers against brothers, and both belong to the jurisdiction of the same prince. And these men come home from battles like these, and tell tales of their exploits like soldiers; they are not punished as robbers and traitors to their country and deserters from their prince. We recoil with horror from an executioner, because he cuts the throats of condemned criminals, although he is paid by order of the law to do it; but men who have left their parents, wives and children to rush off to war uncompelled, not for honest wages but asking to be hired for some infamous butchery – when these men go home they are almost more in general favour than if they had never gone away. (334–5)

Erasmus dwells on the attractions of licensed violence. He cites two motives for enlistment in a rhetorically significant order: first, the prospect of 'small profit'; then, with greater emphasis, the opportunity for 'infamous butchery.' Soldiers fight under the aegis of the state, but their fratricidal acts against other men reduce them to 'robbers and traitors.' The reference to gladiators implies the idea of war as spectacle. Erasmus makes the striking suggestion that, as in gladiatorial combat, the civilian population expresses an admiration for acts of cruelty that makes it complicit in the soldiers' violence. Men who return from the wars impress their neighbours by recounting their exploits and are received at home with appreciation and respect. The common soldier's 'favour' pays tribute to the epic warrior's honour and fame. His self-glorifying tale is a low version of the classical narratives that conserve and disseminate the reputation of heroes.

Erasmus presents a moralist's view of the lower ranks. In imaginative literature several genres shape the presentation of common soldiers. In Cervantine texts on this theme, critics have identified patterns associated with autobiography, confession, miracle narrative, romance, and the theatrical *entremés*.[7] Such patterns illuminate the uses of structure and perspective in narratives about soldiers, as well as the connections between them and other works on warfare and its codes of conduct. The structures of romance and miracle narrative can be traced in both *El casamiento engañoso* and the captive's tale, although with different emphases. The two episodes featuring Ginés de Pasamonte play on the conventions of confessional writing and popular theatre. In addition, the Spanish picaresque lends itself to fictions about soldiers, criminals, and other figures from the lower tiers of society. As Peter Dunn has shown, the picaresque is not a precise generic category, but rather a set of textual practices that Spanish authors developed by 'invading' other kinds of writing (16). In this context picaresque fiction draws on texts that describe the disorder and instability of military life. The social pressures that shape its low mimetic characters correspond to common motives for enlistment: poverty, restlessness, vagrancy, impatience with social restrictions, a propensity for violence. Literary *pícaros* share with common soldiers the desire to survive and to improve themselves in the face of adverse circumstances. As Anne Cruz observes in her recent study of the picaresque novel and changing social attitudes towards poverty, the military aspect is present in the form from its origins (*Discourses* 167–8). Lázaro de Tormes tells us in his account of his childhood that his father died in service as a muleteer in a military expedition against the Moors (*La vida de Lazarillo de Tormes* 92); Guzmán de Alfarache ends his rogue's progress when he is sentenced to the Spanish galleys (Alemán II.3.7, 2: 438–41). Cruz also argues that over the course of its history the picaresque develops an 'enlarging focus, which takes the *pícaro* from begging and swindling throughout the Spanish countryside to the greater expanse of the Hapsburg theatres of war' (*Discourses* 164). Cruz notes that the protagonists of late picaresque fictions follow the itinerary of the military road that led from Castile through Italy to Flanders (187–8), in a movement that relegates Spain's indigent men and vagabonds to its imperial armies (205). This analysis stresses the relationship between literary history and the increasing demands of military policy and recruitment in the seventeenth century. In its shifting responses to issues of social concern, the late picaresque novel redefines the urban *pícaro* as a common soldier and dispatches him to the wars. The picaresque has a clear influence on the literary representation of military experience among the lower ranks, and on the understanding and reception of texts that deal with soldiers' lives.

Strategies for representing and containing disorder are central to current views on the reception of the picaresque and related low mimetic forms. Recent studies have suggested that early modern readers found this material appealing for its imaginative containment of disturbing social forces. Cruz argues that the popularity of the picaresque attests to the capacity of contemporary readers to remain indifferent to socially marginal groups, even as they consumed imaginative works that described the harsh conditions under which such groups lived. On this reading, the picaresque offers 'yet another example of unintended complicity between literary texts and the dominant ideology' (*Discourses* 205). In a parallel argument, Peter Dunn has proposed that this literature addresses 'the *anxiety of others toward* the marginal' and attempts to control by imaginative means 'the violent and deceitful reality of urban life' (305, 303). Dunn's sketch of an anthropology of the picaresque, grounded in Victor Turner's work on rituals and freedom,[8] defines the threat that the groups portrayed in the literature of low life posed to the established social order and outlines the strategies of containment that such texts employ.

Dunn's review of Turner merits summary in some detail. Turner takes as his point of departure the classic work on rites of passage by Arnold van Gennep. Of the three stages isolated by van Gennep – separation, transition, and incorporation – Turner focuses on the central or liminal phase, 'a stage of betwixt and between ... of being neither one thing nor the other' (Dunn 308). He considers the internal dynamics of this stage, stressing the sense of comradeship, or 'communitas,' that arises among those who participate jointly in significant rituals that mark their separation from the rest of society. He also notes that in complex societies certain groups may remain for extended periods in a borderline state that limits reintegration into the larger social order. Among the members of such groups a 'collective identity' prevails, in that 'all are sustained by their communitas, that sense of an overriding community with higher obligations and allegiance to some more compelling ethos than the laws and conventions that normally bind them to their fellow citizens' (Dunn 309). Turner proposes specific terms to describe the conditions isolated in his analysis: 'liminoid' for the state of sustained liminality, and 'antistructure' for the collective ethos that defines the group in opposition to the prevalent value system (309). Dunn suggests that the picaresque and its analogues present a literary projection of various liminoid groups in the society of early modern Spain and use traditional techniques of comedy and satire to contain the social threat that they represented, 'a seductive concept of freedom that was at odds with the established order' (310).

This analysis can be applied to military matters in Spanish fiction. In the terms of Dunn's anthropology of the picaresque, soldiers represented in early modern society a liminoid group, possessed of social privileges and collective values that confirmed their separation from the civilian population. The practices through which soldiers asserted their particular status and sense of identity – defiance of the sumptuary laws, casual violence, sexual licence, admiration for risk-taking and cleverness – presented well-known dangers to Spanish society, particularly when recruitment or desertion brought common soldiers into contact with civilians.[9] Like other liminoid groups, soldiers enjoyed an attractive and perilous freedom that challenged the norms of a highly stratified social order. The broad humour and ironic heroism of such late picaresque texts as *Marcos de Obregón* (1618) and *Estebanillo González* (1648) show that the containing strategies of humour and mockery also apply to the disorderly lives of common soldiers. In Cervantes's case, however, narratives about soldiers are less marked by straightforward mock-heroism. Dunn claims that Cervantes differed from many of his contemporaries in that 'he did not shirk the dangerous fascination, the allure of freedom projected by gypsies, criminal societies, and other travelling charlatans' (311), and this observation can be extended to his presentation of soldiers and of criminals destined for service in the king's galleys. In his texts picaresque conventions intersect with features of soldiers' autobiographies and oral tales. Cervantes admits the disorder that marks these characters and the fascination that their marginal lives hold for others.

The goatherd Eugenio's tale of lost love illustrates the seductions that soldiers can practise through the display of gaudy finery and the telling of heroic tales. Don Quixote and his companion encounter Eugenio in the countryside, and his narrative begins in a nearby village, where he lives among other rich and honourable peasants. Leandra, the daughter of one of his neighbours, is possessed of extraordinary beauty and attracts a multitude of suitors from the village and beyond. Eugenio and his friend Anselmo believe that their various positive qualities – a shared social circle, unquestioned lineage, youth, wealth, and wit – grant them a favoured place among the suitors. Leandra's father submits their claims to her judgment, respecting her right to choose between them without paternal constraint. Leandra, however, appears to make no decision, and her father offers neither commitment nor refusal to either one of the two suitors. This stalemate ends through the unexpected intervention of Vicente de la Rosa, a native of the village who has returned after twelve years of foreign service in Spain's armies. Vicente makes a bold display of colourful clothes, glass trinkets, and fine steel chains. He tells extravagant stories of his own heroic deeds, traces on his body the invisible scars of gunshot wounds, strums the guitar, and writes long ballads on local events. His presence holds the villagers in rapt attention and overturns Leandra's exemplary reticence. In an inversion of Zoraida's careful scrutiny of Ruy Pérez from the seclusion of her father's house, Leandra watches Vicente from a window and is drawn to his easy charms:

> Enamoróla el oropel de sus vistosos trajes; encantáronla sus romances, que de cada uno que componía daba veinte traslados, llegaron a sus oídos las hazañas que él de sí mismo había referido, y, finalmente, que así el diablo lo debía de tener ordenado, ella se vino a enamorar dél, antes que en él naciese presunción de solicitalla. (I. 51, 593)

> The glitter of his showy attire took her fancy, his ballads bewitched her (for he gave away twenty copies of every one he made), and the tales of the exploits he told about himself came to her ears. In short, as the devil no doubt had arranged it, she fell in love with him before he had hit upon the notion of courting her.

Leandra disappears from the village and is found three days later in an isolated cave. She tells her rescuers that Vicente gave her a false promise of marriage and then robbed and abandoned her. Although she states that she has not lost her virginity, her father is well aware of the force of opinion and sends her to a convent. Faced with the loss of Leandra, the two suitors retire to the countryside to tend their animals and express their passions in song, lamenting the loss of Leandra or complaining of her inconstancy. Other suitors soon join them, filling the valley with flocks of sheep and making its limits sound with poems of lament and complaint dedicated to Leandra. Eugenio claims that in these new circumstances he and Anselmo have maintained their eminence among the suitors, since they have taken up general themes: Anselmo sings only of absence; Eugenio, of the fickleness and inconstancy of all women.

Conventional literary patterns are close to the surface of this narrative. By retiring to the countryside to sing of the object and the experience of lost love, the suitors take up roles typical of characters in Iberian pastoral romances and eclogues and align themselves with the long history of European pastoral poetry. Anselmo 'complains in song' ('se queja cantando'); he and Eugenio express their passions in 'laments' ('querellas'); the sheepfolds that the suitors have set up and the songs of love and loss that they sing have transformed the countryside into the Arcadia ('la pastoral Arcadia') of classical literature. Eugenio's naming of Arcadia deliberately invokes literary tradition, and his narrative has a self-conscious relationship to earlier pastoral writings.[10] Like the other pastoral episodes in *Don Quixote*, this narrative also combines diverse generic conventions. Where Don Quixote's encounter with the sheepflocks juxtaposes pastoral with epic and chivalric romance, Eugenio's story puts pastoral in contact with picaresque fiction and other low mimetic forms. The stimulus that sends Eugenio and Anselmo into the green world of pastoral – Leandra's flight and abandonment – follows from the arrival in the village of Vicente de la Rosa. Through Leandra and Vicente, Cervantes illustrates the seductive influence of soldiers and their tales.

Eugenio reports that Vicente first impressed the villagers through his colourful clothes, trinkets, and chains, all articles of personal adornment closely associated with common soldiers in the early modern period. They are, in effect, portable assets, since they enabled soldiers to carry wealth on their persons and make a conspicuous display of the social privileges they enjoyed, in defiance of the sumptuary laws that applied to civilians.[11] Vicente shows his separateness not only in his finery but also through his general conduct in the village. He uses the same form of address with everyone, boasts that he has no lineage beyond what he has gained through his deeds, and recognizes no obligations to his social superiors. Among his former neighbours Vicente asserts his membership in the community of soldiers. In Hale's formulation, the rough sodality of this group mirrors the idealized equality of the pastoral world.[12]

By Eugenio's account, Vicente's tales describe the deeds that he now claims as the basis of his status and identity:

> Sentábase en un poyo que debajo de un gran álamo está en nuestra plaza, y allí nos tenía a todos la boca abierta, pendientes de las hazañas que nos iba contando. No había tierra en todo el orbe que no hubiese visto, ni batalla donde no se hubiese hallado; había muerto más moros que tiene Marruecos y Túnez, y entrado en más singulares desafíos, según él decía, que Gante y Luna, Diego García de Paredes y otros mil que nombraba; y de todos había salido con vitoria, sin que le hubiesen derramado una sola gota de sangre. (I. 51, 592)

> He used to sit on a bench under the big poplar tree in our town square, where he would keep us all hanging open-mouthed on the stories he hold of his exploits. There was no country on the face of the globe he had not seen or battle he had not been engaged in. He had killed more Moors than can be found in Morocco and Tunis, and fought more single combats according to his own account than Gante and Luna, Diego García de Paredes, and a thousand others he named, and out of all he had come vitctorious without losing a drop of blood.

Like Erasmus in *War is sweet to those who have not tried it*, Cervantes paints the bravado of soldiers' tales and their riveting effect on civilians. For both authors, a tale of this kind depends on the context of oral performance and responds to the narrator's desire to mark his special status and to make good war's promise to enhance one's reputation. Through his claims to heroic feats that rival the deeds of Spain's noble commanders, Vicente tells an unlikely story.[13] His account of his achievements is the tribute that roguery pays to the old martial virtues of honour and fame.

Vicente's gifts are not limited to storytelling. He impresses the villagers with his strumming on the guitar and by writing popular poetry.

Although his efforts centre on direct oral or musical performance, the multiple copies that he prepares of each of his ballads suggest an interest in having his art survive in written form, an aspiration that he shares with other picaresque characters. His performances, however, present a low-grade and dubious aspect, both in the excessive claims of his stories and in the elements of his extravagant appearance. Observing him over time, the villagers realize that he assembles new finery each day by shuffling the different pieces of three suits of clothes. In composing his tales and songs and in fashioning his self-presentation, Vicente de la Rosa represents the poet as trickster, a figure of the popular artist who cares only for pleasing his audience.

Eugenio's narrative juxtaposes pastoral romance, a widely read genre in sixteenth-century Iberia, with picaresque, a form of ascending popularity when Cervantes was writing the first part of *Don Quixote*. This episode can be discussed in relation to the interaction and the projected reception of the two forms. Like the story of the sheepflocks, it illustrates the implication of warfare in the idealized world of pastoral literature. The intrusion of a returned soldier transforms Leandra's village suitors into shepherd-poets. Despite the established motif of retirement to a green world of peace and leisure, the recruiter's drum is never far from the idle hill of summer. Eugenio also invites us to compare the effects of low mimetic tales and ballads with those of pastoral laments. Perhaps the most that can be said of Vicente's artistic efforts is that they attract the attention and erotic interest of the sheltered Leandra. Where pastoral records the failure of the shepherd-poet to move his beloved with his harmonious verses, Eugenio's narrative shows us that soldiers' tales and songs, however improbable and dubious in quality, can win fair love. Low art is seductive because it conveys the dangerous attractions and rough privileges of army life in Italy and Flanders. The effects of the tales that soldiers tell, in social and aesthetic terms, is a topic that Cervantes revisits in his other texts concerning the lives of those who fight in the lower ranks of Spain's armies and on the benches of her galleys.

El casamiento engañoso frames the ensign Campuzano's first-person narrative of his marriage to the beautiful and protean Estefanía de Caicedo and introduces the life story that the dog Berganza relates to his canine companion Cipión in the linked *novela*, *El coloquio de los perros*. Campuzano's narrative plays on the motif of the deceiver deceived. The two partners to the marriage – a soldier from the Army of Flanders and a woman who presents herself as a reformed sinner – are low mimetic types, and each enters into the rituals of courtship and matrimony with dubious intentions. L.J. Woodward has remarked that the model of interaction in their tale is 'the conjuror's trick' (84), and Ruth El Saffar has noted that they operate on a pattern of false exchange, in which 'what each wants is real items in exchange for false ones' (35). For both the central and the secondary characters, the plot unfolds in a complex sequence of such exchanges, ending in Estefanía's flight and Campuzano's discovery in his body of the symptoms of syphilis. In a final turn of falsity, the bodily pleasures that the soldier has enjoyed during his brief marriage lead to the pain of venereal disease and its treatment. Campuzano's narrative is a story of deceit and disease, framed in terms that engage the conventions of popular literary forms and the oral features of contemporary soldiers' tales. It registers the disorder that soldiers and their companions bring to their home communities, but it also presents storytelling as a medium of aesthetic pleasure and recreation, particularly through its relationship to the remarkable narrative of the talking dogs.

Many features of picaresque fiction can be traced in *El casamiento engañoso*: first-person narrative in a confessional mode, settings and characters conventionally associated with the lower strata of urban society, attention to the forms of display and cunning required for getting along in the social underworld. In addition, its central theme and point of view are decidedly picaresque. Deceit is a traditional theme often revisited in picaresque texts; a digression in *Guzmán de Alfarache* describes deceit as a disease endemic to humanity and divides its manifestations into four categories.[14] In matters of formal technique, this *novela* exploits a narrative perspective strongly linked to picaresque models. El Saffar has commented that the text accounts for the striking appearance of the convalescent Campuzano, as described in its opening sentence (34); the ensign's illness and its effects constitute a *caso* that the *novela* explains and justifies. Francisco Rico has identified such narration from a single point of view, in which 'the effect of all the principal constituent elements was to account for the hero's ultimate situation,' as a defining technique of the picaresque novel (71). These picaresque features interact with the linguistic practices and social values of the oral soldier's tale, and with patterns and conventions drawn from miracle narratives, pastoral, romance, and contemporary theatre.[15]

In its initial pages *El casamiento engañoso* engages various generic conventions and evokes a general environment of dislocation and disorder. A soldier leaves the Hospital of the Resurrection in Valladolid and proceeds uncertainly through the city, supporting himself with his sword; he encounters a friend on the street, who expresses astonishment at finding him in Valladolid rather than on active service in Flanders and at seeing his obvious physical weakness. The dialogue of the two men reveals their names and their offices in society – 'señor alférez Campuzano' (Ensign Campuzano) and 'señor licenciado Peralta' (Licentiate Peralta) (281–2) – and initiates Campuzano's explanation of the circumstances that have brought him to the place and condition in which Peralta has met him. Maurice Molho has proposed that this encounter has an allegorical resonance, since the offices of ensign and licentiate represent the two sides of the traditional debate over the claims of arms and letters (82). The context in which the characters meet suggests that this topic will be revisited from a low mimetic perspective. The setting of the city street is typical of farce and low comedy.[16] As Francisco Sánchez has noted, the common soldier and the poor licentiate are figures who mediate between the modes of the theatrical *entremés* (as professional types open to burlesque treatment) and the picaresque (as characters who seek work or service in an urban milieu) (174). At the same time, Campuzano's presence and physical appearance point to several registers of disorder, including specific social tensions between soldiers and civilians and a more comprehensive sense of displacement. El Saffar comments that Campuzano is 'thoroughly out of kilter' (18); Forcione remarks more generally that the text's opening presents 'a world in which things seem to have been violently wrenched out of their normal functions, contexts, and relationships' (*Mystery* 86). In this disordered environment Campuzano relates his soldier's tale of adventure and misfortune.

Soldiers' tales in early modern Europe depended on oral delivery, a medium to which modern scholarship has no direct access. Written accounts by soldiers who served in the Mediterranean and Flanders nonetheless indicate the principal features that such stories presented in their Spanish versions. As Margaret Levisi has shown, these texts were clearly intended for private purposes rather than for publication, and each appears to have been composed in written form 'after previous rehearsals in oral format' (112, 114). As a representative text of this kind, Contreras's *Discurso de mi vida* (1630) illustrates the concerns of enrichment and reputation that motivate the personal narratives of soldiers and the techniques of self-presentation that they use in telling their tales.

A striking feature of Contreras's narrative is his eagerness to reckon up the rewards that the soldier's life has brought him. Randolph Pope has noted that Contreras's proud tracing of the pattern of his life – an ascent from childhood poverty to important offices in the army and in the Order of Malta – inverts the scheme of autobiographical narration common to confessional texts and to many picaresque fictions, in which a repentant narrator reviews the errors of his or her past life (153). Pope also remarks on Contreras's candour in conceding that he has followed a life of arms in large part so that he can enrich himself through privateering in the Mediterranean (157, 165). The *Discurso* refers to the forms of wealth acquired by preying on maritime trade, and describes the allocation of spoils and gifts to Contreras on various occasions. Contreras is also eager to acquire the typical soldier's swords, capes, chains, and other finery. An encounter with a bailiff in Córdoba confirms the importance of this finery as a mark of special status. The bailiff challenges Contreras for wearing clothing inappropriate to his social station: '¿Cómo trae ese coleto?' (How can you be wearing this doublet?); Contreras conveys a soldier's contempt for civil authority in his laconic response: 'Puesto' (On me) (Contreras 76). For a man of modest social origins, military life affords both uncommon rewards and unusual opportunities for public display.

The *Discurso* is also attentive to the less material attractions of a military career. By his own account Contreras possesses qualities of character that underwrite his contentment and success in the life of arms, most notably a gift for ingenuity and a propensity for physical violence. Contreras makes it clear that his profession demands a quick wit, and he prides himself on his use of 'industria' (cleverness, ingenuity), both in entrapping adversaries at sea (58–9, 138) and in asserting command over his subordinates (138). An impulsiveness towards violence presents itself at an early stage and reappears at regular intervals in the course of his narrative, starting with his assault on a classmate at school and continuing when he draws his sword to resolve questions of honour and status (77, 172–3). This appetite for arms clearly shapes his early inclination to military service. The young Contreras announces that he prefers the call of the king's recruiter to the practical apprenticeship that his mother has arranged for him (20), and he takes consistent pleasure in the exercise of arms. As Pope has argued, Contreras finds in military necessity a justification for his predisposition to violent acts (153).

The nexus of violence and the soldier's life also asserts itself in Contreras's accounts of his interactions with women.[17] The *Discurso* reports on sustained relationships with three women: a camp-follower whom Contreras maintains in Malta, a prostitute who follows him from Écija to Valladolid, and a widow in Sicily to whom he is married for a period of a year and a half. The material satisfactions of military existence are important in each instance. Contreras sustains and enriches the household in Malta with the proceeds of his expeditions in the Mediterranean, and his brave bearing and soldier's finery attract his lovers in Écija and Sicily (80, 94). In all three relationships jealousy and betrayal lead to violence, as rivals challenge Contreras's claims to sexual possession and withdraw before his physical force.

The *Discurso* also confirms the view that soldiers tell stories in order to enlarge their reputations at home. In describing his feats at sea and his eventful private life, Contreras rarely misses an opportunity to emphasize his courage or trace the ascendant trajectory of his life. This tendency is no doubt due in part to the sense of social purpose that informs his text; as Levisi has shown, the soldiers who have left written accounts of their lives are from the lower ranks, and they write in the hope of securing some 'practical gain' from their social superiors (112). Such attention to the narrator's dominance over others is also characteristic of oral composition. Anthony Zahareas has found common narrative strategies in picaresque fiction and in modern case histories of social offenders; similar parallels can be drawn between soldiers' tales and the oral narratives of black speakers from modern inner-city neighbourhoods recorded and analysed by William Labov.[18] The motives that inform Contreras's conduct correspond closely to the lower-class values of the inner-city informants – 'toughness, smartness, trouble, excitement, autonomy, and fate' (244) – and his text can be divided into a series of what Labov calls 'narratives of personal experience' (354). In a narrative of this kind 'the speaker becomes deeply involved in rehearsing or even reliving events of his past' as he recounts a dramatic episode centred on an experience of 'serious danger' (354). Contreras repeatedly recalls events that have placed his life at risk, and he makes frequent recourse to the same lexical and syntactic means that Labov's informants use to 'evaluate' the importance of their stories. In Labov's view such 'evaluative devices' convey that the narrative is 'worth reporting,' that the events it records are truly 'strange, uncommon, or unusual' (371). The *Discurso* presents many common features of oral narration: verbal intensifiers that stress the remarkable or unique character of specific events (Contreras 27, 35, 36, 97, 141), explications of the speaker's prominence and general reputation (29, 52, 151), apostrophes and commands addressed directly to the reader (37, 49, 175), and colloquial oaths and expletives.[19] Contreras uses these linguistic devices to assert the value of his narrative and convey a soldier's concern with reputation and respect for the life of arms.

The ensign's narrative in *El casamiento engañoso* recalls the linguistic devices, social values, and personal concerns of the soldier's tale. Campuzano deliberately alerts Peralta to the novelty of the story he has to relate: 'le daré cuenta de mis sucesos, que son los más nuevos y peregrinos que vuesa merced habrá oído en todos los días de su vida' (I shall give you an account of these events which are likely to be the strangest and most incredible you have heard in all your life) (282). On several occasions he draws attention to the extraordinary aspect of characters and events: the striking beauty of Estefanía's snow-white hands, the sensual extravagance of the six-day idyll that follows their wedding, the fall into penury and discord after Doña Clementa's return, and the sudden shock of learning about Estefanía's deception. The narrative refers to knowledge of Valladolid that Campuzano and Peralta have in common – 'aquella Posada de la Solana' (that Solana Inn) (283), 'el tiempo en que se dan los sudores en el Hospital de la Resurrección' (the time for them to offer sweat treatment in the Hospital of the Resurrection) (292) – and its recurrent reversals and rapid movement from one episode to the next hold the auditor's attention. Campuzano presents in himself qualities prized by common soldiers – toughness, smartness, a capacity for violence – and Estefanía clearly possesses her own measure of 'industria.' These evaluative devices evoke the context of oral performance and support Campuzano's claim that his tale is unusual and so worth the telling.

The affinity with the soldier's tale emerges with particular force at certain key moments in the narrative. Campuzano begins his story in an inn, a setting strongly associated with low mimetic narrative forms and with the disorderly conduct of common soldiers, and he shares with other experienced soldiers a desire to display external signs of wealth and status. Doña Estefanía wears a fine veil that both conceals and reveals her facial features, and she shows additional marks of beauty and riches: 'una muy blanca mano, con muy buenas sortijas' (a very white hand, which wore very good rings) (283). Campuzano himself remarks on the fine figure that he cut in the public space of the inn:

> Estaba yo entonces bizarrísimo, con aquella gran cadena que vuesa merced debió de conocerme, el sombrero con plumas y cintillo, el vestido de colores, a fuer de soldado, y tan gallardo a los ojos de mi locura, que me daba a entender que las podía matar en el aire. (283–4)

> At that time, I myself was rather flash, wearing that big chain that you have seen on me, a hat with feathers and hatbands, a coloured jacket, as befits a soldier, and so splendid was I in the eyes of my own delusion, that I believed that I could have any woman I wanted.

These items of finery announce Campuzano's status as a soldier and inspire his confidence in attracting Estefanía's attention and erotic interest. The large chain and the ribbons that adorn his hat are also tangible measures of his wealth, a point that the text reiterates after the marriage when Campuzano displays his collection of chains and ribbons to his new bride (286). The ensign stresses his remarkable appearance through a Latinate superlative ('bizarrísimo'), and his language assumes a similar evaluative tone in the later description of his finery ('mi magnífica cadena' [my magnificent chain]). The promise of wealth informs the entire action of the tale. Mutual enrichment is the principal motive for the courtship and marriage of Campuzano and Estefanía. The term 'hacienda' (property, wealth) appears repeatedly in the text, both to predict the wealth that they intend to accumulate and to describe the resources that Campuzano is anxious to retain when they find themselves expelled from the house of their nuptial luxuries.

The discovery of Estefanía's deception leads to the threat of physical violence and, finally, to a sense of disgrace that places the two partners at risk. In an act that parallels Contreras's repeated recourse to violence against his sexual partners, Campuzano first seizes his sword and sets out in search of his errant wife, 'con prosupuesto de hacer en ella en ejemplar castigo' (with the intention of meting out to her an exemplary punishment) (290). When he returns alone to find that she has escaped with his chains and ribbons, Campuzano appears to experience the limits of desperation, equating the empty chest that lies before him with a coffin and evoking through his rhetoric a state of mental anguish: '¡Aquí fue ello! ¡Aquí me tuvo de nuevo Dios de su mano!' (What a mess! Here again God came to my aid!) (290). Although the items that he has lost are counterfeit objects of little financial value, his subsequent claim that Estefanía has fled in the company of a man who witnessed their marriage under the false pretext of familial ties suggests sexual betrayal and a challenge to male honour.

On this reading the soldier's tale provides the central frame through which *El casamiento engañoso* accommodates elements drawn from other narrative forms. That the chain of deceit and false exchange should end in the syphilis that Campuzano claims to have contracted from his bride reinforces the text's strong military inflection. The association of soldiers, prostitutes, and disease is well attested in the visual art of the period, as well as in historical documents on conditions of military service. Keith Moxey has studied the representation of common soldiers and camp-followers in such woodcuts as Erhard Schön's *The Baggage Train of Death* (Nuremberg, 1532), which portrays an ensign marching with his standard held aloft and a female companion on his arm, and *The Mercenary's Whore*, attributed to Martin Weygel (Nuremberg, 1660), in which a written gloss offers an explicit warning against 'the French disease.'[20] Geoffrey Parker has shown that Spanish authorities accepted that the Army of Flanders could not maintain itself without prostitution; officials calculated estimates of the number of prostitutes required for each company of men and made provision for treating venereal diseases in military hospitals and for formally discharging soldiers afflicted with 'incurable illness' (*Army of Flanders* 175–6, 169). Campuzano's ailment is not a wound that confers honour, but it is nonetheless a hazard closely associated with the lives of soldiers in Flanders and elsewhere. Although *El casamiento engañoso* should not be reduced to the sordid story of an ensign and a prostitute, this narrative frame is significant, since the interplay of forms and conventions in the text explores the implication of literary genres in the cultural sphere of the soldier's tale.

The courtship of Campuzano and Estefanía presents a marked instance of interplay among genres. The 'luengos y amorosos coloquios' (long, tender conversations) (284) of this process end in the careful dialogue through which the two characters assess and negotiate the terms of their marriage. Francisco Sánchez comments that their shared intent to advance in society by exploiting external 'signs of wealth and status' marks this scene as picaresque (169). Dunn argues that both characters 'play out their unconvincing drama of desire' by 'acting out the scripts of debased cultural codes, courtly and domestic' (230). The range of allusion here, however, is not limited to the picaresque; the dialogue that leads to their marriage evokes and engages recognizable conventions from romance and pastoral literature.

Estefanía acknowledges the errors of her past but is quick to announce her desire to contract an honourable marriage and to describe the assets, in material resources and feminine virtues, that she can bring to such a match. She assigns a respectable monetary value to her household and stresses the ease with which her goods can be transformed into cash. By her own account, her intention is to attract a husband who will take over her resources and enable her to complete the transformation of her moral life: 'Con esta hacienda busco marido a quien entregarme y a quien tener obediencia; a quien, juntamente con la enmienda de mi vida, le entregaré una increíble solicitud de regalarle y servirle' (With this wealth I am seeking a husband to give myself to and to obey; as well as mending my ways, I will devote an enormous effort to pleasing him and serving him) (285). When she elaborates on her readiness to surrender her assets and her will to a suitable husband, Estefanía enumerates the traditional talents of a submissive woman: excellence in cooking, thrift, effective household management, and the manual skills consistently recommended by moralists for idle female hands – spinning and weaving. Through her resolution to marry, and the catalogue of virtues enlisted to make this claim convincing, Estefanía promises to transform herself from a sinner into an ideal wife.

Estefanía's proposal reveals itself as a fiction well before her marriage unravels. Although Campuzano claims that his bride redeemed her promise of domestic virtue during their six-day sojourn of married leisure, the luxuries of this period have more in common with the profligacy of soldiers on leave than with the modesty held to characterize the household of a good wife. That Estefanía is engaged in constructing her own narrative lends a particular resonance to her references to spinning and weaving. As Carolyn Heilbrun has argued, classical literature supplies famous cases of women who tell their own stories through weaving in order 'to reveal, to engage, to counter male violence' (103). In opposition to this model, Estefanía weaves a fiction that asserts a strong desire to accept the conventional narrative of women's lives. In Heilbrun's formulation, tradition offers women 'the marriage plot,' according to which they 'might only wait to be desired, to be wed, to be forgotten' (108). Estefanía declares that she has aligned her expectations with a strong version of this plot, in which marriage represents the goal of both narrative and female desire. This pattern of marriage as closure, typical of romance and prevalent in many of the *Novelas ejemplares*, determines the shape of the fiction that Estefanía projects.[21]

Campuzano answers with a fiction of his own, one that offers a similar promise of financial well-being and domestic contentment. He assigns to his chain, jewellery, and soldier's finery – all objects easily converted into cash – a value comparable to the assets that Estefanía has claimed to possess in her own name. In keeping with the demand for male authority implicit in Estefanía's fiction, he proposes a plan for their household: by moving from Valladolid to the countryside, they may shepherd well their joint resources:

> eran suficiente cantidad para retirarnos a vivir a una aldea de donde yo era natural y adonde tenía algunas raíces; hacienda tal, que, sobrellevada con el dinero, vendiendo los frutos a su tiempo, nos podía dar una vida alegre y descansada. (286)

> [they] were sufficient to go off and live in the village where I was born and where I had some roots. This property, with the money added on, and selling fruit in season, could provide us with a happy and peaceful life.

Just as Estefanía has extended the prospect of a comfortable household, Campuzano invites his bride to join him on the prosperous side of the rags-to-riches life of the common soldier. In addition, his proposal evokes one of the most enduring ideals of the pastoral tradition. To retreat from the city to a village; to reside on the property associated with one's family; to live comfortably on the returns of a modest capital and the fruits of one's lands: these are the distinguishing features of the pastoral retirement celebrated in Horace's second *Epode* and elaborated with invention by Renaissance authors. The proposal for modest retirement attests to Cervantes's long and intense engagement with pastoral literature. In the context of Campuzano's story, it again suggests the implication in the pastoral world of its polar opposite: the violent theatre of warfare.

The pressure of these forms imparts an ironic cast to the evocation of romance and pastoral. The picaresque motive of deceit underlies the entire process of negotiating the marriage, and Campuzano's dream of pastoral self-sufficiency bears a marked resemblance to a famous piece of wishful invention from picaresque fiction: the impoverished squire's description of his estate in the third tractate of *Lazarillo de Tormes*. Campuzano's vague projection of the resources available in his native village recalls the squire's proud account of the inheritance that he possesses in houses that are no longer standing and doves that his ruined dovecot will never produce. Barry Ife has remarked that the squire's defence of his wealth and social position 'reminds us once again that one of the most effective adjuncts to the creation of a facade is the creative mendacity of language' (107), and the parallel with Campuzano's plan suggests that the idyllic village of his projected retirement may be simply another false front of picaresque lineage.

The treatment of spiritual narrative shows a similar tendency to ironic play. Recent readings have argued that *El casamiento engañoso* engages the patterns of confession and of miracle narratives in order to contain the varieties of deceit and disorder that constitute its principal subject. El Saffar claims that through the discursive processes of 'confession and re-creation' Campuzano releases himself from his experience of evil and emerges as a 'redeemed sinner' (20); Forcione tells us that 'the containing frame of a Christian miracle' orders and controls the lawlessness that the ensign has recorded in his tale (*Mystery* 141). In this text, however, Cervantes qualifies his reliance on such spiritual models. Campuzano claims that his discourse is not confessional: 'aunque estoy diciendo verdades, no son verdades de confesión, que no pueden dejar de decirse' (although I am telling the truth, it is not the whole truth, and nothing but the truth, as in the case of confession) (286). Comparison with Pedro de Rivadeneira's *Vida de Ignacio de Loyola* suggests that in recounting his affairs in Valladolid, the ensign does not conform to the pattern of a reformed former soldier. Ignatius enters the career of arms in pursuit of honour and glory; he is wounded at the siege of Pamplona; reading the lives of Christ and the saints during his recuperation, he turns to spiritual things and starts on the pilgrim's road to Monserrate and Jerusalem. Campuzano begins as an ensign on recruitment in the streets of Valladolid; he succumbs to syphilis before embarking on active service in Flanders; in hospital he occupies his mind with the harried lives of the talking dogs Cipión and Berganza and on recovery he returns to the gates of the city. Where Ruy Pérez de Viedma traces the romance pattern of a saint's life in recovering his miraculous liberty, Campuzano reports on the disorderly lives of soldiers in urban society.

The ensign's disposition towards his own experience also qualifies its moral and spiritual force. Forcione places particular emphasis on his 'mysterious sleep' in the Church of San Llorente and on his treatment for syphilis in the Hospital of the Resurrection (*Mystery* 103, 143). The spiritual resonance of these scenes is undeniable. Campuzano's sleep forestalls the physical vengeance that he intends to exact from Estefanía; his forty days of sweating present a penitential aspect, particularly in opposition to the 'false paradise' of his brief and opulent honeymoon.[22] The stability of the ensign's reformation, however, remains open to question. Edwin Williamson has claimed that his 'moral status' is 'equivocal' and that his 'state of mind at the time of his conversation with Peralta does not suggest spiritual regneration' (115). Such uncertainty can be consistent with confessional narrative. Dunn

(180) and Forcione (*Mystery* 144) both note that *Guzmán de Alfarache* ends before the repentant protagonist embarks on a reformed life and argue that an ending of this kind is not in itself a sign of insincerity or moral failure. *El casamiento engañoso* may also ask us to be content with 'the promise of a new life' (*Mystery* 144). Campuzano's expression of resolve for the future, however, seems more appropriate to the ways of a soldier than to the life of a reformed sinner. After recounting his surrender to charity and his cure in the hospital, the ensign offers this conclusion to Peralta: 'Dicen que quedaré sano si me guardo; espada tengo, lo demás, Dios lo remedie' (They say I'll be fine if I look after myself; I have a sword; as for the rest, it's in God's hands) (292). The phrase 'espada tengo' suggests a soldier's confidence in the instruments of his trade, the expression 'Dios lo remedie' has a formulaic cast, and the statement as a whole has a tone of low-grade Stoicism. Campuzano faces his fate in a spirit of self-assertion and pragmatism that diminishes the force of his conversion.

Throughout his narrative Campuzano is faithful to the practices and values that define the community of common soldiers. In the terms of Dunn's analysis of the picaresque, he asserts his membership in a liminoid group, marked by a disorderly freedom from the laws and conventions that bind others. By following the pattern of the soldier's tale, Cervantes portrays the attractions and dangers of military life in the lower ranks. His *novela* explores what other low mimetic genres attempt to neutralize and control: the full measure of social distinctness that marks the sodality of common soldiers and other such groups.

In the last analysis, however, Campuzano's narrative is not the whole story. His account of deception and reversal completes the pattern of picaresque narration in that it offers a retrospective explanation of the striking condition in which he finds himself when he first meets Peralta. The ensign is lame, yellowish, weak from his long treatment; his dealings with Estefanía have brought him to this state. After Peralta has heard the sequence of mutual deceptions unfold, he responds with a telling quotation from Petrarch's *Triumph of Love*: 'Che chi prende diletto di far frode; / Non si de' lamentar s'altri l'inganna' (For he who takes delight in fraudulence / May not lament if he too be deceived) (291). The citation of humanist authority has the appearance of a closing gesture. Petrarch's lapidary verses confirm the impression that the false courtship and marriage have supplied the events that Campuzano intended to share with his companion and that his extraordinary tale has now ended.

After the ensign has completed this story, he nonetheless reiterates and intensifies his initial promise of novelty: 'doy por bien empleadas todas mis desgracias, por haber sido parte de haberme puesto en el hospital donde vi lo que ahora diré, que es lo que ahora nunca vuesa merced podrá creer, ni habrá persona en el mundo que lo crea' (I consider all my misfortunes to have been valuable to me in that they brought me to the hospital where I witnessed what I shall now recount to you, which you will not be able to believe now or ever, nor is there anyone else in the world who will believe it) (292). For all that it reveals of Campuzano's designs and desires, the marriage story is simply a prelude to the true tale of wonders: the dialogue of the talking dogs that the ensign heard and recorded in the hospital. This interlinking of two narratives, each offering its own series of reversals and recognitions, is typical of Cervantes's fiction and invites us to consider the ways in which *El coloquio de los perros* illuminates or qualifies the uses of the soldier's tale in *El casamiento engañoso*.

The two *novelas* share many features of picaresque narrative. Critics have long recognized Cervantes's interest in this form in *El coloquio de los perros*. Gonzalo Sobejano has isolated the main features that define this generic affiliation: the use of first-person narration, the succession of masters, the final state of dishonour or dependence on charity from which the protagonist relates his life, the tracing of a personal history from infancy to maturity, the use of memory as a unifying device, the stress on the vagaries of luck and fortune.[23] The picaresque themes of deceit and violence repeatedly assert their presence in the text. Cipión proposes to Berganza a contract based on the central principle of picaresque narration – 'que esta noche me cuentes tu vida y los trances por donde has venido al punto en que ahora te hallas' (that tonight you will tell me the story of your life and the events that led you to the point where you are now) (301) – and in Berganza's account the stages of his life offer a lesson in the human propensity for disorder and the need for deception. Theft and violence are endemic to the slaughterhouse district in Seville of which Berganza retains his first memories, and they recur among each of the social groups that he encounters: shepherds, petty officials, soldiers, gypsies, Moriscos, and actors. Despite Cipión's cautions concerning backbiting and traditional satire directed against the trades and offices of human society, Berganza draws general conclusions from his experience, wondering at the seemingly irremediable faults of his masters and commenting on the threat that covetousness and misplaced ingenuity present to the public order: 'que esto del ganar de comer holgando tiene muchos aficionados y golosos' (for many people are keen supporters of the idea of earning one's keep by doing next to nothing) (333). Berganza's description at the end of his narrative of his vain attempt to urge measures against the plague of prostitution in Valladolid returns us to the social sphere of *El casamiento engañoso*, in which deceit is rampant and venereal disease is a commodity that can be offered in a market of false exchange (358). The colloquy that Campuzano overhears in the hospital presents a panorama of the underworld of soldiers, prostitutes, and confidence-artists that he inhabits.

Berganza's sojourn with a company of infantry offers explicit comment on the place of soldiers among the social types whom he surveys. Berganza encounters the company on recruitment in Mairena; four of the soldiers are former companions of the corrupt bailiff whom Berganza has just abandoned in Seville, and they adopt him with the intent of making a small profit from his abilities. Berganza quickly learns a series of carnival tricks – dancing, jumping, turning in pirouettes – and the soldiers tour him through each new town as the 'perro sabio' (wise dog). Like other picaresque characters Berganza accepts his relationship of mutual dependence with his new masters, but he comments acutely on their social status and their arrogant treatment of the civilian population:

> Iba la compañía de rufianes churrulleros, los cuales hacían algunas insolencias por los lugares do pasábamos, que redundaban en maldecir a quien no lo merecía; infelicidad es del buen príncipe ser culpado de sus súbditos por la culpa de sus súbditos, a causa que los unos son verdugos de los otros, sin culpa del señor; pues aunque quiera y lo procure no puede remediar estos daños, porque todas o las más cosas de la guerra traen consigo aspereza, riguridad y desconveniencia. (332–3)

> The company was made up of thugs and deserters who sometimes behaved badly in the places we passed through, causing those who did not deserve it to be cursed; the good prince has the misfortune to be blamed for his subjects and for the harm they inflict on one another, though it is no fault of his; and even if he wants and tries to remedy this, he cannot, because most things to do with war involve hardship, suffering and unpleasantness.

Conflict between soldiers and civilians is a constant in early modern Spain, aggravated by the practice of billeting armies in local houses and often remarked upon in reforming treatises and literary texts. The terms of Berganza's complaint recalls Erasmus's lament on the sins of common soldiers in *On the War against the Turks*:

> what can we hope for if we are encumbered with the sins of all our sinful soldiers? Their mercenary outlook incites them to commit every outrage, as they set out for war intent on plunder and return to plunder more, sometimes more ruthless towards their own people than towards the enemy; they cart their whores round with them, they get drunk in camp, play dice, forswear themselves, quarrel, fight; in fact, they are only attracted to war by the freedom it confers to commit crimes and pay the hope of booty. (327)

Erasmus and Cervantes coincide in decrying the havoc that soldiers wreak upon civil society and the propensity that they display to violence and to the gratifications of casual sex and easy money. Comparison of these two laments nonetheless reveals a significant difference in emphasis. Erasmus proposes that armies are amenable to moral and spiritual reform, and urges the rulers of Europe to take a leading role in this task. In relation to the war against the Turks, he is quick to argue that the princes of Christendom can expect no victory if they shirk their moral duty: 'Much of the responsibility for ensuring that our soldiers are as they should be falls upon their commanders, especially our monarchs' (327). Berganza, in contrast, expresses no such confidence in the reformation of common soldiers. He laments that the prince will be held accountable for the conduct of his armies, but he refuses to cast responsibility upon those who govern and command. In Berganza's view the insolence of soldiers is one of the brutal realities that war brings in its train. The cruelty of warfare is inevitable, as is the harshness that it inculcates in those whom the prince recruits to fight on his behalf. To ask that soldiers on the march abandon their habits of violence and disorder is to struggle against an evil that admits no remedy. Berganza grounds his judgment of the soldiers whom he serves in a direct and unsentimental view of war and its consequences.

By juxtaposing written and oral forms, *El casamiento engañoso* and *El coloquio de los perros* explore the implication of various Renaissance genres in the culture of soldiers and warfare. The first of these *novelas* engages the pattern of the soldier's tale, and both works comment on the persistence in civil society of the disorder and violence of the king's armies. Given the context in which literary works about the lower tiers of society were produced and consumed, such a clear-sighted presentation of soldiers as a liminoid group is unusual, and confirms Dunn's description of Cervantes (in conjunction with the author of *Lazarillo de Tormes* and Mateo Alemán) as one of early modern Spain's 'great disturbers of the reader's peace' (300). Yet Cervantes does not limit the effects of soldiers' tales to disturbance and disorder. In the closing pages that complete the narrative frame that unites the two *novelas*, a final recognition invites us to reconsider Campuzano's relation to his tale. As Dunn has observed, the complex temporal sequence of these texts finally reveals that their main theme is the friendship of Campuzano and Peralta, a friendship renewed when the two men meet unexpectedly on the streets of Valladolid and intensified through the act of storytelling (229–30). Forcione has shown that the frame celebrates their friendship in association with such humanist values as 'charity, conviviality, and good will' (*Mystery* 144). This relationship of equality marks a departure from historical soldiers' narratives. Common soldiers told tales to those above or beneath them on the social scale for pragmatic ends; Campuzano shares his stories with an equal for the purposes of friendship and entertainment. In the closing moments of *El coloquio de los perros* a soldier affirms his convivial relations with someone outside his normal social sphere, and his companion suggests in turn that the primary appeal of a soldier's tale can rest not on its assertion of strength and superiority over others but on positive aesthetic values: 'Yo alcanzo el artificio del *Coloquio* y la invención, y basta' (I see the art of the Colloquy and its invention and that is enough) (359). This gesture confirms and revisits the allegory of arms and letters implicit in the professions of the two characters. The case of Campuzano and Peralta reframes the humanist debate on this topic in terms of the mutual pleasures of the imagination. Through the stories that they share, ensign and licentiate celebrate a bond of friendship and equality.

Campuzano and Vicente de la Rosa share an awareness of the advantages of military life. Through their finery and their tales they make a public display of flashy goods, soldier's bravado, and sexual adventurousness. In their conduct they respond to the motives that led peasants, vagabonds, and the urban poor to enlist under the banner of the king's recruiters. Ginés de Pasamonte, in contrast, has not enlisted by choice. A criminal sentenced for the second time, he is destined to ten years of forced service in the galleys of Spain's navy. These circumstances shape his role as a storyteller and the purposes of the narratives that he creates. Where Vicente and Campuzano assert their identity before civilians, Ginés engages in verbal competition with other convicts. He affirms his superiority in part by claiming that the story of his life has cash value, and he shows a general interest in making his performances pay. He produces stories for pragmatic ends, ones that extend to an intent to control his own destiny by avoiding the forced service to which he has been condemned. In his practical concerns, Ginés is a figure for the popular artist. In his desire to shun the violence and deprivation of the galleys, he is a trickster, anti-heroic in temperament and confident in the force of his ingenuity.

Ginés de Pasamonte first appears as one of a group of some twelve men who are bound together by a long iron chain and marching under an escort of four armed guards. This striking sight preoccupies Don Quixote, despite the clear explanation that he receives from his squire, who identifies the group's function and destination: 'Ésta es cadena de galeotes, gente forzada del rey, que va a las galeras' (That is a chain of galley slaves, on the way to the galleys by force of the king's orders) (I. 22, 268). Sancho's immediate recognition of the men as convicts, or *forzados*, and his knowledge of the form of servitude imposed on them suggest that he has seen such groups before. Given the logistical arrangements in early modern Spain for holding prisoners and delivering them to the coast, it is likely that rural peasants and villagers would have had some familiarity with this aspect of the penal system. Criminals sentenced to the galleys were held in one of several central prisons until sufficient numbers had been assembled to make it feasible to have them escorted to the coast; a group was then bound together with iron collars and a long chain and marched to one of the standard embarkation points (Cartagena, Málaga, Puerto de Santa María), along unchanging routes that had been fixed in the early sixteenth century.[24] For Sancho, the chain of convicts is a familiar entity in an institutionalized system of criminal offences and penalties. Don Quixote, in contrast, objects to the violation of the men's will and sees in their condition an appeal to his chivalric duty to right wrongs and defend the oppressed. The dissonance between squire and knight follows from Don Quixote's rejection of a modern system of justice based on legal codes and on institutional procedures and penalties. His attitude is played out to dramatic effect when he takes action towards the end of the episode, attacking the armed guards and freeing the convicts in a scene of comic chaos and confusion. In this action Don Quixote responds to the striking visual appearance of the enchained convicts, as well as to the brief stories that they tell about themselves.

Once Sancho has explained why the men are in chains, Don Quixote asks one of the guards for more detailed information: 'querría saber de cada uno dellos en particular la causa de su desgracia' (I should like to know from each of them separately the reason of his misfortune) (I. 22, 266). Here Don Quixote shows his typical curiosity about human particularity, a quality that later elicits the life narratives of such characters as Cardenio and Dorotea. The guard responds by inviting him to question the prisoners:

> Aunque llevamos aquí el registro y la fe de las sentencias de cada uno destos malaventurados, no es tiempo éste de detenerles a sacarlas ni a leellas; vuestra merced llegue y se lo pregunte a ellos mesmos, que ellos lo dirán si quisieren, que sí querrán, porque es gente que recibe gusto de hacer y decir bellaquerías. (I. 22, 266)

> Though we have here the register and certificate of the sentence of every one of these wretches, this is no time to take them out or read them. Come and ask the men themselves. They can tell if they choose, and they will, for these fellows enjoy dirty tricks and talking about them.

This statement acknowledges the concern of the Hapsburg state with an extensive paper apparatus of registers and legal documents and with the proper use of such written instruments.[25] Rather than producing the convicts' official records at an inappropriate time, the guard tells Don Quixote to approach the prisoners directly so that each one may describe his crime and sentence in his own words. This may be a question of formal protocols, but the guard also expects to derive some amusement from Don Quixote's dialogue with the prisoners, since he believes that they enjoy saying roguish things ('bellaquerías'). Before Ginés de Pasamonte describes his past experience and present ambitions, the dialogue presents five of the other convicts. Three speak for themselves and two allow others to speak for them, in brief narratives that demonstrate a notable capacity for verbal display and invention.

In each case, the initial effect of the narrative is to disguise or diminish the criminal acts that the convicts have committed. The first says that he has been condemned to the galleys for being in love ('por enamorado'); the second, as a 'canary,' or musician ('por canario, digo, por músico y cantor' [because he is a canary, I mean as a musician and singer]). The third has been sentenced for lack of money ('por faltarme diez ducados' [for the want of ten ducats]). The fourth has been a broker in the affairs of others, and the fifth has amused himself with women within and beyond his circle of kin ('con dos primas hermanas mías, y con otras dos hermanas que no lo eran mías' [with a couple of girl cousins of mine, and with a couple of sisters who were not mine]). Don Quixote expresses his sympathy, given that the men seem to have been sentenced to harsh servitude on such slight grounds, yet as the narratives unfold the impression of relative innocence proves to be deceptive. The object of the lover's affections was a laundry basket that he stole. The singer confessed under torture to stealing livestock. The third convict lacked money to bribe the court officials at the time of his trial. The fourth has been both an agent in moneylending and a sexual procurer, and the fifth has practised a dubious and immoral sexual calculus. The convicts do not deny the crimes that they have committed, but they describe them in an inventive language, playful in tone and rich in metaphors.

In its lexicon and its functions, the convicts' language presents the essential features of what the linguist Michael Halliday has called an anti-language. Halliday states that an anti-language is generated by an anti-society, 'a society that is set up within another society as a conscious alternative to it' (570). A standard feature of anti-languages is the recasting of the lexicon, with a focus on words related to the activities and values that define specific subcultures. The emphasis on shared values allows the users of an anti-language to create and sustain an alternate social reality, through interactions based on verbal competition and the marking of identity and difference in a social hierarchy. Activities of construction and assertion are central because of the inverse relationship between the subculture and the dominant social order: 'The anti-language arises when the alternative reality is a *counter*-reality, set up *in opposition to* some established norm' (576). An anti-language is the verbal medium that sustains the collective ethos or 'antistructure' that Victor Turner assigns to liminoid groups. Metaphor is central to the maintenance of anti-societies and anti-languages. Halliday observes that 'the anti-society is, in its structure, a metaphor for society' and that 'an anti-language is a metaphor for everyday language' (578). In anti-languages, 'this metaphorical quality runs all the way up and down the system' (578) in various forms of linguistic variation (phonological, morphological, semantic). An anti-language offers the speakers who adopt and maintain it a lexicon transformed through metaphors.

One of the examples that Halliday discusses is *grypserka*, a highly developed anti-language used among Polish prisoners. Halliday notes the continuity between the social system of the prisons and the criminal subculture outside of them, as well as the use of the anti-language to sustain social values and assert differences in status (572–3). In *grypserka*, as in other similar anti-languages, relexicalization centres on criminal activity, providing 'new words for types of criminal act, and classes of criminal and of victim; for tools of the trade; for police and other representatives of the law enforcement structure of the society; for penalties, penal institutions, and the like' (571). The narratives that Cervantes assigns to his convicts show these features. They use two expressions that are clear instances of Spanish thieves' slang, or *germanía*, in that they require verbal glosses. The first convict refers to his sentence of three years in the 'gurapas' and then explains to Don Quixote, 'gurapas son galeras' (*gurapas* are galleys) (I. 22, 267). Concerning the second convict, condemned as a 'canario' and 'cantor,' one of the guards tells Don Quixote, 'Señor caballero, cantar en el ansia se dice entre esta gente *non santa* confesar en el tormento' (Sir, to these wicked men, to sing when you're in trouble means to confess under torture) (I. 22, 267). The variation of 'gurapas' for 'galeras' uses a phonological process typical of anti-languages to provide an alternate term for the penal institution of the galleys.[26] The phrase 'cantar en el ansia' employs a metaphor to relexicalize the judicial processes of torture and confession. The metaphorical cast of an anti-language runs through the statements of all five convicts, as they describe a range of acts associated with the commitment and prosecution of crimes: theft, confession, bribery, sexual procurement, and sexual misconduct. Their language exploits semantic ambiguities (using 'corredor' in its two senses of 'agent' and 'procurer')[27] and appeals to knowledge that the convicts share within their subculture (omitting the word 'calles' in the expression 'habiendo paseado por las acostrumbradas' [having paraded through the usual ones] to describe the traditional shaming of sentenced criminals by parading them through city streets). The convicts engage in verbal competition and mark differences in status. The third convict plays on the lexicon of the first when he refers in his sentence to 'las señoras gurapas' (their ladyships the *gurapas*). The five narratives show an increasing degree of ingenuity and complexity, as the convicts attempt to outdo one another. Most are boastful of their crimes, but a guard reports that they are abusive towards the criminal who confessed under torture, on the general principle that one can say 'no' as easily as 'yes.' Just as soldiers' tales mark their separateness from civilians who are bound by social conventions and restrictions, the convicts' narratives assert and sustain a criminal subculture that exists in opposition to the dominant culture of law-abiding citizens. In Cervantes's fiction, convicts and common soldiers also share a pragmatic acceptance of circumstances and a trust in their own abilities. The prisoner who laments his lack of money for a bribe concludes, 'pero Dios es grande: paciencia, y basta' (but God is great. Patience – there, that's enough) (I. 22, 268), and the contriver of the sexual calculus speaks in similar terms: 'castigo es de mi culpa; mozo soy; dure la vida, que con ella todo se alcanza' (it is the punishment of my fault. I am a young man; let life only last, and with that all will come right) (I. 22, 270). Like the ensign Campuzano, the convicts confront their condition in a spirit of low-grade Stoicism.

Ginés de Pasamonte also attempts to assert his place in the convicts' social hierarchy. Bound with chains, fetters, and manacles, he makes an impressive sight that suggests that he is particularly dangerous or notorious, and one of the guards explains that his crimes exceed the total sum of those committed by all the other convicts in the chain. In conversation with Don Quixote, Ginés proves less willing than his fellow convicts to offer a verbal account of himself. To the guard's statement that he has two names – Ginés de Pasamonte and Ginesillo de Parapilla – he protests that the first one is accurate both onomastically and toponymically. To Don Quixote's general curiosity about the captives and their sentences, he first responds with an intriguing refusal:

> Señor caballero, si tiene algo que darnos, dénoslo ya, y vaya con Dios; que ya enfada con tanto querer saber vidas ajenas; y si la mía quiere saber, sepa que yo soy Ginés de Pasamonte, cuya vida está escrita por estos pulgares. (II. 22, 271)

> If you, sir, have anything to give us, give it to us at once, and God speed, for you are becoming tiresome with all this inquisitiveness about the lives of others. If you want to know about mine, let me tell you that I am Ginés de Pasamonte, whose life has been written by these fingers.

Several motives lie behind this brief statement. In the first instance, Ginés asserts that he is more important than the other convicts by refusing to tell his story. He joins the others in his readiness to receive any alms that the knight has to give, but he dismisses any wish to inquire into their lives as unseemly. The expression that he uses to reprove Don Quixote's curiosity – 'saber vidas ajenas' – recalls the preoccupation in picaresque fiction with gossip and slander, as well as Cipión's repeated warnings against backbiting in *El coloquio de los perros*.[28] Ginés's refusal, however, does not necessarily follow from a general unwillingness to reveal the details of his life experience. The crucial point lies in his preference for written over oral communication. In effect, he declares that he is simultaneously living and recording the events and circumstances that he has known; his life is both the sum of his experiences and the book that he is writing about them, under the title *La vida de Ginés de Pasamonte*. The primary value that he assigns to his book is monetary. When a guard explains that the manuscript has been left in pawn for two hundred *reales*, Ginés announces his firm intention to retrieve it. He prefers to report his experience in written form because he expects to make money from his book, and he refuses to give an oral account of himself on the principle that what can be sold at a profit should not be given away for free.

Ginés's statements in praise of his book indicate its generic affiliations. When Don Quixote asks if the book is good, Ginés replies by comparing it to popular prose narratives:

> Es tan bueno ... que mal año para *Lazarillo de Tormes* y para todos cuantos de aquel género se han escrito o escribieren. Lo que le sé decir a voacé es que trata verdades, y que son verdades tan lindas y tan donosas, que no pueden haber mentiras que se le igualen. (II. 22, 271–2)

> It's so good ... that it will show up *Lazarillo de Tormes* and all of that kind that have been written or ever will be written. All I will say about it is that it deals with facts, and facts so pretty and amusing that no lies could match them.

Ginés announces the association of his *Vida*, and of the convicts' narratives in general, with picaresque fiction. As Claudio Guillén has noted, the reference here to *Lazarillo de Tormes* and to other books of the same kind is one of the first testimonies to readers' awareness of a common body of low mimetic narratives centred on the lives of rogues and criminals, an attitude inspired by the popularity of Mateo Alemán's *Guzmán de Alfarache*, published in two parts (1599, 1604) at the time of the composition of the first part of *Don Quixote*.[29] Despite the direct mention of *Lazarillo de Tormes* (1543) – a text generally regarded as the first example of the Spanish picaresque – Cervantes's narrative recalls Alemán's widely read and influential book. Dunn suggests that 'Ginés de Pasamonte' is an alias or pseudonym that the character Ginesillo has chosen for its phonetic echo of 'Guzmán de Alfarache' (217). In his general situation Ginés also resembles the central character of Alemán's fiction, who reveals to the reader that he is writing his confessional narrative from the bench of a Spanish galley. Cervantes engages here in various kinds of literary play and parody. A standard picaresque text poses as a truthful first-person narrative although it is clearly a fiction; Cervantes offers us a convict bound for the galleys who claims to be writing the true history of his own life. Unlike Alemán's hero, Ginés is unrepentant of his past and expresses little regret over his second criminal sentence, since the galleys will grant him sufficient ease ('sosiego') to return to writing his book. Ginés also sets out a discursive paradox. As he explains to Don Quixote, his method of composition posits an exact correspondence of life and letters, which means that his book can never be completed: '¿Cómo puede estar acabado … sin aún no está acabada mi vida?' (How can it be finished … when my life is not yet finished?) (I. 22, 272). Facing his condition with Stoic tenacity and a sense of comedy, he knows the value of a jest at a time when jests are few.

Critical discussion of Ginés de Pasamonte has centred on Cervantes's reaction to *Guzmán de Alfarache*, largely in terms of a relationship that Guillén has described as one of genre and counter-genre.[30] On this reading, *Don Quixote* is in part a creative response to the emerging popular genre of picaresque fiction. Dunn's recent analysis offers a nuanced account of the Cervantes's complex reframing of diegetic and mimetic issues raised by Alemán's narrative. Ginés de Pasamonte resembles Don Quixote in that 'he is both a reader and a writer of his life' (214). He has interpreted the patterns of picaresque fiction 'as desirable modes of action' and as models that he can imitate and surpass in his life (214). He also recalls Don Quixote in his aspiration to transform his experience into 'total discourse,' eliminating 'the difference between story and diegesis' (214). Given this design, Ginés fails to grasp that confessional narrative depends on a particular temporal scheme. In the case of both Lazarillo and Guzmán, the narrator has marked off a period of his life and tells the story of that time from a perspective that grants it structure and significance. Ginés, in contrast, can see no end point other than his own demise and 'wants, absurdly, to hoard his pages until his dying breath' (216). Cervantes's convict and writer has 'stolen the echo' of the name of a famous fictional *pícaro* without understanding the meaning of his narrative, and he illustrates a particular flaw in the partial imitation of literary models. In the form of imitation that Ginés has adopted, 'Guzmán's literary example will produce charlatans and mountebanks' (219).

The range of generic allusions in the presentation of Ginés de Pasamonte, however, is not limited to the picaresque. In his view of the galleys as a place where he will find sufficient ease to resume the composition of his manuscript, Cervantes's convict offers a variant of the motif of retreat for the purposes of reflection and writing. He resembles the noble Pedro de Aguilar in his intention to write while he is serving in the galleys. Although his low mimetic convict's narrative contrasts sharply with Aguilar's heroic sonnets on the defenders of La Goleta, both characters present an unexpected version of the pastoral tradition of creative retirement, in which the *otium* of classical pastoral is transposed to the galleys. Ginés also recalls the traditions of the theatre. As Dunn has noted, he bears the Spanish version of the Latin 'Genesius,' the name of a Roman actor who converted to Christianity, died as a martyr, and became the patron saint of actors (218). In his dual names and his range of generic associations, Ginés evokes the figure of the artist as a shape-changer, a role appropriate to the place that he claims for himself in the anti-society of the convicts.

The name and role that Ginés assumes in Part II of *Don Quixote* confirm his association with the theatre. He appears at one of the inns where Don Quixote and Sancho have taken lodging, disguised as Maese Pedro, an itinerant entertainer who travels from one village to another with a divining monkey and a set of puppets. Maese Pedro invites the villagers to put questions to his monkey at a price, in a carnival turn that recalls Berganza's role as the 'perro sabio' among the company of soldiers in *El coloquio de los perros*. With his set of puppets he stages repeated performances of a single play that draws its plot and characters from Iberian ballads on a heroic incident from the Carolingian cycle: Don Gaiferos's rescue of his beloved Melisendra from captivity among the Moors in Sansueña. When he offers to set up his puppet theatre at the inn, the innkeeper is delighted, since he knows 'the famous puppeteer' by reputation and describes his show as a fine and well-produced play, at least by the local standard (II. 25, 234). In its romance plot and popular venue Maese Pedro's puppet show presents typical features of popular Spanish theatre in Cervantes's time. The description of the performance in *Don Quixote* depicts the heroic rescue of Melisendra in a comic light, in part by juxtaposing popular romance with the conventions of classical epic.

Cervantes's narrator begins the account of the puppet show by citing the famous half line that opens the second book of Vergil's *Aeneid*, in Gregorio Hernández de Velasco's Spanish translation (1555; rev. 1574):

'Callaron todos, tirios y troyanos' (All fell silent, Tyrians and Trojans) (II. 26, 239). In Vergil's text this verse marks a moment of expectation and attentiveness in the court of Tyre, as Aeneas prepares to recount at Dido's request the fall of Troy and his flight from the burning city:

> Conticuere omnes intentique ora tenebant;
> inde toro pater Aeneas sic orsus ab alto:
>   Infandum, regina, iubes renouare dolorem,
> Troianas ut opes et lamentabile regnum
> eruerint Danai, quaeque ipse miserrima uidi
> et quorum pars magna fui. quis talia fando
> Myrmidonum Dolopumue aut duri miles Vlixi
> temperet a lacrimis? (II. 1–8)

> The room fell silent, and all eyes were on him,
> As Father Aeneas from his high couch began:
> 'Sorrow too deep to tell, your majesty,
> You order me to feel and tell once more:
> How the Danaans leveled in the dust
> The splendor of our mourned-forever kingdom –
> Heartbreaking things I saw with my own eyes
> And was myself a part of. Who could tell them,
> Even a Myrmidon or Dolopian
> Or ruffian of Ulysses, without tears?'

Vergil uses standard rhetorical techniques to announce the epic themes of warfare and male heroism. The silence of the audience at the court and Aeneas's sorrow at the prospect of recalling the destruction of his ancestral city emphasize the gravity of his subject and its stylistic demands. The rhetorical question that he poses – who, even among the enemies of Troy, could relate these events without weeping? – is a formulaic device intended to elicit the sympathy of his listeners and stress the burden of his tale. In its martial theme and high stylistic register, this statement consciously marks the seriousness of epic narrative. The Spanish translation cited by Cervantes adds a gloss to the opening half line that makes explicit its performative context. To Vergil's 'all fell silent' Hernández adds 'Tyrians and Trojans,' identifying the epic audience. As the account of the puppet show unfolds, it plays on the ironic contrast between the high form of classical epic and the low mimetic features of popular theatre.

This contrast emerges in the context of performance, in the actions of the characters, and in the techniques of representation. The puppet show takes place in a rural Spanish inn, and its spectators are the innkeeper and his modest guests, a group entirely unlike the leaders of Tyre and Troy. Although the show begins with an impressive chorus of martial sounds, it soon displays an anti-heroic cast typical of low mimetic forms. Many of the details of its staging are anachronistic, and the puppets are shown to act in ways that undercut their heroic status. Don Gaiferos plays backgammon in Paris, indifferent to the captivity of his beloved; Charlemagne threatens to strike the negligent knight with his sceptre; Melisendra spits and wipes her mouth on her sleeve after an impudent Moor has dared to steal a kiss. Given the chaotic events on stage, the silence of the audience does not last long. Don Quixote becomes a garrulous spectator, interrupting the performance to protest at its digressions and inaccuracies. His attitude shifts, however, when Don Gaiferos and Melisendra take flight from Sansueña with the Moors in close pursuit. Suddenly convinced of the reality of what he is seeing, Don Quixote draws his sword and, in a flurry of 'cuts, slashes, downstrokes, and backstrokes,' destroys Maese Pedro's puppets. The Vergilian 'conticuere omnes' is a joke with a satisfyingly long fuse, which unfolds from the initial dissonance between the citation and its context to Don Quixote's intervention in the stock role of the boastful and gratuitously violent soldier.

The account of the puppet show invites us to consider both the contrast between classical epic and low mimetic popular theatre and the extent of the artistic effects that they may hold in common. Aeneas holds the Tyrian court in awed silence as he relates the sad history of Troy's fall, while Maese Pedro cannot control his audience and struggles to keep his show going against a barrage of objections and interruptions. In its abrupt conclusion Maese Pedro's performance nonetheless attests to the mimetic efficacy of art, even in conditions that seem unpromising. After Don Quixote has destroyed the puppets, he recognizes his error but explains that he acted in good faith:

> Real y verdaderamente os digo, señores que me oís, que a mí me pareció que todo lo que aquí ha pasado que pasaba al pie de la letra: que Melisendra era Melisendra, don Gaiferos don Gaiferos, Marsilio Marsilio, y Carlomagno Carlomagno: por eso se me alteró la cólera, y por cumplir con mi profesión de caballero andante, quise dar ayuda y favor a los que huían, y con este buen propósito hice lo que habéis visto. (II. 26, 247)

> In very truth I assure you gentlemen now listening to me that everything that has taken place here seemed to me to take place literally. Melisendra was Melisendra, Don Gaiferos Don Gaiferos, Marsilio Marsilio, and Charlemagne Charlemagne. That was why my anger was aroused, and to be faithful to my calling as a knight-errant I tried to aid and protect those who fled. These good intentions of mine produced what you have seen.

Don Quixote has surrendered himself to the theatrical illusion, showing himself to be as susceptible to the popular stage as he is to the printed word. His actions are mad in that he crosses the essential boundary between the audience and the actors, but his conviction that the characters before him have substance is central to our experience of the theatre. As Don Quixote tells Sancho after their encounter with the actors of *Las cortes de la muerte*, for the duration of a dramatic performance the actors on stage *are* what they appear to be (II. 12, 121). It is striking that the puppet show creates this illusion despite its poor technical quality and its numerous improbabilities and anachronisms. Maese Pedro offers a case study in the boundary conditions of art. Although his show does not inspire the respect and awe accorded to epic poetry, it nonetheless produces an adequate mimetic effect.

In his changes of name and his forays into picaresque fiction and public theatre, Ginés de Pasamonte represents the popular artist as trickster. He also conforms to this model in the motives that he reports for his creative activity. He assesses his *Vida* in terms of its cash value, and he tells Don Quixote that he will not correct the improprieties of his puppet show so long as they do not affect the willingness of his audience to pay: 'que como yo llene mi talego, siquiera represente más impropiedades que tiene átomos el sol' (as long as I fill my pocket, it's no matter if I show as many inaccuracies as there are motes in a sunbeam) (II. 26, 244). His preoccupation with monetary gain reflects the early modern critique of popular forms for reducing literature to a marketable commodity. It is clear, however, that for Ginés the profitable uses of narrative are not solely financial. As a convict he is well aware that he is bound for the galleys, and storytelling offers him a means of delaying or re-directing his journey.

The text of *Don Quixote* tells us more about the Spanish galleys for which Ginés and his fellow convicts are bound, although it is not quick to disclose this information. Towards the end of their travels Don Quixote and Sancho spend several days in Barcelona (II. 61–6). This episode places the two central characters for the first time in an urban centre, in contact with conditions of early modern culture that Don Quixote has set aside or denied. The city affords them their first view of the sea and of the galleys that move on its surface, and in the course of their stay they visit one of the ships. Here, as elsewhere in Barcelona, they are spectators rather than actors, and in this case they find what they see and hear hard to understand and at times frightening. When Sancho boards the galley, the oarsmen lift him off his feet and pass him over their benches from the stern of the ship to the prow and back, in a ritualized action that recalls the violent death of Barbarroja's son at the hands of his crew in the captive's tale. Once the galley sets out for sea Sancho is frightened at every aspect of its navigation: the noise of the ship's yard as it is lowered and raised, the sight of the half-naked slaves and convicts at the oars, the scourge of the boatswain, the apparently lifeless silence of the crew. He perceives the men aboard the ship as 'diablos' (devils) and 'demonios' (demons) and the galley itself as a place of negative enchantment: 'Ahora yo digo que éste es infierno, o, por lo menos, el purgatorio' (I say this is hell, or at least purgatory) (II. 63, 524). Schooled in literary conventions through his long journey at Don Quixote's side, Sancho equates the galley with the demonic lower world of romance. Its operations, however, have a more prosaic explanation. The galley is an instrument of modern warfare; the silence and obedience of its crew are central to the structure of command and military discipline. Such order is of course at odds with Don Quixote's ethos of individual heroism and with the instinct for peace and bodily pleasure that marks Sancho's peasant character. In its discipline and contained violence, the galley reveals the destiny that awaits Ginés de Pasamonte. Chained to an oarsman's bench, he will make his essential but non-heroic contribution to Spain's naval adventures, in a task that parallels the role of Lázaro de Tormes's father as a muleteer in the army of Charles V.

The description of the galley in Barcelona leads us to question Ginés's earlier statements about his current sentence and his *Vida*. It seems unlikely that service in the galleys will furnish him with leisure for writing, or that he will make any progress on his manuscript. As Dunn has argued, Ginés makes these claims in terms that raise doubts about their veracity (213). Ginés states that the truths recorded in his manuscript are 'tan lindas y tan donosas' (so pretty and amusing) that no lies can match them. Given the standard opposition in Renaissance poetics between the attractive surfaces of fiction and the hard substance of truth, this assertion of aesthetic superiority suggests that the 'truths' of Ginés's manuscript are not so true as he claims. This tension undermines even his assertion concerning the prior sentence that he has served in the galleys. The phrase in which he makes this claim – 'ya sé a qué sabe el bizcocho y el corbacho' (I know by this time the taste of the biscuit and the lash) (I. 22, 272) – owes more to the phonetic and metaphorical play of the convicts' anti-language than to the direct statement of truths. As Ginés deploys his strategies of verbal display and diversion, the tale that he tells Don Quixote takes on the bravado and mendacity of a rogue's narrative or a soldier's tale.

As convict and trickster, Ginés embraces popular forms that offer a modest financial profit and some practical advantages appropriate to his way of life. When Don Quixote sets the convicts free in Part I, he asks them to carry their chains to Dulcinea and to tell her of his great adventure in liberating them. Ginés replies that it is impossible for them to comply with this request, since the convicts must flee one by one to elude the authorities who will come to pursue them. The manuscript and the puppet show are activities compatible with the isolated and constrained existence of a fugitive. On the road with his pen and his puppets, Ginés can pass from one village to the next, filling his purse and saving his skin. His strategies of evasion and diversion have an obvious benefit. Through writing and performance Ginés can postpone for an extended period his destiny as an unwilling oarsman in the Hapsburg navy. The king's law has condemned him to the royal galleys; by means of literary activities, he has directed his life to a very different end: the galleys of a printed book. If Ginés must end up *en galeras* he hopes to determine which kind of *galeras* these will be. In this context his bravado and ingenuity are understandable and, to some degree, attractive. The motive for his anti-heroic conduct is not cowardice, but a reasonable desire to forestall his fate in the galleys and avoid exposure to the risks of modern warfare. Popular art enables Ginés to play for time against the threat of death.

Cervantes presents his common soldiers and convicts as practised schemers. These characters use visual display and linguistic devices to assert their separate identity as members of violent subcultures. Skilled in storytelling and verbal competition, they rely on their ingenuity and on their mastery of artifice. The false captives of the *Persiles*, in contrast, are new to the arts of narrative and display. Given their inexperience, they are unable to defend their story of suffering in Algiers and on the galleys of its corsairs against the pointed questions of a village official who has direct experience of captivity. The discovery that their claims about Algiers are inventions exposes them to punishment as vagabonds who are exploiting for their own benefit the public desire to give alms for the redemption and relief of Christian captives. The judicial threat here is genuine, but the false captives win over the local justices by changing their story and expressing an intent to enlist in the Army of Flanders. A shift in the terms of the false captives' narrative allows them to avoid a sentence of forced military service and to establish a relationship of compassion and conviviality with their judges.

The two false captives appear in a Spanish village that the narrator of the *Persiles* chooses not to name. They are wearing the typical clothing of men recently ransomed from captivity, and they have set out on the ground beside them objects that offer evidence of recent imprisonment in Algiers: a painted cloth that shows the city and its surroundings and two large chains, 'insignias y relatoras de su pesada experiencia' (emblems and witnesses of their harsh experience) (343). One of the two cracks a whip in the air, as he addresses a crowd of villagers 'con voz clara y en todo estremo experta lengua' (with a clear voice and a most able tongue) (343). The attention to physical signs and gestures, to the receptiveness of the crowd, and to the speaker's eloquence stresses the peformative and affective aspect of the relationship between the captives and the villagers.

The eloquent captive focuses his discourse on the painted map of Algiers. He begins with a general characterization of the city as a centre of vice and crime, and then turns to specific images on the map: the port; an Algerian galley with twenty-two benches of oarsmen; the corsair captain Dragut, holding aloft a bleeding arm that he has severed from one of his crew; four Christian galleys in pursuit of Dragut's ship. The captive controls the attention of his audience through directive phrases – 'Esta, señores, que aquí veis pintada, es la ciudad de Argel' (This city, sirs, that you see painted here is Algiers); 'estas cuatro galeras que aquí veis' (these four galleys that you see here) – and he gradually narrows the visual focus to two beleaguered galley slaves on a common bench, which he claims to be past images of himself and his fellow former captive.[31] He also invites his audience to imagine the harsh words of Dragut as he menaces and insults his Christian crew. The gloss of the images on the map is intended to move the villagers to charity through a vivid appeal to the senses of sight and hearing. For all his eloquence, however, the captive recognizes the reductions and restrictions of the painted image. He describes the port of Algiers as an image 'deste pequeñuelo puerto que aquí va pintado' (of this little harbour that is painted here) and Dragut's galley as 'este bajel que aquí veis reducido a pequeño, porque lo pide así la pintura' (this ship that here you see reduced to a small size, because this is what the art of painting requires).[32] He qualifies with 'quizá' (perhaps) his exhortation that the villagers attend with their inward 'ears' to the menacing words that a visual image cannot supply. Evoking the experience of captivity presents some further difficulties. The terms in which the captive describes Algiers are so generic that they convey no specific knowledge of the city. The image of the severed arm uses what Elaine Scarry has called a language of agency to displace suffering from a human subject to an isolated body part and so distances the audience from the events that are meant to evoke its sympathy. The painting of Algiers is central to the appeal that the false captives present, but it has limitations that affect their performance.

It is the misfortune of the false captives that one of the two local justices, or *alcaldes*, identifies himself as a former captive who spent five years in Algiers and rowed in Dragut's galley. When his questions about the fate of Dragut's ship and the topography of the city reveal the ignorance that underlies the gloss on the painted map, the *alcalde* declares that he has exposed the two youths as contrivers of a deceitful scheme to appropriate alms for self-interested purposes and states his intention to sentence each of them to a hundred lashes and a term of service in the galleys. The *alcalde* exercises a rough and summary justice. On criminals who have falsely presented themselves as former slaves in the galleys of the Algerian corsairs, he has decided to impose a sentence of penal servitude as *forzados* in the navy of the Spanish monarchy.

Faced with the prospect of this sentence, the eloquent youth offers a different account of himself and his companion. He admits that they are not captives returned from Algiers and reveals that they are both students who have left university with the goal of trying their fortunes in Italy and Flanders:

> quiero que sepa el señor alcalde que nosotros no somos cautivos, sino estudiantes de Salamanca, y en la mitad y en lo mejor de nuestros estudios, nos vino gana de ver mundo y de saber a qué sabía la vida de la guerra, como sabíamos el gusto de la vida de la paz. (347)

> I want your Honour the Mayor to know that we are not captives, but students from Salamanca, and at mid-way and in the best part of our studies, we felt the wish to see the world and to know what the life of war was like, since we had experienced the pleasures of the life of peace.

To the threat of forced service in the galleys the youth opposes voluntary enlistment in the infantry. That the students come from Salamanca suggests that they have begun a formal preparation in law, and their decision to abandon their studies may reflect the declining opportunities for *letrados* in a bureaucratic sector declining in size and increasingly attractive to members of the nobility (Serés 117–18). The familiar motives of adventurousness and a desire for change are also at play. Prompted by a desire to see new parts of the world and to know a different kind of life, the two students have taken to the road that leads to Flanders. Here their knowledge of legal traditions allows them to temper the rigour of the local *alcalde*. The eloquent youth appeals to the concept of equitable judgment, reminding the *alcalde* that a prudent judge must balance justice against mercy. In mitigation of their attempt to misappropriate alms, he explains the circumstances of their scheme. The painted cloth is a prop that the students purchased from other false captives; the purpose of their rhetorical performance is to raise money to support themselves during their journey; the funds that they have raised are minimal. The claim that neither their crime nor the damage that it has caused should invoke judicial rigour receives a favourable hearing. The second of the *alcaldes* states that he cannot agree to the sentence that his fellow judge intends to impose and offers instead to entertain the students in his house and to aid them in their journey, on the condition that they proceed directly to their destination. The first *alcalde*, now moved to compassion, offers to take the youths to his own house and share with them his knowledge of Algiers. The prospect of public shame is transformed into a gesture of good will and hospitality.

Forcione has described the adventure of the false captives as a theatrical episode that recreates the mimetic limitations and the performance conditions of Maese Pedro's puppet show. The pattern of rapid movement to a crisis, a 'moment of potential disaster and highest comic intensity' that is resolved through a fortunate reversal, is drawn from the traditional Spanish interlude, or *entremés* (Cervantes, *Aristotle* 170). Like the itinerant puppeteer, the false captives evoke through their performance a lower world of captivity and invite the audience to take action in order to release the characters in the dramatic tableau from a condition of bondage. In both cases weaknesses in the quality of staging and narration raise questions related to verisimilitude and the engagement of the audience. The false captives resemble Maese Pedro in their attempt to earn a living through a trickster's display, but when their performance is challenged they resort to an honest appeal rather than to the skills of defiance and bravado through which the puppeteer defends his art.[33]

As in other texts, Cervantes draws in unexpected ways on the conventions of satire. The framework of the *entremés* accommodates central Cervantine themes: the interaction of arms and letters, the tempering of justice with mercy, the renunciation of revenge through acts of kindness (Forcione, *Cervantes, Aristotle* 171). The presentation of the *alcaldes* and of the false captives shifts over the course of this brief episode. In satirical narratives and interludes from early modern Spain, the village *alcalde* is a stock figure, subject to petty corruption and deaf to the qualities of justice.[34] The first of the *alcaldes* conforms to this pattern in his summary judgment, but he turns against type when he responds with compassion and generosity to the appeal for clemency. The young student anchors his argument in the skills and wit that he and his companion will bring to the soldier's life, to the benefit of king and commonwealth:

> dejen a los míseros que van su camino derecho a servir a su Majestad con la fuerza de sus brazos y con la agudeza de sus ingenios, porque no hay mejores soldados que los que se transplantan de la tierra de los estudios en los campos de la guerra; ninguno salió de estudiante para soldado, que no lo fuese por estremo, porque cuando se avienen y se juntan las fuerzas con el ingenio y el ingenio con las fuerzas, hacen un compuesto milagroso, con quien Marte se alegra, la paz se sustenta y la república se engrandece. (349)

> release these poor men who are on the straight road to serve his Majesty with the force of their arms and the sharpness of their wits, because there are no better soldiers than those who move from the homeland of studies to the battlefields of war; no one left the student's life to be a soldier who was not the best of soldiers, because when force is reconciled and combined with wit, and wit with force, they make a wondrous compound, with which Mars rejoices, peace is maintained, and the commonwealth is enlarged.

Since students possess both the strength of youth and the acuity that studies can impart, they will make the best soldiers, prepared to serve the king in his wars and guarantee his peace. This account of enlistment as a moral option, in opposition to a life of fraud and vagrancy, recalls the variant of satire that assigns a positive value to military service.

In pardoning the students whom he was so eager to condemn, the *alcalde* does not so much condone their fraud as accept their arguments in mitigation and recognize the ingenuousness that they must remedy before they proceed further on the road to Flanders. Eloquence and an appeal to clemency have inspired compassion and engaged the rites of hospitality, enabling the students to redirect their destination away from forced service in the galleys.

Through common soldiers returned from military campaigns, convicts bound for the galleys, and false captives on the road to Cartagena, Cervantes presents narratives that reflect the experience of those who served in the lower ranks of Spain's imperial forces. The tales and performances of these characters are variants of anti-romance. They follow the general model of picaresque fiction, but they engage other forms, from the classical genres of epic and pastoral to popular theatre and the oral pattern of the soldier's tale. They also imitate the languages of contest and display that sustain the structures and values of a subculture of military service that exists in opposition to the dominant social order. Cervantes recognizes both the dangers and the attractions of this anti-society. His texts take the measure of the violence and disorder that soldiers and convicts bring to civil society. At the same time, they explore the effectiveness and practical uses of oral performance and popular narrative. Vicente de la Rosa holds the villagers spellbound with his tales of high heroism, although they recognize that his riches are deceptive and his stories improbable. Through the invention and artifice of the interlinked narratives that Campuzano presents to his companion Peralta, the two men celebrate the values of friendship and conviviality. In his *Vida* and his puppet show, Ginés de Pasamonte offers popular entertainment and avoids the penal servitude to which he has been sentenced. Through the inventive accounts that they offer of themselves, the false captives in the *Persiles* dissuade the local authorities from sending them to the galleys and engage the rites of hospitality. If Cervantes is invested in the possibilities of heroic conduct in restrictive circumstances, he also shows an interest in the uses of narrative under limiting conditions. The performances of his characters in village squares, urban lodging houses, and country inns confer the pleasures of artifice and of community.

Conclusion

Alfred supposed bits of dream would always work out through him now – the way that tiny shrapnel splinters would sometimes break up through his skin, finally leave him.

A.L. Kennedy, Day (2007)

The canonical literature of war centres on grand designs. Homeric epic celebrates heroic figures from a remote past who demonstrate the moral and physical qualities of male excellence in close combat. The goal of the Homeric hero is to be the best among peers, an attainment that garners the fame that preserves men's names against the force of time. The heroes are also founders of ruling houses, and their stories trace the lineage of families marked by warfare and its aftermath. The epic of battle and siege finds its counterpart in classical tragedy, with its focus on the difficulties of homecoming and the effects of violence and retribution on ruling families. In the *Aeneid* imperial ideas assert themselves among the grand themes of epic. By engaging the didactic tradition of the poet who describes the principles of natural philosophy, Vergil projects a cosmic order that sustains the myths and images of Rome's imperial state. His epic provides cosmological origins for Roman dominion and places the particular events of Roman history within the overarching structure of the universe. The shield of Achilles is an icon that celebrates Rome's wars of conquest and expansion and the triumph of Augustus as emperor of all the world.[1] For many of Vergil's successors the hero's task and identity are linked to questions of secular authority. Renaissance epic accepts a range of heroic themes, and among its prominent concerns are the practice and legitimacy of imperial rule. The tradition that informs the theory and practice of received kinds in Cervantes's time links canonical genres of war to the ethos and acts of martial heroism, the fame of warriors, and the idea of empire.

Cervantes's works in canonical forms express some detachment from these high mimetic concerns, questioning the application of heroic codes to wars waged under state command and the stability of the fame traditionally offered as the reward for singular acts of valour. In *La Numancia* the Roman general Cipión exhorts his troops to renew their commitment to an ethos of heroism that favours the exercise of direct force against the enemy, and he challenges the Numantians to meet his soldiers in open battle. His campaign against the city of Numantia, however, operates through encirclement and attrition, tactics that cannot be reconciled with his stated ideals of heroic conduct. While Cipión's strategic approach spares Roman lives and satisfies his obligations as a leader who must answer to the Roman Senate, it diminishes his claim to heroic status and shifts the moral weight of the conflict to his enemies. Through their fidelity to force and valour, the Numantians make themselves worthy of Fame's accolade. Cipión's tragic reversal illustrates the tensions between the traditional ethos of heroism and the exigencies of a regime that extends its authority on an imperial scale. In *Don Quixote* the interaction of pastoral with higher genres questions the values and rewards of heroic conduct and the motives over which wars are engaged. The pursuit of reputation, whether through military achievement or literary production, is shown to be uncertain, grounded in shifting values and extending fragile returns. Practical pastoralists turn to forms of violence that disrupt the aspirations that Don Quixote has derived from epic poetry and the romances of chivalry. The residents of a village take up arms against neighbours who have offended them, discharge their violence on a scapegoat, and celebrate a victory that the ancients would have commemorated with a monument. The combination of historical kinds questions the codes of valour and fame associated with high mimetic forms.

Through non-canonical genres Cervantes explores less elevated modes of heroism and more customary rewards of military service, stressing conduct appropriate to the conditions of early modern warfare and the community of common soldiers. His works on armed conflict and captivity in the Mediterranean mark a turn to the form of Greek romance and a shift to an ethos of spiritual heroism. Here

Cervantes's characters experience raids and campaigns in the long run of Spain's endemic conflict with the Ottomans and confront battles at sea and captivity in Algiers with constancy and endurance. Fidelity to these values rests on devotional methods and practices. The captives in *El trato de Argel* pray to the Virgin Mary for deliverance, and in *Los baños de Argel* the captives' sufferings replicate figural patterns of exile and martyrdom. The narrative of Ruy Pérez de Viedma in *Don Quixote* affirms the value of constancy. Ruy Pérez enlists for a life of service in the king's armies, falls into captivity at the battle of Lepanto, witnesses the failure of Spain's defences at Tunis and La Goleta, and escapes from Algiers through the redemptive agency of the saintly Zoraida. He sees at first hand the limitations of the traditional heroic ethos, and he adopts a fortitude that leads him, through the ascending movement of romance, to reunion and reconciliation with his original community in Spain.

Cervantes's engagement with soldiers and picaresque fiction contemplates other kinds of community. In *Don Quixote, El casamiento engañoso*, and *El coloquio de los perros*, common soldiers share a culture of violence and freedom that marks their separation from civil society and invites storytelling and public display. Vicente de la Rosa captivates his neighbours and wins Leandra away from her village suitors through his soldier's finery and his tales of exploits in distant battles. The ensign Campuzano tells a story of double deception that displays the bravado of military cultures and ends in gestures that speak to the pleasures of artifice and companionship. Ginés de Pasamonte, convict and author, dedicates himself to forms of popular art, confident that by pleasing a broad audience he will realize material gains and defer his sentence of forced service in the king's galleys. For the false captives in the *Persiles*, the intent to join the community of soldiers deflects the rigour of the law and elicits hospitality from a local justice who was set to condemn them to the galleys. The view from the lower ranks embraces attitudes of fortitude and invention that foster an ethos of community among common soldiers and contrast with the elevated codes of epic and tragedy.

Cervantes proposes that the conditions of early modern warfare demand heroism on a reduced scale. In the sieges of Flanders and the endemic wars of the Mediterranean, appropriate conduct rests on constancy and on a sense of community with those who share the experience of violence and subjection to a life of force. The captive captain, the veterans of Flanders, and the picaresque characters who trade in tales of conflict and captivity practise the fortitude and sodality of common soldiers. The scale of heroism is a question that also underlies many of the adventures of Don Quixote. Dian Fox has described Cervantes's novel as 'a work of fiction that is itself essentially occupied with historical changes in the conception of what constitutes heroic behavior' (20). Don Quixote sets out to perform heroic acts that will secure his fame as a warrior. He regards knight-errantry as a form of knowledge, and he sees his own career as analogous to the poet's progress from the low realm of pastoral to the epic of martial accomplishments. Over the course of his adventures, however, he realizes that the heroism he hopes to exercise is out of time and place and that he must conduct himself according to other norms. An episode that shows this aspect of Don Quixote is his encounter with the carved images of four Christian saints (II. 58).

Don Quixote and Sancho encounter the holy images shortly after their departure from the house of the duke and the duchess. They arrive at a green meadow, where a group of labourers have spread their capes on the ground and are seated together eating, surrounded by several flat objects, each one covered with a white sheet. In conversation with Don Quixote, the labourers explain that they are transporting religious images carved in wooden relief to their village, where they will be placed in an altarpiece that is under construction. They comment on the quality and the cost of the images, noting that out of respect for their pristine condition and fragility they are carrying them draped on their shoulders. At Don Quixote's request they remove the coverings one by one to reveal the images of four apostles and martyrs: St George, St Martin, St James, and St Paul. The representation of these figures follows well-known iconographical conventions, and Don Quixote immediately recognizes and admires the images, praising each saint as a knight-errant who devoted himself to divine matters rather than to earthly challenges and adventures. Don Quixote concludes his remarks with a summary statement comparing the accomplishments of these saintly knights to his own. Sancho expresses his satisfaction with this new kind of adventure and its unusual place in the journeys that he has undertaken with his master.

This scene is characteristic of Cervantine fiction in its engagement of multiple literary models. The meadow is a pastoral setting, and the sharing of food suggests the pastoral rites of hospitality and conversation. Although Don Quixote and Sancho do not eat with the labourers, their encounter nonetheless recalls other episodes in which they are received by rural characters to whom Don Quixote speaks on pastoral themes. The selection of the saints reflects Cervantes's interest in forms that cross the boundary between high and low art. The labourers are constructing an altarpiece in their village, and they have chosen images that engage a strong popular tradition in early modern Spain. At the same time, images of these saints appear in the work of sculptors and court painters. Each one of the labourers' four saints evokes a broad range of visual representations. Patterns from the romances of chivalry also present themselves here. Don Quixote follows his habitual practice of finding correspondences to his favourite romances in the events and images that he encounters, identifying the saints as knights whose holy acts can be compared to chivalric feats of arms.

The generic diversity of this episode raises challenging questions of interpretation. Clemencín argues that Don Quixote's perception of the saints as knights-errant follows from his madness and has a comic effect. On this reading his discourse is a mock encomium that praises religious figures in misconceived terms drawn from the romances of chivalry (1836a). Don Quixote, however, is by no means alone in equating religious faith with force of arms, a relationship that can be traced in the history of specific saints and in the development of Christian evangelism. As Clemencín observes, saints' lives tell us that St George and St Martin were both Roman soldiers before they converted to Christianity (1835b). Three of the saints mentioned in this episode enjoyed special status as patrons and defenders of peoples and nations in early modern Europe: St George in Catalonia, St Martin in France, and St James in Spain. The four saints can be placed in a context of reception and representation that explains the connection between sanctity and the life of arms and warfare. We can consider the terms in which the saints are described and the significance that Don Quixote assigns to each one, particularly when he compares their acts to his own experience. Don Quixote's encounter with these sacred images reflects back on his practice of interpreting the world through the romances of chivalry and modifies his understanding of his own martial ideals.

The association of sainthood with feats of arms is clearly marked in the first three images. St George appears on horseback, transfixing a serpent coiled beneath him with his lance 'con la fiereza que suele pintarse' (with all that fierceness that is usually painted) (II. 58, 471). This traditional iconography informs a long tradition of paintings and sculptures, including art produced for courtly display and political purposes. In two separate paintings of St George (both ca 1504–6), Raphael shows the mounted saint attacking the dragon with lance or sword, against the background of a wooded landscape. Titian evokes these images in his equestrian portrait *Charles V at Mühlberg* (1548), in which the emperor bears a lance as an emblem of his determination to defend Christianity against its enemies. Don Quixote engages this iconography, describing St George as one of the best 'knights-errant' in the 'army of heaven' (II. 58, 472). The image of St Martin also displays a widely diffused incident from the saint's life: his act of giving half his cape to a beggar. In El Greco's painting of this scene (1597–9), prepared for the Chapel of St Joseph in Toledo, St Martin leans down from his mount, extending his cape to the beggar with his right arm. El Greco shows the saint in the damascened armour of a Spanish nobleman, and in the background stands the imperial city of Toledo, a familiar setting that presents St Martin as a timeless exemplar of Christian charity. Don Quixote describes this saint in terms that he knows well as a reader of romances, praising him as 'one of the Christian adventurers,' liberal and brave. *Santiago Defeating the Moors* (1609), a monumental painting by Juan de Roelas for the Cathedral of Seville, shows the miraculous apparition of St James as Spain's militant patron at the ninth-century battle of Clavijo, trampling the Moorish enemies of Ramiro I. Don Quixote calls St James 'a knight, and of the squadrons of Christ' (II. 58, 472).[2]

The account of the image of St Paul again stresses the conventional character of the labourers' representations: 'descubrieron otro lienzo, y pareció que encubría la caída de San Pablo del caballo abajo, con todas las circunstancias que en el retablo de su conversión suelen pintarse' (they raised another cloth which it appeared covered Saint Paul falling from his horse, with all the details that are usually given in representations of his conversion) (II. 58, 472). This standard iconography has an evangelical purpose. The dramatic circumstances presented here lend force to the pivotal moment of St Paul's life: his conversion on the road to Damascus. In responding to the image, Don Quixote remarks on St Paul's status as convert and apostle, describing his transformation from the greatest enemy of Christ's church to its strongest defender. As 'teacher of the Gentiles,' educated in Christ's own school, St Paul also possesses an excellence in letters that complements the true knight's martial skills. The attributes that Don Quixote identifies in the four knights – strength in St George, liberality and charity in St Martin, courage in St James, fortitude and learning in St Paul – confirm his view that his chosen profession is an art and a science that encompasses other skills and forms of knowledge.

Don Quixote's personal concerns and preoccupations are most pronounced in the summary statement that follows his specific remarks on each of the saints. He speaks here on the meaning that he has drawn from this new encounter:

> Por buen agüero he tenido, hermanos, haber visto lo que he visto, porque estos santos y caballeros profesaron lo que yo profeso, que es el ejercicio de las armas; sino que la diferencia que hay entre mí y ellos es que ellos fueron santos y pelearon a lo divino, y yo soy pecador y peleo a lo humano. Ellos conquistaron el cielo a fuerza de brazos, porque el cielo padece fuerza, y yo hasta agora no sé lo que conquisto a fuerza de mis trabajos; pero si mi Dulcinea del Toboso saliese de los que padece, mejorándose mi ventura y adobándoseme el juicio, podría ser que encaminase mis pasos por mejor camino del que llevo. (II. 58, 473)

> I take it as a happy omen, brothers, to have seen what I have; for these saints and knights were of the same profession as myself, which is the calling of arms. Only there is this difference between them and me, that they were saints, and fought with divine weapons, and I am a sinner and fight with human ones. They won heaven by force of arms, for heaven suffereth violence; and I, so far, know not what I have won by dint of my sufferings; but if my Dulcinea del Toboso were released from hers, perhaps with improved luck and a sounder mind I might direct my steps in a better path than I am following a present.

Don Quixote compares himself to the saints and takes note of temporal and spiritual distinctions. Despite his claim that the saints share with him the practice of arms, he insists on the difference between their spiritual conquests in the past and the human challenges that he faces in the present. Paraphrasing Matthew 11:12, he contrasts his own deeds in this world with their holy acts, a high standard that reveals the uncertain nature of his accomplishments. This recognition suggests a shift in the equation of sainthood and knight-errantry, at least as it applies to Don Quixote's pursuit of valour and renown. In the course of his novel adventures in Part II, Don Quixote has lost confidence in the martial ideals that have shaped his conduct and considers other models that will set him on a different path, in anticipation of his conversionary renunciation of the romances of chivalry at the end of his life.[3] His experience encompasses a range of heroic models in the literature of war, from the singular ethos of epic warriors and chivalric knights to the fortitude of Spanish captives and common soldiers who save what they can of art and sodality for pay. On the road that leads to the modern city of Barcelona, Don Quixote contemplates common cause with Ruy Pérez de Viedma and his companions, whose constancy guides them from the demonic world of Algiers to the fulfilment of liberty and community.

Notes

Introduction

1 Characters in *Don Quixote* who present a striking appearance and who speak of themselves in terms that engage models from popular art include the galley slave Ginés de Pasamonte (I. 21) and Don Quixote's neighbour Sansón Carrasco, in his disguise as the Knight of the Mirrors (II. 14). Bound with an extraordinary apparatus of chains and manacles, Ginés is a picaresque anti-hero who is composing a narrative of his own life. Attired in arms with an adornment of green plumes and many small mirrors, Sansón imitates the style of knights in the romances of chivalry. Don Quixote's encounter with Don Diego de Miranda (II. 16) illustrates the importance of dress and physical appearance in indicating aspects of character and social standing. As Jaime Fernández has noted, the meeting with the page is unusual in that the sense of wonder is not mutual; unlike other secondary characters in Part II, the page expresses no reaction at Don Quixote's remarkable appearance (97).
2 Clemencín identifies the reference to Suetonius, *Life of Caesar* I. 87 (1658a).
3 Don Quixote speaks of this natural inclination before he embarks on his third set of adventures (II. 6), when he describes to the women of his household the two worthy paths that men can follow in their lives: 'Dos caminos hay, hijas, por donde pueden ir los hombres a llegar a ser ricos y honrados: el uno es el de las letras; otro, el de las armas. Yo tengo más armas que letras, y nací, según me inclino a las armas, debajo de la influencia del planeta Marte' (There are two roads, my daughters, by which men may reach wealth and honors; one is that of letters, the other that of arms. I have more of arms than of letters in my composition, and, judging by my inclination to arms, was born under the influence of the planet Mars) (II.

6, 83–4). Serés comments on Don Quixote's sense of a 'common vocation' with the page and his appeal here to a 'fraternity of arms' (126).
4 Geoffrey Parker outlines in detail the logistics for the transport of troops and material from Spain to the Lowlands in *The Army of Flanders and the Spanish Road* (80–105).
5 Cervantes engages the strain of satire that places a positive value on military life through his presentation of the career of Tomás Rodaja/Rueda in *El licenciado Vidriera* (Rupp). Serés notes the parallels between Rueda and the page, both forced from the court to pursue their fortunes in military service (128).
6 Don Quixote identifies 'espilorchería' (meanness, stinginess) as a borrowing from Italian. Clemencín notes that Spanish courtiers who had visited Rome introduced this word into their courtly circles at home (1658a). By using this term, Don Quixote claims a familiarity with court culture and emphasizes the interests and attitudes that he shares with the page.
7 This statement is intended to have classical authority, but the attribution that Don Quixote supplies is not reliable. As Clemencín notes, this statement does not appear in the extant plays of Terence (1658a–b).
8 The encounter with the page is one of several episodes that suggest the full extent of the culture of letters that Don Quixote has acquired through his obsessive reading habits. The romances of chivalry have filled his imagination, but his library contains other kinds of imaginative literature – pastoral romances, lyric poetry, vernacular epic verse – and his learning extends to Renaissance ethnographical lore and medieval astronomical theory. In the framework of Cervantes's fiction, it is likely that the page elicits knowledge of soldiers and military values that Don Quixote has garnered from classical and humanist texts.
9 Fussell discusses the literary models that English soldiers applied to their experience in the First World War, to sustain their endurance in trench warfare and to communicate what they had seen and heard to others (155–74). He comments on the popularity among soldiers of the *Oxford Book of English Verse* and on the uses of lyric poetry: 'there are moments in war memoirs when vignettes of rural irony seem the result of a conflation between Hardy and Housman' (164). Hynes includes movies among the popular forms that shaped the expectations and experience of soldiers in the Second World War (30).
10 Hynes draws these phrases from *A Rumor of War*, Philip Caputo's book on his service with the Marines in Vietnam, and he focuses his study on the life writings of common soldiers from the twentieth century. Hynes nonetheless argues that soldiers' narratives present a common pattern over time, one centred on a retrospective account 'of doing and being done to' (3).

11 In his essay on biographical studies of Cervantes, Alberto Sánchez offers a concise account of the documentary and literary evidence and of the conclusions concerning dates and events that can be drawn from it. As Garcés has noted, a detailed and valuable source for Cervantes's life in Algiers is the *Información de Argel*, a collection of testimonies from Cervantes himself and from twelve of his fellow captives concerning his fidelity to Christianity and his conduct towards others in captivity.
12 Garcés surveys the attestations to Cervantes's religious and moral character in the *Información de Argel* (99).
13 Plutarch engages this trope when he describes the conditions of Coriolanus's campaign for the consulship in Rome: 'it was the custom with those who stood for the office to greet their fellow-citizens and solicit their votes, descending into the forum in their toga, without a tunic under it. This was either because they wished the greater humility of their garb to favour their solicitations, or because they wished to display the tokens of their bravery, in case they bore wounds.' Coriolanus initially wins popular support by showing the scars of the many wounds that he has incurred in campaigns for Rome (*Life of Caius Marcius Coriolanus* 14, 15).
14 This discussion of historical factors that qualify Parker's arguments concerning the revolutionary character of military change in early modern Europe follows Black, *European Warfare* 32–54.
15 As Parker has noted, the Dutch attributed their discovery of the volley technique to a study of the methods of warfare recorded in Roman historical texts and military manuals (*Military Revolution* 19). This claim offers one indication of the influence of a humanist culture of writings on military techniques, grounded in classical sources and diffused through the medium of print.
16 Hale studies the representation in visual art of soldiers and of military actions in *Artists and Warfare in the Renaissance*.
17 Frye comments on the ideological cast of medieval chivalric romance, in which the adventures and quests of knights from the courts of Arthur and Charlemagne 'form a ritualized action expressing the ascendancy of a horse-riding aristocracy' and 'express that aristocracy's dreams of its own social function, and the idealized acts of protection and responsibility that it invokes to justify that function' (*Secular Scripture* 56–7).
18 This discussion of the formal poetics of genre and its interaction with creative practice follows Guillén, 'On the Uses of Literary Genre.'
19 Fowler provides a useful survey of the features of literary texts that are generally taken to differentiate one genre from another (60–72).
20 In Fowler's formulation 'kinds' are historical genres, often traceable to classical origins, that are defined by a substantial critical consensus (56).

Cervantes's fictions respond to his awareness of these canonical kinds as they are classified and categorized in Renaissance poetics.
21 De Armas has discussed the influence on Cervantes of the *Rota Virgilii*, or Vergilian Wheel, a schema in medieval poetics that relates the phases of a literary career to the principal genres and styles of Vergil's poetry: pastoral, georgics, epic. In de Armas's view, Caliope's song in *La Galatea* announces a 'career program' based on this schema that culminates in the Christian epic of the *Persiles* ('Cervantes and the Virgilian Wheel' 273–4, 282).
22 Frye outlines the generic features of Menippean satire in his synoptic account in the *Anatomy of Criticism* of continuous prose forms (309–12).
23 Modern criticism of Cervantes has explored in detail his engagement with the principles and debates of Renaissance literary theory. Two foundational studies in this area are Riley, *Cervantes's Theory of the Novel* (1962), and Forcione, *Cervantes, Aristotle and the* Persiles (1970).
24 Riley's 'A Question of Genre' describes the key features of romance and novel in Cervantes and the interplay of the two forms in his fiction, with particular attention to *Don Quixote* and the *Novelas ejemplares*. Frye comments on the novel as 'a fictional approach to history' and on the 'sense of temporal context' that tends to define the form in European literature (*Anatomy* 306–7).
25 Keith discusses the central place of Latin epic in the curriculum of canonical texts and rhetorical exercises that shaped male identity and gender relations in the social and political elite of ancient Rome (8–35).
26 This discussion of the *Persiles* as a work that both engages and questions the privileged conventions of epic poetry follows Armstrong-Roche's comprehensive analysis of this text in relation to classical epic and to the sophisticated and influential model of Heliodorus's Greek romance. Armstrong-Roche describes the reception of the *Ethiopica* by sixteenth-century writers and critics as 'a fascinating chapter in the history of attempts to achieve the ever-elusive reconciliation of the classical and the popular' (6), and he stresses the importance of epic as a 'creative opportunity' through which Cervantes explores contemporary discourses of empire, religion, and politics (8–9). His reading of Persiles and Maximino as characters who revisit and recast the traditional figure of the epic hero (167–204) is of particular relevance to the thematics of warfare.
27 The processes of generic change outlined here are described in Fowler (170–90).
28 Curtius traces the theme of arms and letters to the ancient topos of *sapientia et fortitudo* (wisdom and courage), applied to the heroes of the epic tradition and to the praise of rulers in medieval panegyrics and mirrors of

princes (167–79). Don Quixote develops this theme by following the parts of an epideictic oration – *exordio, narratio, argumentatio, refutatio,* and *peroratio* – and by applying traditional rhetorical formulas intended to move and persuade an audience (Curtius 69–71, 85–9).

29 Hale refers to this passage from Paré's *Apologie and Treatise* in his discussion of the high rates of casualties from deaths in combat, injuries, and infections in the armies of early modern Europe (*War and Society* 120).

30 A humanist statement on the reconciliation of arms and letters can be located in the discourse of Count Ludovico da Canossa in Book I of Castiglione's *Libro del cortegiano* (1528). In setting out the qualities of the ideal courtier, Count Ludovico argues that this figure must be knowledgeable in the area of letters and invokes a traditional argument that places value on letters and poetry because they preserve and transmit the glory that is won through feats of arms: 'Sapete che delle cose grandi ed arrischiate nella guerra il vero stimulo è la gloria ... E che la vera gloria sia quella che si commenda al sacro tesauro delle lettere' (You know that in war what really spurs men on to bold deeds is the desire for glory ... And it is true glory that is entrusted to the sacred treasury of letters) (I. 43, 86). Count Ludovico affirms the importance of arms in defining the courtier's identity – 'estimo che la principale e vera profession del cortegiano debba esser quella dell'arme' (I judge that the first and true profession of the courtier must be that of arms) (I. 17, 51) – but he stresses the use of arms in sports and courtly spectacles and states that the courtier should avoid the seriousness and pride of the professional soldier (I. 21–2, 56–8). In contrast with Cervantes's interest in the conditions of early modern warfare, Castiglione accommodates accomplishments in arms and letters to the forms of role playing and festivity that shape the social world of the Renaissance courtier (Rebhorn 16–17).

31 Cervantes's *Novela del curioso impertinente* (*Story of Ill-Advised Curiosity*) – a short narrative intercalated into the text of *Don Quixote* (I. 33–5) – provides a passage in praise of the courage of early modern soldiers under the conditions of siege warfare that parallels the discourse on arms and letters. Here Lotario marshals logical and rhetorical arguments in an attempt to persuade his friend Anselmo that he should not test the fidelity of his wife, Camila, including an appeal to the grounds on which difficult actions should be undertaken: 'las que se intentan por Dios y por el mundo juntamente son aquellas de los valerosos soldados, que apenas veen en el contrario muro abierto tanto espacio cuanto es el que pudo hacer una redonda bala de artillería, cuando, puesto aparte todo temor, sin hacer discurso ni advertir al manifiesto peligro que les amenaza, llevados en vuelo de las

alas del deseo de volver por su fe, por su nación y por su rey, se arrojan intrépidamente por la mitad de mil contrapuestas muertes que los esperan' (those undertaken for the sake of God and the world together are those of brave soldiers, who no sooner see in the enemy's wall a breach as wide as a cannon ball could make than, casting aside all fear, without hesitating or heeding the manifest peril, borne onward by the desire of defending their faith, their country, and their king, they fling themselves dauntlessly into the midst of the thousand opposing deaths that await them) (I. 33, 406).

32 Presberg discusses the generic features of the mock encomium and its importance as a vehicle of paradoxical discourse in Renaissance culture (27–35).

1. Warriors: Epic and Tragedy

1 The *Iliad* establishes as a central theme of epic the attainment and commemoration of male excellence through singular acts of valour and violence in war. Hardie's comments on the defining features of the Homeric hero make this point clear: '"Best" means, above all, "greatest" in battle; the *aristeia* "(deeds of) excellence" is the label attached to the typical Iliadic episode in which one of the great heroes demonstrates his prowess single-handed in battle' (*Epic Successors* 3). An influential study of the uses of politics and history in Vergilian epic and subsequent texts in this tradition is Quint's *Epic and Empire*. Quint proposes that Latin epic connects narrative structure with an ideology of imperial or dynastic power and that the persistence of epic as a form transmits this pattern through time: 'the equation of power and the very possibility of narrative is a defining feature of the genre' (15).

2 Bakhtin comments on the connection in epic between the concepts of excellence and familial and national origin: 'the world of the epic is the national heroic past; it is a world of "beginnings" and "peak times" in the national history, a world of fathers and of founders of families, a world of "firsts" and "bests"' (13).

3 The recasting of Homeric heroes in Athenian tragedy establishes a long-standing and productive linkage between the two genres. Renaissance writers on poetics confirm this association by according tragedy an elevated position in the hierarchy of genres, often immediately adjacent to epic (Fowler 220).

4 Frye identifies the dual temporal cycle as an aspect of encyclopedic form when he defines epic in relation to his inclusive theory of genres (*Anatomy* 318). He comments on the isolation of the tragic hero and the restriction of his freedom when he discusses tragedy as a specific kind of paradigmatic

narrative (*Anatomy* 208, 212). Frye's analysis suggests some of the principles of selection that govern tragedy's relationship to epic.
5 This discussion of the revisiting in Latin epic of themes and structures from Greek tragedy follows Hardie, *Epic Successors* (20–32, 53–6, 58–60). Hardie's reading of violence and sacrifice in the *Aeneid* stresses Vergil's 'radical contamination of epic with tragedy' (21) and his engagement with the *Oresteia* (27).
6 Nicolopulos offers parallel comment on the importance of Italian models for learned epic in Spain and their assimilation to privileged classical kinds: 'Iberian poets of the period were turning to the Italian *romanzi*, particularly the *Orlando furioso*, for a modern paradigm of dynastic and patriotic epic. Ariosto had become, indeed, the sixteenth-century Virgil: the preferred model for imperialistic epic' (80).
7 Schmidt's 'Development of *Hispanitas*' reviews the historiography of the siege as it informs *La Numancia*, with particular attention to the praise of Numantian valour and sacrifice by Roman historians and the exemplary treatment of the episode by such humanist writers as Antonio de Guevara, Ambrosio de Morales, and Fernando de Herrera.
8 This account of popular theatre as a central factor in the literary career that Cervantes initiates upon his return from captivity follows Canavaggio's biography (*Cervantes* 114–25). Kahn's study places Cervantes in the generation of Spanish dramatists active between 1570 and 1590, prior to the striking popular success of Lope de Vega and the *comedia nueva*, and suggests that in *La Numancia* Cervantes may be continuing a nascent 'attempt at forming a new Spanish national theatre' (127).
9 In the *Adjunta al Parnaso* Cervantes attests to his inclination for the theatre, speaking of the number and quality of the plays that he has written: 'a no ser mías, me parecieran dignas de alabanza, como lo fueron *Los Tratos de Argel, La Numancia, La gran Turquesca, La Batalla Naval, La Jersusalén, La Amaranta o la del Mayo, El Bosque Amoroso, La Unica y La Bizarra Arsinda*, y otras muchas de que no me acuerdo' (if they were not mine, they would strike me as worthy of praise, as were *Los Tratos de Argel, La Numancia, La gran Turquesca, La Batalla Naval, La Jersusalén, La Amaranta o la del Mayo, El Bosque Amoroso, La Unica y La Bizarra Arsinda*, and many others that I do not remember) (1:182–3; I cite Vicente Gaos's edition of Cervantes's *Poesías completas* for the linked texts of the *Viaje del Parnaso* and the *Adjunta al Parnaso*). Canavaggio assigns the composition of *La Numancia* to the period between 1581 and 1585, a date consistent with the chronologies proposed for Cervantes's *comedias* in historical scholarship on his life and works (*Cervantès dramaturge* 18–22).

10 De Armas refers to *La Numancia* as an early expression of Cervantes's sustained interest in the canonical and political dimensions of epic and in 'overgoing' earlier versions of the form ('Cervantes and the Virgilian Wheel' 270).
11 The close combat between Paris and Menelaus in Book III of the *Iliad* establishes a pattern in epic for attempts to resolve conflicts of armies through single combat. Paris defines the terms of his challenge to Menelaus (III. 67–75), and Hector conveys these conditions to Agamemnon and the Greek commanders (III. 86–94). The combat is carefully staged but inconclusive, since the goddess Aphrodite intervenes to save Paris from Menelaus's rage (III. 314–82). In Book XI of the *Aeneid* the Trojans and the indigenous defenders of Latinus's city signal the possibility of reducing their conflict to a combat between the two principal combatants. After the death of Pallas, Aeneas insists that Turnus should present himself in battle (XI. 113–18), and in a council of war Turnus declares that he will accept if the Trojans issue a challenge to single combat (XI. 434–44). Harris notes the tradition of combat by champion in Roman history, describing Scipio Aemilianus as 'the last known monomachist' (38–9). The most influential account of a nocturnal assault in classical epic is the expedition of Nisus and Euryalus against Turnus's encampment in the *Aeneid* (IX. 176–449).
12 Given its date of publication (1594), Tasso's *Discorsi* cannot have directly shaped Cervantes's conception of epic and tragedy in the composition of *La Numancia*. The text is useful, however, for its retrospective view of the Neo-Aristotelian tradition that informs Cervantes's general understanding of the forms and purposes of imaginative literature and as a reflection on the poetics of Renaissance epic by a recognized master of the form. The interest in the theory and practice of Neo-Aristotelian poetics that Cervantes shares with Tasso is discussed at length in Forcione, *Cervantes, Aristotle and the* Persiles.
13 Critical commentary on *La Numancia* has drawn attention to the interplay of epic and tragic patterns in its characters and structure and to the dual focus of its tragic plot. Simerka stresses the relationship of its two dominant genres to warfare and, in particular, to 'the effects of war on individuals' (111). Casalduero reads the play as the tragedy of Numantia and its defenders, articulated through the characters of Morandro, Teógenes, and Viriato (282). De Armas's seminal article argues through comparison to Aeschylus's *The Persians* that Cipión and his generalship can be interpreted as the play's tragic subjects ('Classical Tragedy'). Casalduero comments on Cervantes's interest here in epic materials (262), and King notes *La Numancia*'s affinities with classical and Renaissance epic (201). Discussion of the interaction between the two genres often stresses the tragic qualification

of epic heroism and imperial ideology. Lewis-Smith describes the play as a synthesis of tragicomedy and the 'nationalistic' variant of epic (20). In *Cervantes, Raphael and the Classics*, de Armas presents a comprehensive study of *La Numancia* and its intertexts in classical tragedy and epic – Aeschylus, Homer, Vergil, Lucan – in the context of the transmission of classical models through Renaissance art.

14 Examples of augury through divine speech in Latin epic include the instructions that Aeneas receives from the household gods who have accompanied him from Troy, redirecting his voyage in search of a new homeland from Crete to Italy (*Aeneid* III. 147–71), and the appearance of the river god of the Tiber at the outbreak of the wars in Latium to assure Aeneas that he will achieve victory by forming an alliance with King Evander and locate through a divine sign the site of the city that he is destined to found (*Aeneid* VIII. 31–65). The sign of a swan escaping from an eagle's attack that the nymph Juturna produces to spur Turnus's troops on to battle against the Trojans (*Aeneid* XII. 247–56) recalls the Homeric convention of avian augury. An instance of augury through necromancy that has exercised a strong influence in the European epic tradition is Erictho's prophecy in Lucan's *Bellum ciuile* (VI. 776–820), a clear intertext for the uses of prophecy and prophetic discourse in *La Numancia*.

15 In his study of the social and political uses of spectacle in Livy's *History of Rome*, Feldherr analyses the pre-battle exhortation to the troops as a representation of the authority of the commander and of Rome itself: 'In cataloguing the forces that guarantee a Roman victory, the general puts forward a general interpretation of the world around him ... Often these arguments amount to a comprehensive representation of the universe and its history demonstrating how everything from the landscape of the battlefield, to the power of the gods, to the ancestral *virtus* of the state is working together on the Romans' behalf' (54). As an example of such discourse, he discusses the conduct of the Roman consul Papirius Cursor before the battle of Aquilonia (X. 38–41), noting the close connection between the affective force of the pre-battle speeches on the two sides – Roman and Samnite – and the outcome of the battle.

16 De Armas outlines the medieval debate concerning the competing virtues of *sapientia* and *fortitudo* – associated respectively with Odysseus and Achilles – and discusses the various ways in which this traditional opposition shapes the scrutiny of heroism and imperial values in *La Numancia* (*Cervantes, Raphael* 101–4).

17 The Numantians take care to assert that they are extending an offer of peace not from fear of Roman military force but from respect for Cipión's

reputation as a distinguished general and confidence in his capacity to negotiate with them on fair and equitable terms. Their appeal to Cipión rests on the convention of the meritorious enemy, whose excellence secures a fair contest between the parties and ensures the value of victory. In relation to the characterization of the Spanish leaders and their opponents in *La Araucana*, Davis comments on 'the convention that military parity between parties is always desirable in epic' (21).

18 The Latin sense of *amistad* as a military or political alliance informs Cipión's response to the Numantian embassy. Lewis and Short's *Latin Dictionary* supplies as one of the meanings of *amicitia* 'a league of friendship, an alliance between different nations,' with examples from Caesar, Sallust, and Livy. Maglione describes amity and enmity as the poles of a conflict that opposes Roman hostility and cunning to the bond of friendship that unites the defenders of Numantia in common interest and loyalty. The ambassadors appeal to Cipión on the grounds of utility, but Cipión rejects their friendship even in this pragmatic form (181).

19 Harris reviews Roman attitudes towards war, explaining the central place of warfare in the formation of Roman aristocratic men and the importance of martial achievements for prestige and advancement in public life. Success in Rome's annual military campaigns led to the gradations of a positive public reputation, 'on one level *laus*, on a higher level *gloria*' (17). Braudy stresses the public and performative character of fame in Roman society and the connection between personal esteem and the public good: 'a whole tradition of storytelling about early Roman history emphasized the virtue of symbolic acts in defense of the essential nature of Rome' (56).

20 De Armas compares the nocturnal expedition of Morandro and Leoncio to the parallel raid by Diomedes and Odysseus in the *Iliad*, noting the focus on open force in the presentation of the young warriors in *La Numancia*: 'Although both episodes show the courage of the two warriors who enter the enemy camp, Cervantes has transformed the Numantian mission to emphasize valor over cunning, *fortitudo* over *sapientia*' (*Cervantes, Raphael* 111).

21 Hardie comments on the significance of Cato's suicide in the *Bellum ciuile* in relation to epic's generic interest in cycles of sacrificial violence: 'In the event the manner of Cato's death was such as to rule out any possibility of a resolution to the sacrificial crisis; turning his hand on himself, acting out the roles of both sacrificer and sacrificed in one person, he confounded utterly the distinction between killer and killed on which the logic of Girardian victimization rests' (*Epic Successors* 31).

22 Walzer argues that through general and willing participation in the military cause that has led to the siege, a civilian population compromises its

immunity from attack: 'political integration and civic discipline make for cities whose inhabitants expect to be defended and are prepared, morally if not always materially, to endure the burdens of a siege' (163).

23 Curtius discusses the rhetorical topos of the *puer senex* (98–101); Avalle-Arce comments on the application of this paradox to the exemplary figure of Viriato ('Poesía' 71).

24 In a reading of *La Numancia* and its scriptural intertexts, Stiegler connects the allegorical figures of Hunger, Disease, and War with the destructive forces of apocalypse in Revelations and Ezekiel (570–1) and relates the Duero's prophecy to the vindication of the just and the founding of a new order of unity and concord: 'the glory of this golden age is described as would be the kingdom of God, as a blessed empire where divine wisdom reigns over a world filled with peace and prosperity' (579).

25 It is significant that the end point of the Duero's prophecy is the settlement between the Spanish Crown and the papacy, following the encampment of Alba's army outside Rome in the spring of 1556 and his negotiations for peace on favourable terms with Pope Paul IV. On this occasion the discipline of the Spanish troops and the success of Alba's diplomacy contrasted with the military and moral disorder of the sack of 1527, and the settlement secured papal cooperation with the Hapsburg monarchy and Spanish influence over Rome. Dandelet's study of Rome during the age of imperial Spain discusses Alba's intervention and its effect on subsequent diplomatic relations (532–57); de Armas comments on the literary treatment of these matters in *La Numancia* ('Las mentiras de Proteo'). Recent criticism of the Duero's prophecy has emphasized the historical and political ambiguities of its protean discourse (Johnson; de Armas, *Cervantes, Raphael* 118–35). Kahn notes that the omission of significant historical developments – in particular, the long Islamic occupation of the Iberian peninsula in the Middle Ages and the recent war in Flanders – qualifies its praise of Spanish imperialism (183–5).

26 The interaction of temporal frames is an epic technique that invites reflection on the historical significance of the siege. In her analysis of the play's narrative mode, Bergmann comments that its 'discourse ... is not one of presence but of projection into the future and reflection on the past' (88). De Armas argues that the Duero's prophecy reconstructs Numantia as the foundational site of 'a new imperial myth' through parallels with classical myths of the origins of Rome and its empire (*Cervantes, Raphael* 120). King interprets the conflict of Cipión's army and the Numantian defenders as an encounter between two distant epochs of Spanish history (216). Endress notes that the play combines the present of the fall of Numantia

and the future of imperial Spain with the super-temporal perspective of the allegorical figures (285).

27 Pagden has characterized *pietas* – a concept that combines the exercise of male excellence with loyalty to the community and the common good – as an aspect of Roman imperial myth that 'allowed the classical theory of empire to be absorbed relatively easily by its Christian successors' (29–30).

28 Frances Yates's influential essay analyses the idea of imperial revival that informed the reign of Charles V and its antecedents in medieval and humanist political thought, stressing the significance of imperial symbolism in a period of conflict and uncertainty. Tanner discusses the uses of myth-making and prophecy to sustain the image of Charles V as world emperor and the survival of these practices and concepts during the rule of Philip II (119–45).

29 Simerka comments that in his defence of the tactics of the siege, Cipión 'asserts that he has created new definitions of the terms "honor" and "glory"' (101).

30 Harris discusses *laus* and *gloria* as aristocratic prerogatives that supported the established structures and customs of Roman society, including the traditional authority of highly ranked families (30). Braudy comments on the tension between personal fame and the objectives and values of the state that emerged in the late Republic, as new forms of aspiration and new grades of public honour compromised the authority of the senatorial class (60–5).

31 Braudy analyses the opposition in the *Aeneid* between the vulgar fame diffused through gossip and rumour and the true fame that rests in destiny and divine sanction, in the context of Vergil's response to a 'crisis of fame' in Roman culture (123–8). Hardie comments on the parallels between the Vergilian personification of Fame and the figures of Envy and Fame in Ovid's *Metamorphoses*: '*Fama* is a puffer-up, an inflator, the producer of imposing presences which are in truth nothing but air' (*Ovid's Poetics* 237). Lida de Malkiel discusses the classical antecedents of the concept of fame in medieval Castile, with detailed reference to Cicero (18–22), Vergil (35–44), Ovid (52–62), and Prudentius (80–6). In his *Peristephanon* (*Crown of Martyrs*) Prudentius links fame to glory and secular praise, as cultivated in the civic and military forms of Roman public life (Lida de Malkiel 81). Lida also notes in a number of influential classical works a Stoic critique of the transitory value of worldly fame, most notably in Roman satire, in Cicero's *Somnium Scipionis* (*Dream of Scipio*) and in Macrobius's commentary on this Ciceronian text (87–95).

32 The appeal to clarity in Teógenes's dying words and in the quality of Fame's voice suggests the higher version of fame that Vergil associates with heroic acts committed under the auspices of divine designs (Braudy 125–6). Cesare Ripa's *Iconologia* sets out the attributes of *Fama Buona* (Good Fame): 'Donna con vna tromba nella mano dritta, & nella sinistra vn ramo d'oliua, hauerà al collo vna collana d'oro, alla quale sia per pendente vn cuore, & hauerà l'ali bianche à gl'homeri' (A woman with a trumpet in her right hand, and with an olive branch in her left, she will have a necklace of gold on her neck, to which a heart will be fixed as a pendant, and she will have white wings on her shoulders) (143). According to Ripa's gloss, the trumpet signifies the universal reach of Fame's voice, and the olive branch shows Fame's goodness and the honesty of men who have won fame through illustrious deeds.

33 Citing parallel passages from *La Galatea*, Lope's *Arcadia*, and Petrarch's *Rime*, Stagg proposes that the line in Fame's song 'de Batro a Tile y de uno al otro polo' (from Bactria to Thule and from pole to pole) yokes the ancient Scythian province of Bactria with the northern island of Thule as the limits of the world known to antiquity ('Cervantes' "De Batro a Tile"'). Armstrong-Roche explains that in Vergil's *Georgics* and the *Persiles* 'Thule marks the limits of empire,' and that the journey from Thule to Rome in the *Persiles* is central to its reversal of the traditional movement of empire from Rome outwards (70–3).

34 Fame's 'canto' points to the convention of epic as song, as in the first line of the *Aeneid* and the opening lines of Ariosto's *Orlando furioso*: 'Le donne, i cavallier, l'arme, gli amori / le cortesie, l'audaci imprese io canto' (I sing of knights and ladies, of love and arms, of courtly chivalry, of courageous deeds).

35 King argues that *La Numancia* dramatizes a conflict between 'a primitive, idealized Spain waging a just war in defense of liberty' and the imperial Spain of Cervantes's time, which fought morally challenging wars in the New World and the Lowlands (216). In King's interpretation, the play questions the endurance of empire under conditions of expansion and unjust rule. Simerka argues that the generic instability of the dramatic action reveals the indeterminacy of Spain, as 'the sign that refers simultaneously to the morally victorious Numantians and to the decadent Roman Empire, its achievements in the early modern period shown to be both epic victories and tragic slaughters' (105). Kahn comments that 'sixteenth-century Spain ... identified itself both with the ancient Roman Empire and the Numantians,' and that this duality shapes the play's 'paradoxical portrayal' of both groups (73–4).

2. Defenders: Pastoral and Satire

1 This account of the generic features of pastoral follows Alpers (44–78, 81–93). The standard critical survey of pastoral in early modern Spanish fiction is Avalle-Arce, *La novela pastoril española*. Finello's *Evolution of the Pastoral Novel* is a recent study that emphasizes pastoral communities and spaces and the representation of rustic customs within the idealized framework of pastoral conventions.
2 Alpers discusses the traditional criterion of low style as a defining feature of pastoral (9). Neo-Aristotelian poetics classifies pastoral as one of 'the eight paradigmatic genres' but places it below such received kinds as epic, tragedy, comedy, and satire (Fowler 220–1).
3 Alpers notes that 'convening' is one of the typical gestures of pastoral literature. In classical and Renaissance poetry, shepherds and herdsmen gather to perform songs and dialogues that offer recompense for the sorrows of displacement and lost love. Pastoral conventions depend on communal experience and 'the idea of coming together' (81). In Spanish pastoral fiction, 'camaraderie and community' are central themes (Finello, *Evolution* 59–73).
4 Alpers remarks that at times 'the herdsman's simplicity is a source of moral authority' (50). By convention, the claim to such authority is essential to the critical stance of the satirist.
5 Representative studies of Cervantine pastoral include Avalle-Arce, *Novela pastoril* 197–231; Cozad; Finello, *Pastoral Themes and Forms*; Forcione, 'Cervantes en busca de una pastoral auténtica'; Lowe; McGaha, 'The Sources and Meaning of the Grisóstomo-Marcela Episode'; Randel.
6 Calliope's song takes fame as one of its central themes and stresses the conjunction of martial and literary excellence in the acquisition of this quality. Various writers are praised for their equal possession of the poetic gifts of Apollo and the bellicose skills of Mars: Alonso de Leiva (stanza 3), Alonso de Ercilla (stanza 4), Diego Osorio (stanza 6), Jerónimo Sánchez de Carranza (stanza 53). These poets represent in themselves and their works the union of arms and letters.
7 Alpers traces the classical antecedents of early modern pastoral literature. Theocritus supplies the model for Vergil's *Eclogues*, and Vergil in turn provides the template for Jacopo Sannazaro's *Arcadia* (1504), a series of eclogues linked through prose passages that initiates the sixteenth-century vogue of pastoral romance (66–7).
8 This discussion of the engagement in Renaissance pastoral with public duties and the concerns of an active life is based on Marinelli (57–74).

9 The interest in Renaissance pastoral literature in public affairs and attainments reflects the influence of Italian models. Florentine civic humanism stresses the pursuit of fame and honours in the secular world and the application of historical and rhetorical studies to politics and government (Martines 268–70).
10 Empson discusses the practice in traditional pastoral of presenting characters from distinct tiers of society: 'the effect was in some degree to combine in the reader or author the merits of the two sorts; he was made to mirror in himself the effective elements of the society he lived in' (12). Alpers comments that this reading of pastoral reflects 'Empson's view that poetry is rhetorical and social' and responds to 'the realities of given societies and historical moments' (37).
11 Fussell uses the term 'satires of circumstance' to analyse scenes in memoirs and literary texts that capture the ironic encounter of innocence and experience among soldiers in the First World War (3–35). As Fussell notes, the concept is general in its application: 'Every war constitutes an irony of situation because its means are so melodramatically disproportionate to its presumed ends' (7).
12 The term *regidor* – generally translated as 'alderman' – refers in early modern Spanish to an official of a city or town who is responsible for managing public funds and resources. The relevant entry in the first edition of the *Diccionario* of the Real Academia Española (1726–39) provides this definition: 'Se llama tambien la persona destinada en las Ciudades, Villas or Lugares para el gobierno economico' (This is also the term for the person appointed for the domestic management of cities, towns, and villages) (5:544b).
13 Source accounts for the first three of these Roman exemplars can be found in Livy's *History of Rome*: II. 10.1–13 for Horatius Cocles; II. 12.1–13.5 for Gaius Mutius Scaevola; VII. 6.1–6 for Marcus Curtius. Suetonius's *Life of Julius Caesar*, I. 31–3, describes his crossing of the Rubicon. Gómara's chronicle describes Cortés's destruction of his ships as an expression of his determination to proceed to Mexico and his decisive command over his troops. Gómara comments on the singular nature of this act and cites a parallel example from naval warfare in the Mediterranean: 'Pocos ejemplos destos hay, y aquéllos son de grandes hombres, como fue Omich Barbaroja, del brazo cortado, que pocos años antes desto quebró siete galeotas y fustas por tomar a Bujía' (There are few examples of this kind, and these are of great men, such as Omich Barbaroja, the one-armed, who a few years before this time destroyed seven galliots and raiding vessels, to take the city of Bujía) (López de Gómara 65–6).

14 Spagnesi provides a detailed account of the renovation and fortification of the Castel Sant'Angelo in the early modern period for the strategic purpose of defending the city of Rome (9–55).
15 Elliott describes the rise of the wool industry in medieval Spain and its central place in the economy of early modern Castile under the direction of the *Mesta*, a general organization of sheep owners 'entrusted with the supervision and control of the elaborate system whereby the great migratory flocks were moved across Spain from their summer pastures in the north to their winter pastures in the south, and then back again in the spring to the north' (32–3, 119–20).
16 Murillo notes that a paradigmatic technique in *Don Quixote* 'places the autonomous character before a visual stimulus' and explores his processing of what he sees through correspondence with the images and situations that he has absorbed from the romances of chivalry and other books from his library (*Critical Introduction* 59).
17 Frye remarks that as comedy is assimilated to romance and to traditional seasonal rituals, we find 'the comic theme of the ritual assault on a central female figure' (*Anatomy* 183). This theme is a stable element in the romance tradition and appears in both dramatic and narrative variants of the form.
18 The standard source in Roman comedy for this stock figure is Plautus's *Miles gloriosus*; the central character in Lope de Vega's *El galán Castrucho* (1598) is a paradigmatic instance of the type.
19 In Frye's view, romance is an essentially subjective form, centred on ideals of heroism and integrity and on characters that correspond to stylized or archetypal figures (*Anatomy* 304–6).
20 In his discussion of the theme of arms in *Orlando furioso*, C.P. Brand comments on the absence of a consistent 'epic tone' in Ariosto: 'the troop-reviews, the siege, the earnest combats in the final cantos reveal in varying degrees an ironic use of hyperbole which reminds us that this is a literary fiction' (88). Ariosto is one of Cervantes's models for the hybridization of epic and chivalric romance and the construction of narratives that reveal themselves as fictions.
21 Redondo comments on the comic and non-heroic wordplay that shapes the proper names in this catalogue (344). 'Timonel' is derived from 'timonero' (helmsman or leader), and 'Carcajona' suggests 'carcajadas' (peals of laughter); hence this putatively unvanquished warrior is a figure of laughter. 'Alfeñiquén' is the augmentative form of 'alfeñique,' a confection of sugar paste, and by extension, a delicate or effete person.
22 This motto admits at least two readings: 'Follow my fortune' and 'My fortune trails along the ground.' The idea of a knight subject to the vagaries

and reversals of fate mirrors Don Quixote's awareness of his own mixed career as a voluntary knight-errant.

23 Quint argues that the depiction of the battle of Actium on the shield that is forged for Aeneas (*Aeneid* VIII. 675–728) presents the conflict between the armies of Augustus and Antony as an encounter between West and East, rewriting the Roman civil war as an imperial conflict with a foreign other. Vergil's descriptions of the opposing forces define this opposition in stark terms: 'The Western armies are portrayed as ethnically homogeneous, disciplined, and united; the forces of the East are a loose aggregate of nationalities prone to discord and fragmentation' (Quint, *Epic and Empire* 27).

24 Lokos (59–99) and Rivers discuss elements of traditional verse satire in the *Viaje del Parnaso*. In a detailed analysis of Cervantes's critical view in this text of literary life in Madrid during his time, Schmidt explains the relationship that it traces between 'sites of literary production' and 'the social structures by which literary value is categorized' ('Maps' 30). In this mock epic, literary reputation proves to be no less mutable and uncertain than the fame of warriors.

25 Anthony Close notes that 'whimsical self-mockery' is one of the basic features of the *Viaje del Parnaso* and, more generally, that Cervantine satire 'has the habit of turning in upon itself' (58, 59). Close's study stresses Cervantes's commitment to *propiedad*, or decorum, in his literary works and his tendency to temper the didacticism and acerbity of satire by shifting its typical themes and techniques to other generic frames. As a result, Cervantine satire is a complex variant of the form, 'as much affected by the tendency to modulate into comedy, fable, and farce as the satire directed at moral or social targets' (56).

26 In Book I of Castiglione's *Libro del cortegiano* Cesare Gonzaga summarizes Lodovico Canossa's views on grace as a definitive attribute of the ideal courtier: 'parmi ... che voi questa sera più volte abbiate replicato che 'l cortegiano ha da compagnare l'operazion sue, i gesti, gli abiti, in somma ogni suo movimento con la grazia; e questo mi par che mettiate per un condimento d'ogni cosa, senza il quale tutte l'altre proprietà e bone condicioni sian di poco valore' (it seems to me that you have repeated several times this evening that the courtier has to imbue with grace his movements, his gestures, his way of doing things and in short, his every action. And it appears to me that you require this in everything as the seasoning without which all other attributes and good qualities would be almost worthless) (I. 24, 59). In their deference and their artful braying, the *regidores* display this quality, and the humour of the episode rests in part on this transposition of courtly habits and values to rustic characters.

27 The peasant-narrator tells Don Quixote that the villagers have often armed themselves and set forth to do battle with those who have offended them. It is possible, however, that their neighbours have not responded to their challenges, and that each of these incidents has ended with the peasants returning to their village. This reading emphasizes the ludic and ritualistic aspect of this conflict.

28 Parker outlines the traditional arrangements for billeting troops on the march that obliged village families to provide food and accommodation to soldiers who chose to lodge themselves in their houses (*Army of Flanders* 87–90). The disruptive impact of soldiers in transit on peasant communities is a standard theme in early modern Spanish literature, as in Calderón's canonical play *El alcalde de Zalamea*.

29 Clemencín identifies the traditional epithets for the residents of Spanish cities and town that Don Quixote cites in his discourse to the villagers (1676b–77a).

30 Kagan discusses the tension between local juridical privileges, or *fueros*, that defined customary law in many Castilian jurisdictions during the Middle Ages and the attempt to establish a centralized code of royal laws based on Roman precedent (*Lawsuits* 23–32). He comments on the challenges in early modern Spain of maintaining and negotiating a legal system marked by 'a hodgepodge of confused laws and competing jurisdictions,' stressing the 'labyrinthine state' of Castilian laws and law courts (31–2).

31 The argument that the monarch is morally bound to engage in due consideration and fair diplomacy before declaring war is central to the formation of the Christian prince and not limited to proponents of natural law theory. In his treatise *On the War against the Turks* (1530) Erasmus concedes that Christian rulers may turn to war as a means of 'judicial retribution,' but sets out doctrinal principles that should constrain their recourse to arms, including the obligation to avoid war 'unless all possible remedies have been exhausted,' the ethical demand not to engage in war for revenge or private motives, and the requirement for 'the consent of their citizens and of the whole country' (319–20). Erasmus appeals to Christian clemency and to arguments that favour persuasion and instruction over the use of force.

32 In this episode Sancho presents the 'victim signs' that René Girard has identified in myths of scapegoating. He is a stranger to the villagers who appears at a time of crisis for their community. He commits a single gesture that leads to a misinterpretation with a sequel of violence. He insults the villagers because they do not share the customs of his home

community, where (at least by Sancho's account) braying is a practice that gives no offence (Girard 32). The expulsion of Sancho and his master confirms the core pattern of persecution: 'the import of the operation is to lay the responsibility for the crisis on the victims and to exert an influence on it by destroying these victims or at least by banishing them from the community they "pollute"' (24).

3. Captains and Saints: Lyric and Romance

1 The influence of Greek romance on early modern literature can be traced to the rediscovery of Heliodorus's *Ethiopian History* in the early sixteenth century (Forcione, *Cervantes, Aristotle* 49–50). Editions and translations of Heliodorus cultivated a taste for ancient romances and for vernacular narratives that imitated their conventions of characterization and plot structure, including Alonso Núñez de Reinoso's *Historia de los amores de Clareo y Florisea* (1552), the first text of this kind in Spanish (Jones 73). In Renaissance poetics the *Ethiopian History* is valued for its unity of subject matter and verisimilitude, in opposition to the loosely articulated narratives and unreal incidents of the romances of chivalry (Forcione, *Cervantes, Aristotle* 85–7). Printed collections of saints' lives circulated widely in early modern Spain, and the *comedia de santos* was a prominent sub-genre of the contemporary public theatre. St Teresa of Ávila comments on saints' lives as reading matter for herself and her siblings: 'Tenía uno casi de mi edad; juntávamos entrambos a leer vidas de santos ... Como vía los martirios que por Dios las santas pasavan, parecíame compravan muy barato el ir a gozar de Dios (no por amor que yo entendiese tenerle, sino por gozar tan en breve de los grandes bienes que leía haver en en cielo); y juntávame con este mi hermano a tratar qué medio havría para esto' (I had a brother of almost the same age; we sought each other's company to read saints' lives ... When I saw the torments that the female saints suffered for God, it struck me that they had purchased the joy of God's presence at a very low price [I was moved not by any love that I understood them to have for Him, but by the thought of enjoying so promptly the great pleasures that I had read existed in heaven]; and together with my brother we considered what means there might be to reach this end) (St Teresa de Jesús, *Libro de la vida* 29a–b). The presence of saints' lives among her father's books is an indication of their popularity.

2 I am indebted to Fussell for the passage from Parker that I have used as the epigraph for this chapter (114). Fussell comments on the 'rhetoric of conversion' that can be identified in Parker's text and in other memoirs of infantry service by his contemporaries (114–15).

3 Canavaggio suggests certain principles for dating the two Algiers plays, despite the conflict among the chronologies proposed for Cervantes's *comedias* and the notorious difficulties of assigning exact dates to most of these works (*Cervantès dramaturge* 18–23). With the exception of Stagg, who argues that Cervantes wrote *El trato de Argel* during his captivity in Algiers and revised it shortly after his return to Spain ('Date and Form'), critics have assigned the first play to the period 1580–4; with the exception of Schevill and Bonilla, who give an early date for *Los baños de Argel* (1588), the chronologies assign the second play to the early seventeenth century. These chronological principles are consistent with the influence of the *comedia nueva* on *Los baños de Argel* and with an increasing authorial scepticism concerning Spanish policy and practice in the Mediterranean.

4 Garcés discusses the numerous connections between Cervantes's fictions and contemporary topographical and historical writings on Algiers, including the antecedents for his characters in such notable historical figures as Aluj Ali (76–7), Hasan Pasha (88–90), and Haji Murad and his daughter (207–11). Allen analyses the interplay of autobiography and fiction through Cervantes's reworking of his military experience in the captive's tale.

5 Critical opinion has defined captivity as the central concern of Cervantes's writings on Algiers. Edward Friedman asserts that 'the fundamental conceptual element' of *El trato de Argel* is 'the idea of captivity' and that *Los baños de Argel* returns to the 'multiple facets' of this theme (71). Fothergill-Payne observes that the first play emphasizes the dangers of regular contact with the infidel (177) and argues that the second maintains this 'documentary' aspect while appealing to the audience's sympathies through more intensive theatrical effects (182). Garcés's analysis of 'the afterlife of trauma' in Cervantes as a mental 'wound' that the survivor revisits places a parallel emphasis on captivity: 'the Cervantine fictions that turn on the motif of captivity represent a poetic mode of witnessing – of accessing reality – when all other forms of knowledge have been precluded' (3, 5).

6 Through the trials of its central characters the captive's tale traces voyages outbound to places marked as alien and inbound to reintegration into a home community; it can also be read as a variant of early modern travel literature. Diane Sieber interprets Ruy Pérez's tale as a text that follows the patterns of ethnographic narrative, presenting his experience in Algiers as an 'encounter with alterity' and recording his voyages through the 'liminal or transitional spaces' of the Mediterranean and its coastal centres (118).

7 Perry discusses theatrical mimes and farces and Greek romances as literary forms that respond to the stratification and urban complexity of

late antique society (54–7). Drawing on Perry's historical analysis, Fuchs describes the ancient romances as texts that 'reflect the fractured and hybrid reality of the Hellenistic and early Roman periods, when the relative cultural homogeneity of Greek civilization gave way to the multiplicity of an imperial world' (*Romance* 23).
8 The cited phrase is from Marshall's study of common rhetorical strategies in Greek romance and early Christian texts (385). Marshall comments on ancient authors' shared command of 'a rhetoric of genre' (375), on the appeal to providence as the motive force of the plot (381), and on the structural patterns of Greek romance in religious writing (385–7). Marshall's analysis focuses on apocalyptic literature, but his observations also apply to the genre of the saint's life. Analogy is a common aspect of structure and meaning in medieval romance and hagiography, and the two kinds of writing influence one another (Vinaver 110–16; Fuchs, *Romance* 59–61).
9 Canavaggio regards Cervantes as sceptical in both plays about the prospect of military action against Algiers. He nonetheless argues that the contrast between the two works – *El trato* ends with a general redemption of the Spanish captives in Algiers, while *Los baños* stresses the sacrificial heroism or the miraculous flight of specific characters – suggests an increasing disillusion with official policy concerning North Africa, in the wake of the final collapse of Spain's large-scale military designs for the area during the government of Philip III (*Cervantès dramaturge* 394, 396–7).
10 In support of his account of Aurelio's lament on the state of war and peace as 'typically Erasmian,' Zimic refers to such widely circulated pacifist treatises as Erasmus's *War is sweet to those who have not tried it*.
11 This account of the gradual disengagement along the Mediterranean frontier follows Hess's chapter on the military and political relations between the Hapsburg and Ottoman Empires from 1530 to 1580 (71–99).
12 Ellen Friedman outlines in detail the funding and official regulation of the redemptionists' trade with North Africa (107, 111–14, 121).
13 A diplomatic transcription of the emperor's letter is available in Fernández Alvarez, *Corpus documental* (2:71–5).
14 The text of this verse epistle is available in Gaos's edition of Cervantes's poetry (*Poesías completas* 2:337–46). Despite questions concerning its attribution to Cervantes, this text establishes a convincing rhetorical and narrative framework for the discourse directed to Philip II in *El trato de Argel*. The speaker appeals to the virtue and good will of his addressee, recounts his brave conduct at Lepanto and his imprisonment in Algiers, and asks to be presented at court so that he may deliver his plea for military action directly to the king. The letter thus invokes Cervantes's experience

to underwrite its petition to royal authority and deploys the topics and divisions of formal epistolary rhetoric. In 'The Curious Case' Stagg describes the discovery of this poem in the private archives of the Conde de Altamira in 1863, in a manuscript identified by contemporary philologists as a sixteenth-century copy of Cervantes's original, and reviews the critical debate concerning its authenticity. Stagg concludes that the epistle is the work of Cervantes, on the grounds of its appearance in an archive rich in documents related to early modern Spanish literature and its prosodic and thematic parallels to other Cervantine texts.

15 Comparative discussion of the two Algiers plays generally centres on dramatic method and the technical changes that Cervantes may have introduced in response to the *comedias* of Lope (including *Los cautivos de Argel*, a text often interpreted as Lope's reworking of *El trato de Argel*). Edward Friedman and Fothergill-Payne both emphasize the heightened dramatic effectiveness of *Los baños*, suggesting that here Cervantes attempts to show by theatrical means what he was content to relate discursively through a series of set speeches in *El trato* (Friedman 61; Fothergill-Payne 182).

16 Ellen Friedman describes the logistics and difficulties of defending Spain's Mediterranean coastline against the activities of the corsairs, at times assisted in their expeditions by expelled Moriscos (33–43, 10–13). To illustrate the dangers to which coastal guards were exposed, she cites the case of Bartolomé Claro of Almuñécar, a sentry captured in the act of giving the alarm during a corsair raid and held in captivity for twenty-three years (37).

17 These moments of separation are not wholly parallel, and the differences between them are due in part to the distinct genres of the two texts. Aeneas suffers an irreparable loss when Creusa dies in the ruins of Troy, and her spirit urges that he undertake his long voyage to Latium. Fernando loses Costanza when she is captured by the corsairs, and he willingly surrenders himself into captivity so that he may follow and rescue her. Aeneas's epic task demands that he abandon Troy to found a new kingdom; Fernando's experience conforms to the typical pattern of romance: trials and adventures followed by the fortunate reunion of lost lovers.

18 Corsairs and janissaries formed two distinct social groups in early modern Algiers, and tensions between the corsair guild and the elite military corps were common. The janissaries' desire to share in the profits of privateering led to their rebellion in 1557 (Hess 77). Fisher has noted that European observers commented on the discipline and good order of the janissary corps, particularly following the visit of Kheir-ed-din's fleet to Toulon in 1543 (67).

19 Blecua discusses Cervantes's use of popular Spanish verse forms (*cancionillas, letras, letrillas, romances*) in his *comedias*, particularly in the works from his second dramatic cycle (190–3).
20 The reference here is to Dathan and Abiram, who unite with Korah to rebel against Moses and Aaron following the Israelites' flight from Egypt and are punished when the earth opens beneath them, consuming them and their followers (Numbers 16:1–35). The captives' song presents these usurping leaders as types of false authority.
21 Frye notes that the typical heroine of romance works through strategies of secrecy and disguise, in accordance with the operation of 'craft or guile' as 'the animating spirit of the comic form' (*Secular Scripture* 74–5). Frye offers the example of Terence's *Andria*, in which most of the action is staged on the street outside the heroine's house. The complex traffic of the stage is closely related to the role of this female figure who remains hidden from view: 'If we turn the action inside out, so to speak, we find ourselves in this silent and darkened room, where the heroine is quietly gathering all the threads of the action into her hands' (*Secular Scripture* 75). In the captive's tale Zoraida plays a parallel role, directing the actions of others from within her father's house until she creates the conditions under which she can fully reveal her Christian identity. Márquez Villanueva comments that the actions taken by Ruy Pérez and his companions depend entirely on her initiative, based on their shared desire for flight to Christian lands (116).
22 The resolution in Juan Palomeque's inn of the conflicted loves of Fernando, Cardenio, Luscinda, and Dorotea offers a parallel example of connecting the ascending movement of romance to a providential design (*DQ* I. 36). In the final scene of reunion and reconciliation, the other characters at the inn persuade Fernando to accept Dorotea's love, in part by appealing to the force of providence that operates behind the mere appearance of events: 'Que considerase que, no acaso, como parecía, sino con particular providencia del cielo, se habían todos juntado en lugar donde menos ninguno pensaba' (They urged him to observe that it was not, as it might seem, by accident, but by a special disposition of Providence that they had all met in a place where no one could have expected a meeting) (I. 36, 453).
23 Sevilla Arroyo and Rey Hazas identify this scriptural reference in their edition of *Los baños de Argel* (Cervantes, *Teatro completo* 226n). The first two books of Maccabees appear in the Vulgate text of the Bible, and the Council of Trent accepted them as canonical.
24 Garcés reviews current scholarship on the date of composition of the captive's tale and concurs with Allen and Murillo in assigning it to 1589–90. Garcés finds support in Murillo's hypothesis that the captive's tale was

written as an independent narrative at this time and later incorporated into the first part of *Don Quixote* (186). This chronology suggests that the captive's tale and *Los baños de Argel* can be read as parallel works that revisit the material and themes of *El trato de Argel*.

25 This account follows *The Secular Scripture* in describing the key concepts in Frye's formulation of romance as 'the structural core of all fiction' (15), particularly 53–4 for 'identity,' 6–15 for 'myth,' and 169–79 for 'recreation' and 'recovery.'

26 From Zoraida's initial appearance at the inn, where she insists that she be called María, a series of terms and images repeat and reinforce her figural association with the Virgin. Critics have noted the clear parallel to Mary and Joseph (Márquez Villanueva 115; Gerli 46; Murillo, 'Cervantes' Tale' 232) and her Marian intervention as guide and liberator of the Christian captives. The name Zoraida ('Star' or 'Pleiades' in Arabic) evokes the Virgin as *stella maris*, the traditional guide to Christian travellers and the 'beacon' in the tale's 'spiritual voyage of deliverance' (Gerli 50). The gold, pearls, and precious stones that adorn her body when she appears in her father's garden recall the Counter-Reformation iconography of the veneration of the Immaculate Conception (Garcés 214). The recognition of her agency in delivering Ruy Pérez and his companions from forced exile in Algiers confirms her figural significance; she is 'transformed into the very incarnation of the Virgin when the Captive calls her '"*señora de nuestra libertad*"' (Garcés 215). The loss of her material wealth during the voyage to Spain further confirms the parallels that link her to the Virgin: 'Zoraida has come down in the world, but her own descent from riches is a descent into humility like that of the Queen of Heaven herself' (Quint, *Cervantes's Novel* 72).

27 Clemencín's commentary identifies these figures as military leaders from Cervantes's time: Diego de Urbina, the captain of the infantry company in which Cervantes served at Lepanto (1363b–64a); Juan Zanoguera, an officer charged with the command of a tower in the defence of Tunis in 1574 (1372a); Gabrio Cervellón, a general in the Spanish infantry and military engineer named governor of Tunis and taken captive after the city's fall (1372a).

28 Scarry argues that torture and war are acts of destruction with a common structure that 'unmakes' the order of civilization by both appropriating and reversing the creative processes that give shape and substance to mental representations (21). Through the operations of this structure, 'the incontestable reality of the body – the body in pain, the body maimed,

the body dead and hard to dispose of – is separated from its source and conferred on an ideology or issue or instance of political authority' (62).
29 This view reflects the general response in early modern Europe to the victory of the Holy League over the numerically superior forces of the Ottomans. Contemporary chroniclers include spiritual factors among the Christians' strategic advantages, and commemorative representations of Lepanto – in such media as paintings, frescoes, engravings, medals, and popular songs – attribute the Christian triumph to divine intervention (Hanson 252–4).
30 Lattimore cites Greek and Latin epitaphs that illustrate this practice under the general category of 'alleviations of death,' since in most cases 'the dead person is represented as speaking to the survivors, telling them to stop lamenting' (217–20).
31 Poetry here assumes its place among the skills and accomplishments that contribute to the shaping of the model courtier, on the pattern of Castiglione and the tradition of courtly manuals inspired by his work. In Spain this model is subject to tensions and contradictions, particularly in relation to the courtier's equal command of arms and letters. Anne Cruz has argued that Garcilaso's poetry attests to an imbalance between the demands of literature and warfare and to a critique of violence that underlies his interest in war's impact on 'the vanquished and the vulnerable' ('Career of the Poet' 195–9). A parallel preoccupation with the social and rhetorical construction of the courtier-poet is apparent in the interactions among the multiple roles and voices of Garcilaso's verse: poet, lover, soldier, shepherd (Cruz, 'Self-Fashioning' 519–20). In her recent study of subjectivity and the politics of form in early modern Spanish court lyric, Leah Middlebrook argues that the sonnet form accommodates 'the complex codes of self-repression, dissembling, and the self-consciously artless postures of sprezzatura' and so offers 'an increasingly suitable allegory of the tension between the nobleman's double identity as a knight and a subject' (52).
32 For the Portuguese monarchy, the defeat at Alcazar-el-Kebir marked a devastating loss of military capacity and material resources. The young king Sebastian fell in battle; aristocratic officers were taken captive in large numbers; significant resources were committed to paying the ransoms demanded by the victors; the king's death led to a crisis of succession. Philip II's military enforcement of his claim to the Portuguese crown in 1580 brought the two nations of Iberia under the rule of a single regime that had no interest in pursuing Portugal's territorial interests in Africa (Lynch 1:306–9).

33 In his 'Canción en alabança de la Diuina Majestad, por la vitoria del señor don Juan' (*Obra poética* 1:244–55) Herrera celebrates the Christian triumph at Lepanto by combining a lexicon of praise in imitation of the Psalms with Italianate *canzone* form.

34 In a typical formulation of this argument, Erasmus argues that 'the Turks have won an immense empire less by their own merits than because of our sins,' and that war against their forces can succeed only if it is waged in a religious spirit and for the ends of peace and Christian unity: 'since God sends the Turks so frequently against us to call us to reform our lives, all the omens will be against us in this war if we take up arms without correcting the errors which have provoked God to punish us through their barbaric cruelty. It is obvious that this has been the case up to now; I am afraid that in the future things will get worse unless we turn wholeheartedly towards the Lord, and offer to him the sacrifice which the psalm suggested' (*On the War against the Turks* 316, 321).

4. Soldiers and Sinners: Picaresque

1 This discussion of methods of recruitment and the opportunities that they offered for deferral and avoidance follows MacKay's analyses of the Crown's interactions with municipal authorities (80–96) and individual subjects (134–46), as well as Geoffrey Parker's account of recruitment and mobilization for the companies of infantry that were sent to Flanders (*Army of Flanders* 35–43). It should be noted that MacKay's study centres on a period in the seventeenth century (1631–43) when demographic factors and repeated levies for military campaigns increased the likelihood of local opposition to the call for men to serve in the king's armies.

2 Parker comments on the popularity of military service in Italy (*Army of Flanders* 33) and on the Crown's reliance on voluntary recruitment for most of the sixteenth century (37). MacKay notes that despite the forms of resistance available to them, many men went willingly to Spain's armies (8).

3 Ruth Pike reviews changes in legislation that extended the range of criminal offences punishable by terms of penal servitude in the galleys (6–7). She notes that 'by the second half of the sixteenth century the normal sentence for convicted male criminals, with the exception of nobles and the clergy, was the galleys' (7). The period of the average sentence was from four to six years.

4 The economic incentives for military service are discussed by Parker (*Army of Flanders* 158–9) and MacKay (8–9).

5 Moxey's chapter on the representation of mercenaries in German popular art (67–100) elucidates the iconography of common soldiers in the sixteenth century. Hale offers a parallel discussion of visual images of soldiers in northern Renaissance art (*Artists and Warfare* 42–72).
6 In his chapter on 'Life in the Army of Flanders' Parker discusses the military customs and conditions of service that created a sense of solidarity and a distinct world view among the common soldiers of Spain's *tercios* (*Army of Flanders* 158–84).
7 In 'A Question of Genre' Riley discusses the importance for Cervantes of genre theory and generic models, with a focus on the broad categories of 'romance' and 'novel.' The discussion in this chapter addresses specific models for each of the texts that centre on common soldiers and other characters associated with the lower ranks.
8 Dunn's analysis of the representation of social structures and marginal groups in the picaresque draws on two studies by Turner: *The Ritual Process* and *Dramas, Fields, and Metaphors*.
9 Parker discusses the notorious lawlessness and disorder of Spanish soldiers, and the contribution of deserters and mutineers to 'the remarkable diffusion of the cult of the *pícaro* in seventeenth-century Spain' (*Army of Flanders* 180).
10 A text that offers a clear antecedent for the amorous verses of Eugenio and Anselmo is the first of Garcilaso's *Églogas*, in which the shepherd-poet Salicio claims to have moved stones, trees, birds, and beasts with his lament for the faithless Galatea and the pastoral *locus amoenus* responds with a compassionate echo when he cries out in the pain of lost love and betrayal (*Obras completas* 264–302, ll. 228–30).
11 Parker states that 'officers in the early modern period usually carried their gold and silver, their wardrobes and their other trappings around with them on campaign' and refers to an auction in 1596 at which a captain's gold chain was sold for 277 escudos (*Army of Flanders* 177).
12 Hale comments on the parallels between the cultured ideals of freedom and equality in pastoral literature and the release from the restraints and hierarchies of civilian life that common soldiers experienced in the 'alternate society' of military service. From this perspective, the armies of early modern Europe could offer the prospect of 'a longed-for "natural" life, unbourgeoisified and unclericized' (*War and Society* 123).
13 Diego García de Paredes was an officer in the army of the legendary Spanish general Gonzalo Hernández de Córdoba and the subject of a book recommended to the innkeeper Juan Palomeque in *Don Quixote* as an antidote

to the pernicious reading matter of the romances of chivalry (I. 32, 394–5). Commentators on *Don Quixote* have not identified Gante and Luna.

14 Alemán, *Guzmán de Alfarache* II.1.3, 2: 63–9. For commentary on the uses of deceit in *Don Quixote* in relation to the treatment of deceit as a comic device in Renaissance literary theory, see Hart, 'Deceit and Decorum.'

15 Recent critical commentary has proposed various generic models for Campuzano's narrative: autobiography (Williamson), confession (Boyd; El Saffar 20–2), the miracle narrative (Forcione, *Mystery* 131–45), and the *entremés* (Francisco Sánchez 163–78). His narrative also presents features of romance: the unfolding pattern of recognitions and reversals, the evocation of sensual pleasures in Campuzano's honeymoon, and the parallelism in the narrative's time frame (four days of courtship, followed by four days between the betrothal and the wedding; six days of marital delight, followed by six of rancour).

16 Compare Dunn's remark on the typical settings of picaresque fiction: 'A street, an inn, a cellar, the entrance to a merchant's store, a bedroom with two entrances, these have always been the locations of farce, low comedy, fabliaux' (129).

17 Pope discusses the various sections of Contreras's *Vida* that address his relations with women (155–7).

18 For the general relevance of Labov's work to the analysis of oral narratives, I am indebted to Ife (92).

19 For comment on Contreras's use of oaths and expletives, see Pope (162) and Levisi (105).

20 Moxey provides reproductions of the woodcuts of Schön and Weygel and discusses their significance (80–4).

21 Cervantes's use of the marriage plot as a projection of 'social and narrative order' is a central subject of Theresa Ann Sears's study of the *Novelas ejemplares* (see esp. 149–65).

22 Forcione has argued that the sensuous details in Campuzano's account of his six-day honeymoon 'recall the false paradises of the type that Cervantes created in the *Persiles* as well as the moral issues generally connected with them' (*Mystery* 137).

23 Sobejano's discussion of picaresque features in *El coloquio de los perros* is part of his extended response to Fernando Lázaro Carreter, Lazarillo de Tormes *en la picaresca*.

24 Pike describes the standard arrangements for the temporary imprisonment of convicted criminals and their transportation to ports of embarkation for the galleys (18–20). At least twelve convicts were required to make up a chain, and this is the number that Don Quixote sees approaching him on the road.

25 The bureaucratic apparatus of the Hapsburg state required standard written information about convicts. When convicts were embarked on a galley, its officials recorded relevant details in the ship's register, comprising 'each man's name, age, place of origin, crimes, sentences, and other pertinent information' (Pike 20).
26 Halliday distinguishes various processes of phonological variation in anti-languages, including metathesis, alternation, back formation, and aspiration (576).
27 For the various senses of 'corredor,' from 'agent' or 'broker' to 'procurer,' see the current edition (2001) of the *Diccionario* of the Real Academia Española (449a–b).
28 In a typical exhortation, Cipión admonishes Berganza not to indulge in gossip and backbiting under the false name of philosophy: '¿Al murmurar llamas filosofar? ¡Así va ello! Canoniza, Berganza, a la maldita plaga de la murmuración, y dale el nombre que quisieres, que ella dará a nosotros el de cínicos, que quiere decir perros murmuradores; y por tu vida que calles ya y sigas tu historia' (You call gossiping philosophy? That's great! Dress up the accursed plague known as gossiping and give it whatever name you like, it will call us cynics, which means gossiping dogs; for heaven's sake keep quiet and carry on with your story) (319).
29 In 'Genre and Countergenre' Guillén argues that the popularity of *Guzmán de Alfarache* led to the rereading of *Lazarillo de Tormes* as a similar rogue's narrative, in the context of the vogue of the picaresque in early seventeenth-century Spain.
30 The standard point of departure for such comparative readings is Blanco Aguinaga's seminal article on modes of realism, which opposes the 'dogmatic realism' of *Guzmán de Alfarache* to the 'objective realism' of *Don Quixote*. Blanco interprets Alemán as a 'closed,' authoritarian author, in contrast with the 'open' and 'objective' perspective of Cervantine fiction. Dunn offers a pointed critical analysis of this argument (208–12).
31 Forcione relates this appeal to visual perception to the tenet in Renaissance poetics that the writer should set the events and places of his narrative before the eyes of his readers (*Cervantes, Aristotle* 172). Robbins notes that contemporary theories of history place a parallel emphasis on the connection of history to sight and knowledge (629–30).
32 Robbins argues that the false captive's recognition of the limitations of the painted image that he displays to the villagers alludes to the Platonic critique of representation as a distortion of truth and undermines the view that 'a historical narrative can be absolutely true to all aspects of reality' (633). Questions of representation and verisimilitude are central to this episode.

33 This discussion of the episode of the false captives as a theatrical performance in the lineage of the popular *entremés* follows Forcione, *Cervantes, Aristotle* 170–2.
34 Fox discusses the conventional attributes of the rural *alcalde* in popular theatre and the oral tradition (158).

Conclusion

1 This discussion of the correspondence in the *Aeneid* between the cosmic order and the ideas and icons of imperial rule follows Hardie, *Cosmos and Imperium* (51–83, 340–76). Hardie traces Vergil's techniques to the ancient tradition of didactic poetry and to early allegorical interpretations of Homer. In a parallel political reading of the *Aeneid*, Quint discusses the opposition between the 'futile repetition' of the Trojans' defeat in Books I–VI and the 'positive repetition' of their past through victory and conquest in Books VII–XII. Quint associates these patterns with the Augustan virtues of *clementia* and *pietas* and with two core tenets of Augustan ideology: 'the injunction to forget a past of civil war (so as to stop repeating it), and the demand that this past be remembered and avenged (and so be repeated and mastered)' (*Epic and Empire* 51–2). Quint's analysis also proposes that Vergil uncovers the contradictions inherent in these tenets and in the foundational narrative of Roman history that they attempt to sustain.
2 De Armas discusses Raphael's paintings of St George and St Michael and Titian's equestrian portrait of Charles V as sources for an iconography of the Christian warrior that Cervantes explores in *Don Quixote* (*Quixotic Frescoes* 120–1). El Greco's *Saint Martin and the Beggar* and its placement of the Chapel of St Joseph, in honour of the patron saint of its founder, Martín Ramírez, are reviewed in Brown et al. (164–8, 241). Kubler and Soria comment on the career in Seville of Juan de Roelas, with an emphasis on his monumental altarpieces (230–1).
3 Fox argues that through his renunciation of folly and his turn to devotional reading, the central character of Cervantes's novel 'finally attains the only type of heroism available to a man of his restricted circumstances' (20).

Works Cited

Alemán, Mateo. *Guzmán de Alfarache*. Ed. Benito Brancaforte. 2 vols. Madrid: Cátedra, 1979.
Allen, John J. 'Autobiografía y ficción: El relato del Capitán cautivo (*Don Quijote* I, 39–41).' *Anales Cervantinos* 15 (1976): 149–55.
Alpers, Paul. *What Is Pastoral?* Chicago and London: U of Chicago P, 1996.
Ariosto, Ludovico. *Orlando furioso*. Ed. Cesare Segre. Milan: Mondadori, 1976.
– *Orlando Furioso*. Trans. Guido Waldman. Oxford: Oxford UP, 1983.
Armstrong-Roche, Michael. *Cervantes' Epic Novel: Empire, Religion, and the Dream of Heroes in* Persiles. Toronto: U of Toronto P, 2009.
Avalle-Arce, Juan Bautista. *La novela pastoril española*. Madrid: Revista de Occidente, 1959.
– 'Poesía, historia, imperialismo: *La Numancia*.' *Anuario de Letras* 2 (1962): 55–75.
Bakhtin, M.M. 'Epic and Novel.' *The Dialogic Imagination*. Trans. Caryl Emerson and Michael Holquist. Austin: U of Texas P, 1981. 3–40.
Bergmann, Emilie. 'The Epic Vision of Cervantes' *Numancia*.' *Theatre Journal* 36.1 (1984): 85–96.
Black, Jeremy. *European Warfare 1494–1660*. London: Routledge, 2002.
– 'Military Revolutions and Early Modern Europe: The Case of Spain.' *Guerra y sociedad en la monarquía hispánica: Política, estrategia y cultura en la Europa moderna*. Ed. Enrique García Hernán and Davide Matti. 2 vols. Madrid: Laberinto, 2006. 1:17–30.
Blake, William. *On Homers Poetry*. *The Poetry and Prose of William Blake*. Ed. David V. Erdman. Garden City NY: Doubleday, 1965. 267.
Blanco Aguinaga, Carlos. 'Cervantes y la picaresca: Notas sobre dos tipos de realismo.' *Nueva Revista de Filología Hispánica* 11.3–4 (1957): 313–42.
Blecua, José Manuel. 'La poesía lírica de Cervantes.' *Sobre poesía de Edad de Oro*. Madrid: Gredos, 1970. 161–95.

Boyd, Stephen. 'Sin and Grace in *El casamiento engañoso y el coloquio de los perros.*' *What's Past Is Prologue: A Collection of Essays in Honour of L.J. Woodward.* Ed. Salvador Bacarisse et al. Edinburgh: Scottish Academic P, 1984. 1–9.

Brand, C.P. *Ludovico Ariosto: A Preface to the* Orlando Furioso. Edinburgh: Edinburgh UP, 1974.

Braudel, Fernand. *The Mediterranean and the Mediterranean World in the Age of Philip II.* Trans. Siân Reynolds. 2 vols. New York: Harper and Row, 1976.

Braudy, Leo. *The Frenzy of Renown: Fame and Its History.* New York: Vintage, 1997.

Brown, Jonathan, et al. *El Greco of Toledo.* Boston: Little Brown, 1982.

Canavaggio, Jean. *Cervantes.* Trans. J.R. Jones. New York: Norton, 1990.

– *Cervantès dramaturge: Un théâtre à naître.* Paris: Presses Universitaires de France, 1977.

Caputo, Philip. *A Rumor of War.* New York: Holt, Rinehart and Winston, 1977.

Casalduero, Joaquín. *Sentido y forma del teatro de Cervantes.* Madrid: Gredos, 1966.

Castells, Ricardo. 'La modernidad y el arte de la guerra en el discurso de las armas y las letras en *Don Quijote.*' *Cervantes* 28.2 (2008): 41–56.

Castiglione, Baldassarre. *The Courtier.* Trans. George Bull. Harmondsworth: Penguin, 1976.

– *Il libro del cortegiano.* Ed. Ettore Bonora. Milan: Mursia, 1972.

Castro, Miguel de. *Vida de Miguel de Castro.* Cossío 487–627.

Cervantes Saavedra, Miguel de. *Don Quixote.* Trans. John Ormsby. Ed. Joseph R. Jones and Kenneth Douglas. New York: Norton, 1981.

– *El casamiento engañoso. Novelas ejemplares* 2:279–95.

– *El coloquio de los perros. Novelas ejemplares* 2:297–359.

– *El ingenioso hidalgo don Quijote de la Mancha.* Ed. Luis Andrés Murillo. 2 vols. Madrid: Castalia, 1978.

– *El trato de Argel. Teatro completo* 843–917.

– *Exemplary Novels/Novelas ejemplares.* Ed. and trans. B.W. Ife et al. 4 vols. Warminster: Aris and Phillips, 1992.

– *Información de Argel.* Transcribed by Pedro Torres Lanzas. 1905. Rpt. Madrid: José Esteban, 1981.

– *La Galatea.* Ed. Francisco López Estrada and María Teresa López García-Berdoy. Madrid: Cátedra, 1995.

– *Los baños de Argel. Teatro completo* 188–283.

– *Los trabajos de Persiles y Sigismunda.* Ed. Juan Bautista Avalle-Arce. Madrid: Castalia, 1969.

– *Novelas ejemplares.* Ed. Harry Sieber. 2 vols. Madrid: Cátedra, 1985–6.

– *Poesías completas.* Ed. Vicente Gaos. 2 vols. Madrid, Castalia, 1973.

- *Teatro completo.* Ed. Florencio Sevilla Arroyo and Antonio Rey Hazas. Barcelona: Planeta, 1987.
- *Tragedia de Numancia. Teatro completo* 918–91.
- *Viaje del Parnaso* and *Adjunta al Parnaso. Poesías completas* 1:47–191.

Cetina, Gutierre de. *Sonetos y madrigales completos.* Ed. Begoña López Bueno. Madrid: Cátedra, 1981.

Cheney, Patrick, and Frederick A. de Armas, eds. *European Literary Careers: The Author from Antiquity to the Renaissance.* Toronto: U of Toronto P, 2002.

Chevalier, Maxime. 'El cautivo entre cuento y novela.' *Nueva Revista de Filologia Hispánica* 32.2 (1983): 403–11.

Cicero. *Pro lege manilia.* Trans. H. Grose Hodge. Cambridge MA: Harvard UP, 1927.

Clemencín, Diego. Commentary on *Don Quijote de la Mancha.* 1833–9. Rpt. in Miguel de Cervantes Saavedra. *Don Quijote de la Mancha.* Ed. Luis Astrana Marín. Madrid: Castilla, 1966. 990–1928.

Close, Anthony. *Cervantes and the Comic Mind of His Age.* Oxford: Oxford UP, 2000.

Colie, Rosalie L. *The Resources of Kind: Genre-Theory in the Renaissance.* Ed. Barbara K. Lewalski. Berkeley, Los Angeles, and London: U of California P, 1973.

Contreras, Alonso de. *Vida del capitán Alonso de Contreras.* Ed. Manuel Criado de Val. Madrid: Taurus, 1965.

Cossío, José María de. *Autobiografías de soldados (Siglo XVII).* Biblioteca de Autores Españoles 90. Madrid: Atlas, 1956.

Cozad, Mary Lee. 'Cervantes and *Libros de entendimiento.*' *Cervantes* 8.2 (1988): 159–82.

Cruz, Anne J. 'Arms versus Letters: The Poetics of War and the Career of the Poet in Early Modern Spain.' Cheney and de Armas 186–205.

- *Discourses of Poverty: Social Reform and the Picaresque Novel in Early Modern Spain.* Toronto: U of Toronto P, 1999.
- 'Self-Fashioning in Spain: Garcilaso de la Vega.' *Romanic Review* 83.4 (1992): 517–38.

Curtius, Ernst Robert. *European Literature and the Latin Middle Ages.* Trans. Willard F. Trask. Princeton: Princeton UP, 1953.

Dandelet, Thomas James. *Spanish Rome 1500–1700.* New Haven and London: Yale UP, 2001.

Davis, Elizabeth B. *Myth and Identity in the Epic of Imperial Spain.* Columbia: U of Missouri P, 2000.

de Armas, Frederick A. 'Cervantes and the Virgilian Wheel: The Portrayal of a Literary Career.' Cheney and de Armas 268–85.

- *Cervantes, Raphael and the Classics.* Cambridge: Cambridge UP, 1998.

- 'Classical Tragedy and Cervantes' *La Numancia.*' *Neophilologus* 58.1 (1974): 34–40.
- 'Las mentiras de Proteo: El duque de Alba, los Colonna y *La Numancia.*' *Theatralia* 5 (2003): 123–32.
- *Quixotic Frescoes: Cervantes and Italian Renaissance Art.* Toronto: U of Toronto P, 2006.

Diccionario de la lengua española. Compuesto por la Real Academia Española. Vol. 5 (O–R). Madrid, 1737.

Diccionario de la lengua española. 22nd ed. Madrid: Real Academia Española, 2001.

Dunn, Peter N. *Spanish Picaresque Fiction.* Ithaca NY and London: Cornell UP, 1993.

Elliott, J.H. *Imperial Spain 1469–1716.* Harmondsworth: Penguin, 1970.

El Saffar, Ruth. El casamiento engañoso *and* El coloquio de los perros. Critical Guides to Spanish Texts 17. London: Grant and Cutler, 1976.

Empson, William. *Some Versions of Pastoral.* 1935. Rpt. London: Hogarth, 1986.

Endress, Heinz-Peter. 'La guerra como asunto, situación, motivo y tema central en *La Numancia.*' *Theatralia* 5 (2003): 283–9.

Erasmus, Desiderius. On the War against the Turks (*De bello turcico*). *The Erasmus Reader.* Ed. Erika Rummel. Toronto: U of Toronto P, 1990. 315–33.

- War is sweet to those who have not tried it (*Dulce bellum inexpertis*). Margaret Mann Phillips. *The Adages of Erasmus: A Study with Translations.* Cambridge: Cambridge UP, 1964. 308–53.

Fagles, Robert. Translator's Preface. *The Iliad.* By Homer. Harmondsworth: Penguin, 1991. ix–xiv.

Feldherr, Andrew. *Spectacle and Society in Livy's History.* Berkeley, Los Angeles, and London: U of California P, 1998.

Fernández, Jaime, S.J. 'La admiración en el *Quijote* y el enigma del paje soldado (*DQ* II, 24).' *Cervantes* 19.1 (1999): 96–112.

Fernández Alvarez, Manuel. *Corpus documental de Carlos V.* 5 vols. Salamanca: Ediciones de la Universidad de Salamanca, 1973–81.

Finello, Dominick. *The Evolution of the Pastoral Novel in Early Modern Spain.* Arizona Studies in the Middle Ages and the Renaissance 25. Tempe: Arizona Center for Medieval and Renaissance Studies/Brepols, 2008.

- *Pastoral Themes and Forms in Cervantes.* Lewisburg: Bucknell UP, 1994.

Fisher, Sir Geoffrey. *Barbary Legend: War, Trade and Piracy in North Africa 1415–1830.* Oxford: Oxford UP, 1957.

Forcione, Alban K. Cervantes and the Mystery of Lawlessness: A Study of El casamiento engañoso y El coloquio de los perros. Princeton: Princeton UP, 1984.

- *Cervantes, Aristotle, and the* Persiles. Princeton: Princeton UP, 1970.
- 'Cervantes en busca de una pastoral auténtica.' *Nueva Revista de Filología Hispánica* 36.2 (1988): 1011–43.

Fothergill-Payne, Louise. '*Los tratos de Argel, Los cautivos de Argel* y *Los baños de Argel*: Tres "trasuntos" de un "asunto."' *El mundo teatral español en su Siglo de Oro: Ensayos dedicados a John E. Varey*. Ed. J.M. Ruano de la Haza. Ottawa: Dovehouse, 1989. 177–84.

Fowler, Alastair. *Kinds of Literature: An Introduction to the Theory of Genres and Modes*. Cambridge MA: Harvard UP, 1982.

Fox, Dian. *Refiguring the Hero: From Peasant to Noble in Lope de Vega and Calderón de la Barca*. University Park: Pennsylvania State UP, 1991.

Friedman, Edward H. *The Unifying Concept: Approaches to the Structure of Cervantes' Comedias*. York SC: Spanish Literature Publications Company, 1981.

Friedman, Ellen G. *Spanish Captives in North Africa in the Early Modern Age*. Madison: U of Wisconsin P, 1983.

Frye, Northrop. *Anatomy of Criticism: Four Essays*. Princeton: Princeton UP, 1957.
- *The Secular Scripture: A Study in the Structure of Romance*. Cambridge MA: Harvard UP, 1976.

Fuchs, Barbara. *Mimesis and Empire: The New World, Islam, and European Identities*. New York: Cambridge UP, 2001.
- *Romance*. New York and London: Routledge, 2004.

Fussell, Paul. *The Great War and Modern Memory*. Oxford: Oxford UP, 1975.

Garcés, María Antonia. *Cervantes in Algiers: A Captive's Tale*. Nashville: Vanderbilt UP, 2002.

Garcilaso de la Vega. *Obras completas con comentario*. Ed. Elias L. Rivers. Madrid: Castalia, 1981.

Gerli, E. Michael. *Refiguring Authority: Reading, Writing, and Rewriting in Cervantes*. Lexington: UP of Kentucky, 1995.

Girard, René. *The Scapegoat*. Trans. Yvonne Freccero. Baltimore: Johns Hopkins UP, 1986.

Greene, Thomas M. *The Light in Troy: Imitation and Discovery in Renaissance Poetry*. New Haven and London: Yale UP, 1982.

Guillén, Claudio. 'Genre and Countergenre: The Discovery of the Picaresque.' *Literature as System: Essays toward the Theory of Literary History*. Princeton: Princeton UP, 1971. 135–58.
- 'On the Uses of Literary Genre.' *Literature as System*. 107–34.

Hale, J.R. *Artists and Warfare in the Renaissance*. New Haven and London: Yale UP, 1990.
- *War and Society in Renaissance Europe 1450–1620*. London: Fontana, 1985.

Halliday, M.A.K. 'Anti-Languages.' *American Anthropologist* ns 78.3 (1976): 570–84.
Hanson, Victor Davis. *Carnage and Culture: Landmark Battles in the Rise of Western Power*. New York: Doubleday, 2001.
Hardie, Philip. *The Epic Successors of Virgil: A Study in the Dynamics of a Tradition*. Cambridge: Cambridge UP, 1993.
– *Ovid's Poetics of Illusion*. Cambridge: Cambridge UP, 2002.
– *Virgil's Aeneid: Cosmos and Imperium*. Oxford: Oxford UP, 1986.
Harris, William V. *War and Imperialism in Republican Rome 327–70 B.C.* Oxford: Oxford UP, 1979.
Hart, Thomas R. 'Deceit and Decorum in Cervantes.' *Modern Language Review* 90.2 (1995): 370–6.
Heilbrun, Carolyn. 'What Was Penelope Unweaving?' *Hamlet's Mother and Other Women: Feminist Essays on Literature*. New York: Columbia UP, 1990. 103–11.
Helgerson, Richard. *A Sonnet from Carthage: Garcilaso de la Vega and the New Poetry of Sixteenth-Century Europe*. Philadelphia: U of Pennsylvania P, 2007.
Herrera, Fernando de. *Obra poética*. Ed. José Manuel Blecua. 2 vols. Anejos de la Real Academia Española 32. Madrid: Real Academia Española, 1975.
Hess, Andrew C. *The Forgotten Frontier: A History of the Sixteenth-Century Ibero-African Frontier*. Chicago and London: U of Chicago P, 1978.
Hynes, Samuel. *The Soldier's Tale: Bearing Witness to Modern Warfare*. New York: Allen Lane-Penguin, 1997.
Ife, B.W. *Reading and Fiction in Golden-Age Spain: A Platonist Critique and Some Picaresque Replies*. Cambridge: Cambridge UP, 1985.
Johnson, Carroll B. '*La Numancia* and the Structure of Cervantine Ambiguity.' *Ideologies and Literature* 3 (1980): 74–94.
Jones, R.O. *The Golden Age: Prose and Poetry. A Literary History of Spain*. London: Ernest Benn, 1971.
Juvenal. *Satires. Juvenal and Persius*. Trans. G.G. Ramsay. Rev. ed. Cambridge MA: Harvard UP, 1940.
Kagan, Richard L. *Lawsuits and Litigants in Castile 1500–1700*. Chapel Hill: U of North Carolina P, 1981.
– *Students and Society in Early Modern Spain*. Baltimore: Johns Hopkins UP, 1974.
Kahn, Aaron M. *The Ambivalence of Imperial Discourse: Cervantes's La Numancia within the 'Lost Generation' of Spanish Drama (1570–90)*. Bern: Peter Lang, 2008.
Keegan, John. *A History of Warfare*. New York: Vintage, 1994.
Keith, A.M. *Engendering Rome: Women in Latin Epic*. Cambridge: Cambridge UP, 2000.

Kennedy, A.L. *Day*. Toronto: Anansi, 2007.
Kernan, Alvin. *Crossing the Line: A Bluejacket's World War II Odyssey*. Annapolis: Naval Institute P, 1994.
King, Willard F. 'Cervantes' *Numancia* and Imperial Spain.' *MLN* 94.2 (1979): 200–21.
Kubler, George, and Martin Soria. *Art and Architecture in Spain and Portugal and Their American Dominions 1500 to 1800*. Harmondsworth: Penguin, 1959.
Labov, William. *Language in the Inner City: Studies in the Black English Vernacular*. Philadelphia: U of Pennsylvania P, 1972.
Lara Garrido, José. *Los mejores plectros: Teoría y práctica de la épica culta en el Siglo de Oro*. Analecta Malacitana 23. Málaga: Universidad de Málaga, 1999.
Lattimore, Richmond. *Themes in Greek and Latin Epitaphs*. Urbana: U of Illinois P, 1962.
La vida de Lazarillo de Tormes, y de sus fortunas y adversidades. Ed. Alberto Blecua. Madrid: Castalia, 1972.
Lázaro Carreter, Fernando. Lazarillo de Tormes *en la picaresca*. Barcelona: Ariel, 1972.
Levisi, Margaret. 'Golden Age Autobiography: The Soldiers.' Spadaccini and Taléns 98–127.
Lewis, Charlton T., and Charles Short. *A Latin Dictionary*. Oxford: Clarendon, 1879.
Lewis-Smith, Paul. 'Cervantes' *Numancia* as Tragedy and Tragicomedy.' *Bulletin of Hispanic Studies* 64.1 (1987): 15–26.
Lida de Malkiel, María Rosa. *La idea de la fama en la Edad Media Castellana*. Mexico: Fondo de Cultura Económica, 1952.
Livy. *History of Rome*. Trans. B.O. Foster et al. 14 vols. Cambridge MA: Harvard UP, 1919–59.
Lokos, Ellen D. *The Solitary Journey: Cervantes's Voyage to Parnassus*. New York: Peter Lang, 1991.
López de Gómara, Francisco. *Historia de la conquista de México*. Mexico: Porrúa, 1988.
Lowe, Jennifer. 'The *Cuestión de amor* and the Structure of Cervantes' *Galatea*.' *Bulletin of Hispanic Studies* 43.2 (1966): 98–108.
Lynch, John. *Spain under the Hapsburgs*. 2 vols. Oxford: Blackwell, 1965–9.
MacKay, Ruth. *The Limits of Royal Authority: Resistance and Obedience in Seventeenth-Century Castile*. Cambridge: Cambridge UP, 1999.
Maglione, Sabatino G. 'Amity and Enmity in Cervantes's *La Numancia*.' *Hispania* 83.2 (2000): 179–88.
Maravall, José Antonio. *Utopía y contrautopía en el* Quijote. Santiago de Compostela: Pico Sacro, 1976.

Marinelli, Peter V. *Pastoral*. London: Methuen, 1971.
Márquez Villanueva, Francisco. *Personajes y temas del* Quijote. Madrid: Taurus, 1975.
Marshall, John W. 'Revelation and Romance: Genre Bending in the *Shepherd of Hermas* and the *Acts of Peter*.' *Rhetorical Argumentation in Biblical Texts*. Ed. A. Eriksson, T.H. Olbricht, and W. Übelacker. Harrisburg PA: Trinity P International, 2002. 375–88.
Martín, Francisco J. 'El desdoblamiento de la *hamartia* en *La Numancia*.' *Bulletin of the Comediantes* 48.1 (1996): 15–24.
Martines, Lauro. *Power and Imagination: City-States in Renaissance Italy*. London: Allen Lane, 1980.
McGaha, Michael D. 'Intertextuality as a Guide to the Interpretation of the Battle of the Sheep (*Don Quixote*, I, 18).' Parr 149–61.
– 'The Sources and Meaning of the Grisóstomo-Marcela Episode in the 1605 *Quijote*.' *Anales Cervantinos* 16 (1977): 33–69.
Meregalli, Franco. 'De *Los tratos de Argel* a *Los baños de Argel*.' *Homenaje a Casalduero*. Ed. Rizel Pincus Sigele and Gonzalo Sobejano. Madrid: Gredos, 1972. 395–409.
Middlebrook, Leah. *Imperial Lyric: New Poetry and New Subjects in Early Modern Spain*. University Park: Pennsylvania State UP, 2009.
Molho, Maurice. 'Antroponimia y cinonimia del *Casamiento engañoso y Coloquio de los perros*.' *Lenguaje, ideología y organización textual en las* Novelas ejemplares. Actas del Coloquio celebrado en la Facultad de Filología de la Universidad Complutense en mayo de 1982. Madrid: Universidad Complutense de Madrid, Université de Toulouse-le-Mirail, 1983. 81–92
Moxey, Keith. *Peasants, Warriors, and Wives: Popular Imagery in the Reformation*. Chicago and London: U of Chicago P, 1989.
Murillo, Luis A. 'Cervantes' Tale of the Captive Captain.' *Florilegium Hispanicum: Medieval and Golden Age Studies Presented to Dorothy Clotelle Clarke*. Ed. John S. Geary et al. Madison: Hispanic Seminary of Medieval Studies, 1983. 229–43.
– *A Critical Introduction to* Don Quixote. New York: Peter Lang, 1990.
Murrin, Michael. *History and Warfare in Renaissance Epic*. Chicago and London: U of Chicago P, 1994.
Navarrete, Ignacio. *Orphans of Petrarch: Poetry and Theory in the Spanish Renaissance*. Berkeley, Los Angeles, and London: U of California P, 1994.
Nicolopulos, James. *The Poetics of Empire in the Indies: Prophecy and Imitation in* La Araucana *and* Os Lusíadas. University Park: Pennsylvania State UP, 2000.
Oliver Asín, Jaime. 'La hija de Agi Morato en la obra de Cervantes.' *Boletín de la Real Academia Española* 27 (1947–8): 245–333.

Orwell, George. *Homage to Catalonia*. 1938. Rpt. Harmondsworth: Penguin, 1966.
Osborne, John. 'St. Peter's Needle and the Ashes of Julius Caesar: Invoking Rome's Imperial History at the Papal Court, ca. 1100–1300.' *Julius Caesar in Western Culture*. Ed. Maria Wyke. Oxford: Blackwell, 2006. 95–109.
Pagden, Anthony. *Lords of All the World: Ideologies of Empire in Spain, Britain and France c. 1500–c. 1800*. New Haven and London: Yale UP, 1995.
Paré, Ambroise. *The Apologie and Treatise of Ambroise Paré*. Ed. Geoffrey Keynes. London: Falcon, 1951.
Parker, Ernest. *Into Battle 1914–1918*. 1964. Rpt. London: Leo Cooper, 1994.
Parker, Geoffrey. *The Army of Flanders and the Spanish Road*. Cambridge: Cambridge UP, 1972.
– *The Military Revolution: Military Innovation and the Rise of the West 1500–1800*. Cambridge: Cambridge UP, 1988.
Parr, James A., ed. *On Cervantes: Essays for L.A. Murillo*. Newark DE: Juan de la Cuesta, 1991.
Pasamonte, Jerónimo de. *Vida y trabajos de Jerónimo de Pasamonte*. Cossío 5–73.
Perry, Ben Edwin. *The Ancient Romances: A Literary-Historical Account of Their Origins*. Berkeley and Los Angeles: U of California P, 1967.
Petrarca, Francesco. *The Triumphs of Petrarch*. Trans. Ernest Hatch Wilkins. Chicago and London: U of Chicago P, 1962.
Petro, Antonia. 'El fallido ritual sacrifical en *La Numancia* de Cervantes.' *Bulletin of Spanish Studies* 82.6 (2005): 753–72.
Pike, Ruth. *Penal Servitude in Early Modern Spain*. Madison: U of Wisconsin P, 1983.
Plutarch. *Life of Caius Marcius Coriolanus*. *Plutarch's Lives*. Trans. Bernadotte Perrin. 11 vols. Cambridge MA: Harvard UP, 1914–26. 4:117–219.
Polybius. *The Histories*. Trans. W.R. Paton. 6 vols. Cambridge MA: Harvard UP, 1922–7.
Pope, Randolph. *La autobiografía española hasta Torres Villaroel*. Frankfurt: Peter Lang, 1974.
Presberg, Charles D. *Adventures in Paradox: Don Quixote and the Western Tradition*. University Park: Pennsylvania State UP, 2001.
Quint, David. *Cervantes's Novel of Modern Times: A New Reading of* Don Quijote. Princeton: Princeton UP, 2003.
– *Epic and Empire: Politics and Generic Form from Virgil to Milton*. Princeton: Princeton UP, 1993.
Randel, Mary Gaylord. 'The Language of Limits and the Limits of Language: The Crisis of Poetry in *La Galatea*.' *MLN* 97.2 (1982): 254–71.
Rebhorn, Wayne A. *Courtly Performances: Masking and Festivity in Castiglione's Book of the Courtier*. Detroit: Wayne State UP, 1978.

Redondo, Augustin. 'Los rebaños de ovejas (I, 18).' *Otra manera de leer el* Quijote. Madrid: Gredos, 1997. 341–6.
Ribbans, Geoffrey. 'Herostratus: Notes on the Cult of Fame in Cervantes.' *Cervantes for the 21st Century/Cervantes para el siglo XXI: Studies in Honor of Edward Dudley*. Ed. Francisco La Rubia Prado. Newark DE: Juan de la Cuesta, 2000. 185–98.
Rico, Francisco. *The Spanish Picaresque Novel and the Point of View*. Trans. Charles Davis. Cambridge: Cambridge UP, 1984.
Riley, E.C. 'Cervantes: A Question of Genre.' *Mediaeval and Renaissance Studies on Spain and Portugal in Honour of P.E. Russell*. Ed. F.W. Hodcroft et al. Oxford: Society for the Study of Mediaeval Languages and Literature, 1981. 69–85.
– *Cervantes's Theory of the Novel*. Oxford: Oxford UP, 1962.
Ripa, Cesare. *Iconologia*. 1603. Hildesheim: Georg Olms, 1970.
Rivadeneira, Pedro de. *Vida de Ignacio de Loyola*. Ed. Vicente de la Fuente. Biblioteca de Autores Españoles 60. Madrid: Rivadeneira, 1868. 9–118.
Rivers, Elias L. 'Genres and Voices in the *Viaje del Parnaso*.' Parr 207–35.
Robbins, Jeremy. 'The False Captives and the Representation of History and Fiction in *Los trabajos de Persiles y Sigismunda*.' *Bulletin of Spanish Studies* 81.4–5 (2004): 627–39.
Roberts, Michael. 'The Military Revolution 1560–1660.' *Essays in Swedish History*. London: Weidenfeld and Nicolson, 1967. 195–225.
Rodríguez García, José María. '*Epos delendum est*: The Subject of Carthage in Garcilaso's "A Boscán desde La Goleta."' *Hispanic Review* 66.2 (1998): 151–70.
Rupp, Stephen. 'Soldiers and Satire in *El licenciado Vidriera*.' *A Companion to Cervantes's* Novelas ejemplares. Ed. Stephen Boyd. London: Tamesis, 2005. 134–47.
Sallust. *Bellum Catilinae*. Trans. J.C. Rolfe. Cambridge MA: Harvard UP, 1931.
Salter, James. *The Hunters*. 1956. Rpt. New York: Vintage, 1999.
Sánchez, Alberto. 'Estado actual de los estudios biográficos.' *Suma cervantina*. Ed. J.B. Avalle-Arce and E.C. Riley. London: Tamesis, 1973. 3–24.
Sánchez, Francisco J. *Lectura y representación: Análisis cultural de las* Novelas ejemplares *de Cervantes*. New York: Peter Lang, 1993.
Scarry, Elaine. *The Body in Pain: The Making and Unmaking of the World*. New York: Oxford UP, 1985.
Schevill, R., and A. Bonilla. 'El teatro de Cervantes: Introducción.' *Comedias y entremeses*. By Miguel de Cervantes Saavedra. Madrid, 1922. 1–158.
Schmidt, Rachel. 'The Development of *Hispanitas* in Spanish Sixteenth-Century Versions of the Fall of Numancia.' *Renaissance and Reformation* ns 19.2 (1995): 27–45.

- 'Maps, Figures, and Canons in the *Viaje del Parnaso*.' *Cervantes* 16.2 (1996): 29–46.
Sears, Theresa Ann. *A Marriage of Convenience: Ideal and Ideology in the* Novelas ejemplares. New York: Peter Lang, 1993.
Selig, Karl-Ludwig. 'The Battle of the Sheep (*Don Quixote* I, XVIII).' *Studies in Cervantes*. Kassel: Reichenberger, 1993. 103–13.
- '*Don Quixote* II, XXIV–XXVIII: La aventura del rebuzno.' *Studies in Cervantes*. 135–40.
Serés, Guillermo. 'Estudiantes y soldados cervantinos: El ingenio, la fuerza y el servicio al Rey.' *Releyendo el Quijote, cuatrocientos años después*. Ed. Augustín Redondo. Travaux du CRES 19. Madrid: Presses de la Sorbonne Nouvelle, Centro de Estudios Cervantinos, 2005. 117–30.
Sieber, Diane E. 'Mapping Identity in the Captive's Tale: Cervantes and Ethnographic Narrative.' *Cervantes* 18.1 (1998): 115–33.
Simerka, Barbara. *Discourses of Empire: Counter-Epic Literature in Early Modern Spain*. University Park: Pennsylvania State UP, 2003.
Sobejano, Gonzalo. 'El *Coloquio de los perros* en la picaresca y otros apuntes.' *Hispanic Review* 43.1 (1975): 25–41.
Spadaccini, Nicholas, and Jenaro Taléns, eds. *Autobiography in Early Modern Spain*. Minnesota: Prisma Institute, 1988.
Spagnesi, Pietro. *Castel Sant'Angelo: La fortezza di Roma*. Rome: Palombi, 1995.
Stagg, Geoffrey. 'Cervantes' "De Batro a Tile."' *MLN* 69.2 (1954): 96–9.
- 'The Curious Case of the Suspect Epistle.' *Cervantes* 23.1 (2003): 201–14.
- 'The Date and Form of *El trato de Argel*.' *Bulletin of Hispanic Studies* 30 (1953): 181–92.
Stiegler, Brian N. 'The Coming of the New Jerusalem: Apocalyptic Vision in Cervantes' *La Numancia*.' *Neophilologus* 80.4 (1996): 569–81.
Suetonius. *Life of Julius Caesar. Lives of the Caesars*. Trans. J.C. Rolfe. Rev. ed. 2 vols. Cambridge MA: Harvard UP, 1998. 1:36–149.
Tanner, Marie. *The Last Descendant of Aeneas: The Hapsburgs and the Mythic Image of the Emperor*. New Haven and London: Yale UP, 1993.
Tasso, Torquato. *Discorsi dell'arte poetica e del poema eroico*. Ed. Luigi Poma. Bari: Laterza, 1964.
- *Discourses on the Heroic Poem*. Trans. Mariella Cavalchini and Irene Samuel. Oxford: Oxford UP, 1973.
Teresa de Jesús, St. *Libro de la vida. Obras completas*. Ed. Efrén de la Madre de Dios and Otger Steggink. Madrid: Biblioteca de Autores Cristianos, 1967. 25–191.
Turner, Victor. *Dramas, Fields, and Metaphors: Symbolic Action in Human Society*. Ithaca NY and London: Cornell UP, 1974.
- *The Ritual Process: Structure and Antistructure*. Ithaca NY and London: Cornell UP, 1969.

Vergil. *The Aeneid*. Trans. Robert Fitzgerald. New York: Vintage, 1990.
– *Opera*. Ed. R.A.B. Mynors. Oxford: Oxford UP, 1969.
Vinaver, Eugène. *The Rise of Romance*. Oxford: Oxford UP, 1971.
Vitoria, Francisco de. *On the Law of War. Political Writings*. Ed. Anthony Pagden and Jeremy Lawrance. Cambridge: Cambridge UP, 1991. 295–327.
Walzer, Michael. *Just and Unjust Wars: A Moral Argument with Historical Illustrations*. 2nd ed. New York: Basic, 1992.
Williams, Raymond. *The Country and the City*. London: Hogarth, 1985.
Williamson, Edwin. 'Cervantes as Moralist and Trickster: The Critique of Picaresque Autobiography in *El casamiento engañoso y El coloquio de los perros*.' *Essays on Hispanic Themes in Honour of Edward C. Riley*. Ed. Jennifer Lowe and Philip Swanson. Edinburgh: Department of Hispanic Studies, University of Edinburgh, 1989. 104–26.
Woodward, L.J. '*El casamiento engañoso y el coloquio de los perros*.' *Bulletin of Hispanic Studies* 36 (1959): 80–7.
Yates, Frances A. 'Charles V and the Idea of Empire.' *Astraea: The Imperial Theme in the Sixteenth Century*. London: Routledge and Kegan Paul, 1975. 1–28.
Zahareas, Anthony N. 'The Historical Function of Picaresque Autobiographies: Toward a History of Social Offenders.' Spadaccini and Taléns 129–62.
Zimic, Stanislav. *El teatro de Cervantes*. Madrid: Castalia, 1992.

Index

Adjunta al Parnaso, 209n9
Aeschylus, 32, 209n5, 210–11n13
Alemán, Mateo, 156, 162, 172, 176, 182–3, 230n14, 231nn29–30
Algiers, 9, 101–2, 105–6, 108–9, 115, 190–1, 222n5
Allen, John J., 222n4, 225–6n24
Alpers, Paul, 66, 216nn1–4, 7, 217n10
anti-languages, 179–81, 189, 194
Ariosto, Ludovico, 16, 32–3, 66, 81–5, 209n6, 215n34, 218n20
arms and letters: as aristocratic and martial ideal, 20, 65, 130, 132, 135, 200, 207n30, 216n6, 227n31; compared as careers, 20–5, 146–7, 176; in early modern warfare, 19–27, 207–8n31; and laws of war, 25; and mock-encomium, 26; as rhetorical topic, 19–20, 163, 193, 206–7n28
Armstrong-Roche, Michael, 17–18, 32, 53, 206n26, 215n33
Army of Flanders, 5, 150–1, 152, 156, 168, 190, 204n4, 228n2, 229nn6, 11
Avalle-Arce, Juan Bautista, 47, 49, 213n23, 216nn1, 5

Bakhtin, M.M., 208n2
baños de Argel, Los, 8, 28, 101–2, 103, 112–22, 123, 127, 197, 222nn3, 5, 223n9, 224nn15, 17, 225–6n24
Bergmann, Emilie, 52, 213–14n26
Black, Jeremy, 10–11, 12–13, 205n14
Blanco Aguinaga, Carlos, 231n30
Blecua, José Manuel, 225n19
Boyd, Stephen, 230n15
Brand, C.P., 218n20
Braudel, Fernand, 105–6, 112
Braudy, Leo, 55–6, 212n19, 214nn30–1, 215n32
Brown, Jonathan, 232n2

Canavaggio, Jean, 103, 112, 209nn8–9, 222n3, 223n9
Caputo, Philip, 204n10
Casalduero, Joaquín, 118, 120, 210–11n13
casamiento engañoso, El, 8, 29–30, 150, 161–3, 166–73, 174, 181, 194, 197
Castel Sant'Angelo (Rome), 72, 75, 76–7, 218n14
Castells, Ricardo, 19

246 Index

Castiglione, Baldassarre, 137, 207n30, 219n26, 227n31
Castro, Miguel de, 153
Cervantes Saavedra, Miguel de, biography, 8–9, 34–5, 101–2, 205nn11–12, 209nn8–9
Cetina, Gutierre de, 135–7, 139
Charles V, 53, 54, 70, 108–12, 134, 135, 141, 200, 214nn27–8, 232n2
Chevalier, Maxime, 123
Cicero, 43, 59
Clemencín, Diego, 199, 203n2, 204nn6–7, 220n29, 226n27
Close, Anthony, 219n25
Colie, Rosalie L., 15
coloquio de los perros, El, 8, 30, 88, 150, 161, 173–6, 181–2, 184, 194, 197, 231n28
common soldiers, culture of, 29, 154–5, 157–8, 160, 175, 189, 194, 197, 229nn6, 9, 12
confessional narratives, 29, 150, 155, 164, 171–2, 183
Contreras, Alonso de, 153, 163–6, 230nn17, 19
Cozad, Mary Lee, 216n5
Cruz, Anne J., 155–6, 227n31
Curtius, Ernst Robert, 206–7n28, 213n23

Dandelet, Thomas James, 213n25
Davis, Elizabeth, 33, 211–12n17
de Armas, Frederick A., 47, 50, 206n21, 210n10, 210–11n13, 211n16, 212n20, 213n25, 213–14n26, 232n2
Don Quixote de la Mancha, characters: Don Diego de Miranda, 88, 203n1; Ginés de Pasamonte, 8, 30, 150, 155, 176–7, 181–9, 192–3, 194, 197, 203n1; Pedro de Aguilar, 130–2, 137, 139, 141, 149, 184; Ruy Pérez de Viedma, 28–9, 101, 122–5, 127–30, 140–7, 149–50, 202; Sansón Carrasco, 203n1; Vicente de la Rosa, 8, 29, 158–61, 176, 194; Zoraida, 102, 122–5, 126–7, 143–7, 225n21, 226n26
Don Quixote de la Mancha, episodes: the braying *regidores* (II. 25–7), 29, 68, 86–99; the captive's tale (I. 49–51), 8, 28–9, 80, 101–2, 122–50, 158, 188, 197, 202, 225–6n24; dialogue with the canon of Toledo (I. 47–8), 17; DQ and Sancho's journey to El Toboso (II. 8), 28, 68, 69–77; DQ's assault on the sheepflocks (I. 18), 28, 68, 77–86, 92; DQ's discourse on arms and letters (I. 37–8), 19–27, 130, 146–7; DQ's discourse on the Golden Age (I. 11), 78, 103–4; DQ's encounter with the actors of *Las cortes de la muerte* (II. 11–12), 187; DQ's encounter with the galley slaves (I. 22), 8, 30, 150, 177–84, 197; DQ's encounter with the images of the saints (II. 58), 198–202; DQ's encounter with the page (II. 24), 3–7, 128, 204n8; Eugenio's tale (I. 51), 29, 150, 158–61, 197; Juan Palomeque's inn (I. 32–46), 19, 126, 147, 225n22; Maese Pedro's puppet show (II. 25–7), 184–7, 189, 192–3; *Novela del curioso impertinente* (I. 33–5), 207–8n31
Dunn, Peter N., 155, 156–8, 168, 171–2, 176, 182, 183, 188, 229n8, 230n16, 231n30

El Greco, 200, 232n2
Elliott, J.H., 218n15

El Saffar, Ruth, 162, 163, 171, 230n15
empire: in the captive's tale,
 140–1; in *La Numancia* 52–5, 61–2,
 210–11n13, 213nn24–5, 213–14n26,
 214nn27–8, 215n35; in Renaissance lyric, 135, 137–40; as subject
 of epic, 32–3, 48–50, 85, 195–6,
 206n26, 208n1, 209n6, 219n23,
 232n1
Empson, William, 67, 217n10
Endress, Heinz-Peter, 34, 213–14n26
enlistment, motives for, 152–5, 176,
 228n2
epic: Cervantes's treatment of,
 16–18, 60–1, 100, 114–16, 147–8,
 184–7, 206nn21, 26, 210nn10, 12,
 210–11n13, 213–14n26, 224n17;
 and courtly lyric poetry, 132–9; in
 early modern Spain, 32–3, 209n6;
 and early modern warfare, 13–14;
 ethos of, 31, 42–3, 115–16, 128–9,
 155, 202, 206n25; and pastoral,
 65–6, 68, 77–86; prophecy in, 52–3,
 211n14; structure and subjects
 of, 31–2, 38–9, 100–1, 195–6,
 208nn1–2, 210n11, 212n21, 232n1;
 and tragedy, 31–2, 36–8, 208n3,
 208–9n4, 209n5
'Epístola a Mateo Vázquez,' 111–12,
 223–4n14
Erasmus, Desiderius, 103, 154–5,
 160, 175, 220n31, 223n10, 228n34
Ercilla, Alonso de, 33, 53

fame: Cipión's generalship and, 38,
 58–60; and the city of Numantia,
 38, 52, 60–1; Don Quixote's desire
 for, 26, 69–70, 78–9; instability of,
 8, 28, 36, 65, 75, 77, 98–9, 219n24;
 as martial value, 31, 132, 155, 160,
 195–6, 215n32; in Roman historical
 and literary sources, 59–60, 70–1,
 73, 212n19, 214nn30–1; secular and
 Christian, 68, 71–7, 201
Feldherr, Andrew, 211n15
Fernández, Jaime, S.J., 4, 203n1
Fernández Alvarez, Manuel, 223n13
Finello, Dominick, 216nn1, 3, 5
Fisher, Sir Geoffrey, 224n18
Forcione, Alban K., 163, 171, 172,
 176, 192–3, 206n23, 210n12, 216n5,
 221n1, 230nn15, 22, 231n31,
 232n33
Fothergill-Payne, Louise, 108, 222n5,
 224n15
Fowler, Alastair, 14–15, 205n19,
 205–6n20, 206n27, 208n3, 216n2
Fox, Dian, 198, 232nn34, 3
Friedman, Edward H., 107, 118,
 222n5, 224n15
Friedman, Ellen G., 223n12, 224n16
Frye, Northrop: *Anatomy of Criti-
 cism*, 14, 31–2, 58, 81, 206nn22, 24,
 208–9n4, 218nn17, 19; *The Secular
 Scripture*, 102, 117, 123–7, 145,
 147–8, 205n17, 225n21, 226n25
Fuchs, Barbara, 102, 106, 144,
 222–3n7, 223n8
Fussell, Paul, 101, 204n9, 217n11,
 221n2

Galatea, La, 65, 206n21, 215n33, 216n6
galleys, 23–4, 152, 187–8, 189, 190–1
galley slaves, 141–2, 177–84, 191,
 228n3, 230n24, 231n25
Garcés, María Antonia, 102, 106, 107,
 111, 125, 127, 144, 205nn11–12,
 222nn3–4, 225–6n24, 226n26
Garcilaso de la Vega: epic and lyric
 in, 100, 132–5; pastoral in, 66–7, 69,

229n10; as soldier-poet, 111, 137, 227n31; and the Spanish literary canon, 111, 139–40
genres, general theory and history of, 14–19, 64, 205nn18–19, 205–6n20, 206nn21–4, 27
Gerli, E. Michael, 127, 146, 226n26
Girard, René, 220–1n32
glory: Cipión and, 38, 56–9; and debate on arms and letters, 207n30; in epic, 32, 52, 77; Numantian valour and, 36, 45, 52, 56, 59; in Roman historical sources, 59–60, 212n19, 214n30; secular and Christian, 71–5, 132
Greene, Thomas, 75–6
Guillén, Claudio, 14–16, 182, 183, 205n18, 231n29
gunpowder weapons, 6, 9–13, 22–3, 25–6

Hale, J.R., 151, 205n16, 207n29, 229nn5, 12
Halliday, Michael, 179–80, 231n27
Hanson, Victor Davis, 142, 227n29
Hardie, Philip, 208n1, 209n5, 212n21, 214n31, 232n1
Harris, William V., 210n11, 212n19, 214n30
Hart, Thomas R., 230n14
Heilbrun, Carolyn, 169
Helgerson, Richard, 134–5
Heliodorus, 17–18, 206n26, 221n1
Hernández de Velasco, Gregorio, 184–5
heroism: and classical epic, 31, 42–3, 115–16, 131–2, 195–6; in early modern warfare, 22–4, 26–7, 102–7, 197–8; martial and spiritual, 8, 28, 103, 106–7, 111–13, 121, 122, 123, 129, 141, 143, 146–7, 196–7; romance and, 29, 101, 107, 141, 196–7; traditional ethos of, 27, 36, 39–45, 51–2, 61–2, 79, 128–9
Herostratus, 70
Herrera, Fernando de, 137–40, 209n7, 228n33
Hess, Andrew C., 105, 223n11, 224n18
Homer, 80, 84, 114, 195, 208nn1, 3, 210n11, 210–11n13, 211n14, 212n20
Horace, 88–9, 97, 170
Hynes, Samuel, 7, 8, 26, 204n10

Ife, B.W., 170, 230n18
Información de Argel, 205nn11–12

Johnson, Carroll B., 213n25
Juvenal, 87, 88–9

Kagan, Richard L., 20, 220n30
Kahn, Aaron M., 39, 46, 55, 58, 209n8, 213n25, 215n35
Keegan, John, 47, 154
Keith, A.M., 206n25
Kennedy, A.L., 3, 7, 195
King, Willard F., 210–11n13, 213–14n26, 215n35
Kubler, George, and Martin Soria, 232n2

Labov, William, 165–6, 230n18
Lara Garrido, José, 32–3, 34
Lattimore, Richmond, 227n30
laws of war, 24–5, 80, 91–2, 93–7, 99, 104
Lazarillo de Tormes, La vida de, 155–6, 170, 176, 182, 183, 188, 231n29
Lázaro Carreter, Fernando, 230n23

Lepanto, battle of, 9–10, 103, 105, 128–9, 140, 223–4n14, 227n29, 228n33
Levisi, Margaret, 163, 165, 230n19
Lewis-Smith, Paul, 47, 50, 55, 210–11n13
licenciado Vidriera, El, 88, 204n5
Lida de Malkiel, María Rosa, 214n31
Livy, 211n15, 212n18, 217n13
Lokos, Ellen D., 88, 219n24
López de Gómara, Francisco, 217n13
Lowe, Jennifer, 216n5
Lucan, 32, 46, 53, 210–11n13, 211n14, 212n21
Lynch, John, 105, 227n32
lyric, 8, 14, 28–9, 100, 101–2, 109–12, 130–40, 204nn8–9, 225n19, 227nn30–1, 228n33, 229n10

MacKay, Ruth, 151–2, 154, 228nn1–2, 4
Maglione, Sabatino G., 212n18
Maravall, J.A., 20, 68–9
Marinelli, Peter V., 66–7, 216n8
Márquez Villanueva, Francisco, 123, 144, 225n21, 226n26
Marshall, John W., 102, 223n8
Martín, Francisco J., 38
Martines, Lauro, 217n9
McGaha, Michael, D., 80–1, 216n5
Meregalli, Franco, 107
Middlebrook, Leah, 227n31
military revolution, 10–14, 205nn14–15
miracle narrative, 29, 155, 171
mock encomium, 26, 74, 199, 208n32
Molho, Maurice, 163
Moxey, Keith, 229n5, 230n20
Murillo, Luis A., 81, 123–4, 218n16, 225–6n24, 226n26
Murrin, Michael, 13–14

Navarrete, Ignacio, 139–40
Nicolopulos, James, 33, 53, 209n6
Novelas ejemplares, prologue to, 9
Numancia, Tragedia de, 8, 27, 33–62, 63–4, 71, 75, 132, 196, 210–11n13
Numantia, history of, 27, 33–4, 209n7, 213–14n26

Oliver Asín, Jaime, 101
Orwell, George, 63, 67
Osborne, John, 76
Ovid, 214n31

Pagden, Anthony, 61–2, 214n27
Pantheon, 72, 75, 76
Paré, Ambroise, 21–2, 207n29
Parker, Ernest, 100, 101, 221n2
Parker, Geoffrey, 11–12, 204n4, 205nn14–15, 220n28, 228nn1–2, 4, 229nn6, 9, 11
Pasamonte, Jerónimo de, 153
pastoral: and picaresque, 159, 161, 170, 184, 194; reflections on fame and the active life in, 8, 14, 26–7, 65, 68, 71, 98–9, 184, 196, 216nn6, 8, 217n9; in Renaissance literature, 16, 66–7, 91, 159, 206n21, 216nn3, 5, 7; rural labour in, 65–6, 68, 86–7; and satire, 27–8, 65, 67, 68, 86–7, 93–4, 216n4; style and subjects of, 64–9, 198–9, 216nn1–2, 217n10, 229nn10, 12; and violence, 27, 29, 65–9, 77, 86–7, 98–9, 100, 114, 161, 170
Perry, Ben Edwin, 222–3n7
Persiles y Sigismunda, Los trabajos de, 8, 17–18, 30, 32, 150, 189–94, 197, 206nn21, 26, 215n33, 230n22
Petrarch, 75, 136–7, 172, 215n33
Petro, Antonia, 46

Philip II, 108, 110–11, 112, 141, 214n28, 223–4n14, 227n32
picaresque: and early modern Spanish society, 14, 156–8; military service and the culture of common soldiers in, 5, 8, 29, 156–8, 197; and soldiers' tales, 29–30, 150, 161; style and subjects of, 162–3, 164, 170, 173–4, 181–3, 231nn28–9
Pike, Ruth, 228n3, 230n24, 231n25
Plutarch, 43–4, 60, 205n13
Polybius, 43
Pope, Randolph, 163–4, 230nn17, 19
popular artist, figure of, 30, 177, 187, 189
popular theatre, 34, 100, 113, 155, 163, 184–7, 192, 209n8, 218n18, 221n1, 224n15, 230n16, 232n33
Presberg, Charles D., 208n32
privateering, 105–6, 113, 224n18
prophecy, 40–1, 52–5, 211n14, 213nn24–5
prostitution, 168
prudence, 40, 47, 50–1

Quint, David, 21, 85, 208n1, 219n23, 226n26, 232n1

Randel, Mary Gaylord, 216n5
Raphael, 200
Rebhorn, Wayne A., 207n30
recruitment, 29, 151–2, 156, 228nn1–2
Redondo, Augustin, 80, 218n21
rhetoric: and the displacement of injury, 106–7, 115, 131–2, 191; and leadership, 39–40, 96, 211n15; structures of, 25, 26–7, 78–9, 92–3, 110–11, 223–4n14; styles of, 15, 64, 90–1, 185; topics of, 19–20, 51, 73–4, 92–3, 108, 185, 206–7n28

Ribbans, Geoffrey, 74
Rico, Francisco, 162
Riley, E.C., 206nn23–4, 229n7
Ripa, Cesare, 215n32
Rivadeneira, Pedro de, 171
Rivers, Elias L., 219n24
Robbins, Jeremy, 231nn31–2
Roberts, Michael, 10, 11
Rodríguez García, José María, 135
Roelas, Juan de, 200, 232n2
romance: and epic, 13–14, 17–18, 81, 83–5, 147–8, 206n26, 224n17; heroism in, 29, 101, 107, 141, 196–7; and Mediterranean cultures, 102, 222–3n7; and novel, 16–17, 206n4; plot and structure of, 80, 101–2, 122, 123–7, 145–6, 169–70, 184, 188, 218nn17, 19, 225n21, 230n15; saints' lives as, 100, 102, 221n1, 223n8; social ascent in, 149–50
romances of chivalry, 17, 23, 74, 77–86, 196, 199–202, 203n1, 204n8, 205n17
Rupp, Stephen, 204n5

Saint Peter's needle (Rome), 72, 75, 76
saints, 73–4, 121, 184, 198–201, 232n2
saints' lives, 28, 100, 101, 102, 122, 147, 171, 199–200, 221n1
Sallust, 55, 59–60, 212n18
Salter, James, 31
Sánchez, Alberto, 205n11
Sánchez, Francisco J., 163, 168, 230n15
satire: Cervantes's views on, 87–9, 193, 219nn24–5; and fame, 28, 68, 86–7, 97–8; and military life, 5, 128, 140, 204n5; and pastoral, 27–8, 65, 67, 68, 86–7, 93–4, 216n4

scapegoating, 28, 68, 97, 99, 196, 220–1n32
Scarry, Elaine, 106, 129, 191, 226–7n28
Schevill, R., and A. Bonilla, 222n3
Schmidt, Rachel, 33–4, 209n7, 219n24
Sears, Theresa Ann, 230n21
Selig, Karl-Ludwig, 81, 85, 92
Serés, Guillermo, 4, 117–18, 203–4n3, 204n5
Sieber, Diana, 222n6
siege warfare, 11–13, 23–4, 46–50, 132–3, 152, 197, 207–8n31, 212–13n22
Simerka, Barbara, 34, 55, 210–11n13, 214n29, 215n35
Sobejano, Gonzalo, 173, 230n23
soldier-poet, figure of, 65, 102, 111–12, 130, 132–7, 139–40, 227n31
soldiers' tales: language of, 165–6; as markers of community, 176, 197; as performance, 154–5, 160–1, 194; purposes of, 150, 158, 160, 163–6
Stagg, Geoffrey, 112, 215n33, 222n3, 223–4n14
Stiegler, Brian N., 213n24
Suetonius, 4, 6, 203n2, 217n13

Tanner, Marie, 214n28
Tasso, Torquato, 27, 36–9, 52, 61, 66, 210n12
Teresa of Ávila, St, 221n1
Titian, 200, 232n2
tragedy, 8, 16, 27, 31–3, 36–9, 52, 58–9, 100, 147, 195–6

trato de Argel, El, 8, 28, 34, 101–2, 103–12, 120, 122, 130, 141, 197, 222nn3, 5, 223n9, 223–4n14, 224n15, 225–6n24
Turner, Victor, 156–7, 179, 229n8
typology, biblical, 28, 112–13, 116–22, 127, 197, 225n20, 226n26

vainglory, 69, 71, 75
Vergil: and empire, 49, 53, 195, 208n1, 209n6, 215n33, 219n23, 232n1; epic conventions in, 80, 84, 114, 135, 184–6, 210n11, 211n14; and the ethos of epic, 31, 42–3, 115–16, 138–9; fame in, 60, 214n31, 215n32; pastoral in, 64, 65–6, 216n7; and poetic career, 206n21; tragedy in, 32, 209n5
verisimilitude, 16–17, 38–9, 231n32
Viaje del Parnaso, 71, 75, 87–8, 98–9, 209n9, 219nn24–5
Vinaver, Eugène, 223n8
Vitoria, Francisco de, 94–7

Walzer, Michael, 47–8, 212–13n22
Williams, Raymond, 65–6
Williamson, Edwin, 171, 230n15
Woodward, L.J., 162

Yates, Frances A., 214n28

Zahareas, Anthony N., 165
Zimic, Stanislav, 47, 103–4, 107, 114, 223n10

TORONTO IBERIC

CO-EDITORS: Robert Davidson (Toronto) and Frederick A. de Armas (Chicago)

EDITORIAL BOARD: Josiah Blackmore (Harvard); Marina Brownlee (Princeton); Anthony J. Cascardi (Berkeley); Justin Crumbaugh (Mt Holyoke); Emily Francomano (Georgetown); Jordana Mendelson (NYU); Joan Ramon Resina (Stanford); Enrique Garcia Santo-Tomás (U Michigan); Kathleen Vernon (SUNY Stony Brook)

1. Anthony J. Cascardi, *Cervantes, Literature, and the Discourse of Politics*
2. Jessica A. Boon, *The Mystical Science of the Soul: Medieval Cognition in Bernardino de Laredo's Recollection Method*
3. Susan Byrne, *Law and History in Cervantes' Don Quixote*
4. Mary E. Barnard and Frederick A. de Armas (eds), *Objects of Culture in the Literature of Imperial Spain*
5. Nil Santiáñez, *Topographies of Fascism: Habitus, Space, and Writing in Twentieth-Century Spain*
6. Nelson Orringer, *Lorca in Tune with Falla: Literary and Musical Interludes*
7. Ana M. Gómez-Bravo, *Textual Agency: Writing Culture and Social Networks in Fifteenth-Century Spain*
8. Javier Irigoyen-García, *The Spanish Arcadia: Sheep Herding, Pastoral Discourse, and Ethnicity in Early Modern Spain*
9. Stephanie Sieburth, *Survival Songs: Conchita Piquer's* Coplas *and Franco's Regime of Terror*
10. Christine Arkinstall, *Spanish Female Writers and the Freethinking Press, 1879–1926*
11. Margaret Boyle, *Unruly Women: Performance, Penitence, and Punishment in Early Modern Spain*
12. Evelina Gužauskytė, *Christopher Columbus's Naming in the* diarios *of the Four Voyages (1492–1504): A Discourse of Negotiation*

13 Mary E. Barnard, *Garcilaso de la Vega and the Material Culture of Renaissance Europe*
14 William Viestenz, *By the Grace of God: Francoist Spain and the Sacred Roots of Political Imagination*
15 Michael Scham, *Lector Ludens: The Representation of Games and Play in Cervantes*
16 Stephen Rupp, *Heroic Forms: Cervantes and the Literature of War*
17 Enrique Fernandez, *Anxieties of Interiority and Dissection in Early Modern Spain*
18 Susan Byrne, *Ficino in Spain*
19 Patricia M. Keller, *Ghostly Landscapes: Film, Photography, and the Aesthetics of Haunting in Contemporary Spanish Culture*
20 Carolyn A. Nadeau, *Food Matters: Alonso Quijano's Diet and the Discourse of Food in Early Modern Spain*
21 Cristian Berco, *From Body to Community: Venereal Disease and Society in Baroque Spain*
22 Elizabeth R. Wright, *The Epic of Juan Latino: Dilemmas of Race and Religion in Renaissance Spain*
23 Ryan D. Giles, *Inscribed Power: Amulets and Magic in Early Spanish Literature*
24 Jorge Pérez, *Confessional Cinema: Religion, Film, and Modernity in Spain's Development Years (1960–1975)*
25 Juan Ramon Resina, *Josep Pla: Seeing the World in the Form of Articles*
26 Javier Irigoyen-Garcia, *"Moors Dressed as Moors": Clothing, Social Distinction, and Ethnicity in Early Modern Iberia*
27 Jean Dangler, *Edging toward Iberia*

Selected Bibliography

A/BIBLIOGRAPHIES

Kerry, Otto *Karl-Kraus-Bibliographie* Munich 1970
- 'Nachtrag zur Karl-Kraus-Bibliographie' *Modern Austrian Literature* 8 (1975) 103–80
Scheichl, Sigurd Paul 'Kommentierte Auswahlbibliographie zu Karl Kraus' in: *Karl Kraus* Text + Kritik, Sonderband, ed. Heinz Ludwig Arnold, Munich 1975, 158–241

B/KARL KRAUS'S WORKS

Kraus, Karl *Die demolirte Literatur* Vienna 1897*
- ed. *Die Fackel* Vienna 1899–1936
- *Die letzten Tage der Menschheit* 2 vols Munich 1964
- *Shakespeares Dramen* Für Hörer und Leser bearbeitet, teilweise sprachlich erneuert von Karl Kraus. 2 vols Vienna 1934–5
- *Werke* 14 vols ed Heinrich Fischer, Munich 1954–67

C/WORKS ABOUT KARL KRAUS

Arntzen, Helmut 'Karl Kraus als Kritiker des Fin de Siècle,' in: *Fin de siècle: Zu Literatur und Kunst der Jahrhundertwende* ed Roger Bauer et al Frankfurt 1977, 112–24
- *Karl Kraus und die Presse* Munich 1975
Bohn, Volker *Satire und Kritik. Über Karl Kraus* Frankfurt 1974
Borries, Mechthild *Ein Angriff auf Heinrich Heine. Kritische Betrachtungen zu Karl Kraus* Stuttgart, Berlin, Cologne, Mainz 1971

* For the articles published by Kraus between 1892 and 1898 in *Wiener Literatur-Zeitung, Die Gesellschaft, Das Rendez-vous, Wiener Tagblatt, Liebelei, Montags-Revue, Wiener Rundschau, Breslauer Zeitung,* and *Die Wage* see Kerry's *Karl-Kraus-Bibliographie* listed above.

Brecht, Bertold *Schriften zur Literatur und Kunst* 3 vols ed. Werner Hecht, Tübingen 1967
Brock-Sulzer, Elisabeth 'Karl Kraus und das Theater' *Akzente* (December 1955) 503–9
Daviau, Donald G. 'Language and Morality in Karl Kraus' "Die letzten Tage der Menschheit"' *Modern Language Quarterly* 22 (1961) 46–54
Deutsch, Otto Erich 'Offenbach, Kraus und die anderen (1931)' *Österreichische Musik-Zeitschrift* 18 (1963) 408–12
Dietze, Walter 'Dramaturgische Besonderheiten des Antikriegsschauspiels "Die letzten Tage der Menschheit" von Karl Kraus' *Philologica Pragensia* 5 (1962) 65–83
Disch, Andreas *Das gestaltete Wort. Die Idee der Dichtung im Werk von Karl Kraus* Zurich 1969
Dürrenmatt, Friedrich 'Die dritte Walpurgisnacht,' in Friedrich Dürrenmatt *Theater-Schriften und Reden* (Zurich 1966) 247–50
Engelmann, Paul *Dem Andenken an Karl Kraus* Vienna 1967
Field, Frank *The Last Days of Mankind. Karl Kraus and his Vienna* London, Melbourne, Toronto 1967
Fischer, Jens Malte *Karl Kraus* Stuttgart 1974
– *Karl Kraus. Studien zum 'Theater der Dichtung' und Kulturkonservatismus* Kronberg/Taunus 1973
Flatter, Richard *Karl Kraus als Nachdichter Shakespeares. Eine sprachkritische Untersuchung* Vienna 1934
Ginsberg, Ernst, 'Karl Kraus und die Schauspieler' *Forum* (August 1961) 229
Grimstad, Kari 'Karl Kraus and the Problem of Illusion and Reality in Drama and the Theater' *Modern Austrian Literature* 8 (1975) 48–60
Hahnl, Hans Heinz 'Karl Kraus und das Theater' Diss. Vienna 1947
– 'Karl Kraus und das Theater' *Wort in der Zeit* 2 (June 1956) 17–20
Hartl, Edwin, 'das Ja und Nein zu Karl Kraus' *Literatur und Kritik* 24 (May 1968) 247f
– 'Verblendete Hellseher und Schwarzseher' *Literatur und Kritik* 41 (1970) 3–14
Heller, Erich 'Karl Kraus: The last days of mankind' in Erich Heller, *The Disinherited Mind. Essays in modern German literature and thought* (Cambridge, 1952) 183–201
Himmel, Hellmuth 'Hugo von Hofmannsthal und Karl Kraus' *Österreich in Geschichte und Literatur* 10 (1966) 551–65
Iggers, Wilma A. *Karl Kraus: A Viennese Critic of the 20th Century* The Hague 1967
Jenaczek, Friedrich 'Protest' *Literatur und Kritik* 41 (1970) 14–21
– *Zeittafeln zur "Fackel". Themen, Ziele, Probleme* Munich 1965
Kars, Gustave 'L'esthétique de Karl Kraus' *Études germaniques* 8 (Oct./Dec. 1953) 252–61
Kohn, Caroline 'Bert Brecht, Karl Kraus et le "Kraus-Archiv"' *Études germaniques* 11 (1956) 342–8
– *Karl Kraus* Stuttgart 1966
Kohn, Hans *Karl Kraus, Arthur Schnitzler, Otto Weininger. Aus dem jüdischen Wien der Jahrhundertwende* Tübingen 1962

Kosler, Hans Christian 'Karl Kraus und die Wiener Moderne' *Text und Kritik* Sonderband Karl Kraus (1975) 39–57
Kraft, Werner *Das Ja des Neinsagers. Karl Kraus und seine geistige Welt.* Munich, 1974
– 'Es war einmal ein Mann. Über die "Dritte Walpurgistnacht" von Karl Kraus' *Merkur* 22 (1968) 926–35
– *Karl Kraus. Beiträge zum Verständnis seines Werkes* Salzburg 1956
Krolop, Kurt 'Bertolt Brecht und Karl Kraus' *Philologica Pragensia* 4 (1961) 95–112 and 203–30
– 'Dichtung und Satire bei Karl Kraus' in Karl Kraus *Ausgewählte Werke* (Munich 1971) III, 651–91
Leschnitzer, Franz 'Ein zweites Gedicht Bertolt Brechts über Karl Kraus' *Neue Deutsche Literatur* 12 (1964) 212–15
Liegler, Leopold *Karl Kraus un sein Werk* Vienna 1933
Mautner, Franz H 'Karl Kraus. Die letzten Tage der Menschheit' in *Das deutsche Drama. Vom Barock bis zur Gegenwart. Interpretationen* 2 Benno von Wiese ed. (Düsseldorf 1964) 360–85
– 'Über Karl Kraus's Komödie Wolkenkuckucksheim: Aristophanes Vögel nach 2300 Jahren' in *Austriaca: Beiträge zur österreichischen Literatur: Festschrift für Heinz Politzer zum 65. Geburtstag* ed. Winfried Kudszus et al (Tübingen 1975) 315–28
Mayer, Hans 'Karl Kraus' in Mayer *Der Repräsentant und der Märtyrer. Konstellationen der Literatur* (Frankfurt/Main 1971) 45–64
Mühlher, Robert 'Karl Kraus und das Burgtheater vor 1890' *Österreich in Geschichte und Literatur* 10 (June 1966) 298–307
Muschg, Walter 'Karl Kraus; Die letzten Tage der Menschheit' in Muschg *Von Trakl zu Brecht. Dichter des Expressionismus* (Munich 1961) 174–97
Nachrichten aus dem Kösel-Verlag. Sonderheft zum 90. Geburtstag von Karl Kraus Munich 1964
Naumann, Michael *Der Abbau einer verkehrten Welt; Satire und politische Wirklichkeit im Werk von Karl Kraus* Munich 1969
Ögg, Franz *Personenregister zur Fackel von Karl Kraus Supplementband zum Reprint der Fackel* Munich 1977
Polacek, Josef 'Egon Erwin Kisch über Karl Kraus' *Literatur und Kritik* 41 (1970) 21–36
Politzer, Heinz 'Die letzten Tage der Schwierigen: Hofmannsthal, Karl Kraus und Schnitzler' *Merkur* 28 (1974) 214–38
Raddatz, Fritz J. 'Der blinde Seher. Überlegungen zu Karl Kraus' *Merkur* 22 (1968) 517–32
Rychner, Max *Karl Kraus* Vienna 1924
Schaukal, Richard *Karl Kraus. Versuch eines geistigen Bildnisses* Vienna 1933
Schick, Paul 'Karl Kraus: Der Satiriker und die Zeit' *Études germaniques* 12 (1957) 240–9
– *Karl Kraus in Selbstzeugnissen und Bilddokumenten* Reinbek 1965 (Rowohlt)

Schmid, Richard 'Die Fackel des Karl Kraus' *Merkur* 28 (1974) 1053–70
Snell, Mary 'Karl Kraus' "Die letzten Tage der Menschheit"' *Forum for Modern Language Studies* 4 (1968) 234–47
Stern, J.P. 'Karl Kraus' Vision of Language' *Modern Language Revue* 61 (1966) 81–4
Sternbach-Gärtner, Lotte [Caroline Kohn] '"Die letzten Tage der Menschheit" und das Theater von Bert Brecht' *Deutsche Rundschau* 84 (Sept. 1958) 836–42
- 'Karl Kraus und das expressionistische Theater' in *Worte und Werte. Festschrift für Bruno Markward zum 60. Geburtstag* ed. G. Erdmann and A. Eichstaedt (Berlin 1961) 398–409
- 'Karl Kraus und Offenbach' *Der Monat* 96 (1956) 55–61
Torberg, Friedrich 'Das Wort gegen die Bühne. Zur szenischen Uraufführung der "Letzten Tage der Menschheit" von Karl Kraus' *Forum* (Aug. 1964) 383–5
Urbach, Reinhard 'Karl Kraus und Arthur Schnitzler. Eine Dokumentation' *Literatur und Kritik* 49 (1970) 513–30
- 'Karl Kraus und Hugo von Hofmannsthal. Eine Dokumentation. I. 1892–1899. II. 1899–1935' in *Hofmannsthal Blätter* I Heft 6 (1971) 447–58. II Heft 12 (1974) 372–424
Wagenknecht, Christian *Das Wortspiel bei Karl Kraus* Göttingen 1965
Weigel, Hans *Karl Kraus oder Die Macht der Ohnmacht* Vienna 1972
Zohn, Harry *Karl Kraus* New York 1971

D GENERAL BACKGROUND

Aristotle *Poetics* trans. Leon Golden Englewood Cliffs 1968
Arntzen, Helmut *Literatur im Zeitalter der Information* Frankfurt/Main 1971
Basil, Otto *Johann Nestroy in Selbstzeugnissen und Bilddokumenten* Reinbek 1967 (rowohlt)
Catholy, Eckehard 'Schauspielertum als Lebensform' *Hebbel-Jahrbuch* 1951, 97–112
Gröning, K. und W. Kließ *Friedrichs Theaterlexikon* Velber bei Hannover 1969
Hadamowsky, Franz 'Die Commedia dell'arte in Österreich und ihre Wirkung auf das Wiener Volkstheater' *Maske und Kothurn* 3 (1957) 312–16
Harding, L.V. *The Dramatic Art of Ferdinand Raimund and Johann Nestroy* The Hague, Paris 1974
Hein Jürgen 'Nestroy-Forschung (1901–1966)' *Wirkendes Wort* 18 (1968) 232–45
Hofmannsthal, Hugo von/Leopold von Andrian *Briefwechsel* Frankfurt/Main 1968
Ihering, Herbert, *Von Josef Kainz bis Paula Wessely* Heidelberg 1942
- *Von Reinhardt bis Brecht. Vier Jahrzehnte Theater und Film* Berlin 1961
Irmer, Hans-Jochen 'Jacques Offenbachs Werke in Wien und Berlin' *Wissenschaftliche Zeitschrift der Universität Berlin. Gesellschafts- und Sprachwissenschaftliche Reihe* 18 (1969) 125–45
Jacob, P. Walter *Jacques Offenbach in Selbstzeugnissen und Bilddokumenten* Reinbek 1969 (rowohlt)

Kindermann, Heinz *Hermann Bahr. Ein Leben für das europäische Theater* Graz, Cologne 1954
Mautner, Franz H. *Nestroy* Heidelberg 1974
Nestroy, Johann *Werke* Munich 1968
Niederle, Bertha *Charlotte Wolter* Vienna 1948
Prohaska, D. *Raimund and Vienna* Cambridge 1970
Raimund, Ferdinand *Sämtliche Werke* Munich 1966
Reichert, Herbert W. 'Some causes of the Nestroy renaissance in Vienna,' *Monatshefte* 47 (1955) 221–30
Richter, Helene *Josef Lewinsky. Fünfzig Jahre Wiener Kunst und Kultur* Vienna, no date
Rommel, Otto *Die Alt-Wiener Volkskomödie* Vienna 1952
Rühle, Gunter *Theater für die Republik (1917–33). Im Spiegel der Kritiker* Frankfurt 1967
Schorske, Carl E. *Fin-de-siècle Vienna. Politics and Culture* New York 1980
Schreyvogl, Friedrich *Das Burgtheater* Vienna 1965
Shakespeare, Wm *Macbeth* New Haven 1954
– *Werke* 5 Darmstadt 1958
Swales, Martin *Arthur Schnitzler. A Critical Study* Oxford 1971
Volke, Werner *Hugo von Hofmannsthal in Selbstzeugnissen und Bilddokumenten* Reinbek 1967 (rowohlt)
Wedekind, Frank *Gesammelte Werke* Munich 1920

Index

Adamus, Franz 269 n.83
Andó, Flavio 8
Andrian-Werburg, Leopold Freiherr von 115, 119, 136
Anzengruber, Ludwig 40, 200, 236
Arbeiterzeitung 71, 162, 283 n.12
Aristophanes 210, 212
Aristotle 272 n.34
Auernheimer, Raoul 158

Bab, Julius 49, 50
Bahr, Hermann xiv, 18–30, 32, 34, 44, 67–8, 71, 87, 90, 115, 119, 127–8, 135–7, 153, 196–7, 202, 224, 260, 265, n.4, 267 n.68ff.
Barnay, Ludwig 9, 48
Bauer, Julius 22–4, 26, 35, 37, 43, 66, 69, 94, 268 n.68
Baumberg, Antonie 32, 87–8, 272–3 n.40
Baumeister, Bernard 9, 10, 37, 43–4, 46–8, 50, 108–9, 115, 130, 184, 199, 245
Beckmann, Friedrich 237
Bekessy, Imre (Emmerich) xiv, 151, 175, 211, 222–4, 259, 278 n.15
Berger, Alfred Freiherr von 84, 115–16, 120, 272 n.38, 275 n.7
Berliner Börsenkurier 69
Berliner Schauspielhaus 180
Berliner Staatsoper 241
Bernard, Tristan 203–4

Bernhardt, Sarah 9
Bezecny, Josef Freiherr von 7
Bien, Erich 130
Bleibtreu, Karl 156, 268 n.69
Blumenthal, Oskar 86
Bohemia 168
Bracco, Roberto 28–9
Brahm Otto 33–4, 37, 185, 249
Brecht, Bertolt xii, 251–7, 282 n.75
Brečka, Hans 158
Breslauer Zeitung 11–12, 266 n.12ff., 267 n.31ff.
Brod, Max 274 n.3
Buchbinder, Bernhard 31, 37, 41, 56, 58–9, 66, 68–9, 86–7, 270 n.11
Büchner, Georg xiii
Budapester Orpheumgesellschaft 98, 106, 120
Bukovics, Emerich von 25–8, 68, 90, 265 n.4
Burckhard, Max 4–7, 41, 153–4
Bürgertheater (Vienna) 148, 150
Burgtheater 3–12, 25, 35, 37, 39–47, 49–55, 59, 60, 67, 70, 106–20, 122, 148, 152–61, 167, 179, 181, 196–7, 199, 215, 236, 245–7, 259, 266 n.8, 269 n.81ff., 272 n.38, 274 n.2, 275 n.7ff., 277 n.7ff., 278 n.18

Café Griensteidl 3, 17–19, 21

Calderon de la Barca, Pedro 4, 47
Carltheater 22, 170, 279 n.26
Castiglioni, Camillo 203–4, 211, 281 n.50
Coleridge, Samuel Taylor xi
Concordia 22–4, 26, 29, 37
Corneille, Pierre 245
Cremieux, Hector-Jonathan 172, 270 n.16

Das Vaterland 84
Davis, Gustav 4
Decsey, Ernst 278 n.18
Delvard, Marya 272 n.29
Deutsches Schauspielhaus (Hamburg) 38, 84, 115
Deutsches Theater (Berlin) 24–5, 33, 122, 249
Deutsches Theater (Prague) 242
Deutsches Volkstheater (Vienna). *See under* Volkstheater
Deutsche Zeitung 25
Devrient, Max 115, 118
Die Gesellschaft 8, 266 n.5ff., 267 n.35ff.
Die Stunde 211, 222–3
Die Truppe 185
Die Wage 7, 266 n.15ff., 267 n.60
Die Zeit 25, 41, 273 n.46
Die Zukunft 92
Dingelstedt, Franz von 269 n.81
Doczi, Ludwig 86
Dollfuß, Engelbert 228, 233, 256–7
Dörner, Erich 238, 242
Dreher, Conrad 10
Dreyer, Max 24
Duse, Eleonora 8, 9

Eisenbach, Heinrich 120
Elbogen, Friedrich 14
Engel, Erich 252
Ernst, Otto 24, 73, 87–8, 272 n.39
Eulenberg, Fürst Philipp zu 273 n.44

Euripides 71
Ewers, Hanns Heinz 128
Extrablatt 69
Eysler, Edmund 148
Eysoldt, Gertrude 83

Fehling, Jürgen 185
Feld, Leo 145
Félix, Elisa. *See under* Rachel
Feuillet, Octave 5
Fischer, Heinrich 252
Frankfurter Zeitung 271 n.18
Fremdenblatt 272 n.29
Friedell, Egon 74, 278 n.18
Friedmann, Armin 234
Friedmann, Oskar 22–3

Gabillon, Ludwig 108
Gabillon-Würzburg, Zerline 108, 152, 154–5, 215, 283 n.21
Gelber, Adolf 271 n.22
George, Stefan 240
Girardi, Alexander 23, 37–8, 40, 43, 52, 56–9, 73, 102, 114–15, 120, 126, 130, 270 n.10
Goethe, Johann Wolfgang von 4, 12, 40, 77, 87, 188, 201, 214, 242, 250, 260, 272 n.27, 278 n.16
Gogol, Nicolaj 15, 278 n.16
Goldmann, Paul 43, 71, 73, 76–7, 90, 135, 272 n.35, 278 n.18
Gorki, Maxim 54
Gottlieb. *See under* Kerr, Alfred
Grillparzer, Franz 200–3, 234
Großmann, Stefan 43, 49, 68, 71
Gundolf, Friedrich 181–3
Gutt, Bernhard 167–9

Halévy, Ludovic 170
Hallenstein, Konwed Alfred 112
Hamburger Schauspielhaus. *See under* Deutsches Schauspielhaus (Hamburg)

author's] lack of familiarity with the theatre ...'[19] That others, too, have reached the conclusion that Kraus's Offenbach adaptations are not ideally suited to the operetta stage is evident in the programme notes to a recent (1972) production of *Perichole* in the Vienna Volksoper. In commenting on why they did not use Kraus's text, the producers wrote:

> Karl Kraus erschien uns allzusehr auf die Erfordernisse der späten zwanziger Jahre zugeschnitten. Wir hatten den Eindruck, sie würde unserer 'Perichole' nicht ganz gerecht. (Darüber hinaus fanden wir, daß ein sprachschöpferisches Genie wie Kraus nicht von einer Nebenseite gezeigt werden sollte, die nicht seine stärksten Leistungen beinhaltet.)

Karl Kraus's version seemed to us to be all too tailored to the demands of the late twenties. We had the impression that it would not do complete justice to our *Perichole*. (Moreover, we felt that, with a linguistically creative genius such as Kraus, we ought not to present a minor aspect of his work which does not show him at his best.)

Evidently, in the eyes of the authors of these programme notes, Kraus himself had been unable to avoid the 'style of the times'!

In 1931, in his programme notes to his 600th lecture, Kraus announced a 'flight from the times': he would no longer fight against the 'triumph of stupidity and shabbiness' but would only sing of it.

> Die Feier des 600. Abends würde dem Sinn des Vortragenden erst erfolgen, wenn er zum 601., dem seines geliebten Vert-Vert, ein ebenso vollzähliges Auditorium versammelt sähe. Sie wäre die Teilnahme an einer Zeitflucht, die die wahre und letzte Beziehung zu der verpesteten Gegenwart bedeutet; sie wäre die Anerkennung der eigeneren Schriften des Autors und des Ranges, den der Vortragende des Theaters der Dichtung sich selbst streitig macht. Hingegen sei man endlich mit ihm überein, daß sich der Triumph der Dummheit und der Lumperei, denen wir alle mit Haut und Haar geopfert sind, nicht mehr bestreiten, sondern nur noch besingen läßt. (F.864/7:5)

The celebration of the 600th evening of readings would only conform to the wishes of the lecturer if he were to have just as many people in the audience for his 601st evening, for his beloved *Vert-Vert*. Such a celebration would be a participation in a flight from the times that signified the true, ultimate connection with the pestiferous present; it would be recognition of those writings of the author that are more completely his own, and of the rank for which the lecturer of the Theater der Dichtung competes with himself. However, let us finally all agree with him that the triumph of stupidity and shabbiness whose victims we all are from top to toe can no longer be fought against, but only sung of.

This escape from the times is mirrored in Kraus's choice of operettas for his repertoire from 1932. He avoided ones such as *Die Briganten*, where the satire could too easily be applied to contemporary times, and chose instead those which, through magic and fantasy (*Die Reise in den Mond*), vaudeville and circus touches (*Vert-Vert, Die Prinzessin von Trapezunt*), or foreign and exotic settings (*Die Kreolin*), could remove him from the cares and growing horrors of Hitler's Europe to the 'never-never land' of Offenbach's works and to the Viennese operetta style of the mid-nineteenth century. By 1935 Kraus even considered removing the last trace of any possibility of relating the operettas to the contemporary world: he suggested that it might be advisable, in an era dominated by Hitler, in which satire was impossible and in which even the contrast between Offenbach's world and Hitler's would throttle laughter, to consider performing Offenbach's music without the text, so that at least the joyfulness of the music could divert us.

> *Seit es Hitler gibt, kann es Offenbach ... nicht mehr geben, weil, was sich im Zeichen jenes abspielt ... das Lachen erdrosselt, wie es den Atem erstickt. Der Einlaß alltäglicher Narrheit aber, die vor dem Unsäglichen nicht verstummt ist, würde durch ihr geringeres Format die große Lücke noch fühlbarer machen ... Wäre sie* [Offenbach's music] *ohne textliche Grundierung und Überleitung möglich ... so empföhle sich – bei aller theatralischen Meisterlichkeit dieser Texte – in solcher Zeit die Isolierung der Musik ... Besser jedoch, von der Zeit durch Heiterkeit – und wenn deren tieferer Sinn ungefühlt bliebe – abzulenken, als durch diese an sie zu erinnern.* (F.909/11:25–6)

Since there is Hitler, Offenbach ... is no longer possible, because what is happening under Hitler's rule ... strangulates laughter just as it chokes our breath. But the addition of everyday folly that is not rendered speechless when confronted with the unspeakable would, by its lesser stature, only make the great void more painfully evident ... If [Offenbach's music] were possible without the foundation of the text and the transitions provided by it ... it might be advisable – in spite of the theatrical brilliance of these texts – to isolate the music in such times ... But even if the deeper meaning of this serene art should remain unnoticed, it is better to distract attention from the times by this serenity than to remind people of the times by means of it.

Even in the case of Offenbach, then, Kraus had come to feel that words were no longer adequate. In the end, his preoccupation with language and ethics seems to have given way to a desire for the more purely aesthetic appeal of music: art had become an escape for him, an ivory tower to which he could retreat before the horror of his times.

Kraus's turning to the past for his models of acting had been clearly evident throughout the 1900s. Almost without exception, the actors whom he admired had been associated with the Burgtheater. In the current period, his memories of Burgtheater performances from the 1880s and 1890s were reinforced (particularly in 1935) by the memoirs of actors, directors, and even critics from that era, which Kraus reprinted.[20] He even sought to trace the roots of the Burgtheater style of acting further back into the past by reprinting what he judged to be an exemplary piece of theatre criticism by the German revolutionary and American statesman Karl Schurz (F.885/7:21–30). Schurz wrote of the great impression that the French actress Rachel[21] had made on him when he had seen her perform in the tragedies of Racine and Corneille in Berlin in 1850. He was especially affected by the elemental power of Rachel – the same quality that Kraus had so admired in Baumeister, Matkowsky, and Mme Wolter. Schurz wrote:

Die elementaren Kräfte der Natur und alle Gefühle und Erregungen der menschlichen Seele schienen entfesselt in dieser Stimme, um darin ihre beredteste, ergreifendste, durchschauerndste Sprache zu finden. (F.885/7:25)

Die Rachel war mir ein Dämon, ein übermenschliches Wesen, eine geheimnisvolle Kraft ... (Ibid, p. 28)

The elemental forces of nature and all the feelings and emotions of the human soul seemed to be released in this voice, in order to find in it their most eloquent, moving, and thrilling expression.

For me, Rachel was a demon, a superhuman being, a mysterious force ...

Schurz's review substantiates Kraus's claim than an actor or actress of genius can have a formative influence on members of the audience. For Kraus, who had never seen Rachel (she had died in 1856), it was Charlotte Wolter who had had that kind of effect on him.

Das glaubt auch der, der in dem Maß der nachgebornen Welt den analogen Eindruck von einem Naturereignis der Wolter verdankt hat ... die Wolter, die von ihrer Zeit als ein jenseits allen Könnertums wirkendes Elementarwesen, als der Inbegriff tragischer Weibnatur empfunden wurde.
(Ibid, p. 21)

[What Schurz is saying] is given credence by a person who, on the reduced scale of later days, is indebted to the phenomenon of Charlotte

Wolter for a similar impression ... Wolter, who was felt by her time to be an elementary force beyond all technical ability, the epitome of the tragic woman.

This claim by Kraus must, of course, be taken with a grain of salt – one has only to read his critiques from 1892 to 1894 to realize that he had on occasion been quite critical of Mme Wolter. However, the details did not matter in 1935. For Kraus, Mme Wolter and her colleagues, as well as the books by or about them, were the mirror of their age (F.912/15:32). In writing about them, Kraus was escaping not just from the contemporary Burgtheater but from a whole era, to find refuge in a theatre in which ethical and aesthetic purposes seemed to complement each other. He reprinted some remarks by Lewinsky on the Burgtheater before 1888 that illustrate this point and show those actors' idealism and commitment to it:

> *Ein starkes und reizvolles Talent bedurfte ja immer einen Zusatz idealen Strebens und eines stolzen Bewußtseins, diesem Tempel der Kunst anzugehören und dadurch ein oberster Träger deutscher Kunst auf diesem Gebiete zu sein, um dem Drange nach Geldgewinn widerstehen zu können.*
> *Wer dies über sich vermochte, schloß sich inniger an diesen Gralstempel, dessen geistiges Wesen im ersten Dritteil dieses Jahrhunderts Schreyvogel gebildet hatte. Durch ihn wurde erfüllt, was Kaiser Josef beabsichtigt hatte, eine Bildungsstätte höchster Art, eine Schatzkammer, in welcher sich die dichterischen Kostbarkeiten der führenden Nationen zusammen fanden ... Diese Idee und der familienhafte Sinn, der an der Scholle festhielt, machten das Burgtheater zu jener einzigen Erscheinung, die sich von allen anderen Theatern unterschied und nur im Théâtre français seinesgleichen hatte.* (F.916:14–15)

An actor with a powerful and attractive talent always needed a touch of ideal ambition and proud awareness of belonging to this temple of art and thereby being one of the foremost champions of German art in this field in order to be able to resist the urge for financial gain. Whoever could do so formed an even closer alliance with this Temple of the Grail, whose spiritual character Schreyvogel had created in the first third of this century. He brought into being what Emperor Joseph had intended – a cultural institution of the noblest kind, a treasure-house in which the poetic treasures of the leading nations were gathered ... This idea and the sense of family which clung to the soil gave the Burgtheater that uniqueness which distinguished it from all other theatres and was only equalled in the Théâtre français.

Of the 'poetic treasures' in the custody of the Burgtheater that Lewinsky referred to, some of the most memorable for Kraus were Shakespeare's plays, as he remembered them from performances in that theatre during his youth. Kraus's criticism of contemporary performances of Shakespeare dramas is predictable. In the essay 'Lear im Burgtheater' (F.906/7:1–28), he attacked Röbbeling's 1935 Burgtheater production with Werner Krauß as guest performer in the title role. Kraus claimed that the production lacked all dimensions of greatness: the actors had scaled down and flattened Shakespeare's characters; most of them were unable to handle the language of the text;[22] the director was guilty of errors in both the staging and the editing.[23] Kraus again referred to the example of Sonnenthal as Lear in the 1889 Burgtheater production, a performance, while recognizing its faults, he now tended to idealize (ibid, p. 13). The implication of his criticism of the current Burgtheater production was that, with Sonnenthal gone and the theatre in the hands of untalented actors and directors, it was now he himself, with his adaptations and readings[24] of the dramas, who was best able to serve both Shakespeare and the old Burgtheater style of acting.

Perhaps Kraus's strangest return to the past was in an article entitled 'Die Handschrift des Magiers (Aus meinen Memoiren)' (F.912/15:34–62). The magician of the title was Reinhardt. *Der Magier* was one of Kraus's favourite terms for the by then world-famous director (another was *der Professor*, a sarcastic and perhaps envious reference to Reinhardt's honorary doctorate). 'Magician' was the catch word by means of which Kraus made fun of Reinhardt's 'magical' capabilities as a director: Reinhardt could put on huge spectacular shows which would dazzle audiences – he had, as Kraus put it, 'a flair for the effect on the masses' ('Sinn für Massenwirkung') (F.912/15:45); he seemed to be able to be everywhere (Hollywood, Paris, London, New York, Salzburg) at once; his rehearsals had an almost ritualistic quality; he seemed to have magic control over his actors, from whom he elicited a completely sycophantic response, and over audiences and the press, who treated him as a genius.

Kraus objected to Reinhardt's use of spectacle and his belief that 'real' scenery and props (such as real grass in *A Midsummer Night's Dream*) constituted 'genuine' theatre. Kraus's major grounds for artistic censure had been, and still were, that the 'play' was lost in the 'show' and that Reinhardt's concept of theatre did not proceed from concerns of language.

Oft nun, wenn ich Theaterleuten beizubringen suchte, wie aus dem Satzbau die Gestalt hervortritt ... war ich nicht nur vergebens bemüht, es zu erreichen, sondern auch zu erfahren, was 'der Professor' [Reinhardt] ... mit den Schauspielern anstelle, daß sie nicht sprechen können. (Ibid, p. 36)

Aber durch die Farbenfreude des Parvenüs, der blauen Dunst bevor-

zugt, des Dekorateurs, der an der 'Schau' der ärgsten Kunstgewerb-
lerzeit fortwirkt, zu einem Element des Spiels vorzudringen; durch die
Spielereien des Attrapisten zur Sprache und zur Sache zu gelangen, war
mir mein Lebtag nicht möglich. (Ibid, p. 37)

Often, when I tried to show theatre people how the form emerges from the sentence structure ... I not only failed to do so, but I could not find out what 'the professor' [Reinhardt] could be doing to the actors so that they could not speak.

The play was impenetrably obscured by the gay colours of this parvenu who prefers the foam to the beer, of this decorator who is still knitting away on the 'show' of the worst era of amateur handicraft; not once have I managed to reach the language and the message of the play through the gadgetry of this mock-up artist.

In 'Die Handschrift des Magiers,' Kraus bolstered his argument for language and against visual effects by quoting from an 1875 critique by Ludwig Speidel and from a remark by Graf Schönborn to the actor Adolf Sonnenthal, both of whom expressed sentiments similar to his own on this score (ibid, pp. 50–3).

As usual, Kraus made his readers aware that it was on ethical as well as artistic grounds that he was criticizing Reinhardt. Reinhardt lived like a prince, while his extras were paid starvation wages (ibid, p. 44). Hailed by the critics as a genius, Reinhardt was making money in the Salzburg Festival, whereas Mozart, the true genius of the festival, had died a pauper (ibid, pp. 43–4). The 'grovelling' of the press and the fans around Reinhardt was morally reprehensible; in fact, Kraus stated, only the moral collapse of the German nation presented a picture that was more undignified than the 'grovelling' in Reinhardt's palatial residence; 'Daß es, nächst dem Kopfsturz der deutschen Nation, kein Bild eklerer Entwürdigung geben könnte als die Kriecherei um Leopoldskron [Reinhardt's castle residence near Salzburg] ...' (ibid, p. 43). This particular remark is typical of Kraus's ability to criticize by insinuation. The two phrases 'Kopfsturz der deutschen Nation' and 'Kriecherei um Leopoldskron' have a common reference point: 'kein Bild eklerer Entwürdigung.' For Kraus, Reinhardt had some of Hitler's sinister charisma. In fact, in another passage, he is even more explicit. Commenting on Reinhardt's dictatorial powers at rehearsals, where the actors seemed to obey him blindly, he remarked that Reinhardt's rule 'bordered on the magical essence of Hitler' (except that Reinhardt's magic was one of silence): 'dies [Reinhardt's] wundertätige Walten ... grenzt an das thëurgische Wesen Hitlers, wovon es sich jedoch durch die völlige Schweigsamkeit der Regie unterscheidet, welche eben den besondern Zauber ausmacht' (ibid, p. 35). [(Reinhardt's) miraculous control ... borders on Hitler's theurgic nature, from which it differs, however, by the complete silence of the direction, which of course constitutes the special magic.] The comment is sarcastic and meant perhaps half jokingly, but the equation is there nevertheless.

The remarks linking Reinhardt and Hitler's Germany are only a few of the many instances in which Kraus tried to represent Reinhardt as typical of all that was wrong with the times. Some of the characteristics of such a type would be banality and a love for the decorative and superficial rather than the essential, and an interest in business and a desire to make money. According to Kraus, the shoe fit Reinhardt rather well, since here was a director who was interested in 'superficial' spectacle rather than 'essential' language and whose cultural ventures were much closer to showbusiness than to 'pure' theatre.

But Kraus had a very peculiar way of going about proving his case. He went back to that disastrous performance of *Die Räuber* in 1893, in which he had done so badly as Franz Moor. He reprinted the programme, which he claimed had come into his hands in 1930 when it had been reprinted in connection with the celebration of Reinhardt's twenty-five years as managing director of the Deutsches Theater in Berlin. For the first time, Kraus's readers discover that it was Max Reinhardt who had played Spiegelberg in that production. The incident obviously still bothered Kraus. He did not fail to mention that he had had no acting instruction, whereas Reinhardt was a student actor. He admitted that Reinhardt 'doubtless made a more favourable impression' (ibid, p. 46), but laid part of the blame for his own failure on his costume and wig, which were far too big for him, all the while asserting that even at that time he was better able to represent an ensemble – as he had done in his 1893 reading of *Die Weber* – than to play a single part: 'und ich wäre, der schon damals besser ein Ensemble als eine Rolle darzustellen vermochte, vielleicht auch dann durchgefallen, wenn mich nicht gleich beim Aufgehn des Vorhangs ein zu weites Kostum [sic] nebst zu weiter Perücke dem Gelächter der anwesenden Freunde preisgegeben hätte ...' (ibid, pp. 46–7). From that time on, he now claimed, he had resolved to achieve 'dramatic effects' without costume and make-up (ibid, p. 47).

Having established this early link with Reinhardt, Kraus went on to claim that it was he who had started Reinhardt on his meteoric rise to fame and fortune, since he had suggested his name to the Berlin naturalist director Otto Brahm, who was in Vienna looking for talented actors for his troupes: 'Er [Brahm] wurde von mir auf den Salzburger Charakterspieler [Reinhardt] ... nachdrücklich aufmerksam gemacht' (ibid, p. 49). He then sketchily traced Reinhardt's career in the theatre (ibid) and finally brought forward his evidence against him: a four-page letter written to him by Reinhardt in 1893, which Kaus reproduced in facsimile (ibid, p. 54–7). In it Reinhardt thanked Kraus for his help and then went on to comment on the theatre. This private and casual letter, then more than forty years old, was Kraus's 'proof' of the bad qualities he had since discovered in Reinhardt and his contemporaries – and on the basis of the handwriting at that.

> *Nicht geistige Leere und Lücke der Bildung ... sondern der untilgbare Charakter einer Schrift, deren perfektem Schönheitsdrang und ausschweifender Banalität jene Mängel wesentlich zugehören, macht das folgende Werk des Anfängers zu einem der fesselndsten Schaustücke des Meisters.* (Ibid, p. 53)
>
> *Hier paart die kaufmännische Energie des Zugs mit dem Hang zum Dekorativen.* (Ibid, p. 61)

It is not [his] emptiness of mind and bad education ... but the indelible character of his handwriting, with whose absolute quest for beauty and excessive banality these defects shared the same essential nature, which makes the following work of the beginner one of the most fascinating revelations of [the character of] the master.

Here a businessman's energy is coupled with a love of the decorative.

The commercialism and the liking for empty pomp and circumstance displayed by Reinhardt's handwriting, Kraus asserted, were equally evident in the director's theatrical ventures, as was the banality displayed in the letter, which was marred by spelling mistakes, the use of abbreviations (some of them wrong), and a general lack of intellectual content.

Kraus then further projected the qualities shown in the letter into space and time and predicted that the dexterity of 'this sales clerk's script' would override the culture of Goethe and the 'purity' of the past:

> *Aber das Staunen, daß in demselben Jahrhundert die Züge, womit jene Feenhand das Goethewort schrieb, und diese Kommisschrift Raum hatten, weicht dem Grauen, daß eben deren Fertigkeit fortwirkt und daß die unbedankte Reinheit dessen, 'was gewesen ist', nicht Bestand hat vor dem Griff, der sich die Geisteswelt zueignet. Selbst die bange Frage, wie lange diese Illusionen noch vorhalten, bis sie zerstört sind mit allem Lebenswert, sie wird übertäubt von den Interessen, mit denen uns der tägliche Betrug die Zeit vertreibt. Daß wir zu lebenslänglichem Reinhardt verurteilt sind, ist gewiß.* (Ibid, p. 62)

But one's astonishment that there was room in the same century for the magnificent handwriting in which Geothe's works were composed and for this sales clerk's calligraphy gives way to one's horror that it is the slickness of the latter which lasts, while the unrewarded purity of that 'which has been' cannot survive in the grip of those who now rule the cultural scene. Even one's anxious question as to how long these illusions can last before they are destroyed along with everything that is of value in life, even this question is silenced by the interests with which daily fraud kills time for us. That we are condemned for life to put up with Reinhardt is certain.

The essay ends on an apocalyptic note: 'Szenenwechsel: "Welch ein greuliches Entsetzen droht mir aus der finstern Welt!" Im Vordergrund Leopoldskron; im Hintergrund zwei wilde Völkerschaften, deren eine die Presse schont und von der andern mit Gas versorgt wird' (ibid). [Scene change: 'What dreadful horror threatens me from the dark world!' In the foreground Leopoldskron; in the background two savage tribes, one of which is coddled by the press but is supplied with [poison] gas by the other one.]

The reader may well be astonished at such a devastating reading of what even at second glance must seem to be an entirely harmless document. The article is true to Kraus's practice of proceeeding from the particular to the general in his evaluation and censure. But this case must seem like the reductio ad absurdum of such a method of criticism. Why would Kraus feel constrained at this point to unearth that old story about his failure as an actor in the *Räuber* performance? The ending of the essay would seem to indicate that he wanted us to take his analysis of the wording and handwriting of Reinhardt's letter seriously. Yet there is a disturbing discrepancy between the half-sarcastic, half-defensive personal aspect of the argument and the grave and frightening conclusions that he draws from the influence of the 'magician.' Kraus's own letters from 1893 (such as his letters to Schnitzler), although in a less florid script, were no less banal and superficial in content and style than those of Reinhardt. The article itself is disturbing in its own banality. There is a tragic irony in the fact that the man who had so eloquently expressed his opposition to Hitler in a ten-line poem and long months of silence should now, in the fall of 1935, devote twenty-eight pages to his own personal trivia.

BERTOLT BRECHT

Even when Kraus had been negatively disposed towards Brecht, he had always found occasion for an indirect compliment. Such was the case in 1927 in the essay 'Mein Vorurteil gegen Piscator' (*F.*759/65:69–71), in which he discussed Brecht's view that the material of some classics could be used to present an up-to-date message, while all those classical works which did not lend themselves to such a use should be left unperformed. Kraus criticized this view and defended the poetry and 'spirituality' (*Geistigkeit*) of the classical repertoire. He added, however, that in view of what the Berlin producers and directors had done to Shakespeare in the last few years, producing Brecht's plays instead might not be so unreasonable (F.759/65:71).

Caroline Kohn writes of an occasion in 1928 when Kraus and Heinrich Fischer attended a rehearsal of Brecht's *Dreigroschenoper*, at which they observed Brecht at work. Kraus was impressed with Brecht's theatrical talent:

> *Kraus wohnte 1928 in Fischers Begleitung einer Probe der 'Dreigroschenoper' bei, bei der Erich Engel die Regie führte, aber Brecht vielfach zur Mitarbeit heranzog. Als Kraus den Dramaturgen und Regisseur Brecht einen Vormittag lang aus einer Loge bei der Arbeit beobachtet hatte, war er von dessen echter Theaterbegabung überzeugt, und bald kam es zur persönlichen Fühlungnahme und freundschaftlichen Annäherung der beiden gleichermaßen für das Theater begeisterten Männer.*[25]

In 1928, Kraus, accompanied by Fischer, attended a rehearsal of the *Threepenny Opera*, in which Erich Engel was the director but frequently asked for Brecht's co-operation. After watching Brecht at work as a dramatist and director all morning from one of the boxes of the theatre, Kraus was convinced of his genuine theatrical talent, and soon these two men who were so enthusiastic about the theatre established personal friendly contact.

Strangely, Kraus made no comment in *Die Fackel* about *Die Dreigroschenoper*. However, in 1929 Alfred Kerr accused Brecht of plagiarism in that work. Brecht had indeed used some lines of K.L. Ammer's translation of the poetry of Villon. Kraus, who normally was opposed to plagiarism and who was critical both of Brecht's attitude towards the classics and of his Marxist sympathies, came to his aid against his old arch-enemy, Kerr:

> *Im kleinen Finger der Hand, mit der er fünfundzwanzig Verse der Ammerschen Übersetzung von Villon genommen hat, ist dieser Brecht originaler als der Kerr, der ihm dahintergekommen ist; und hat für mein Gefühl mit allem was ihn als Bekenner dem Piscatorwesen näher rückt als mir ... mehr Beziehung zu den lebendigen Dingen der Lyrik und der Szene als das furchtbare Geschlecht des Tages, das sich nun an seine Sohlen geheftet hat.* (F.811/19:129)

In the little finger of the hand which took the twenty-five lines from Ammer's translation of Villon Brecht is more original than Kerr, who found him out. And for all that he is closer in my view to the practices of Piscator than to me, he has more relation to the living essence of poetry and theatre than those horrible ephemerals who now cling to his soles.

Similarly, in 1931 Kraus stated that Kerr's literary protégés could not measure up to Brecht: 'Doch alle zusammen können sie das Wasser ... nicht dem einen Brecht reichen, selbst wenn er sich als sein eigener Vampir mit Doktrinen das Blut abzapft: es bleibt immer noch so viel, um das Gedicht von Kranich und Wolke und die Gerichtssitzung in 'Mahagonny' hervorzubringen ...' (F.847/51:78). [But all of them together are not fit to hold a candle to one Brecht ... even though, like his own vampire, he sucks his blood away with doctrines: there will always be enough left to create the poem about the crane and the cloud and the court-room scene in *Mahagonny* ...] The works mentioned in this quotation were included in Kraus's Theater der Dichtung; in an introduction to a reading of them one year later, Kraus reaffirmed his support of Brecht.

> *Der Vortrag aus Bert Brecht, mit dem weder eine Übernahme seines Weltbilds noch seines Begriffes vom Theater beabsichtigt ist, erfolgt aus mehrfachen Gründen. Der maßgebendste dürfte wohl der sein, daß ich ihn für den einzigen deutschen Autor halte, der – trotz und mit allem, womit er bewußt seinem dichterischen Wert entgegenwirkt – heute in Betracht zu kommen hat ...* (F.868/72:36)

Several reasons led to this reading from Bert Brecht, with whom I share neither world view nor theatrical concept. The most important reason is probably that I consider him to be the only German author whom one can take seriously today – and this in spite of and along with everything he does consciously to inhibit his worth as a poet ...

He hastened to add that it was the 'purely poetic value' of Brecht's works that he valued, the didacticism of which transcended Brecht's own didactic concept (ibid, p. 37).

Brecht's attitude towards Kraus can be discovered, at least in part, in his *Schriften zur Literatur und Kunst*. In 1926 he wrote:

> *Dieser Karl Kraus, der von der Allgemeinheit erstaunlich wenig geschätzt wird, kann sich doch nicht heute und nicht morgen die wirkliche Achtung der Besten erringen, da gerade der Geruch nach Vorzugsschüler auf gutem Niveau unangenehmer als der eines Unholdes ist. Kraus ist ein Beispiel dafür, daß aus der Antithese nichts herauskommt! Ein so aktives Gegenteil wie K. eines so schlechten Menschen, wie Kraus nicht ist, ist merkwürdiger- und beruhigenderweise noch keineswegs gut. Er legt immerfort ein anderes corpus non delicti auf den Tisch, der sich unter seiner Last schon biegt. Aber da es den Ansichten der Pessimisten zum Trotz so viele Verderbtheiten gibt, triumphiert er niemals ganz. Er wird einfach freigeschwiegen. Auch macht man ungern Aufhebens von Leuten, die durch Behebung eines Übelstandes überflüssig würden.*[26]

This Karl Kraus, who is astonishingly little regarded by the general public, is unable today and will remain unable tomorrow to gain the real esteem of the best people, since his aura of being an A student and the teacher's pet is more unpleasant than that of a rogue. Kraus is an example that nothing comes from an antithesis. Such an active opposite as K. to such a bad person as Kraus is not, is strangely and reassuringly not good. He keeps on putting another corpus non delicti on the table which is already groaning under its weight. But since, in spite of the views of the pessimists, there is so much corruption, he never triumphs completely. He is simply ignored and thus allowed to go his own way. Also, no one likes to make a fuss about people who would become superfluous if the abuse [they protest against] were to cease.

In a longer series of comments around 1934 ('Über Karl Kraus'), Brecht especially praised Kraus's technique of quoting without commentary in *Die Fackel*, as well as his criticism of language and his censure of the contemporary belief in progress. He asserted:

Lebend in einer Zeit, die unermüdlich fast unschilderbare Scheußlichkeiten hervorbringt, übt et eine Kritik von höchstem Standpunkt aus. Die Kräfte in diesem Kampf scheinen zunächst allzu ungleich. Aber nach einigem Nachdenken kann man erkennen, daß Kraus in drei bis vier Jahrzehnten viel erreicht hat: Es ist den finsteren Kräften zumindest nicht gelungen, die großen Bilder der Reinheit zu verwischen und die Begriffe der Sittlichkeit selber zu entfernen.[27]

Living in a time which tirelessly brings forth almost indescribable horrors, he practises a criticism of the highest standard. The forces in this struggle seem at first to be all too unequal. But after some reflection one can see that Kraus has accomplished very much in three to four decades: at least the forces of darkness have not succeeded in wiping out the great images of purity and in removing the concepts of morality.

In a poem written between October 1933 and July 1934 and entitled 'Über die Bedeutung des zehnzeiligen Gedichtes in der 888. Nummer der Fackel (Oktober 1933),'[28] Brecht showed his appreciation of the silence with which Kraus bore witness against the times. The following is the last stanza of the poem:

Als der Beredte sich entschuldigte
daß seine Stimme versage
trat das Schweigen vor den Richtertisch
nahm das Tuch vom Antlitz und
gab sich zu erkennen als Zeuge.[29]

When the eloquent man apologized for the fact that his voice was giving out, Silence stepped before the judge's bench, removed the veil from her face and declared herself a witness.

But after Kraus's long explanation of his silence (F. 890/905), Brecht wrote another poem about him, 'Über den schnellen Fall des guten Unwissenden,' which remained unpublished until 1961 and in which Kraus is represented as a person of good intentions, but one whose ignorance (presumably, his political naiveté) is such that he does more harm than good:

Als wir den Beredten seines Schweigens wegen entschuldigt hatten
verging zwischen der Niederschrift des Lobs und seiner Ankunft
eine kleine Zeit. In der sprach er.

Er zeugte aber gegen die, deren Mund verbunden war
und brach den Stab über die, welche getötet waren.
Er rühmte die Mörder. Er beschuldigte die Ermordeten.
Den Hungernden zählte er die Brotkrusten nach, die sie erbeutet hatten.
Den Frierenden erzählte er von der Arktis.
Denen, die mit den Stöcken der Pfaffen geprügelt wurden
drohte er mit den Stahlruten des Anstreichers.
So bewies er
wie wenig die Güte hilft, die sich nicht auskennt
und wie wenig der Wunsch vermag, die Wahrheit zu sagen
bei dem, der sie nicht weiß.
Der da auszog gegen die Unterdrückung, selber satt
wenn er zur Schlacht kommt, steht er
auf der seite der Unterdrücker.

Wie unsicher ist die Hilfe derer, die unwissend sind!
Der Augenschein täuscht sie. Dem Zufall anheimgegeben
steht ihr guter Wille auf schwankenden Beinen.

Welch eine Zeit, sagten wir schaudernd
wo der Gutwillige, aber Unwissende
noch nicht die kleine Zeit warten kann mit der Untat
bis das Lob seiner guten Tat ihn erreicht!
Sodaß der Ruhm, den Reinen suchend
schon niemand mehr findet über dem Schlamm
wenn er keuchend ankommt.[30]

When we had excused the eloquent man for his silence, a short time passed between the recording of this praise and its arrival. In that time he spoke.

He bore witness, however, against those whose mouth was gagged and condemned those who were killed. He praised the murderers. He blamed the murdered. He reproached the hungry for the crusts of bread they had grabbed. To the freezing he told stories of the Arctic. Those who were beaten by the sticks of the priests he threatened with the steel rods of the house-painter [Hitler].

In this way he proved how little goodness helps when it does not know what's what, and how little the wish to say the truth can do with a person who does not know the truth. He who set out to fight against oppression, well-fed himself – when he arrives at the battle, he stands on the side of the oppressors. How unsure is the help of those who are ignorant! Appearances fool them. Left to chance, their good will stands on shaky legs.

What a time, we said shuddering, when the goodwilled but ignorant person cannot wait that little time with his misdeed until the praise for his good deed has reached him! So that fame, seeking one who is pure, no longer finds anyone above the mud when, gasping, it arrives.

Krolop suggests that the basic theme of the two poems was developed further in Brecht's 'Fünf Schwierigkeiten beim Schreiben der Wahrheit,' as well as in his 'Pariser Rede' of 1935 and 'Madrider Rede' of 1937, in which Brecht tried to come to terms with the problems faced by an anti-Fascist writer in his fight against barbarism.[31] Jenaczek has many reservations about the second poem; why, he wonders, did Brecht not publish it? Why did he leave it in what is so obviously an unfinished state? What conclusions can be drawn from this about his attitude toward the poem? He also criticizes Krolop and some Marxist critics for what he considers to be a too biasedly Marxist and overly simplistic interpretation of Kraus and his motivations. For example, Jenaczek writes:

Es ist ... einfach unrichtig, zu behaupten, Kraus sei 'dollfußfällig' geworden. Kraus bejaht in Dollfuß nur den entschlossenen 'Anschluß'-Gegner; darin zeigt er ihn der 'europäischen Staatsmannschaft' als das Vorbild, das den Galuben bestätige, 'Hitler-Sigasax' werde einer gemeinsamen militärischen Intervention aller europäischen Staaten weichen müssen. Innenpolitisch dagegen hat Kraus Dollfuß immer nur als das kleinere ubel bezeichnet – das kleinere, gemessen an dem von außen drohenden größeren, Hitler – und betont, daß keine andere Gemeinsamkeit zwischen seinem Denken und dem des Kanzlers bestehe ...[32]

It is simply not right to assert that Kraus had kow-towed to Dollfuß. Kraus affirmed in Dollfuß only his *determined* opposition to the annexation of Austria by Germany; *in this regard* he showed him to 'European statesmanship' as an example confirming the belief that 'Hitler-Sigasax' would have to give in to a common military intervention by all European states. In the field of *internal politics*, however, Kraus always merely called Dollfuß the lesser evil – lesser in comparison with the greater one threatening from outside, Hitler – and he insisted that [the opposition to Hitler] was all that his views had in common with those of Dollfuß ...

In failing to understand why Brecht decided not to publish his second poem about Kraus, Jenaczek displays a surprising degree of blindness towards the realities of the 1930s. Evidently, Brecht was motivated in writing the poem by a profound feeling of disappointment with Kraus's self-centred and repetitive apologia; to publish this poem, however, would have meant to attack an ally in the fight against Naziism and thus to commit a mistake of which Kraus himself was so often guilty.

Conclusion

There are three ways in which theatrical illusion functions: as make-believe, as revelation of reality, and as delusion. The creator of farces and operettas delights in make-believe, in creating a world as we might like it to be, without making any attempt to convince us that this is the way the world really is. The dramatist or performer of the second type uses illusion to illustrate moral truths. Finally, the playwright can pretend to use the magic of transformation to discover an enhanced reality while in fact only creating a dream world corresponding to his own wishes. In Kraus's case we can sense a natural development from one phase to the next. The motivating force behind this development is Kraus's obsession with power: Kraus the performer achieves a sense of power both from his ability to transform reality and from his ability to move or influence an audience.

A crude but perhaps useful way to illustrate this development is to compare Kraus's life with that of a magician who is caught up in the dynamics of his work. We begin with the magician who is content to astound his audience with the standard magician's trick of pulling rabbits out of a hat. He may then become tempted by an even more extraordinary possibility of theatrical transformation: he can pull not only rabbits out of that hat but great moral truths as well. If the magician is a humble man, he will realize that moral truths are complex – they are painted in mixtures of greys and pastels rather than in primary colours. But chances are that the magician is still principally interested in showing off his powers as a transformer and in impressing his audience. He will then distort these truths so that they have a striking dramatic quality. He will use sharp antitheses, and will present a vivid picture of a reality that is peopled by heroes and villains only.

But how is it possible for a hat to even *seem* to produce a moral truth? The answer is that in the theatre the magician has not only hats but words to play with. And it is the power of the word that enables him to assume the role of the preacher – not the true dispenser of wisdom, but the old-style evangelist who beats the drum and thunders hell-fire and brimstone.

What happens, however, when the moral truths no longer receive the applause of the audience and the house empties? The magician then easily falls prey to the temptations of the failed idealist. He may, for example, turn so far inward that he can convince himself that his power of illusion-making is the source of meaning itself, a rationalization which protects him from the fact that his illusions were not able to reveal reality. Or he may retreat completely into silence.

From what we have seen of Kraus's life and development, I think this schema is partially valid.

Kraus's delight in the theatre was evident very early in his life, as was the theatrical streak in his nature. His theatricality expressed itself primarily in his extravagantly dramatic way of presenting ideas in essays, critical reviews, and lectures. In the early 1890s, Kraus was also actively involved in the make-believe of theatre, either as theatre critic or, less often, as performer or reciter. And as a critic he was primarily interested in the performance of the actors or in the mechanics of the plays, and based his remarks for the most part on aesthetic criteria.

After 1899, with the beginning of the publication of *Die Fackel*, a strong moralistic streak in Kraus became increasingly evident. Purely artistic theatre or drama criticism now became rarer in his writing. All criticism had to serve and become subordinate to an ethical purpose: that of exposing and criticizing contemporary Austrian society. His information now came increasingly from newspapers rather than his own reading of plays or visits to the theatre, and a large part of his comments consisted of ridicule or censure of the writings of other critics. Artistic weaknesses, both in the critiques quoted from other newspapers and in the dramas or performances reported on, were now interpreted by Kraus as symptoms of ethical flaws, and artistic strength was often seen as evidence of strength of character. Faulty use of language by a dramatist or a drama critic was traced back by Kraus time and again to a shortcoming in the man's character, and an actor's great performance was attributed more to his fine personality than to his artistic skill. In the 1920s and 1930s a significant theme in his works was his moralistic adulation of the great Burgtheater actors he had seen in his youth. During the same period his negative criticism extended from individual plays or performers to the whole of society – the play or performer manifested (in Kraus's eyes) the surrounding corruption. This was particularly evident in his short essays of 1916 and 1917 on war plays. Another way he conducted his attacks was by using his readings of Shakespeare to underline the moral poverty of contemporary Viennese productions and his recitations of Nestroy to satirize Austrian society in general. During his lecture-recitations as well as in *Die Fackel* he often made direct references to contemporary figures such as Bekessy and Schober, references which actually amounted to full-scale campaigns of vituperation.

Kraus's growing reliance on ethical criteria in his evaluations often led him into untenable critical positions. In his treatment of Harden, he had tried to prove that stylistic weaknesses revealed ethical flaws in the writer. However, Kraus shifted the emphasis even further from artistic to ethical standards. By 1915 he was able to say that a poem was good until he found out who had written it: 'Ein Gedicht ist so lange gut, bis man weiß, von wem es ist' (F.406/12:131). Such a statement was the reverse of his previous view that a writer's style revealed his ethical flaws. In fact, the establishment of objective aesthetic criteria was rendered impossible by such a view and artistic criticism was made absurd.

Ironically, criticism which depended so heavily on ethical criteria or on an ethical interpretation often led Kraus to make unfair and, therefore, unethical judgments. This was evident in the case of Hofmannsthal, whom Kraus no longer judged on his artistic merits after 1899. Kraus even boasted about *not* having read a particular work of his. Thus, Hofmannsthal was damned because of his association with Bahr and Reinhardt and because of his work in the Ministry of War from 1914 to 1918.

Within the area of criticism to which this book is limited, we have seen that Kraus was sometimes quite wrong in his literary judgment. The reasons for such misjudgments were often of a personal nature, which he then rationalized as objective, rational criticism. It does not seem unfair to suggest that most of those who held up under Kraus's ethical scrutiny were either writers of undoubted merit who were no longer alive, such as Shakespeare, Goethe, Raimund, and Nestroy, or more recent writers who appealed to Kraus on ethical grounds and whose aesthetic merits he then tended to extol somewhat beyond reasonable proportions (in particular, Frank Wedekind).

We must not, however, exaggerate the analogy between Kraus and a megalomaniacal magician. No doubt, it is a matter for regret that Kraus, who was, after all, the contemporary of some very major writers and the eyewitness of much that has stood the test of time, found so much to object to and so little to praise in the first three decades after the founding of *Die Fackel*. There can, however, be no question that the ceaseless polemics he engaged in were motivated at least in part by a fine sense of justice, by a moral indignation that even in its quixotic aberrations compels one's respect and admiration. The failings and faulty judgments that we so frequently come across were not merely those of a theatrical virtuoso. They also sprang from an excess of zeal, from an ethical sensitivity that left him no choice but to speak out where he saw injustice done. It may well be argued that his need to pose as a prophet and cast himself in the role of the knight-in-shining-armour compelled him to seek out causes, to dwell on the sins of his contemporaries rather than their virtues. Such an argument, however, can quite easily be turned around, and it may well be fairer to claim that a man so thin-skinned where moral impropriety was concerned needed theatricality both to shield himself and to make himself heard. In any case, it cannot be doubted that the battles he staged on the pages of *Die Fackel* in his best years were waged to reveal a truth, and that the society he castigated so ceaselessly in his theatrical criticism as well as throughout his writings ultimately revealed its basic corruption by the almost total lack of resistance to the Nazis both before and after their take-over, and thus – if not in all details, at least in the overview – proved him right. It is all the more tragic that the prophet of doom lost his grip on reality when doom finally came.

When it did, the tragic ending of the magician in our schema has a biting relevance for Kraus. As the Nazi tide began to rise, Kraus's first reaction was silence. It was as if he had lost all faith in the power of theatre to ennoble the world, and he had excellent grounds for losing that faith since it was precisely the very theatricality of the Nazi movement that supplied its inexorable dynamic. He had even lost faith in the power of words. He took refuge in Offenbach's music, even to the extent of suggesting that words might not be necessary to Offenbach's 'supreme art' – the art of the totally escapist operetta. He had entered the garden of the aesthete and locked the gate behind him. Fortunately he died two years before the Storm Troopers arrived to smash down the gate and to put the torch to all the values that Kraus had stood for.

APPENDIX

A Chronology of *Die Fackel*

Die Fackel no.	Volume	Year	Number of issues published
1 –36	1	1899/1900	36
37 –72	2	1900/1901	36
73 –99	3	1901/1902	27
100–134	4	1902/1903	35
135–158	5	1903/1904	24
159–178	6	1904/1905	20
179–200	7	1905/1906	20
201–222	8	1906/1907	20
223–249	9	1907/1908	19
250–278	10	1908/1909	18
279–300	11	1909/1910	15
301–320	12	1910/1911	10
321–346	13	1911/1912	14
347–371	14	1912/1913	10
372–397	15	1913/1914	12
398–405	16	1914/1915	5
406–417	17	1915	2
418–453	18	1916/1917	7
454–473	19	1917	4
474–507	20	1918/1919	4
508–530	21	1919/1920	4
531–567	22	1920/1921	8
568–594	23	1921/1922	5
595–612	24	1922	3
613–648	25	1923/1924	4
649–685	26	1924/1925	5
686–723	27	1925/1926	6
724–756	28	1926/1927	7
757–777	29	1927/1928	5
778–805	30	1928/1929	5
806–833	31	1929/1930	5
834–851	32	1930/1931	4
852–872	33	1931/1932	4
873–887	34	1932	3
888	35	1933	1
889–905	36	1934	2
906–922	37	1935/1936	6

The volumes of *Die Fackel* begin in April.

Notes

PREFACE

1 See my article 'Karl Kraus and the Problem of Illusion and Reality in Drama and the Theater,' *Modern Austrian Literature* 8 (1975) 48–60.
2 Schiller, 'Die Schaubühne als eine moralische Anstalt betrachtet,' *Ästhetische Schriften* (Paderborn 1961) 12–13
3 Büchner, *Leonce und Lena* (Stuttgart 1969) 58
4 I have used *Die Fackel* as the basis for my study. For the division into chapters, I have followed the pattern set by Friedrich Jenaczek in his *Zeittafeln zur 'Fackel'. Themen, Ziele, Probleme* (Munich 1965), but with three minor changes. First, whereas Jenaczek's major concern was obviously the criticism contained in *Die Fackel* (for example, his first chapter only covers the years 1899 to August 1902), I have included the early criticism in chapter 1, and then divided this chapter into two sections: the pre-*Fackel* period and the first two years of *Die Fackel*. Second, I have ended this chapter in June 1901, with the major break in publication of the periodical. The crisis which, at least in part, brought about the nervous exhaustion that necessitated this break was the Bahr/Bukovics case in early 1901, in which Kraus had his knuckles rapped publicly for the first time. After this incident, Kraus's style of criticism was somewhat less brash.

The third slight divergence from Jenaczek concerns the period from September 1909 to 1918, which Jenaczek has divided into two sections, since he considered the war years to require discussion in a separate chapter. As my own study is limited to a consideration of Kraus's theatricality and his theatre and drama criticism, I have devoted only one chapter to the years 1910–18, since I see his censorious comments on war plays in 1916 and 1917 as being the logical conclusion of the kind of criticism he made earlier in that decade.

CHAPTER 1

1 Paul Schick, *Karl Kraus in Selbstzeugnissen und Bilddokumenten* (Reinbek 1965) 23

2 Ibid, 29
3 Ibid, 30
4 *Die Fackel* (Vienna: Verlag 'Die Fackel,' 1899–1936) no. 912–15, p. 47. Future references to this periodical will be given in the text, stating the number of the issue and the page: (F.912/15:47).
5 See *Die Gesellschaft* 1893, no. 2, 234.
6 Ibid, 233
7 *Das Magazin für Litteratur* 1893, no. 26, 422
8 *Die Gesellschaft* 1892, no. 8, 1061–1. It is interesting to contrast this opinion with the views that Kraus held on this particular point from 1908, when he proclaimed, for example, that the Burgtheater had never been a literary stage, that it had 'always' been an actors' theatre, and that these actors were best served by Scribe and Sardou (see chapters 2 and 3)
9 Ibid, 1060
10 Ibid, no. 11, 1508
11 Ibid, 1894, no. 3, 384–5
12 'Aus vollkommenster Unkenntniß aller Tradition hat er sich bald eine Art seichter Modernität herausgeschlagen, die gleich mit aller Tradition es aufzunehmen erklärt, ein Litteraturinteresse, das beim "Heurigen" anfängt,' *Breslauer Zeitung* 1897, no. 58, 3
13 Ibid, no. 202, 3
14 Ibid
15 *Die Wage* 1898, no. 4, 74–5
16 Ibid, no. 43, 719
17 Ibid
18 *Die Gesellschaft* 1893, no. 2, 234–5
19 Ibid, 234
20 Ibid, 235
21 Ibid, 1892, no. 11, 1509
22 Ibid, 1893, no. 2, 233
23 Ibid, no. 5, 648
24 Ibid
25 Ibid, 1892, no. 8, 1063
26 'Sie werden an ihrer Schlichtheit Schaden nehmen, wenn sie in Schlichtheit "reifen", die Fühlung mit dem heimatlichen Boden verlieren und dafür die schlechten Manieren der Virtuosen erlernen. Man hüte sich, die immerhin merkwürdige und in der Geschichte des Theaters bedeutungsvolle Erscheinung agirender Bauern zur "Specialität" zu erniedrigen, von der zu der Orpheum-Pikanterie der "neunjährigen Soubrette" nur mehr ein Schritt ist' *Neue Freie Presse* 12 August 1894, 5
27 *Die Gesellschaft* 1893, no. 2, 234
28 *Wiener Rundschau* 1897, no. 13, 511
29 *Breslauer Zeitung* 1897, no. 340, 1

30 *Wiener Rundschau* 1897, no. 13, 512
31 'Herr Reicher soll fürder die Litteratur in Ruhe lassen und sich brav an den Svengali in "Trilby" halten,' *Breslauer Zeitung* 1897, no. 340, 1
32 Ibid, no. 714, 2
33 See pp. 8–9.
34 *Breslauer Zeitung* 1897, no. 202, 3
35 *Die Gesellschaft* 1892, no. 6, 800
36 *Wiener Literatur-Zeitung* 1892, no. 4, 19–20
37 Ibid
38 Ibid
39 *Das Magazin für Litteratur* 1893, no. 20, 324
40 *Breslauer Zeitung* 1897, no. 240, 2
41 Ibid
42 Ibid
43 Ibid
44 *Die Gesellschaft* 1893, no. 5, 650
45 Ibid, 649
46 Ibid
47 Reinhard Urbach, 'Karl Kraus und Arthur Schnitzler,' *Literatur und Kritik* 49 (1970) 514–15
48 *Das Magazin für Litteratur* 1893, no. 18, 294. See also *Die Gesellschaft* 1893, no. 1, 109–10.
49 Urbach, 'Karl Kraus,' 523
50 Ibid
51 Ibid
52 Karl Kraus, *Die demolirte Literatur* (Vienna 1897) 17. This pamphlet was first published in four instalments in *Wiener Rundschau* November 1896 to January 1897.
53 *Breslauer Zeitung* 1897, no. 271, 3
54 See p. 144.
55 *Die Gesellschaft* 1892, no. 6, 800
56 Ibid
57 *Breslauer Zeitung* 1897, no. 271, 3
58 *Die Gesellschaft* 1893, no. 5, 630
59 See note 52 (chapter 1)
60 '[Napoleon war] kein Held, sondern .. auch ein Mensch ... eine Erkenntnis, die wir uns mit einem Abend voll Langeweile erkaufen,' *Die Wage* 1898, no. 1, 17
61 *Wiener Rundschau* 1897, no. 9, 354
62 Ibid, no. 13, 513
63 Ibid, 514
64 I could find no evidence to support this statement by Kraus in the Munich papers of that period.
65 See also F.2:30.

66 See F.43:16–25 ('Vom Wechselgastspiel').
67 Kraus made no allowance for possible differences in aesthetic value of the plays by Holzer and Schnitzler. He admitted that he did not know Holzer's play, nor, from what he had seen of his previous work in the Raimund-Theater, was he tempted to become acquainted with it. But the question as to whether the Schnitzler play was good and merited defence by the critics did not even enter Kraus's purely ethical argument.
68 On the other hand, Kraus insisted that the six critics defending Schnitzler had been very personally motivated: 'Es ist zu auffallend, daß diese Gesellschaft [that is, the other critics] nur dann, wenn sie gerade mit dem Autor persönlich befreundet und mit dem Director gerade persönlich verfeindet ist, prinzipiell die Autorenrechte wahrt ... Man hört ordentlich, wie die protestierenden Herren Bahr und Bauer bei der Nachricht von der definitiven Ablehnung des Schnitzler'schen Stückes erschreckt ausrufen: Was heute Schnitzlern passiert ist, das kann morgen auch uns passieren; das "erfüllt uns mit aufrichtiger Besorgnis" für uns und für die anderen heranwachsenden Talente ...' (F.53:4–5).
69 Kraus questioned whether Bahr had not also plagiarized Karl Bleibtreu when gathering material for his play *Josephine*. See F.67:22.
70 Presumably this referred to the caricature of Kraus.
71 Kraus's argument that changing styles are evidence of fraudulence is, of course, ludicrous. In that case, Picasso would have to be the most fraudulent of artists.
72 It is interesting to note that Kraus did not criticize Gerhart Hauptmann's use of detail in the stage directions and descriptions of setting in his naturalistic plays.
73 See Schick, *Karl Kraus*, 40.
74 The Christian-Socialist (anti-Semitic) press as yet escaped the brunt of his ire, probably because it was not so powerful. But in *Die Fackel* no. 57 (p. 25) he stated that the purging campaign the anti-Semitic press was waging in the Viennese theatre was only one of principle. In individual cases they were just as bad as the liberal press: 'Im Einzelfalle sind die Herren [der antisemitischen Tagespresse] mit den "verjudeten" Theatern zumeist geradeso versippt wie ihre liberalen Collegen.' Kraus lamented the fact that the anti-Semitic editors had reached such heights of objectivity 'von der aus sie mindestens das Wirken der schlechten und schädlichen Juden mit vorurtheilsloser Nachsicht betrachten können.' (Ibid, 27)
75 See p. 10.
76 He defended himself by stating that he at least had drawn the boundary lines for such 'art' – that is, it was to be practised on home ground only, and not sent off on trips and exposed to the world by impresarios.
77 Kraus again showed himself to be inconsistent in his criticism, for he had admired Hauptmann's dialect plays (such as *Die Weber* and *Der Biberpelz*) and had praised the naturalness of the dialogue.
78 Schreyvogl, *Das Burgtheater* (Vienna 1965) 67

79 Ibid, 106
80 Ibid, 67
81 Dingelstedt was director of the Burgtheater from 1871 to 1881. His productions depended heavily on spectacular theatrical effects.
82 Kraus gave no references for these quotations.
83 They were Franz Adamus's *Die Familie Wawroch* and Theodor Wolff's *Die Königin*.

CHAPTER 2

1 Bahr called Lewinsky's interpretation '(einen) ebenso läppischen als hämischen Einfall' (F.104:21–2). The occasion provided Kraus with the opportunity to show Bahr's stupidity as a critic (according to Kraus, the *Dovrealte* was played in the mask of Ibsen throughout Norway), and to praise Lewinsky's artistic integrity, seriousness, and honesty.
2 Lewinsky mentioned that he was unaccustomed to the recognition he had found in *Die Fackel* of 31 January 1905.
3 Koźmian was originally from Poland; by 1905, he had lived fifteen years in Vienna.
4 Sonnenthal had already been criticized by Kraus for accenting the word *Vater* in the line 'Dein Wunsch ist des Gedankens Vater, Heinrich' from *Henry IV*. This moved the spectators, but was rhetorically incorrect.
5 See p. 36.
6 Other critics, however, tended to stress the neo-romantic aspect of Kainz's style. See Herbert Ihering, *Von Josef Kainz bis Paula Wessely* (Heidelberg 1942) 7–15.
7 See his comments on Lewinsky and Matkowsky.
8 Kraus opened the article in *Die Fackel* no. 175 (p. 17) with a quotation from *Hamlet*, II.2. 'nun ist übrig,/Daß wir den Grund erspähn von dem Effekt,/Nein, richtiger, den Grund von dem Defekt;/Denn dieser Defektiv-Effekt hat Grund.' The lines are spoken by Polonius to the queen. The English version, including the lines immediately preceding, runs thus: 'Madam, I swear I use no art at all./ That he [Hamlet] is mad, 'tis true; 'tis true 'tis pity;/And pity 'tis 'tis true: a foolish figure,/ But farewell it, for I will use no art./Mad let us grant him, then; and now remains/That we find out the cause of this effect,/Or rather say, the cause of this defect,/For this effect defective comes by cause.' The opening line, 'I swear I use no art at all' (although not quoted by Kraus), has a particularly ironic effect if it is applied to the Berlin naturalistic style. That 'this defect' in the case of Hamlet was madness could also be considered a stab at Naturalism.
9 Kraus's conservatism is worth noting. In an article in *Die Fackel* no. 156 (pp. 1–6) he defended the royal family's right to forbid the performance of Hauptmann's *Rose Bernd* since it offended a royal princess. (The Hofburgtheater was, after all, a court theatre.) 'Der Freiheitspöbel möchte immer das Unvereinbare vereinen. Anstatt sich in seiner Art zu freuen, daß der Hof nicht hauptmannfähig ist,

greint er jetzt, weil Hauptmann nicht für hoffähig erklärt wurde ...' Kraus also interpreted Nestroy in a very conservative, anti-liberal fashion (F.88:17 and F.89:31–2). See also Jens Malte Fischer, *Karl Kraus. Studien zum 'Theater der Dichtung' und Kulturkonservatismus* (Kronberg/Taunus 1973)

10 Kraus saw Girardi's leaving as a sign of the decay of the times; it was, in his eyes, more of a cultural than a theatrical loss to Vienna. He began one aphorism with the incredulous question 'Girardi in Berlin?' There were two aspects which bothered Kraus. First, Vienna was so influenced by the Berlin naturalist style that there was no room left for genuineness (that is, for a genuine talent and personality such as Girardi's). Therefore, genuineness (*Echtheit*) had to go to Berlin, where there was room for everything. Second, for Berliners, the Viennese culture was ethnographically interesting, so that, in sending Girardi to Berlin, Vienna had sent all that was characteristic of its culture to the world fair, to be seen and admired by all (F.241:23–4). Kraus later referred to the complete indifference of the Viennese to losing Girardi as '(ein) kultureller Skandal, der nur zufällig in der Theatersphäre spielt' (F.246/7:39). Viennese tradition and culture were to be used by the machine age (Berlin), which had no tradition and culture of its own, and in such an environment the genuineness of this culture would vanish, leaving only decorative effects. Girardi's fate would be akin to that of the *Schlierseer* (see chapter 1), though on a higher level, since it was questionable how long Girardi could remain 'genuine,' once cut off from his cultural roots.

11 The pun on *Buchbinder* is untranslatable: *Buchbinder* means bookbinder, but refers as well to the critic-playwright Bernard Buchbinder.

12 This notoriously inane snippet of blank verse is ascribed in Buchmann's *Geflügelte Worte* to Hans Adolf von Thümmel.

13 These are roles in plays by Nestroy that Nestroy, who was very tall and thin, had played himself.

14 This article was originally published in *Simplizissimus*.

15 He gave as an example a family of circus artists in Offenbach's *Prinzessin von Trapezunt*, who unfortunately inherited a baronetcy. The father then had to slip quietly into the kitchen in order to secretly eat fire and the son felt compelled to jump over the table to sit down on a chair. Family life was threatening to disintegrate – until they again stood together on the stage, *being* a family of acrobats.

16 It may seem peculiar that he rescued such eminently 'theatrical' vehicles as the operettas of Offenbach in his non-theatrical Theater der Dichtung. In this article he did not distinguish between 'old' style operettas by Strauß or by Offenbach. However, in a previous article, 'Libretti' (F.172:6–10), he made a distinction between the libretti of Strauß's operettas, which gave the singer-actor room to extemporize, and the texts of Offenbach operettas (by Meilhac, Cremieux, and Nuitter), which were wittier (*geistvoller*). This was basically the same distinction as the one he made between stage drama and literary drama.

17 For an interesting comment on the importance of the feuilleton writer in Viennese bourgeois society at the turn of the century, see Carl E. Schorske, *Fin-de-Siècle Vienna. Politics and Culture* (New York 1980) 9.
18 See F.83:5–6. Kraus later used his two-column comparison technique to show the mediocrity of Lothar's play and to suggest the complicity of the *Neue Freie Presse* in the 'success' of the play. The *Neue Freie Presse* stated that the Munich performance of Lothar's *König Harlekin* had been a success, but offered no criticism and mentioned only the full house and the fact that the author had appeared on stage at the end of the performance. Kraus juxtaposed the critique of the play in the *Frankfurter Zeitung*, which stated that the play had not been well received. The fool (Harlekin) had merely posed as a man of the Renaissance, and the tragedy had turned into satire (F.85:21).
19 Ironically, at one point Kraus had to defend Buchbinder. After Buchbinder was forced to leave the *Neues Wiener Journal*, the other Viennese critics no longer feared him and so felt safe to reject his plays. Kraus considered all of Buchbinder's plays equally bad, but commented on the other critics' lack of morality. 'Etwas Scheußlicheres als diese Hetzjagd auf einen, der keinen Revolver hat, *bloß weil* er keinen mehr hat, etwas Elementareres als dies Geständnis, daß ausschließlich das geschäftliche Cliqueninteresse das öffentliche Urteil bestimmt, läßt sich nicht ersinnen.' (F.151:27)
20 Kraus still championed actors and actresses who were used and abused by theatre directors and critics alike (see F.148:4–9).
21 His attitude towards Schiller as a playwright was mixed. He protested against the pairing of Goethe and Schiller by literary critics, since neither could then stand as an individual. And he defended Schiller against Otto Weininger, who had linked Schiller and journalism. Kraus stated that this did not apply to everything by Schiller. In Schiller's defence, he cited two early poems. One, 'Der Venuswagen,' was worthy of Wedekind, in Kraus's opinion; the other was called 'Die Journalisten und Minos' (F.180/1:39–50). The choice, however, is more indicative of Kraus's penchant as a critic than of Schiller's literary or dramatic importance.
22 For example, Gelber's changes in *Troilus and Cressida*, mentioned in *Die Fackel* no. 93, 15–19
23 Kraus very much minimized any contact Nestroy had had with the stage in a professional capacity, as actor, director, or playwright.
24 To a lesser extent *Rose Bernd* was also an exception. See *Die Fackel* no. 155 (pp. 19–20) for Kraus's defence of this play against the critics.
25 It must be kept in mind that many Austrian writers at that time were proud to be called *Heimatkünstler* and that the term had more positive connotations than its English equivalent, 'regional artist.'
26 Kraus obviously admired Strindberg as a writer – much of the Swedish writer's prose was published in *Die Fackel*. However, he mentioned very little about Strindberg, the dramatist, in these years.

27 'Löscht' ich so der Seele Brand,/Lied es wird erschallen;/Schöpft des Dichters reine Hand,/Wasser wird sich ballen' (F.195:26). (Quoted from Goethe's *West-östlicher Divan*.)
28 See 'Maximilian Harden: Ein Nachruf' (F.242/3:26–7). Kraus insisted Wedekind's friendship with Harden was dependent on his *not* reading Harden's periodical *Die Zukunft*.
29 Kraus was also involved with cabaret theatre in 1906, when he was the director of a one-act sketch at the Cabaret zum Nachtlicht. He had never used *Die Fackel* to promote the cabaret and had thus, he felt, preserved his independence as a critic. However, the engagement met with disaster when Kraus was physically attacked by an actor, Herr Henry, for his criticism of Marya Delvard, an actress who was also associated with the cabaret. Kraus felt that his satirical exposé (F.201:26–8) of Marya Delvard's exaggerated idea of her own greatness was justified, since he did not criticize her until she had given an interview to the *Fremdenblatt* – that is, until she had entered his realm of the newspaper. (F.203:22)
30 This was evident in other articles from this period, which later appeared in the collection *Sittlichkeit und Kriminalität* (1908).
31 The pun on which the effect of the original passage depends – *Dirne* (prostitute) and *Dirndl* (which can mean both 'lass' and 'dirndl dress') – is lost in the translation.
32 Even in *Erdgeist* Lulu embodied for Wedekind, as for Kraus, an idea rather than a person – that is, the earth-spirit of woman's sexuality.
33 Even the alleged importance of the portrait must be questioned, for it does not appear in Act I at all, and it is not until Act III that the portrait becomes an integral rather than a decorative part of the play. In the final act not only does Lulu's former beauty contrast with her present extreme squalor, but, in rescuing the picture and smuggling it into London, Gräfin Geschwitz demonstrates her devotion to Lulu by a dramatic deed that we the audience can perceive and react to.
34 See chapter 6 of Aristotle's *Poetics*.
35 Goldmann had protested against perversity on the stage. Kraus countered that no one knew what Goldmann meant by perverse (F.217:23).
36 See F.226:13–14. Kraus reprinted Nordau's damning review in the *Neue Freie Presse* of Wilde's *Salome* (which had been produced in Paris). All of Nordau's criticism was on moral, not literary, grounds.
37 Presumably he could have seen the Berlin production with another actress in the title role.
38 Berger was an Austrian who later became director of the Burgtheater.
39 Kraus praised the 'ehrliche Lehrhaftigkeit' of *Helden der Feder* (F.102:17) and the 'didaktische Gewandung' of *Die Gerechtigkeit* (F.122:2).
40 In the case of the dramatist Antonie Baumberg, the critics' lack of scruples was violently attacked by Kraus. Kraus had already praised her as a promising

dramatic talent. However, her plays had never achieved success on stage, since neither the liberal nor the anti-Semitic press would support her. Finally in 1902, after three failures of what Kraus considered to be good plays, she committed suicide. Kraus blamed the press for this death. 'Eine begabte Frau, das erste außerhalb der Clique gewachsene dramatische Talent, hat sich aus der Welt fortgemacht, weil drei Einacter nach der zweiten Aufführung vom Repertoire des Deutschen Volkstheaters abgesetzt wurden' (F.100:11). '(Sie) wurde zwischen den Parteien zermalmt' (F.102:27).

41 That is from the middle of p. 3 to p. 13. Even most of p. 1 is taken up by a quotation from his criticism of Madjera's play in Die Fackel no. 102.
42 Kraus pointed out that the dramatic weakness of the work lay in the indecisiveness of the author's intention; Hawel swayed for four acts between the standpoint of the liberal phrasemonger and the uncle who despised politics. Not until Act v was his intent clear.
43 See F.162:24–8.
44 The Eulenberg and Moltke trials
45 See F.2:8 and F.69:23–5.
46 See also F.118:3 – 'Hier mußte wirklich "alles ruiniert" werden; denn jeder Versuch, die Tagespresse literarisch zu heben, würde der heillosen Schlechtigkeit ihrer ethischen Natur nur eine höhere Weihe geben.' In the same article, Kraus noted that he could probably ironically be blamed for the founding of a new Viennese newspaper, Die Zeit, which claimed to have a clear style. Kraus stated that this was only 'die Ablösung des blumigen Schmockstils der alten Blätter durch die nüchterne Mauschelweis der Herren Singer und Kanner [editors]' (ibid, 8).
47 Kraus had already taken exception to Harden's calling Wedekind's *Frühlings Erwachen* 'einen Lenzmimus' in which 'das Männern der Knaben und das Böckeln der Mädchen' is described.
48 In 'Maximilian Harden: Ein Nachruf' (F.242/3) Kraus was concerned with writers and intellectuals who had been taken in by Harden's legendary pose of revolutionary fighter (even though they might never have read a line of Harden), and who saw a parallel to the martyrdom of Oscar Wilde in the fact that Harden had had to spend a few months in jail for his accusations against Graf Moltke. Kraus showed a great distrust of their critical abilities vis-à-vis a 'literary personality.'
49 See F.251/2:15–18, F.254/5:41–8.
50 F.118:1 ff
51 F.232/3:44, F.244:23–4
52 For example, an essay in Die Fackel no. 292 (pp. 16–32) entitled 'Rhabarber'

CHAPTER 3

1 Kraus's praise of Nestroy's use of language was counterpointed in this period by his severe censure of Heine, whose wit Kraus considered to be shallow and in

whose (in his opinion) superficial use of language he claimed to see the origins of the twentieth-century phenomenon of *Feuilletonismus*. See Kraus's essay 'Heine und die Folgen,' which formed the highlight of his first public lecture in Vienna in May 1910, and which was subsequently printed both in pamphlet form and in *Die Fackel* no. 329/30 (September 1911).

2 In 1912 he wrote: 'Die letzten zwei Jahre ... habe ich fern einer Wiener Bühne verlebt ...' (F.343/4:20). Of the Burgtheater, he wrote in 1917: 'Jetzt gehe ich wieder erst in zehn Jahren ins Burgtheater' (F.445/53:62).

3 Here, a parallel can probably be drawn between Nestroy and Kraus. In the essay 'Der kleine Pan stinkt schon' (F.324/5:50–60), Kraus cited a criticism of his style made by Max Brod. Brod had stated: 'Ein mittelmäßiger Kopf dagegen, wie Karl Kraus, dessen Stil nur selten die beiden bösen Pole der Literatur, Pathos und Kalauer, vermeidet, sollte es nicht wagen dürfen, einen Dichter ... zu berühren' (ibid, 57). Kraus countered with the asurance that he *never* avoided the two opposite poles of pathos and pun: '(ich begnüge) mich damit ... ihn [Brod] mit der Versicherung zu verblüffen, daß mein Stil diese beiden bösen Pole nicht nur selten, sondern geradezu nie vermeidet. Ob es die höchste oder die niedrigste Literatur ist, den Gedanken zwischen Pathos und Kalauer so zu bewegen, daß er beides zugleich sein kann, daß er eine feindlich Mücke in die Leidenschaft mitreißt, um sie im nächsten Augenblick in einem Witz zu zertreten, darüber lasse ich mich mit keinem lebenden Deutschen in einen Wortwechsel ein.' (Ibid, 58)

4 Here, Kraus drew a parallel between Wedekind and Nestroy: 'Der Schauspieler hat eine Rolle für einen Dichter geschrieben, die der Dichter einem Schauspieler nicht anvertrauen würde. In Wedekind stellt sich ... ein Monologist vor uns, dem gleichfalls eine scheinbare Herkömmlichkeit und Beiläufigkeit der szenischen Form genügt, um das wahrhaft Neue und Wesentliche an ihr vorbeizusprechen und vorbeizusingen. Auf die Analogie im Tonfall witzig eingestellter Erkenntnisse hat einmal der verstorbene Kritiker Wilheim hingewiesen. Der Tonfall ist jene Äußerlichkeit, auf die es dem Gedanken hauptsächlich ankommt, und es muß irgendwo einen gemeinsamen Standpunkt der Weltbetrachtung geben, wenn Sätze gesprochen werden, die Nestroy so gut gesprochen haben konnte wie Wedekind,' (F.349/50:9). He went on to cite a sentence from Wedekind that could as well have been written by Nestroy, and two from a Nestroy play that displayed Wedekind traits. But his assertion that similarity of cadence or accent (*Tonfall*) was an indication of similarity of outlook is not convincing.

5 In fact, Kraus was even willing to admit that a critic (presumably himself) could have been misled by hatred of the Jewish liberal press into a temporary lack of appreciation for Sonnenthal: 'es war möglich, daß ein Ressentiment gegen eine jüdische Presse, die längst die Vertretung der Verfallszeit übernomen hatte, seinen ehrwürdigen Resten unrecht tat.' (Ibid, 36–7)

6 See pp. 46–7.

7 The one certain exception occurred in 1917, when he saw the Arno Holz produc-

tion of *King Lear* in which Wüllner and Reimers performed. Kraus wrote that this was his first visit to the Burgtheater in ten years (F.445/53:62). However, it is possible that he saw the production of *Richard III* in 1910, when Berger was managing director of the Burgtheater. See his comment in *Die Fackel* no. 311/12 (p. 4): 'ich habe mit Wehmut die welken Blätter betrachtet, die zur Totenklage der Königinnen in "Richard III." von den Soffitten fielen.' It is also possible, however, that he read about this piece of stage business in a newspaper critique of the play.

8 See Kraus's remark in 1907: 'Herr Reimers wird neuestens aus seiner dekorativen Tüchtigkeit, die für Herolde und ähnliche unbewegte Begleiter einer Staatsaktion langt, in eine gefahrvolle Natürlichkeit gelockt.' (F.239/40:30)

9 This last point was particularly accentuated in another, shorter article about the Burgtheater's Swiss tour entitled 'Es war einfach überwältigend.' Kraus first quoted from a newspaper: 'Das Wiener Burgtheater und somit die österreichische Kunst hatte *mitten* im Krieg einen *unblutigen* Kultursieg im neutralen Ausland errungen!' He then remarked: 'Verwundet wurde niemand. Aber ich bekenne offen und ehrlich und auf die Gefahr hin, daß ich bei meinem nächsten Versuch, das Burgtheater zu betreten, hofftentlich nicht hineingelassen werde: daß ich eine blutige Niederlage von Burgschauspielern in Zürich ... einem Weltkrieg vorgezogen hätte!' (F.457/61:77)

10 Friedrich Schreyvogl, *Das Burgtheater* (Vienna, 1965) 120
11 See p. 84.
12 See also F.326/8:59–63.
13 Schreyvogl, *Das Burgtheater* 113. Wüllner had played Lear in 1917 in the production of that play so criticized by Kraus. See F.484/98:88–91.
14 Schreyvogl, *Das Burgtheater* 113
15 F.445/53:60; F.454/6:8.
16 See F.445/53:62–3. See also the article entitled 'Ein Staatsverbrechen an Shakespeare und Jugend' (F.484/98:88 ff) in which he reprinted a lettter he had sent to the Ministry of Culture and Education, protesting against the performance of Lear which was given free of charge for high-school students and pointed out the inadequacies of the production. He asked for a list of all students given invitations to the Burgtheater performance, in order that he might invite them to his public reading of the play. His purpose was pedagogical: to restore the image of the poet's original intention to youth, which had been led astray. 'Hat ihn [Kraus himself] zu seiner ersten "Lear"-Vorlesung die Absicht bestimmt, die Spuren der Unkunst zu verwischen, und ist ihm dies ohne jeden Apparat theatralischer wie publizistischer Inszenierung ... gelungen, so liegt ihm nun umsomehr der Wunsch am Herzen, einer irregeführten Jugend das dichterische Urbild wieder herzustellen.'
17 That Kraus's concept of drama was more aural than visual is obvious in his *Theater der Dichtung*. See also F.150:1 – 'Aber mir ist's nicht vergönnt, Kunstwerke als Betrachter zu genießen; eine unselige Hellhörigkeit zwingt

mich, den Stimmen zu lauschen, die aus der Tiefe dringen ...' and F.241:1 – 'Mein Gehör ermöglicht es mir, einen Schauspieler, den ich vor zwanzig Jahren in einer Dienerrolle auf einen Provinztheater und seit damals nicht gesehen habe als Don Carlos zu imitieren. Das ist ein wahrer Fluch. Ich höre jeden Menschen sprechen, den ich einmal gehört habe.'

18 See also F.462/71:173.
19 The title (lit., 'Limits of Mankind') is – ironically – borrowed from a Goethe poem.
20 *Der mährisch-schlesische Korrespondent* (22 October 1913)
21 This at least is the date given by Kraus in *Die Fackel*; unfortunately it has proved impossible to verify it.
22 For example, 'Worte zum Gedächtnis des Prinzen Eugen,' written at the end of 1914
23 F.339/40:30–1
24 F.400/3:60
25 See Martin Swales, *Arthur Schnitzler. A Critical Study* (Oxford 1971).
26 Kraus continually reminded his readers that he was one of the few in the camp of the enemy who took a stand against the lie. In his essay 'Weltgericht' (written at the end of October 1918) he wrote: 'daß die schmutzige Zumutung der Macht an den Geist: Lüge für Wahrheit, Unrecht für Recht, Tollwut für Vernunft zu halten, von mir tagtäglich mühelos abgewiesen wurde. Denn der bessere Mut war der meine, im eigenen Lager den Feind zu sehen!' (F.499/500:2–3)

CHAPTER 4

1 See Hans Weigel, *Karl Kraus oder Die Macht der Ohnmacht* (Vienna 1972) 250. 'Immer stärker trat das vorgelesene dramatische Wort gegenüber den "eigenen Schriften" in den Vordergrund. Immer kleiner wurden aber auch die Säle dieses Theaters der Dichtung. Die zunehmende Isolation ist aus dem Vorlesungskatalog zu ersehen, der immer häufiger den Festsaal des Architektenvereins nennt, dann den kleinen Saal, den Karl Kraus Offenbach-Saal nannte, schließlich den ganz abseitigen Ehrbar-Saal in der Mühlgasse 30.'
2 Helene Richter, *Josef Lewinsky. Fünfzig Jahre Wiener Kunst und Kultur* (Vienna, no date)
3 Rachel (1821–58), whose real name was Elisabeth Félix, was reputedly one of the greatest French tragediennes of the nineteenth century.
4 Wildgans later returned for a second term as managing director from July 1930 to the end of 1931.
5 See F.640/8:167 ff.
6 Kraus did not censure all contemporary efforts at staging Nestroy. He commended Jarno's production of *Eine Wohnung zu vermieten* at the Lustspieltheater. In *Die Fackel* no. 676/8 (p. 31) he stated that the necessary theatrical, poetic, and metaphysical dimension would have been present in a performance of *Lumpaziva-*

gabundus by actors such as Kneidinger (who had performed in Jarno's production of *Eine Wohnung zu vermieten*) and Oskar Sachs (whose portrayal of Knieriem Kraus remembered from twenty years before – F.622/31:112). However, it must be noted that *Eine Wohnung zu vermieten*, which had not had any success during Nestroy's time, had been 'rescued from oblivion' by Kraus, who included it in the repertoire of his Theater der Dichtung, and that he had originally been asked to direct the production at the Lustspieltheater. As he himself, with little modesty, stated: 'Wohl der einzige Ertrag des Theaterfestes war die von mir angeregte Aufführung von Nestroys "Eine Wohnung zu vermieten" ... jenem theatralischen Meisterstück, das von der zeitgenössischen Kritik totgetreten wurde und seit damals nicht auferstanden war. Die Verantwortung des Regisseurs (die ich ursprünglich nicht abgelehnt hatte) zu übernehmen, war mir im unverschuldet späten Zeitpunkt meiner Rückkehr nach Wien ... unmöglich ...' (F.668/75:64). Here, Kraus's subjectively biased criticism is apparent, for, along with his own readings of Nestroy in his Theater der Dichtung, this performance, in which he was an interested party, was the only one that received his approval.

7 *Im Burgtheater spielen s' den Nestroy und*
  Man ist im Himmel, nämlich auf dem Hund.
  Im Haus voll Würde und von stolzem Wuchs
  Woll'n sie sich mit ihm machen einen Jux.
  Und wenn s' den Z'riss'nen spiel'n in diesem Haus,
  Kommt nur der Titel als a Ganzer 'raus.
  Doch den Lumpazi bringen s' erst zu sich,
  Denn den spiel'n s', wie sich's g'hört, ganz liederlich.
   Die Leut hab'n a Freud' beim Nestroy sein' Schaden:
   Der Leim der ist trocken und mit'n Zwirn hat's ein' Faden.
  Beim Knieriem sein' Lied da wurde mir bang,
  Bei dem Humor steht d' Welt auf kein' Fall mehr lang.
  Doch ich hör' s' vor Begeisterung schrei'n –
  Nein, die Welt fällt auf jeden Fall 'rein 'rein 'rein 'rein 'rein 'rein,
  Die Welt fällt noch lang lang herein. (F.676/8:1)
8 Friedrich Jenaczek, *Zeittafeln zur "Fackel." Themen, Ziele, Probleme* (Munich 1965) 56.
9 See also F.676/8:57.
10 See F.717/23:106–7. The dialect was that of Darmstadt. Kraus indicated in the programme notes that he felt it to be his 'duty as an honest man' (*Ehrenpflicht*) to show that Karl [sic] Zuckmayer's *Der fröhliche Weinberg* was but a watered-down version of the Niebergall play.
11 Kraus had (unsuccessfully) invited the Burgtheater actors to his readings of Raimund's *Der Bauer als Millionär* – see F.668/75:53.
12 In the pages following, Kraus included his praise of Lewinsky's biography and reprinted some of that actor's letters to him.

13 The remark occurred in a conversation with Otto Kerry in Vienna on 30 May 1972.
14 See his comment on his readers in *Die Fackel* no. 546/50 (p. 71): 'Eine der unangenehmsten Begleiterscheinungen der Fackel sind ihre Leser.'
15 Weigel contends that in 1925 at least (during his campaign to drive Bekessy from Vienna) Kraus was more than a prophet, in that he tried to make the authorities act. 'Karl Kraus wollte einst vom Schreibtisch forteilen und in die Vorgänge draußen eingreifen. Diesmal tat er es. Er stellte eine präzise Forderung. Er sagte nicht nur, was zu sagen war, er zog eine Konsequenz. Er war nicht mehr jener Prophet, den die Existenz des Üblen bestätigt. Er ging dem Übel gerade an den Leib. Er wollte in unmittelbarer Relation Ursache einer Wirkung sein.' Weigel, *Karl Kraus* 287. That, however, the witness he bore as prophet could awaken strength in others is evidenced by the influence he had on many intellectuals in Israel during the Second World War. See the foreword by Elazar Benyoetz to the reprint of Paul Engelmann's *Dem Andenken an Karl Kraus* (Vienna 1967) 4: 'Daß zur Zeit der furchtbaren Vernichtung in Europa, als das Chaos sich vollzog, einige in Israel lebende, auf wunderbare Weise gerettete Juden sich weiter mit Kraus beschäftigen konnten, ist kein Mißverständnis des Mannes, dem zu Hitler nichts einfiel. Es zeigt vielmehr, daß sie eben nichts mechanisch übernommen, sondern in einer Weise von Kraus gelernt hatten, die ihnen mitten im Chaos einen Halt gab, der sich als Haltung im gelebten Leben bezeugen konnte.'
16 Kraus read plays or scenes from plays by Goethe, Raimund, Niebergall, Gogol, Hauptmann, and Wedekind, as well as his own plays.
17 Kraus's preoccupation with Nestroy was especially evident until 1925; after that, much of his critical and creative energy went into the 'discovery' of Offenbach and the reworking of Offenbach operettas.
18 Kraus continued his fight against the critics and literary historians who, beginning with Friedrich Hebbel, and with the exception of Ludwig Speidel, could not see or would not admit that Nestroy was a great writer and only saw in him an adapter of French farces or a comic who turned out 'vehicles' to show off his acting talent (see also F.608/12:45). As Kraus wrote in his short article 'Nestroy und die Literatur': 'Da kann ich mich auf den Kopf stellen, bei der Literatur setze ich Nestroy nicht durch' (F.595/600:53). Even a critic such as Egon Friedell, who was quite sympathetic towards Nestroy, did not get off without some criticism from Kraus, who accused him of superficiality in the book of Nestroy quotations that Friedell published (F.613/21:51-3). As for the press critics, who were paid to publish what Kraus considered to be worthless opinions, Kraus accused Löwy of factual inaccuracy (F.668/75:67 ff) and misquoting (F.622/31:109-10); Goldmann of inaccuracy, lack of proper respect, and lack of competence (F.640/8:81); and both Salten and Decsey of lack of critical judgment (F.622/31:110-11) – Salten, because he thought Nestroy's plays were dead, and Decsey because he did not share Kraus's prejudice against the quality of acting of the Burgtheater and judged

that theatre's performance of *Einen Jux will er sich machen* in 1923 to be 'genuinely Viennese.' Even newspaper critics who were Nestroy's contemporaries received their share of criticism from Kraus for disregarding the intrinsic value of the plays and contributing to their failure when Nestroy hit too close to home with his satire (see F.781/6:55–6).

19 See F.781/6:53. *Das Notwendige und das Überflüssige* was published in 1920. In 1925 Kraus published his version of *Der konfuse Zauberer* based on the play by that name, to which Kraus added lines from an unpublished Nestroy manuscript, *Der Tod am Hochzeitstag oder Mann, Frau, Kind* (which was, according to him, 'obviously' a sketch for *Der konfuse Zauberer* – see F.679/85:39–40). For Kraus, reworking these plays afforded relaxation from the polemical work, which he considered to be his duty (ibid, 40).

20 *Grundlosigkeit* can of course mean both 'unfathomable depth' and 'unreasonableness,' but the two meanings support each other in this passage: if we could subject life to rational analysis, it would not be unfathomable.

21 See F.349/50:23.

22 His allusions to 'der Spiegelmensch' (F.679/85:47), while obvious to anyone familiar with the Kraus/Werfel feud, would be lost to many reading Kraus's added verses in the 1980s.

23 For example, in Knieriem's 'Kometenlied' (F.608/12:46 ff)

24 See Jenaczek, *Zeittafeln* 34: 'Erst dank Karl Kraus wurde der hohe Rang und die Bedeutung der Kunst Nestroys erkannt, und anerkannt.' The most concrete evidence of renewed interest in Nestroy was the publication of the critical edition of his works by Fritz Brukner and Otto Rommel between 1924 and 1930.

25 See Schick, *Karl Kraus* 21.

26 There is, however, no proof that Kraus really saw this performance at the Carl-Theater.

27 Jenaczek, *Zeittafeln* 56

28 See Lotte Sternbach-Gärtner (Caroline Kohn), 'Karl Kraus und Offenbach' in *Der Monat* 96 (Berlin 1956) 57.

29 It is worth remembering that when Kraus himself was lampooned on the stage, he thought that this was improper and appealed to the authorities to protect him.

30 F.806/9:62–3. Reprinted from *Der Anbruch* (March 1929)

31 For example, with the exception of his readings before 1900

32 Karl Kraus, *Werke* 11, *Sittlichkeit und Kriminalität* (Munich 1963) 11

33 Karl Kraus, *Shakespeares Dramen* (Vienna 1934) Vol. I, xiii–xiv

34 In the 1930s Kraus often wrote about the problems he encountered in adapting Shakespeare. See F.908 and F.909/11:16–19.

35 *Erste Hexe.* Wann kommen wir drei uns wieder entgegen,
　　　　　　　Im Blitz und Donner, oder im Regen?
　Zweite Hexe. Wenn der Wirrwarr stille schweigt,
　　　　　　　Wer der Sieger ist, sich zeigt.

Cf. Schiller's version:
> Erste Hexe. Wann kommen wir drei uns wieder entgegen,
> In Donner, in Blitzen oder in Regen?
> Zweite Hexe. Wann das Kriegsgetümmel schweigt,
> Wann die Schlacht den Sieger zeigt.

36 'Dazu aber bedarf der Nachdichter gar nicht der Kenntnis des Originals, sondern bloß des Vergleichs jener unzulänglichen Ergebnisse philologischer Bemühung.' Shak. I. ix.

37 For a negative view of Kraus as an adapter of Shakespeare, see Richard Flatter, *Karl Kraus als Nachdichter Shakespeares. Eine sprachkritische Untersuchung* (Vienna 1934).

38 The plays were performed in Berlin and Vienna (March and April 1924).

39 The example he gives of Hamlet in modern dress ('Hamlet im Smoking') was Jeßner's production of the play.

40 This affirmation occurs at the end of a long passage in which Kraus criticized the Berlin Expressionist directors for updating the classics in their productions. Kraus obviously allied himself with 'jene Epigonen': 'Det Janze [sic] aber mit der aus dem unvermeidlichen Untergang des Abendlandes bezogenen Sicherheit, daß alles, was die Zeit bietet und was im "Querschnitt" der Gehirne die Impotenz kubisch erhöht zeigt, nun mal auch auf das Theater gehört und daß schließlich nicht wir Regisseure für den Humbug verantwortlich sind, sondern die Zeit, deren Betonfestigkeit uns über alle Wortproblematik hinweghilft, deren amoralische, dynamoralische Tüchtigkeit unsere stärkste Hilfe ist gegen die Betriebsstörung durch jene Epigonen, die noch heute auf dem Schein bestehen, den sie für das Wesen in Kunst und Natur halten.' (F.676/8:32–3)

41 See Jens Malte Fischer, *Karl Kraus. Studien zum 'Theater der Dichtung' und Kulturkonservatismus* (Kronberg/Taunus 1973).

42 See F.668/75:90.

43 See Gröning & Kließ, *Friedrichs Theaterlexikon* (Hannover 1969) 346: 'Reinhardts Auffassung vom Theater als großem Fest, als letzten Endes unpolitische ... gesellschaftsverbindende und überhöhte Lebensäußerung erscheint sowohl als Nachfolge österreichisch-barocker Vorstellungen wie als Erfüllung des großbürgerlichen, luxuriösen Kunstbegriffs.'

44 See Weigel, *Karl Kraus* 280.

45 F.743/50:53–8

46 Kraus even (belatedly) praised Kainz for his performance of the Fool in *Lear*: 'unter den vielen (seiner Leistungen) schien mir sein Narr im "Lear" die Bühnengestalt nicht zu verkümmern' (F.622/31:121).

47 Kraus had satirized this 'musicality' in one of the topical verses that he composed for Offenbach's *Pariser Leben*:
> Ich möchte gern zum Moissi gehn,
> Weil der Gesang zum Herzen dringt,

Und das Chantant möcht' ich besehn,
Wo abends er den Hamlet singt. (F.759/65:31)
Ironically, in his book *Karl Kraus* (New York 1971) 101, Harry Zohn writes of Kraus's voice that 'in its musicality, vibrancy, and striking expressiveness ... was somewhat reminiscent of that of the actor Alexander Moissi ...' He does not, however, mention on whose authority he makes such a statement.
48 This ethical-aesthetic link between *Persönlichkeit* and art was even more striking when Kraus discussed some of Moissi's writings (F.743/50:57–8).
49 Originally, this essay was published in *Die Fackel* no. 182 (pp. 1–18). It was reprinted in the collection of essays entitled *Literatur und Lüge* (Vienna 1929).
50 Castiglioni was portrayed in Kraus's play *Die Unüberwindlichen* under the thin disguise of Camillioni. See Schick, *Karl Kraus* 112.
51 Hofmannsthal's play was performed in the cathedral in Salzburg.
52 See also F.613/21:8. Here Kraus made an equally unsavoury pun on the title *Der Unbestechliche*.
53 Kraus claimed to be quoting from an interview with Shaw printed (with photos of Shaw in swimming trunks) in a magazine called *Der Abend*. However, characteristically he gave no issue or page number.
54 Weigel, *Karl Kraus* 293
55 See p. 38.
56 See Jenaczek, *Zeittafeln* 49: 'Nach Ansicht von Karl Kraus ist das Drama nicht aufführbar (Brief vom 8. XII. 22 ...).'
57 Karl Kraus, *Die letzten Tage der Menschheit* (Munich 1964) I, 5
58 Weigel, *Karl Kraus* 201: 'Bei den Spielszenen sehnte man sich nach den Kraus-Vorlesungen zurück. Die Andeutung war mächtiger gewesen, als die Realisation sein konnte. Auch in den Vorlesungen Helmt Qualtingers und auf seinen Platten erstehen das Werk und sein Geist reiner und richtiger als in der Dreidimensionalität.'
59 Karl Kraus, *Werke* 14, *Dramen* (Munich 1967) 90
60 For example, his remarks on Wedekind and Nestroy noted in chapter 2
61 Quoted in H.H. Hahnl's dissertation 'Karl Kraus und das Theater' (Vienna 1947) 117
62 Weigel, *Karl Kraus* 237–8
63 See chapter 3, pp. 145 ff.
64 Kraus, *Dramen* 56–7
65 Ibid, 101
66 Ibid, 103
67 Ibid, 106–7
68 Ibid, 103
69 Ibid, 108
70 *Wolkenkuckucksheim* is the exception.
71 Hahnl notes that Kraus's drama is a kind of monologue: 'Das Drama Kraus', An-

griff, Vision oder Reflexion in der elastischen Formel des Aphoristen, ist ein schauspielerisch konzipierter Monolog.' Hahnl, 'Karl Kraus' 139.
72 Tom Prideaux in *Life*, 14 July 1972, 22
73 See Leopold Liegler, *Karl Kraus und sein Werk* (Vienna 1933) 378 ff.
74 See Weigel, *Karl Kraus* 225. See also Lotte Sternbach-Gärtner, 'Karl Kraus und das expressionistische Theater,' in *Worte und Werte*, eds G. Erdmann and A. Eichstaedt (Berlin 1961) 407–9.
75 Sternbach-Gärtner, ibid, 408–9. See also Lotte Sternbach-Gärtner, 'Die letzten Tage der Menschheit und das Theater von Bert Brecht,' in *Deutsche Rundschau* 9 (Baden-Baden 1958) 836 f.
76 The Berlin critics' reports were reprinted on pp. 2–51, and those of the Viennese critics on pp. 128–48.
77 Kraus, *Die letzten Tage der Menschheit* II, 264
78 Kraus did in fact use slides at some of his lectures during the war years. See F.400/3:46.
79 Weigel, *Karl Kraus* 234
80 Ibid, 237
81 Ibid, 238
82 It is interesting to note that Kraus hated all attempts (such as those by Piscator) at creating a 'revolutionary' theatre in Berlin.
83 His attack against Kerr at that time occurred in a series of articles, which incorporated the phrase 'der kleine Pan stinkt' – see F.324/5:50–60.

CHAPTER 5

1 Two further volumes of Shakespeare adaptations were promised but never appeared.
2 Kraus preferred actors, such as Peter Lorre and Helene Weigel, to singers for his Offenbach broadcasts.
3 It is a stunning illustration of Kraus's political blindness that he found nothing better to do with his time at this desperate stage in the history of Europe than to attack the moderate political Left.
4 Frank Field, *The Last Days of Mankind. Karl Kraus and His Vienna* (London 1967) 195–6
5 Paul Schick, *Karl Kraus in Selbstzeugnissen und Bilddokumenten* (Reinbek 1965, rowohlt) 129
6 Since 1914, Kraus had already read scenes and songs from Raimund's *Der Verschwender, Der Alpenkönig und der Menschenfeind*, and *Das Mädchen aus der Feenwelt oder Der Bauer als Millionär*.
7 In 1920 Kraus had mentioned Raimund's 'powerlessness in the presence of the spirit of the times' and, although admiring him, called him 'antiquated': 'Was insonderheit die Wirkung Raimunds anlangt, so bitte überzeugt zu sein, daß ich

mir seiner Ohnmacht vor dem Zeitgeist, dessen Opfern oder Bekennern, vollkommen bewußt bin und ihn für noch weit antiquierter halte als die Verehrer des Alfred Kerr es tun. Und dennoch stehe ich lieber zu Raimunds "Jugend" als einer, deren Erlebnis die Hysterie ist und deren Weltanschauung der Mangel an Ehrfurcht' (F.546/50:12–13). There is a terrible irony in this remark, for now it could just as easily be applied to the Kraus of 1935–6. He, too, was 'powerless before the spirit of the times' and was considered by many to be 'antiquated.'
8 In his programme notes to a reading of *Der Verschwender*, Kraus divulged that around 1891 he had been a guest actor in a public performance of the play by a school for actors. He had played Wolf in Act III. See F.909/11:51.
9 The article was originally published in the *Wiener Zeitung* 30 January 1936.
10 *Eisenbahnheiraten oder Wien, Neustadt, Brünn* had already been praised by Kraus in 1901. See F.88.
11 2 March 1935
12 See F.847/51:43–4 regarding his one and a half year court battle (which he lost) against the music critic of the *Arbeiterzeitung*.
13 Ibid, 41–3
14 This letter was first published in *Stimmen über Karl Kraus* (Vienna 1934), a collection of articles and letters written in praise of Kraus on the occasion of his sixtieth birthday.
15 These were: a programme of Offenbach excerpts under the title of *Der König ihres Herzens*, in the Johann Strauß-Theater in Vienna in 1931, Reinhardt's productions of *Die schöne Helena* and *Hoffmanns Erzählungen*, Mehring's version of *Die Großherzogin von Gerolstein*, and the 1932 Prague production of *Madame l'Archiduc*.
16 It is again worth noting that Kraus is no longer in control of his language: in the clause 'ohne die diese Wirkung ...' In this passage, the relative pronoun 'die' has no meaningful antecedent, and the reader has to guess the intended meaning.
17 Hans Weigel, *Karl Kraus oder Die Macht der Ohnmacht* (Vienna 1972) 245–6
18 Ibid, 248
19 Ibid, 247
20 See especially F.912/15:21–33, F.916:11–16.
21 See also Zerline Gabillon's remarks about Rachel reprinted in 1926 in F.743/50.
22 'Die Bühne ist ... besät mit den Sätzen, die sie [die Schauspieler] "fallen lassen," hauptsächlich Zitaten. Herr Werner Krauß unterscheidet sich von den anderen wenigstens dadurch, daß er deutlicher macht, was er fallen läßt. Wenn er als Lear "O Höll und Tod" oder gar "Pest, Rache, Tod, Verderben" sagt, so sind es klare Feststellungen seiner Unzufriedenheit' (F.906/7:22). 'Das erhöhte Theater verlangt die Fähigkeit, aus der Sprache zu gestalten. Heute aber entsteht Charakteristik auf Kosten der Sprache oder es werden Verse von einem verkleideten Herrn mit mehr oder minder richtiger Betonung aufgesagt.' (Ibid, 23)

23 Not only had the director added lines (ibid, 5) but he had, in Kraus's opinion, cut the speeches in such a way as to simplify the thought and flatten both poetry and tragedy. When Kraus listened for the lines:
Gott, wer darf sagen: schlimmer kann's nicht werden?
's ist schlimmer nun als je.
Und kann noch schlimmer gehn; 's ist nicht das Schlimmste,
Solang' man sagen kann: dies ist das Schlimmste.
he heard only:
Gott, wer darf sagen: schlimmer kann's nicht werden?
's ist schlimmer nun als je. (Ibid, 4)

24 Kraus was not the only one in Vienna at the time who gave a one-man show of Shakespeare readings. Ernst Reinhold had received much critical acclaim for his dramatic recitations. They differed from those of Kraus in that Reinhold made use of lighting effects and a podium draped in purple. He did not use a text but recited whole plays by heart in English. In Kraus's opinion, this was sheer nonsense and gimmickry. 'Die freie Rede wie das Englisch wird mich zwar nicht beirren, aber ich vermute, daß es die andern Hörer beirrt, sowohl die, die es nicht verstehen, wie die, die es verstehen, und solche, denen bloß die Gedächtnisleistung imponiert. Mir ja nicht: der sie im Vorhinein für Unfug und für Manöver der Ablenkung hält' (F.857/63:92). For Kraus, it was indispensable to have the text in his hand, even though he insisted that he knew the plays by heart. It was as if the book formed the necessary barrier between him and his audience, which only the characters whom he brought to life could cross. 'Denn es kommt darauf an, das sichtbare Buch so unsichtbar zu machen, daß nur die Gestalten sichtbar werden, die daraus hervortreten ... Das Buch ist unerläßlich' (ibid). Nevertheless, the critical praise that Reinhold received for his performances rankled Kraus, especially when the newspapers claimed that Reinhold was the first to give such readings, completely ignoring Kraus's unique pioneering in that field (F.909/11:19 ff).

25 Caroline Kohn, *Karl Kraus* (Stuttgart 1966) 120
26 Bert Brecht, *Schriften zur Literatur und Kunst* ed. Werner Kraft (Tübingen 1967) I, 58–9
27 Ibid, III, 66–7
28 Quoted in Friedrich Jenaczek, *Zeittafeln zur "Fackel". Themen, Ziele, Probleme* (Munich 1965) 121–2
29 Ibid, 122
30 Quoted by Kurt Krolop in his article 'Bertolt Brecht und Karl Kraus,' *Philologica Pragensia* 4 (1961) 226–7
31 Ibid, 229–30
32 Jenaczek, *Zeittafeln* 137–8

Harden, Maximilian xiv, 28, 44, 77, 90–6, 116, 127, 129, 224, 260, 273 n.47ff.
Hartmann, Ernst 51, 108, 199
Hartmann-Schneeberger, Helene 9, 10, 108
Hauer, Karl 74–5
Hauptmann, Gerhart 4, 6, 13–16, 33, 43, 54, 71, 75–7, 97, 135, 154, 192–3, 203–4, 249, 268 n.72ff., 269 n.9, 271 n.23, 278 n.16
Hawel, Rudolf 89, 273 n.42
Hebbel, Christian Friedrich 9, 20, 75, 87, 124–5, 144, 201, 278 n.18
Heine, Albert 115, 118, 155
Heine, Heinrich 69, 94, 100, 273 n.1
Heller, Hugo 134, 135
Herterich, Franz 155–6
Herzl, Theodor 71
Hitler, Adolf 134, 228–9, 231–2, 248–9, 251, 256–7
Höfer, Irma von 148
Hoffmann, Ernst Theodor Amadeus 77
Hofmannsthal, Hugo von 13, 18–19, 39–40, 73, 89, 90, 135–9, 145, 195–6, 200, 204–6, 240, 260, 281 n.51ff.
Hohenfels, Stella von 51
Holz, Arno 3, 274 n.7
Holz, Arthur 117–18
Holzer, Rudolf 27, 268 n.67
Homma, Hans 46
Hopp, Julius 170

Ibsen, Henrik 6, 9, 23, 41, 43–4, 74–5, 117, 124–5, 154, 269 n.1

Jarno, Josef 73, 81, 276 n.6
Jeßner, Leopold 180, 185–6, 188, 195, 280 n.39
Johann Strauß-Theater 283 n.15
Josefstädter Theater. *See under* Theater in der Josefstadt
Jung-Wiener Theater zum lieben Augustin 69, 73, 77

Kadelburg, Gustav 86
Kainz, Josef 12, 36, 38, 43, 46, 49–52, 59, 110–12, 115, 158, 180, 185, 198, 200, 269 n.6, 280 n.46
Kaiserjubiläums-Stadttheater 31
Kalbeck, Max 37, 72, 90
Kalmar, Annie 38, 83, 211, 215
Kanner, Heinrich 273 n.46
Karczág, Wilhelm 73
Karlweis, C. (pseudonym of Karl Weiß) 22, 26, 85–6
Keim, Franz 4
Kerr, Alfred 90, 208, 224, 252–3, 282 n.83, 283 n.7
Kleines Theater 54
Kleist, Heinrich von 14, 41
Knaack, Wilhelm 237
Kneidinger, Karl 277 n.6
Kózmian, Stanislaus von 45–6, 269 n.3
Krastel, Fritz 108, 112
Kraus, Karl:
– Theater der Dichtung xiv, 60, 66, 97–8, 105, 121–5, 135, 151–2, 154, 159–84, 194–5, 203, 210, 212, 217, 219, 225, 227, 233–45, 253, 270 n.16, 275 n.17, 277 n.6
– works: *Die chinesische Mauer* 130, 176; *Die demolierte Literatur* 17, 20, 38, 267 n.52; *Die Dritte Walpurgisnacht* 229–32; *Die Fackel* xiv ff.; *Die letzte Nacht* 210, 214, 218; *Die letzten Tage der Menschheit* 99, 144, 176, 194, 210–13, 217–18, 220, 232, 281 n.56ff., 282 n.75; *Die Sprache* 226; *Die Unüberwindlichen* 175, 211–13, 217–18, 222–3, 281 n.50; *Literatur oder Man wird doch da sehn* 210–12, 214, 217; *Sittlichkeit und Kriminalität* 176, 178, 272 n.30, 279 n.32; *Traumstück* 185, 210–13, 217–18; *Traumtheater* 185, 211–13, 215–18; *Wolkenkuckucksheim* 210, 212, 281 n.70; *Worte in Versen* 242

Krauß, Werner 247, 283 n.22
Křenek, Ernst 176–7
Kunststelle 220, 222–3

Landesberg, Alexander 86
Lehar, Franz 128
Leon, Victor 66, 87
Lewinsky, Josef 12, 34–7, 44–7, 108, 152–4, 187, 199, 246, 269 n.1ff., 277 n.12
Liegler, Leopold 236
Liliencron, Detlev von 3
Loos, Adolf 226
Lorre, Peter 282 n.2
Lothar, Rudolf 68–9, 271 n.18
Löwy, Siegfried 69, 278 n.18
Lustspieltheater 276 n.6

Madjera, Wolfgang 87, 272 n.39, 273 n.41
Maeterlinck, Maurice 18, 34–5, 41
Magazin für Litteratur 17, 267 n.39ff.
Martin, Karlheinz 185, 192–3
Matkowsky, Adalbert 44, 47–50, 130, 184, 187, 198, 245, 269 n.7
Medelsky, Lotte 85, 156
Mehring, Walter 239, 283 n.15
Meilhac, Henri 170, 172, 270 n.16
Meyer-Förster, Wilhelm 117
Michel, Robert 115
Millenkovich, Max von 115, 118
Mitterwurzer, Friedrich 9–10, 108
Moissi, Alexander 185, 195, 198–200, 280 n.47, 281 n.48
Moltke, Kuno, Graf 273 n.44
Mosenthal, Salomon von 86
Moser, Gustav von 5
Mozart, Wolfgang Amadeus 238, 248
Müller, Hans 117, 145–6
Müller-Guttenbrunn, Adam 31–2, 74
Münchener Neueste Nachrichten 23–4

Nestroy, Johann Nepomuk xiv, 21, 58, 62, 71, 73–4, 98–105, 110, 121, 123–5, 142, 145, 151, 157–8, 160, 162, 164–70, 175–7, 179, 200, 212, 227, 233–7, 259–60, 270 n.9ff., 273 n.1, 274 n.3ff., 276 n.6, 277 n.7, 278 n.17ff., 279 n.18, 281 n.60; *Das Notwendige und das Überflüssige* 164, 279 n.19; *Der böse Geist Lumpazivagabundus* 40, 50, 56, 59, 156, 165, 169, 233, 237, 276 n.6, 277 n.7, 279 n.23; *Der konfuse Zauberer* 160, 164–5, 279 n.19; *Der Talisman* 164–5, 169, 195, 200, 236; *Der Tod am Hochzeitstag oder Mann, Frau, Kind* 279 n.19; *Der Tritschtratsch* 169; *Der Zerrissene* 101, 169, 277 n.7; *Die beiden Nachtwandler* 164–5; *Einen Jux will er sich machen* 169, 277 n.7, 279 n.18; *Eine Wohnung zu vermieten* 164, 276 n.6; *Eisenbahnheiraten oder Wien, Neustadt, Brünn* 74, 235, 283 n.10; *Freiheit in Krähwinkel* 104; *Judith und Holofernes* 124, 166–7; *Liebesgeschichten und Heiratssachen* 235; *Weder Lorbeerbaum noch Bettelstab* 164
Neue Freie Presse 5, 28, 30–2, 47, 70–1, 81, 84, 86, 91, 116, 128, 222, 266 n.26, 271 n.18, 272 n.36
Neues Wiener Journal 69, 109, 271 n.19
Neues Wiener Tagblatt 25
Niebergall, Ernst Elias 160, 277, n.10, 278 n.16
Nietzsche, Friedrich 75
Nissen, Hermann 41
Nordau, Max 85, 272 n.36
Novelli, Ermete 48
Nuitter, Charles 172, 270, n.60

Offenbach, Jacques xiv, 21, 43, 66, 97, 151–2, 160–2, 164, 170–7, 179, 213, 226–7, 233–5, 237–44, 261, 270

295 / Index

n.15ff., 278 n.17, 282 n.2, 283 n.15;
Blaubart 170–1; *Die Briganten* 175,
244; *Die Creolin* 244; *Die Großherzogin von Gerolstein* 239, 283 n.15;
Die Prinzessin von Trapezunt 244, 270
n.15; *Die Reise in den Mond* 244;
Die schöne Helena 65, 171, 283 n.15;
Hoffmanns Erzählungen 211, 283
n.15; *Madame l'Archiduc* 170, 238–9,
242, 283 n.15; *Pariser Leben* 171–3,
175–6, 280 n.47; *Perichole* 170, 227,
237, 241–3; *Vert-Vert* 170, 227, 237,
243–4
Ohnet, Georges 5
Olden, Hans 4

Paulsen, Max 155–6
Pinter, Harold 64
Pirandello, Luigi 207
Piscator, Erwin 185–9, 191, 218, 251, 282
n.82
Poe, Edgar Allan 77

Rachel (=Elisa Félix) 154, 245, 276 n.3,
283 n.21
Racine, Jean Baptiste 245
Raimund, Ferdinand 3, 21 40, 52, 74,
233–5, 260, 277 n.11, 278 n.16, 282
n.6ff., 283 n.8
Raimundtheater 5–6, 25, 268 n.67
Reicher, Emanuel 11, 12, 20, 33, 267
n.31
Reimers, Georg 49, 111–12, 115, 118, 275
n.7ff.
Reinhardt, Max 34–5, 54, 98, 122–3, 128,
138, 171, 185, 194–8, 200, 203–4, 207,
218, 227, 247–51, 260, 280 n.43, 283
n.15
Reinhold, Ernst 284 n.24
Rilke, Rainer Maria 240
Rittner, Thaddäus 77
Röbbeling, Hermann 247

Robert, Emmerich 51, 108, 198
Rossi, Ernesto 48
Rößler, Karl 121
Rott, Max 120

Sachs, Oskar 277 n.6
Salten, Felix 69–70, 72, 77, 110, 156, 158,
162, 197, 206, 278 n.18
Salzburg Festival 195, 248
Sardou, Victorien 5, 125, 266 n.8
Scher, Peter 171
Schiller, Friedrich xii–xiii, 3, 17, 46, 70,
181, 185–6, 188–9, 201, 227, 236–7,
249, 251, 271, n.21, 276 n.17, 280 n.35
Schlegel, A.W., Translations of Shake-
speare's plays. *See under* Shakespeare
Schlenther, Paul 7–8, 27, 40, 50, 67, 115
Schlierseer 10, 32–3, 37, 270 n.10
Schnitzler, Arthur 16–18, 27, 38–9, 89,
117, 139–45, 204–5, 251, 267 n.47, 268
n.67
Schober, Johann 151, 175, 211, 223–4,
259
Scholz, Wenzel 57–8
Schönthan, Franz von 15
Schreyvogel, Joseph 246
Schurz, Carl 245
Schütz, Friedrich 43, 68, 70, 81, 84–5
Scribe, Eugène 5, 125, 266 n.8
Secessionsbühne 34
Shakespeare, William xiv, 36, 40–1, 50,
57, 59–60, 71, 74, 86, 121, 125, 128,
152, 160, 164, 177–84, 190, 194, 217,
226–7, 233, 235, 240, 246–7, 252,
259–60, 279 n.34, 280 n.36ff., 284
n.23ff.; *A Midsummer Night's Dream*
247; *Coriolanus* 177; *Hamlet* 63, 127,
177, 179–82, 186, 188–90, 217, 269 n.8,
280 n.39; *Henry IV* 40, 61–2, 178, 269
n.4; *Henry VI* 178; *Julius Caesar* 51;
King John 49, 178; *Lear* 9, 37, 48,
117–18, 121–2, 127, 177–9, 181, 247,

275, n.7ff., 280 n.46, 283 n.22; *Love's Labour's Lost* 177–8; *Macbeth* 121–3, 128, 152, 161, 177–8, 181, 183–4, 230, 279 n.35; *Measure for Measure* 51, 177–8; *Othello* 48–9, 59, 112, 127; *Richard II* 49, 198; *Richard III* 116, 275 n.7; *The Merry Wives of Windsor* 46, 178; *The Taming of the Shrew* 121–2; *The Winter's Tale* 121–2, 177; *Timon of Athens* 177–8, 227; *Troilus and Cressida* 177, 271, n.22
Shakespeare, translations by Schlegel and Tieck 177, 181–4
Shaw, George Bernard 117, 144–5, 207–10, 281 n.53
Singer, Wilhelm 30, 273 n.46
Skoda, Albin 148–9
Sonnenthal, Adolf von 12, 23–4, 36–7, 44, 47–8, 61–2, 106, 108–9, 112, 115, 130, 152, 199, 247–8, 269 n.4, 274 n.5
Sonn- und Montagszeitung 71
Sophocles 4, 217
Speidel, Ludwig 5, 116, 248
Staatstheater (Berlin) 185
Stein, Leo 86
Steiner, Gabor 127
Sternberg, Julian 43
Strakosch, Alexander 38
Strauß, Johann 66, 172, 270, n.16
Strauß, Richard 136, 195
Strindberg, August 11–12, 77, 134, 271, n.26
Sudermann, Hermann 16, 41, 89–90

Thaller, Willi 58, 157
Theater an der Wien 73, 170
Theater in der Josefstadt 34, 81, 195, 203
Théâtre français 246
Théâtre libre d'Antoine 9
Thimig, Hugo 8, 115, 117–18
Thoma, Ludwig 54, 89

Trebitsch, Siegfried 145
Tressler, Otto 113–15, 118
Treumann, Carl 237
Trianontheater 78
Triesch, Gustav 5, 72
Triester Zeitung 130

Viertel, Berthold 185, 218
Villon, François 252
Volksbühne (Berlin) 188, 218
Volksoper (Vienna) 235–6, 243
Volkstheater (Vienna) 5–6, 14, 24–5, 34, 37–8, 40, 46, 67–8, 71, 83, 85, 131–2, 273 n.40

Wagner, Richard 89
Walden, Herwarth 117
Wedekind, Frank 43, 71, 74–5, 77–81, 97, 134–5, 203, 215, 260, 272 n.28ff., 273 n.47, 274 n.4, 278 n.16, 281 n.60
Weigel, Helene 282 n.2
Weinberger, Charles 86
Weininger, Otto 271 n.21
Weiß, Karl. *See under* Karlweis
Werfel, Franz 210, 214, 240, 279, n.22
Werner, Fritz 149
Wiener Allgemeine Zeitung 69, 71
Wiener Literatur-Zeitung 267 n.36ff.
Wiener Rundschau 11, 33, 266 n.28, 267 n.30ff.
Wiener Zeitung 283 n.9
Wildbrandt, Adolf 4
Wilde, Oscar 43, 72, 81–5, 116, 272 n.36, 273 n.48
Wildenbruch, Ernst von 57
Wildgans, Anton 155, 276 n.4
Wittmann, Hugo 112
Wolff, Theodor 269 n.83
Wolter, Charlotte 4, 8–12, 34, 36, 45–7, 108–9, 152, 161, 215, 245–6
Wüllner, Ludwig 117, 275 n.7ff

Zacconi, Ermete 11, 48
Zuckerkandl, Bertha 69

Zuckmayer, Carl 277 n.10
Zweig, Stefan 73

This book

was designed by

ANTJE LINGNER

and was printed by

University of

Toronto

Press

www.ingramcontent.com/pod-product-compliance
Lightning Source LLC
Chambersburg PA
CBHW030304080526
44584CB00012B/440